REVAMPING AFRICAN FOREIGN POLICIES IN THE 21ST CENTURY

Ingredients, Tools & Dynamics

Joram M. Biswaro

Abraham K. Nyuon

Samson S. Wassara

Africa
World Books
Pty Ltd

A Note from the Publisher

The publisher wishes to acknowledge and thank Dr Douglas H. Johnson for his invaluable help and support for Africa World Books and its mission of preserving and promoting African cultural and literary traditions and history. Dr Johnson and fellow historians have been instrumental in ensuring that African people remain connected to their past and their identity. Africa World Books is proud to carry on this mission.

Copyright © 2021
Joram M. Biswaro, Abraham K. Nyuon, Samson S. Wassara

Edited by Michele Poff, PhD
Accomplish, LLC
Research-driven strategic communication, USA

ISBN: 978-0-6451109-4-4 (Hardcover)
978-0-6451109-5-1 (Paperback)

Cover design, typesetting and layout : Africa World Books

Synopsis

In modern world, no state or country can remain isolated from the global community. It is a global village. Nations are interdependent. None lives on an island. Hence, each and every state/nation should have an effective and vibrant Foreign Policy to manage the highly complex issues of current statecraft. The ongoing debate on theoretical and conceptualization of the dynamics of issues in Foreign Policy, its formulation, decision making principles, conduct, guidelines, national interests etc. have continued to raise a heated discussion among academics, diplomats, and international relations pundits.

It is in light of this pertinent debate that this book attempts to contribute. Its main thrust is revamping of African Foreign Policies within the context of the Continental's Agenda 2063. It is further argued that based on agreed common Foreign Policies benchmarks as stipulated in this continental blueprint, the political, and socio-economic development of Africa, will progressively and significantly change and therefore Africa claiming its rightful place in the international community during the 21st century.

The authors of Revamping African Foreign Policies in the 21st century have written an innovative work that is vast in scope, deep in analysis, impressively well researched, and functionally timely. Its coverage goes deep into the ancient roots of African diplomacy and navigates through national policy, to regional and international dynamics.

The book ends with a powerful chapter on revamping foreign policy, defined as "revitalizing, changing, or re-arranging the existing policy strategies to reflect the contemporary African context in the interest of the people by improving where Africa has been disadvantaged". The book concludes with high sense of optimism given the appropriate Pan-African, committed as well as visionary leadership coupled with immense resources, this is doable and achievable. The symbiotic relation is inevitable. However, mutual respect is paramount. It can be done, play your part. Let us walk the Talk.

Dedication

This book is dedicated to the memory of the late Prof Samson Samauel Wassara who passed on during the initial stage of writing the manuscript of this book. His commitment during the conception of the idea, inspired the remaining two of authors to carry on this project to its logical conclusion.

CONTENTS

ABBREVIATIONS AND ACRONYMS

AAAA: Addis Ababa Action Agenda
ACCORD: African Centre for the Constructive Resolution of Disputes
AEC: African Economic Community
AFCFTA: African Continental Free Trade Agreement
AfDB: African Development Bank
AGA: African Governance Architecture
AIDA: Accelerated Industrial Development of Africa
AISA: Africa Institute of South Africa
ALCSP: Arab League Collective Security Pact
AMCOMET: African Ministerial Conference on Meteorology
AMESD: African Monitoring of the Environment for Sustainable Development
AMISOM: African Union Mission in Somalia
AMU: Arab Maghreb Union
ANC: African National Congress
APRMUCG: African Peer Review Mechanism and Unconstitutional Change of Government
APSA: African Peace and Security Architecture
ARCSS: Agreement on Resolution of Conflict in South Sudan
ASEAN: Association of South East Asian Nations
ATAF: African Tax Administration Forum
AU: African Union
AUC: African Union Commission
AUCPCC: African Union Convention on Preventing and Combating Corruption
AUMR: African Union Master Roadmap
AUP: Africa Union Passport
AYCPAC: African Youth Community of Practice on Anti-Corruption
BIAT: Boosting Intra-Africa Trade

BRICS: Brazil, China, India, Russia and South Africa
CAADP: Common African Agriculture Development Pragramme
CABRI: Collaborative African Budget Reform Initiatives
CAR: Central African Republic
CARIFTA: Caribbean Free Trade Association
CCR: Centre for Conflict Resolution
CIA: Chief Intelligence Agency
CITES: Convention on International Trade of Endangered Species
COMESA: Common Market for Eastern and Southern Africa
COVID 19: Corona Virus 2019
CPA: Commonwealth Parliamentary Association
CPCC: Convention on Preventing and Combating Corruption
DDG: Deputy Director General
DDR: Disaster Risk Reduction
DFA: Department of Foreign Policy
DISCOS: Distribution to Final Consumers
DRC: Democratic Republic of Congo
EAP: East Africa Parliament
EAP: Encyclopedia Africana Project
ECCAS: Economic Community of Central African States
ECOMOG: Economic Community of West African States Monitoring Group
ECOWAS: Economic Community of West African States
EEC: European Economic Community
EPA: Economic Partnership Agreement
EPLF: Eritrean People's Liberation Front
EPRDF: Ethiopian People's Revolutionary Democratic Front
EU: European Union
FDI: Foreign Direct Investment
FDRE: Federal Democratic Republic of Ethiopia
FP: Foreign Policy
FPA: Foreign Policy Analysis
FPAM: Foreign Policy Analytical Model
FTA: Free Trade Agreements
GATT: General Agreement on Tariffs and Trade
GDP: Grow Domestic Product
GGWSS: Great Green Wall for the Sahara and Sahel Initiative
GNU: Government of National Unity
GSP: Generalised System of Preference
IAE: Inter-African Embassies
IATF: Intra-African Trade Fair

IBRD: International Bank for Reconstruction and Development
IBSA: Rise of Middle Power
ICC: International Criminal Court
ICGLR: International Conference on the Great Lakes Region
ICT: Information communication Technology
IGAD: Intergovernmental Authority on Development
IGADD: Intergovernmental Authority on Drought and Development
IGD: Institute of Global Dialogue
IGO: Intergovernmental Organizations
IIMMP: Imaginary Ideal Machine for Making Policy
IJR: Institute for Justice and Reconciliation
IL: International Law
IMF: International Monetary Fund
IMTC: International Military Training Cooperation
IO: International Organization
IOR-ARC: Indian Ocean Rim-Association for Regional Cooperation
IPP: Independent Power Producers
IPPF: Infrastructure Project Preparation Facility
IR: International Relations
ITO: International Trade Organization
JPA: Juba Peace Agreement
LPA: Lagos Plan of Action
MAF: Model as an Analytical Framework
MDC: Movement for Democratic Change
MEA: Multilateral Environmental Agreements
MESA: Monitoring for Environment and Security in Africa
MFN: Most Favoured Nations
MILF: Moro Islamic Liberation Front
MNC: Multinational Corporations
MOFAIC: Ministry of Foreign Affairs and International Cooperation
MPFA: Migration Policy Framework
NACFP: National Advisory Committee on Foreign Affairs or Policy
NAM: Non-Alignment Movement
NCP: National Congress Party
NEPAD: New Partnership for Africa's Development
NGO: Non-Governmental Organisation
NIF: National Islamic Front
NSC: National Security Council
OAU: Organization of African Unity
ODA: Overseas Development Assistance

OECD: Organisation for Economic Co-operation and Development
OIC: Organisation of Islamic Countries
OPEC: Organization of the Petroleum Exporting Countries
OPM: Organization Process Model
PAeN: Project, Pan African e-network
PAFTRAC: Pan-African Private Sector Trade and Investment Policy Committee
PAP: Pan-African Parliament
PAPSS: Pan African Payment and Settlement System
PAVeU: Pan African Virtual and e-University
PCAS: Policy Coordination and Advisory Service
PCP: Popular Congress Party
PIDA: Programme for Infrastructure Development in Africa
PKO: Peacekeeping Operations
POA: Programme of Action
PPCA: Parliamentary Portfolio Committee on Foreign Affairs
PPP: Public- private partnership
PRC: People's Republic of China
PTA: Preferential Trade Agreements
R2P: Responsibility to Protect
RAM: Rational Actor Model
REC-RM: Regional Economic Communities and Regional Mechanism
REC: Regional Economic community
REC: Regional Economic Councils
REC: Regional Economic Councils
SAATM: Single African Air Transport Market
SACU: Southern African Customs Union
SADC: Southern African Development Community
SADCC: Southern African Development Coordination Conference
SAFA: South Africa foreign policy analysis
SAIIA: South African Institute of International Affairs
SANDF: South African National Defence Force
SME: Small and medium enterprises
SPLA/M: Sudan People Liberation Army/movement
SPLM-N: Sudan People Liberation Movement -North
STC: Scientific and Technical Committee
TAC: Technical Aids Corps
TDCA: Trade, Development and Cooperation Agreement
TFP: Total Factor Productivity
TFTA: Tri-Partite Free Trade Agreement
TPLF: Tigray People's Liberation Front

UAE: United Arab Emirates
UK: United Kingdom
UN HABITAT: United Nations Human Settlements Programme
UN: United Nations
UNAMID: United Nations Mission in Darfur
UNDP: United Nations Development Programmes
UNECA: United nations Economic Commission for Africa
UNEP: United Nations Environmental Programme
UNGA: United Nations General Assembly
UNITA: National Union for the Total Independence of Angola
UNMISS: United Nations Mission in South Sudan
UNSC: United Nations Security Council
US: United States
USA: United States of America
USSR: United Soviet Socialist Republics
WTO: World Trade Organization
WWI: World War I
ZANU-PF: Zimbabwe African National Union – Patriotic Front

PREFACE

The authors of *Revamping African Foreign Policies in the 21ˢᵗ Century* have written an innovative work that is vast in scope, deep in its analysis, impressively well researched, and functionally timely. Its coverage goes deeply into the ancient roots of African diplomacy and stretches from national policy, to regional and international dynamics. The book ends with a powerful chapter on revamping foreign policy defined as "changing or re-arranging the existing policy strategies to reflect the African context in the interest of the people by improving where Africa has been disadvantaged". The authors explain that "revamping African foreign policy refers to an improvement of an old idea or a newer into a better version from something that was disfavoured to get new life through repair and restoration." I am deeply honoured to have been asked to write a Foreward for the book and it is my pleasure to do so.

A great deal of work has obviously gone into preparing this book. The breadth and depth of the scholarship is very impressive. And the coverage of African foreign policy traced back to ancient times into the foreign policies of modern African states, as represented by case studies selected from all the regions of the continent, is laudable. The combination of the scholarship and country-specific empirical studies makes this a major contribution to the field of foreign policy and diplomatic practice in Africa.

Having said that, I would like to make a few observations that I hope might be useful in guiding the reader. My first observation is that the book contains a vast literature review in which the references become so overwhelming that it is at times difficult to discern the link to the major threads or themes of the book. This challenge must be viewed in the wider perspective of the study as targeting mixed audiences and policy objectives. The target readership should include scholars, policymakers and practitioners. There is much in the book that offers the opportunity for strategic intellectual and functional selectivity for the readers.

This leads to my second observation. I discern two major interwoven and complementary clusters or themes in the book. The first comprises theoretical issues, backed by the vast literature review. The second is a more empirical and operational discussion of the issues and relating them to cases from a select number of countries. I believe that the reader would benefit more fully from the book by connecting these two major themes.

Given the diversity of the targeted readership and policy objectives, this might require diligently selective focus on some major themes in the first part of the book, and connecting them to the themes of the second part, depending on the particular interests of the reader. This admittedly demanding exercise should help the reader understand how the theoretical themes guide or explain their application in the second part of the book. That would not only integrate the book more clearly to the reader, but would also substantiate the interconnectedness of the book, and sustain the logical flow and the momentum for the reader.

My third observation relates to the second part of the book that comprises the case studies of the foreign policy of a select number of countries. This is a concrete reflection of the practical experience of the countries concerned that is of great contemporary interest. However, as noted in my earlier comment, this will require diligence on the part of the reader to make the connection with the theoretical themes covered in the first part. Again, efforts in this exercise will vary with the particular interest of the reader. Furthermore, while each case study stands on its own, it is worth considering the structures of the case studies along the same issues or themes to combine the specificity of each case study with the commonalities of the concepts and their practical applications.

1. Ancient Roots of African Diplomacy

I was intrigued by the coverage of the pre-colonial roots of African foreign policy. This is a fascinating area which calls for greater attention than it has so far received. It is an aspect of a wider area of pre-colonial system of governance, constitutionalism, and Africa's relationship to the outside world that needs to be more thoroughly studied. Colonialism assumed a vacuum in every aspect of pre-colonial life in Africa. The Europeans invaders decided to fill that alleged vacuum as a moral justification for their imperialist intervention. While there were clear economic motivations behind the invasion of Africa, foreign rulers tried to legitimize their rapacious occupation with the mission of 'civilizing' the 'dark continent'.

The authors make a strong case against the assumption that diplomacy is a novel concept in Africa. They observe: "The origin of African diplomatic relations could be traced to early times of its existence until the period of the Trans-Atlantic trade in slaves, ivory, beads and other goods. Treaties were ratified solemnly, widely accepted protocol, regulated negotiations, sanctions were provided for the observance of treaties and embassies were sent to Europe with emissaries performing official diplomatic duties. These diplomatic activities went on in the pre-colonial period covering a period of four or five hundred years up to the last decade of the nineteenth century before the partition and the establishment of colonies. Pre-colonial Africa too could trace the origin of its Diplomatic relations to the same period".

The authors go on to argue that pre-colonial Africa had its diplomacy practiced in different forms until it was interrupted and to some extent destroyed by colonialism. As most of this history was not documented, it posed intellectual challenges. "The debate that ensued between the early post independent African intellectuals and their counterparts in the west, from different disciplines in defense of African history must be seen within this context. For example, the first generation of African lawyers, the likes of Francis Deng, argued in defense of African jurisprudence. This was in response to the western scholars who contended that the continent had no legal system. This argument was factually incorrect."

The authors conclude their elaborate review of specific accounts of the diplomatic history of some African pre-colonial states with the following statement: "It is thus clear that pre-colonial Africa, far from being a chaotic, backward 'Dark Continent' as depicted by early colonial historians, was home to sophisticated political organization, ranging from Empires and Kingdoms to city-states and chieftaincies. Democracy among these centrally organised political entities produced a rich tapestry of relations, and was facilitated by abundant trade and the existence of customary law".

2. Parallels with African Jurisprudence

The authors' argument about the ancient roots of African diplomacy is reminiscent of what I encountered in the study of African customary law to which the authors refer. The general assumption was that African customary law was not law because it did not have institutions of enforcement, such as courts, the police, and the military, that characterize the concept of law as viewed from the Western jurisprudential perspective. The first generation of African scholars therefore endeavoured to interpret African institutions to establish similarities with Western institutions to justify their claim that African law was indeed law even by Western institutional standards. As the authors note, I was among the early students of African law. In the end, the result was a hybrid between the authenticity of African tradition and linkage with the Western-oriented concepts.

There are discernible similarities between this jurisprudential scholarship on African law and the presentation of pre-colonial African foreign policy and diplomacy, which cites parallels between historical African diplomatic experience and contemporary Western concepts and practice of diplomacy, as African legal scholars tended to do. While the comparison with Western practice is interesting and indeed unavoidable, I believe that there is a need for an original and authentic contribution to be made by investigating African indigenous theory and practice of foreign policy and diplomacy. The book takes innovative and encouraging steps in that direction, but more research is obviously needed. As is the case with the study of African Constitutionalism, I make this point as an aspiration, since I realize that exploring that past may not be easy or practical, but it is nonetheless called for and would be very interesting and valuable.

3. Nature of Foreign Policy

The authors correctly observe, "Foreign policy of any country is an extension of domestic policy". They list domestic factors such as internal politics, geography, form of government, leadership, and public diplomacy among the domestic factors pertinent to formulating foreign policy. They link these with external factors, such as regional integration and international organization, as pertinent.

The overriding and interrelated objectives of foreign policy are two-fold: to protect and safeguard the sovereignty, territorial integrity, security and stability of the country; and to ensure regional and international cooperation in promoting peace, security, stability and socio-economic development. They postulate that development as an objective must prioritize the eradication of poverty, disease and illiteracy, and generate constructively managing resources toward enhancing inclusive growth and prosperity for all the people of the country.

I was attracted by the authors' focus on what they see as the three pillars of foreign policy: "the 'end', the 'ways', and the 'means. The end consists of a vision of a desired outcome or set of interests in interacting with another state/ actor; the ways, consists of the strategies and ideas (e.g., diplomatic tactics, coercion), to pursue these desired interests; and the means, consists of the available resources at a state's disposal (e.g., economic, military)". Stated differently, this means clarifying the objectives of foreign policy, the institutional framework for pursuing them, and the resources availed in support of the policy implementation.

Diplomacy is the principal tool for pursuing foreign relations objectives, regionally and internationally. While the foreign policy of a country and its diplomatic tools need to be dynamic, flexible and open to continuous reassessment, readjustment, and change, national interest remains paramount and constant. Contrary to popular belief, diplomacy is more than being elegantly dressed and well spoken, although those are important elements. For diplomacy to be most effective, it should be based on representing and advocating a positive domestic agenda, with confidence and conviction. A diplomat cannot be confident, credible and effective if he or she does not enjoy the full support of the pertinent national leaders and related institutions. He or she must also be well equipped with up-to-date reliable information. Without these ingredients, a diplomat cannot be convincing or effective.

Diplomacy is a two-way process transmitting a message to outside interlocutors and reflecting back to the national decision-makers the message from the outside world, with recommendations for corrective measures as needed. I have always maintained that a diplomat by and large represents both his/her country and the country of accreditation. Success means bringing the two countries closer together.

Let me give an example in which I was personally involved as Ambassador to a number of Western countries, including the Scandinavian countries, Canada and the United States, and as Minister of State for Foreign Affairs of the Sudan from 1972 to 1983. In 1972, the Addis Ababa Agreement ended the seventeen-year civil war that had cost the lives of two million people, displaced over four million internally, and forced an additional one million into refuge abroad, a tragic situation that was a source of grave concern to friendly countries around the world.

We used that negotiated agreement to win international support for consolidating peace, security, and stability. We projected the agreement as having replaced war with a robust regionally equitable development program for which we needed international support. We presented the Sudan to the outside world as a meeting ground for racial, ethnic, cultural, and religious diversities in Africa, and a bridge to the Middle East. Sudan became a model and an agent for the promotion of regional peace and security, with positive international ripple effects. That vision appealed to Western democracies, especially the United States. Sudan became third after Israel and Egypt as the recipient of US economic and security assistance. Sudan unfortunately lost that privilege when President Jaafar Nimeiri, who had ironically championed the Addis Ababa Agreement in the first place, unilaterally abrogated the Agreement ten years later. The country returned to war in 1983, spearheaded by the Sudan People's Liberation Movement and its army, SPLM/A. That war lasted for over twenty years until it was ended by the Comprehensive Peace Agreement in 2005.

The foreign policy of the Republic of South Sudan and the diplomatic tools for pursuing it must be seen in the context of the long liberation struggle of South Sudanese against successive foreign rulers in pursuit of the ideals of freedom, liberty and dignity for all, without discrimination. It was the failure to achieve the ideals of New Sudan that the liberation movement became a struggle from the Arab-Islamic internal colonialism.

Ironically, the objectives of South Sudanese independence movement that should continue to guide post-independence foreign policy of South Sudan have much in common with the African independence struggle and its relevancy to the foreign policy of African states. As the authors of state, "The foundation of African foreign policy lay in the struggle for social and political equality and freedom from economic exploitations and racial discrimination. The cornerstone of African foreign policy was the liberation of African territories still under colonial rule to full independence, the struggle against apartheid and settler colonialism in South Africa and continuous struggle against neo-colonialism". These ideals, which represented the Vision of the New Sudan that the SPLM/A postulated for the country, must still be seen as providing the guiding principles for building South Sudan as a modern nation, united in its vision and mission, with respect for diversity, inclusivity and equality. To be credible as a basis for a successful foreign policy, the country must be seen to be sincerely pursuing those ideals.

Given the current situation in the country, which has already alienated many former friends and partners of South Sudan, what the country needs is a strategic engagement with the international community in a frank constructive analysis of the conditions in the country and a constructive exchange of views on how to get the country out of its quagmire and chart a way to sustainable peace, security, stability and nation building.

4. Partnership Toward Shared Objectives

The authors of *Revamping African foreign policies in the 21st century* succinctly elaborate the interconnection between national and international dimensions of foreign policy and the emergent issues of global concern, such as the degradation of the environment and pandemic diseases. As they observe, "In the modern world, no state can remain isolated from the global community. With the rise of globalisation, the concept of statecraft has been reshaped and the interdependency between and among the nations has grown to a new height. The network is so visible that an action and decision of one state is bound to affect the fate of another. Even the domestic matters or instability of a particular state pose far-reaching consequences for the entire region or even the whole world. Indeed, globalisation and other forces of modernization, notably trans-boundary and global environmental changes, mean that more of what was once purely national is now the subject of foreign policy. Hence, each and every state should have an effective and vibrant foreign policy to manage the highly complex issues of modern statecraft".

The authors argue that it is the responsibility of national sovereignty to provide for the socio-economic welfare of citizens and to seek international cooperation to enhance its capacity to fulfil that national obligation. This requires states to enter into partnership with other states in order to harness resources needed to meet domestic needs. As the authors note, "No nation, no matter how powerful and richly endowed, has ever achieved economic prosperity and ensured a high standard of living for its citizens without active involvement in the channel of international trade".

Another area of importance is the image a state projects as a basis for international cooperation which comprises political, economic and cultural dimensions. One of those dimensions is "national prestige (e.g., national honour, respect and so forth). The degree of influence a nation can wield on others depends on the extent to which such a state is able to conduct its affairs consistent with a high sense of self-respect, process and national honour. The implication here is that a state that fails to maintain a high degree of acceptable reputation in the international system risks disrespect and even isolation in the community of nations".

It is not surprising that Ambassadors live in relatively prestigious accommodations, dress elegantly, entertain lavishly, and carry themselves with an air of affluence. All that is to project their status as representatives of their head of State and the country. It is sometimes impressive for an Ambassador to be conspicuously modest to reflect the needy realities of a poor developing country or to make an ideological socialistic statement. So, the popular criticism of diplomats as spendthrifts of scarce resources is a misreading of the obligations of their representational status. In the African tradition, even a relatively poor host will lavishly entertain guests to project hospitality and generosity as noble attributes of pride and dignity.

But as the saying goes, charity begins at home. A state must first meet the essential needs of its people before it projects an image of pride and dignity externally. Even more ominous is the failure to provide physical protection and respect for human rights and humanitarian standards. If a state fails to live up to the normative principles of 'Sovereignty as Responsibility' or its reformulated version, 'The Responsibility to Protect', and does not request or welcome international assistance, with the result that its people suffer and die in masses, the world is not going to stand by and watch without embarking on some form of intervention. The most effective way of protecting national sovereignty is to discharge the responsibilities of sovereignty. National sovereignty can no longer be used as a barricade against justified international humanitarian action.

Those were the normative principles that guided me in carrying out my UN mandates as Representative of the Secretary General on Internally Displace Persons, IDPs, for twelve years, and as Under-Secretary-General and Special Advisor for the Prevention of Genocide for five years. I recall an experience I had when, as Representative of the Secretary General on IDPs, I visited an African country that was torn apart by genocidal conflict. A burly Minister of Interior, who was notorious for his hostility to the UN, began to preach to me about African pride and dignity, and how they would not allow foreigners to infringe on their national sovereignty in the name of human rights protection. After listening patiently, I responded, politely but firmly, "Mr. Minister, as an African myself, I could not agree with you more on what you said about African pride and dignity. But African pride and dignity must include all Africans. Dignity cannot be enjoyed by some Africans, while others are excluded and denied that dignity". My UN staff could not believe the way I talked to the Minister. But to our happy surprise, his response was remarkably calm and seemingly understanding. Our relations became cordial from that time on. He apparently saw the point.

5. The Role of Culture

If foreign policy is an extension of domestic policy, as the authors correctly underscore, then it should be grounded in the cultural values of the country concerned. Culture is more than song and dance, language or art; it is the sum-total of societal norms and patterns of behaviour that constitute a way of life or social order. It can be assumed that every cohesive society has an integrated, coherent and established system based on fundamental values and institutional structures that constitute the foundation of its public order. That foundation stipulates the principles that determine the way a society governs itself and mobilizes and utilizes its human and material resources and allocates responsibilities.

Over a long period of experience, trial and error, this eventually results in a functional framework of optimum communal acceptance by broad consensus and establishes a system that is stable, self-sustaining and resistant to disruptive change. Such shocks as war may be so severe as to shatter the existing order, necessitating the development of a new logic for reforming the system and determining a reallocation of functional roles. That might entail fundamental reforms in such areas as gender relations and the role of youth. But change must be a process of incremental reform, not the obliteration of what was existing to be replaced by something radically new and threatening to the stability of the social order.

My interest in legal anthropology and the study of customary law literature was not a purely academic or scholarly exercise. I believed strongly that knowledge of our culture(s) should be applied to the challenges of nation-building and development. South Sudanese societies are among the most thoroughly studied by world-renown anthropologists who have left a wealth of knowledge that has not been sufficiently studied, far less applied, by South Sudanese scholars, policymakers and practitioners.

Such notions as acephalous political systems, stateless societies, tribes without rulers, the segmentary lineage system, balanced opposition, and ordered anarchy, which were central to anthropological description of the Nilotic societies, which Oxford anthropologists and their colleagues in related academic institutions championed, have built in them concepts of governance, democracy, respect for human rights, and constitutionalism that, if applied, could help build an admirable model African state.

I believe that was what the colonial rulers did when they adopted the policy of indirect rule, which post-Colonial administrations abandoned as part of colonial exploitation of culture as a tool of domination. The culturally-oriented approach I am envisaging is what the chairman of my doctoral dissertation at Yale Law School, Professor Harold Lasswell, helped me dub as the strategy of 'transitional integration.'[1]

6. Models of African Cultural Values

The authors of *Revamping African foreign policies in the 21st century* underscore the importance of cultural values in these words: "The nature and manner of our family values, political socialization, indoctrination, and our personal experience shape our values because they form the standards against which our conducts and of others are weighed. In the process of formulation of foreign policy, therefore, values serve justification for actions and goals for policymakers. Belief could be viewed as propositions that policymakers hold to be true, even if they cannot be verified. In a foreign-policymaking context, such beliefs are valuable because they become the unexamined assumptions upon which numerous policy choices are made".

---

1   Francis Mading (1971)

Without stipulating the cultural values of any one particular system as a model for emulation by others, the Dinka normative principles of Cieng, which I believe are widely shared by South Sudan's ethnic communities, postulate living harmoniously and cooperatively together with others. The Dinka normally refer to the concept as Cieng baai, and the word baai applies equally to family, home, village, community, tribe and country. Cieng as a normative principle is almost identical to the now world-famous Bantu principle applies to the principles of Ubuntu as a concept of shared humanity in which the interests of the individual are viewed in harmony with communal solidarity and the ideals of humankind.

A similar concept prevails in the indigenous culture of Ethiopia. Prime Minister Abiy Ahmed Ali, in his acceptance speech for the Nobel Peace Prize, invoked the Amharic concept Medemer, which means togetherness for synergetic unity, peace, and reconciliation. Prime Minister Abiy Ahmed saw Medemer as a concept of social compact of love, forgiveness and reconciliation. According to the Prime Minister, this normative concept stipulates that you are your brother's or sister's keeper. He called on the Ethiopians to use the best of their past to build a new culture and implicitly to develop a system of governance and constitutionalism based on that culture.

Among the Akan people of Ghana, the concept of 'Personhood', which has also been well studied and documented, embodies similar moral principles. According to the renown Ghanian philosophy scholar, Kwasi Wiredu, the Akan perceive personhood as constituting an individual within a community that expands from the family to the lineage, clan, nation, country, and humanity. Members in these concentric circles are expected to share rights and privileges that match obligations based on the reciprocal Golden Rule of *do unto others what you would have them do unto you*. Clearly, the concept is a potential guiding principle for good governance and constitutionalism.

In Rwanda, the concept of *Gacaca*, which has been used as a method of addressing the disputes associated with the 1994 genocide to lessen the burdens of the tribunals formally carrying out the trials of genocide, is a traditional way of "discussing together on a grass patch". As a means of resolving conflicts and promoting unity and harmony in the community based on customary laws, codes and institutions, Gacaca has much in common with the concepts applied in other regions of Africa.

These values belie the Eurocentric perception of Africa as lacking cultural values and indeed history worthy of recognition, and therefore requires external importation of ideas to fill the vacuum. As the authors observe, "Much of the rhetoric of African diplomacy is informed by its history of marginalization and exploitation: a relationship vis-a-vis the rest of the world that infers continental vulnerability. But contemporary African diplomacy is not just born of negative experiences. It is also infused with traditional values that Africans and the Diaspora share: a seamless approach to the passage of time, respect for culture, tradition and authority, predilection for collective, unhurried decisions, and the prioritization of community rather than individuals". The authors cite the case of South Africa to emphasise the values enshrined in the concepts that promote societal selflessness, such as *Harambee* (Swahili word for "pulling together") and *Ubuntu* (Ngun word for "being human").

Ubuntu was often invoked as the African moral foundation of reconciliation based on interdependence that led to the eradication of the apartheid system in South Africa. The authors give the example of the South African government's most recent foreign policy document, 'Building a Better World', places emphasis on the Diplomacy of Ubuntu'.

The fact that these values are largely aspirational, reflecting what can at best be only partially achieved in practice, does not negate their importance as normative principles that guide performance. In fact, these concepts describe both what should happen and what in fact happens, what ought and what is.

7. Building a Future from the Past

It is my belief that these cultural principles, which form a holistic model of the social order, should be relevant to the formulation of a culturally oriented normative framework of good governance, conflict prevention, peace, security, stability, development and nation building. But the challenge is not only within the African state, because cultural values and the principles of constitutionalism are relevant to the functioning of local communities, national institutions, sub-regional organizations, the continent-wide African Union, the United Nations, and a wide array of governmental and non-governmental organizations. To the extent that membership and participation in these various entities and organizations includes states which comprise cultural diversities, the fundamental norms on which communities and organizations are founded and guide their operations are, and should be, subject to the challenges posed by cross-cultural differences. These differences need to be reconciled, harmonized and rendered mutually accommodating and enriching through inter-communal and inter-state cultural dialogue.

In his Foreward to my book, *Identity, Diversity and Constitutionalism in Africa,* former President of Nigeria, General Olusegun Obasanjo, advocated a similar objective. He wrote, "I share Dr. Deng's view of an Africa that builds on its time-tested cultural ideals, and institutionalized practices … I might also note that these values have much to offer not only Africa but the world as a whole. Just as Western democracy enshrines certain universal values, so does the African worldview. In a world where every community is increasingly obliged to acknowledge and interact with often very different communities, the traditional African focus on building consensus instead of fostering competition has obvious relevance. Equally, the African concern to root the individual within the community, is highly pertinent to societies in which migration, and industrialization have generated atomic isolation, and alienation".

What is stipulated here is not a return to the past, but building a future on the sound foundations of the past. It is a strategy of transitional integration, by which traditional values and institutions are reinterpreted, to facilitate a culturally oriented development, toward a better future. What I am advocating here echoes what the Founding Fathers of African independence aspired to achieve. Although the current situation in Africa is largely one of disconnect between the prevailing Eurocentric governance systems and the indigenous African cultural values and institutions, the need for cultural orientation has been an unheeded call by the Founding Fathers from the inception of independence from the colonial yoke. This was reflected in the normative visions they declared: Nkrumah's Consciencism; Nyerere's Ujamaa; Kaunda's Humanism; Kenyatta's Harambee; Senghor's Negretude'; and Mobutu's Authenticite'.

However, these normative concepts, though sincere, tended to be politically motivated and aimed at legitimizing otherwise authoritarian rule. The priority objectives of fostering national unity and accelerating socio-economic development were used to justify one party system, 'African socialism', leadership without term limits, and denial of human rights, fundamental freedoms and civil liberties. Our objective should be to honour and pursue their legitimate aspirations reflected in their slogans while avoiding the political manipulation of those noble postulations. To give one specific example, it is time African leaders stopped seeing human rights as a reflection of European values imposed on Africa. As UN Secretary General Kofi Annan once said, this is insulting to the African value system, for human rights are African rights and reflect the ideals of our African value system.

8. Evolution of African Policy Agenda

African engagement with the international community has gone through several phases. The first phase marked the liberation struggle against colonial domination, which began to bear fruits with the waves of independence in the 1950s, beginning with the Sudan in 1956, followed by Ghana in 1957. After these two front-runners, the flood of independence became unstoppable, although ending racial domination in Southern Africa, in particular apartheid in Namibia and South Africa, persisted into the mid-1990s. As the authors note, "The OAU encouraged its members to support liberation movements in Southern Africa in countries like South Africa, Zimbabwe, Namibia, Angola, Mozambique and Western Sahara. African countries coordinated their foreign policy actions in international organisations like the United Nations to secure independence of colonial territories, to impose sanctions against apartheid South Africa and its isolation from in the international system".

The second phase focussed on continuing the fight against neocolonialism and fostering partnership in economic development and nation building. Neocolonialism persists in African systems of governance and constitutionalism. It is self-evident that post-independence constitutions in Africa were modelled after the constitutions of the colonizing countries. It is also a fact that colonial authorities only put in place the basic institutional structures of the constitutions of their home countries, without adhering to their ideals. Paradoxically, the constitutions bequeathed to the post-colonial state contained those lofty principles which the colonialists themselves never observed. For the same reason, the independence leaders were not familiar or comfortable with those principles. They were indeed resentful of limitations on their powers. These constitutions were often overthrown by military coups with little or no tears shed.

A third phase in the African decolonization, often labelled as a second wave of liberation movements from within, aims at promoting indigenous concepts of democratization and respect for fundamental rights and civil liberties by developing home-grown African constitutions and related principles of constitutionalism with the popular involvement of the people. Constitution-making is more credible and effective when it is an exercise by the people, in self-reflection, self-projection, and self-realization. The reality, however, is that even when the people participate in the drafting of constitutions, the substance remains basically reflective of the centralized power structure. Constitutionalism in Africa essentially remains a transplantation of legal rules, institutions, and customs from external sources. The prevailing tendency is to adopt a constitution as a matter of formality, but otherwise ignore, undermine, amend or even abrogate it unceremoniously

Africa has continued to introduce reforms in the development of normative frameworks in a wide variety of areas. As the authors observe, "African Union (AU), which succeeded the OAU in July 2002 in Durban ... has instituted principles of peace in the Protocol on Peace and security, principle of post-conflict reconstruction and principles of development by establishing the New Partnership for Africa's Development (NEPAD). The AU has introduced principles in the area of governance, which have implications for African foreign policy. They are the African peer review mechanism and unprincipled and unconstitutional change of government. African countries are careful about their policy directives outside their territorial boundaries."

Redrafting post-colonial constitutions has so far not involved introducing genuinely substantive reforms. A constitutional identity for Africa should entail more than dressing up Eurocentric constitutional models with colourful African garbs, and envisage constructing a constitutive order that genuinely reflects the cultural values and institutions that represent African world view. It must reflect the qualification for leadership based on recognized cultural values, stipulate the manner in which decisions are taken through popular consensus-building, emphasize persuasive power over coercive imposition, and foster 'respect' and 'deference' for good leadership rather than fear of oppressive exercise of power.

9. Africa in the Global Dynamics

Since the African independence movement in the 1950s, the world has constantly gone through changes that are continuously challenging African diplomacy. Africa was initially the beneficiary of the end of the Second World War which resulted in a new global order under the United Nations. Although dominated by the victorious powers and challenged by the emergence of the Cold War, United Nations maintained relative peace and security globally. The new World Order promoted self-determination and independence for the colonized territories and universalized respect for human rights and fundamental freedoms, but the United Nations Security Council remained conspicuously dominated by the victorious Permanent Five who have resisted reforms of the system for decades.

During the Cold War, global peace and security was paradoxically maintained through the bi-polar control mechanisms and confrontation of the two Super Powers, the United States and the Soviet Union. Conflicts around the world, national and regional, were seen as extensions of the proxy global confrontation of the Super Powers. While relative peace precariously prevailed among the major powers, fearing the mutual threat of nuclear weapons, Third World countries became embroiled in internal and regional wars that were both managed and sometimes aggravated by the Cold War rivalry of the Super Powers. These wars massively displaced populations internally and forced large numbers into refuge across international borders, and caused untold humanitarian crises.

The end of the Cold War initially raised hopes that an even more effective global peace and security would emerge. Conflicts were now being seen in their proper context as internal and regional and not distorted as proxy wars of the Super Powers. This was a positive development. But that also ended dependency on the Super Powers whose strategic interests behind the bi-polar control mechanisms of the Cold War no longer applied. The burden now shifted to the countries or regions concerned to assume primary responsibility. Human rights and humanitarian concerns and mutually beneficial economic relations became the bases of engagement between the developed and developing world.

This necessitated a fundamental change in perceptions of national sovereignty which became increasingly stipulated as the responsibility to protect and assist the populations under state jurisdiction, with international assistance as needed. Manifest failure to protect or seek needed international assistance triggers a more robust international humanitarian intervention which is now more associated with the concept of the Responsibility to Protect, popularly known by the acronyms RtP or R2P. Although based on the same three pillars of Sovereignty as Responsibility, which include state responsibility, assistance to the state as needed, and a residual remedial intervention in case of manifest state failure, Responsibility to Protect tends to be viewed as advocating international intervention and is therefore resisted by the weaker states of the Third World. In either case, sovereignty is ceasing to be a barrier against international involvement in a country whose people are in need of supplementary or alternative source of protection for its citizens.

Following the end of the Cold War, the outbreak of international terrorism invaded the world and generated a new polarization between the perpetrators of terrorism and those fighting it. A new trend toward globalisation also emerged that tended to dichotomized the world into those who benefit from it and those it leaves behind. The world became torn between globalisation and localization.

Amidst these tumultuous developments appeared the Coronavirus (Covid-19) that has now paradoxically reaffirmed globalisation through pervasive infection while fragmenting the world in isolationist response to the pandemic. What prevails today is a global upheaval and uncertainty about the state of the world and its future. The challenge is how to manage this crisis situation.

10. Framing a Humanizing Global Order

In *Revamping African foreign policies in the 21ˢᵗ century*, the authors have laid a broad inclusive framework to guide relations between Africa and the international community. This is an innovative work that opens doors for creatively searching for strategies to address the myriad challenges facing Africa in forging cooperation and partnership in a paradoxically united and yet fragmented world. Building on illustrative principles implicitly enshrined in International Bill of Rights and other human rights and humanitarian instruments, as well as a wide array of international normative frameworks, a policy-oriented approach to African dialogue with external interlocutors could be developed around four inter-related fundamental principles that are connected to four interlinked levels of participation. These principles are: identity, dignity, diversity and equality; and the correlative levels are: local, national, regional and global.

Identity is a fundamental attribute of every person and group, a subject of legal and constitutional recognition and protection. It is the foundation of humanity. Dignity, however defined, is a universal value of shared humanity, which is why universal human rights norms are grounded in human dignity. Diversity at the point of contact with other groups raises the issue of comparison and discrimination. This generates a quest for equality and non-discrimination, a central norm of human rights. The goal then is to reverse tensions and conflicts emanating from mismanaged adversity and promote inclusivity based on mutual understanding, respect, unity, harmony and cooperation, often expressed in terms of the rule of law and equality before the law. These should be among the Pillars of Constitutionalism and international relations.

The United Nations guiding principle of sovereign equality of all nations, big and small, must also entail mutual respect for all peoples and their cultures. But this means that representatives of cultures or civilizations enter into this global interaction of give and take with a clear sense of the fundamental values which should guide their negotiating positions. Intrinsic in this should be clear sense of self awareness about one's identity, the principles of self-esteem and dignity associated with that identity, respect for each other in the diversity of the interactive parties, and a deep and sincere recognition of the overriding principle of equality. These fundamental principles should guide relations at the local, national, regional and global levels. They should be among the cardinal rules of an all-embracing community of human-kind that should be enshrined and widely disseminated as core elements in a global code of conduct.

While these are operational or negotiating guidelines, the book concludes with a powerful statement of the substantive goals and objectives of 'revamping' African Policy within the framework of the AU agenda 2063, which is "the current blueprint which guides both aspirations and flagship projects of the continent". The authors state that "All the AU member states have signed, ratified, acceded and domesticated the blueprint into their National Development programmes" They also observe that some of the goals of the AU Agenda 2063 coincide with the UN- SDGs. The authors argue that the foreign policies of African states must be realigned to accommodate the Agenda 2063 and give as examples programmes like African Peace and Security Architecture (APSA), Programme on Infrastructure Development in Africa (PIDA), Common African Agriculture Development Programme."

The seven 'aspirations' of the Agenda 2063 as put in a 'nutshell' by the authors include: "(i) A prosperous Africa based on inclusive growth and sustainable development, (ii) An integrated continent politically united, based on the ideals of Pan-Africanism and the vision of Africa's renaissance, (iii) An Africa of good governance, democracy for human rights, justice and rule of law, (iv) A peaceful and secure Africa, (v) Africa with a strong cultural identity, common heritage, values, and ethics., (vi) An Africa whose development is people driven, relying on the potential of African people, especially its women and youth, and caring for children, (vii) Africa as a strong, united, resilient and influential global player and partner".

In addition, the Agenda 2063 has 15 fast-track or flagship projects which have been identified as key to accelerate Africa's economic growth and development as well as promoting a common identity by celebrating Africa's history and vibrant culture. The flagship projects are: "Integrated High Speed Train Network (aims to connect all African capitals and commercial centres), Pan African Virtual and e-University (PAVeU), African Commodities Strategy, African economic Forum, African Continental Free Trade Area, (AfCFTA), African passport, and Free Movement of People, Silencing the Guns by 2020, Grand Inga Dam Project, Pan African e-network, (PAeN), Africa Outer Space Programme, Single African Air Transport Market, (SAATM), African Financial Institutions, Great Museum of Africa, Cyber Security, and Encyclopaedia Africana Project (EAP)."

While regional and international partnership is crucial to the development of Africa, and therefore a principal objective of African foreign policy, the core principle of foreign policy as an extension of domestic policy must remain pivotal to a well-grounded, confident, sovereign, internationally respected and effective foreign policy. Africa must know itself, its unifying identity, and the core cultural values of that identity as bases for engaging with international partners. Africa must prioritise developing its vast natural resources to achieve at least food sufficiency and promote prosperity for its people. Africa must end its current image as the richest continent of the poorest populations. From a foundation of rich natural endowment and well-grounded self-confidence, Africa can then reach out to partners in trade and economic cooperation on the basis of mutual respect, shared interests and responsible sovereignty.

There can be no pride in a sovereignty that depends on foreign handouts to meet basic needs and even to keep domestic peace and security. Africa now depends on international peacekeeping operations that are often tenuous, not entirely dependable, and get terminated in a panic when the going gets tough. Under those exigencies, foreigners that are supposed to provide protection barricade themselves or exit the afflicted African country to safety, leaving Africans to slaughter themselves, as the world shamelessly witnessed in Rwanda in 1994.

It is not easy to build a sense of pride and dignity in a people whose history has mostly been one of enslavement, domination, humiliation and dehumanisation. But that only makes the challenge of overcoming this dehumanising legacy a formidable task and success in doing so a most rewarding and gratifying achievement. There is no alternative to Africans assuming the front line of the fight against injustice and gross inequality, and stop Africans from continuing to be the primary victims of physical insecurity, gross violations of human rights and suffering the ills of poverty – hunger and disease. Africa must assume primary responsibility for ensuring peace, security, stability, development and prosperity for its people, with external partnership based on equality and mutual respect.

The guiding principle must be to approach 'Sovereignty as Responsibility', and not as a barricade against remedial action by the concerned world when national authorities manifestly fail to protect or assist their own needy populations. The best protection for national sovereignty is to discharge the responsibilities of sovereignty and if lack of capacity dictates otherwise, to invite or accept international support in the exceptional case of unmet needs proving to be beyond the means of the state concerned to provide protection and assistance for its needy citizens.

The authors of *Revamping African foreign policies in the 21st century* have written a book that impressively covers in great depth a wide scope of issues and raises an array of questions which they have elaborately answered. But they have also left much room for thought and the challenge of thinking creatively about the issues they have raised. This Foreward is the product of my effort, albeit modest, to meet that challenge in recognition and appreciation of the honour of having been invited to make a contribution to this innovative and laudable project of national, regional and global importance.

By Dr. Francis Mading Deng Majok

INTRODUCTION

The ongoing debate on theory and conceptualization of the dynamics of issues in foreign policy, its formulation, decision-making principles, guidelines and national interests have continued to raise a heated discussion among academics, diplomats, and international relations pundits. Several schools of thought have emerged. Some contend that foreign policy formulation and its decision is meaningless. Others argue that it goes without saying because everyone knows it; therefore, studying is a waste of time. There are also those who see it as a new area of inquiry, and thus studying it is inevitable. This uncertainty has provoked and continues to pre-occupy many scholars and researchers in the field.

In the modern world, no state can remain isolated from the global community. With the rise of globalisation, the concept of statecraft has been reshaped and the interdependency between and among nations has reached new heights. The network is so visible that an action and decision of one state is bound to affect the fate of another. Even the domestic matters or instability of a particular state pose far-reaching consequences for the entire region or even the whole world. Indeed, globalisation and other forces of modernization, notably trans-boundary and global environmental changes, mean that more of what was once purely national is now the subject of foreign policy. Hence, each and every state should have an effective and vibrant foreign policy to manage the highly complex issues of modern statecraft.

This lead scholars like to observe that even a decision to have no relations with a particular state is also a foreign policy. A state without a foreign policy has been compared to a ship in the deep sea without any knowledge of direction.[2] Thus, foreign policy leads a state in fulfilling its national interests and acquiring rightful place among community of nations. Like small states studies, the first problem that one faces in the study of foreign policy is the problem of

---

2   Feliks Gross (2008),

definition or clear meaning of the term. When used, it is either out of context or entails a different meaning. In the same note, it has been called a "neglected concept", adding that "this neglect has been one of the most serious obstacles to providing more adequate and comprehensive explanation of foreign policy"[3]. He believed that part of the reasons for this neglect is that "most people dealing with the subject have felt confident that they knew what foreign policy was."

In some countries, the legislature also has considerable effects on foreign as well as other areas of public policy, most often in liberal democracies. States with stronger unitary executive branches of government and which lack parliamentary sovereignty have weaker legislative involvement with foreign policy, except in cases of autocracy where one ruler handles major decisions on all national policy as the autocrat is the legislature. Elections and other shifts in government makeup can change the course of foreign policies, even on areas with long periods of consistency, when new leadership comes in with new goals and different views on national interests. Foreign policies of countries have varying rates of change and scopes of intent, which can be affected by factors that change the perceived national interests or even affect the stability of the country itself. The foreign policy of a country can have a profound and lasting impact on other countries and on the course of international relations as a whole, such as the Monroe Doctrine conflicting with the mercantilism policies of 19th-century European countries and the goals of independence of newly formed Central and South American countries.

Literally, the term *foreign policy* is composed of two individual words, *foreign* and *policy*. The word '*foreign*' came from the Latin word "foris" and "forus" meaning "outside" and the word '*policy*' originated from the Old French word "policie" meaning "civil administration". Therefore, the literal meaning of the phrase 'foreign policy' is the administration of the outside activities or strategy to manage the issues that exist beyond territorial boundaries of a state. According to the *Oxford Dictionary*, foreign policy is "a government's strategy in dealing with other nations." Putting it more comprehensively, *Encyclopedia of Britannica* defines foreign policy as the "General objectives that guide the activities and relationships of one state in its interactions with other states." It further explains that "the development of foreign policy is influenced by domestic considerations, the policies or behaviour of other states, or plans to advance specific geopolitical designs". As for *Brockhaus Encyclopedia* (1967), foreign policy is the institution for managing a state's relations with other states, with the aim of preserving its own independence and promoting its welfare.

Yet these dictionaries only begin to answer the vexing question: What is

---

3   Charles Herman (2018),

foreign policy? From an historical perspective, the nature of international relations before the 1917 Revolution was violently characterized by the Crimean Wars and World War I. Be that as it may, war is always an extension of politics. These wars were the result of violent politics and diplomats were sent to foreign countries while gunboats were anchored in the harbour, hence, "Gunboat Diplomacy". This violence was at times accompanied with collaboration if necessary and such kind of collaboration manifested itself in events like the 1884/85 Berlin Conference, Chaired by Chancellor Bismarck, for the partition of Africa; or the formation of League of Nations.

World War I, accelerated and facilitated inter alia the revolutionary battles for the working class. The result was the Great October Revolution in 1917, which for the first time in history brought the working class in power. The impact of this revolution in international relations was that, with the emergence of a socialist state, the question of self-determination and national liberation assumed a class dimension.[4]

Furthermore, after the treaty of Westphalia in 1648, and the end of the First and Second World Wars, the international system has witnessed a proliferation in the number of nation states. The end product of this development was thus, the creation of an interaction between these nation states. In addition, the establishment of United Nations and the process of decolonization that liberated many states into sovereign entities further provided the impetus to interrelationships. Furthermore, the modern world of "globalisation", the "widening, deepening and speeding up of global interconnectedness", has increased these interrelationships or interactions among states. Hence, there is unanimity among scholars today on the necessity of a "foreign policy" for each state, since no state will want to function in complete isolation. In this connection, a theoretical and historical framework is necessary.

The term foreign policy has been defined in various ways by scholars; however, they are certain that it is concerned with behaviour of a state towards other states. Hermann for instance, defined foreign policy as "the discrete purposeful action that results for the political level decision of an individual or group of individuals. It is the observable artifact of a political level decision. It is not the decision, but a product of the decision." By this, it can be seen that Charles Hermann (1978) defines foreign policy as the behaviour of states.

Literally, the term *foreign policy* is composed of two individual words, *foreign* and *policy*. The word 'foreign' came from the Latin word "foris" and "forus" meaning "outside" and the word 'policy' originated from the Old French word "policie" meaning "civil administration". Therefore, the literal meaning of the

---

4   S.S. Mushi and K.Mathew,(1981).

phrase 'foreign policy' is the administration of the outside activities or strategy to manage the issues that exist beyond territorial boundaries of a state.".

In our view however, foreign policy is not only to change, but also to oversee continuation of the behaviour at different times. It is concerned both with the change and the status quo as far as they serve the national interest. For example, Gambia's decision to break off diplomatic ties with Taiwan in 2013 was a change in the foreign policy of the Gambia. In addition, no reasons were given for the decision, nor further details provided in the official press release other than stating that it was in the "national interests" of the Gambia. In the same vein, Gambia's decision to resume diplomatic relations with China is a shift in her foreign policy towards a continuation of that relationship with an old ally.

Foreign policy refers to the comprehensive and effective design of a state to deal with matters beyond its territorial borders. It is a complete plan to materialize the national objectives and multiply the national gains. Making this comprehensive plan or the policy is a complex process and is usually prepared by the top political leadership with the help of senior bureaucrats. The procedure of decision making as well as policy outcomes generally depend upon the working style of leadership, the structure of the decision-making unit, as well as the nature of other internal and external factors. In an autocratic system, for example, the decision-making process is generally a one-act play where the supreme leader plays the decisive role, whereas in the democratic setup, the decision-making process is the sum of overall consensus. It is, therefore, essential to know how a nation's foreign policy is formulated and the factors responsible for the successful and effective foreign policy that can guide the country to achieve its national interest. The debate continues.

Thus, in view of such a variety of definitions as to what is meant by 'foreign policy', one may be tempted to conclude by defining a foreign policy as consisting of three parts: the 'end', the 'ways', and the 'means'. The end consists a vision of a desired outcome or set of interests in interacting with another state/ actor; the ways consists of the strategies and ideas (e.g., diplomatic tactics, coercion) to pursue these desired interests; and the means consists of the available resources at a state's disposal (e.g., economic, military). Therefore, a foreign policy is a vision of a desired outcome or set of interests in interacting with another state/ actor, the strategies and ideas used in achieving these goals, and the available resources at a state's disposal in guiding her interaction with other states.

Foreign policy-making often involves responding to a crisis of the international community. For instance, during the Tsunami in South and Southeast Asia nations in 2004, the whole world came forward in the reconstruction process. More currently, the ongoing COVID-19 pandemic has affected and attracted world attention. Addressing these conceptual gaps in foreign policymaking, George Modelski (1962) defines "foreign policy as the system of activities evolved by communities for changing the behaviour of other states and for adjusting their own activities to the international environment". Here the activities are not limited to the state, but address the whole community including various organizations or groups. Foreign policy must throw light on the ways states attempt to change and succeed in changing the behaviour of other states." Modelski noted only those aspects of policy that aim at the change in the existing behaviour of states, as the primary objectives of foreign policy.

James N. Rosenau (1974) views foreign policy as an adaptive behaviour and contended that it "consists of all the attitudes and activities through which organized national societies seek to cope with and benefit from their international environment. According to Walter Carlsnaes (2002) "Foreign policies consist of those actions which, expressed in the form of explicitly stated goals, commitments and/or directives, and pursued by governmental representatives acting on behalf of their sovereign communities, are directed towards objects, conditions and actors-both governmental and non-governmental – which they want to affect lie beyond their territorial legitimacy."

Other scholars have, however, defined foreign policy as an activity of the State with which it fulfils its aims and interests within the international arena. This simple definition requires explanations and additions in order to allow us to understand how we interpret the concept of foreign policy and what foreign policy actually is.

Worth noting is the fact that there is a consensus among scholars that foreign policy serves as an intersection point of domestic and international politics. Thus, from here we can say that the foreign policy of every state is influenced by mainly two determinants: international or external, and domestic or internal. These are considered factors which help in shaping and moulding foreign policy. However, the linkage between international and domestic determinants has long been a widely debated topic in the field of international relations and Foreign Policy Analysis (FPA) in particular. Be that as it may, domestic and external politics are 'interdependent' and could spill over into each other. Robert Putman and others propagate the idea of two-level games. In this respect, the two have symbiotic relations.

While both levels of analysis make convincing arguments, their influence between domestic and international determinants of foreign policies varies among states and the political environment in which these states exist. This school recognizes the heterogeneous character of states. In other cases, domestic determinants are more important and influential. Nonetheless, there is a general agreement that the foreign policy of a country reflects its internal policy, and that foreign policy is an extension of the internal policy.

The fragmentation of international relations has however, put a huge challenge in defining foreign policy as well as foreign policy decision making. Analysing in general, foreign policy includes a wide range of activities and strategies under which a sovereign state interacts with other international players. A careful study reveals that the meaning of the concepts varies from scholar to scholar.

Going by literal meaning, the term *foreign policy* can be divided into two different words. The term *'foreign'* refers to things that exist beyond the territorial boundaries and *'policy'* can be referred to as the guidelines and approaches to achieve the objectives. Therefore, foreign policy can be defined as the principles and guidelines to achieve the objectives existing outside the territorial border. But, the meaning of foreign policy in modern time is not restricted to this simple definition and the concept is changing rapidly along with the world's political environment. Thus, the modern concept of 'foreign' is associated with deep and multidisciplinary approaches relatively different from scholar to scholar. Hence, the simple meaning of foreign policy can be calculated as the sum of a state's strategy to strengthen its national capacity, the approach to attain the national goal and the tools to deal with the other elements of the world. It is the state's desire to avoid any conflict without compromising the national goals or interests. In a narrow sense, 'foreign policy' is the official relationship between two states. Traditionally, foreign policy referred to the course of action taken by the government, more precisely by the Foreign Ministry, to deal with foreign countries. But the rise of globalisation has downplayed this argument where dealing with the outer world became more complex. The internationalization of life took this issue beyond the matter of diplomat to diplomatic interactions.

Throughout this discourse, the concept of national interest has been featured. This calls for a clear scrutiny and understanding (as we shall see later) of what those interests are and how far we can hope to draw the means at our disposal. Anything less than this falls short of being a national foreign policy." Similarly, according to Padelford and Lincoln (1977)" "foreign policy is the key element in the process by which a state translates its broadly conceived goals and interests into concrete courses of action and to attain these objectives and preserve its interests." In other words, foreign policy involves both a formulation as well as the approach to achieve the objectives. Cecil V. Crabb offers a simple yet very effective definition of foreign policy. For him, "reduced to its most fundamental ingredients, Foreign policy consists of two elements: national objectives to be achieved, and means for achieving them." Though the scholars differ in the goal and the means, both are integral parts of foreign policy and carry equal importance. The main objective of the foreign policy is to optimally maximize the national interest, to maintain the state sovereignty and defend its border by enhancing its capacity.

Summarizing the above definitions, it is clear that most of the scholars limited the definition of foreign policy to the official relation between the states and recognized the state as the only actor in the foreign policy decision making. But in the 21st century, non-state actors such as MNCs, NGOs as well as other international and ultra-national organizations are also playing an active role in shaping foreign policies of the states and influence their international politics in many ways. For example, the 9/11 terrorist attack has definitely been the major factor in reshaping the behaviour of the statecraft of the United States of America. Even disproving the standing definitions, the United States has recently started negotiating with the non-state actors, the Taliban leaders for the settlement of the Afghanistan issue. Of course, the US had similar negotiations with the Barbary pirates of the Mediterranean Sea in the 18th century. Besides, non-state actors, and non-human factors such as earthquake, Tsunami or prolonged famine also are considered as the major determinants of foreign policy of a nation. Amnesty International for example, has been constantly perusing, directing and criticizing nation states over any human rights violation by the respective governments.

Although managing external relations is the salient feature in defining foreign policy, many contemporary studies highlight that the domestic environment also plays a significant role in determining the foreign policy of a state. Hence, as observed before, the significance of the internal and external factors has been the center of debate for years. While one section stresses upon internal structure such as internal leadership, domestic political set-ups and nature of decision making environment, others highlight the importance of international environment and world political order. This debate in some quarters is called levels of analysis. The details on this is addressed in the relevant chapter in this work. As argued above, to us, they are interdependent.

From the earlier discussions on defining Foreign Policy and the subsequent analysis on decision making, one can synthesize what foreign policy decision-making is. To put it simply, foreign Policy decision-making is the amalgamation of two different concepts: 'foreign policy', the external behaviour of a country; and 'decision making', meaning choosing the right options. Therefore, foreign policy decision-making can be referred to as the sum total of a governmental decision to guide its national interests. In other words, foreign policy decision-making is the process to reach a conclusive approach to address the outstanding foreign policy complexity. In words of Mintz and DeRouen (2010) "Foreign Policy Decision Making (FPDM) refers to the choices individuals, groups and coalitions make that affect a nation's action on the international stage".

Similarly, Goldstein and John Pevehous (2010) define "foreign policy decision making as a steering process in which adjustments are made as per the feedback from the outside world. Decisions are carried out by actions taken to change the world, and then information from the world is mentioned to evaluate the effects of these actions." According to Janice Gross Stein, "the foreign policy process is a process of decision making. States take actions because people in governments – decisionmakers – choose those actions". Valerie Hudson is one of the strong advocates of this view. Policy-making has been defined as the process by which governments translate their political vision into programmes and actions to deliver 'outcomes' – desired change in the real world.

According to B. Raman (2012), "Decision making in foreign policy involves the analysis and assessment of past and current date, in the light of our past experience and that of others, who had dealt with similar situations, in order to identify the need and available options for action in the future and the likely implications of each of those options for the protection and promotion of our national interests." From the above definitions, it can be determined that Foreign Policy decision-making is the process of searching for the best alternative costs and consequences and as well as attempting to choose the best course of action; however, sometimes leaders can make bad choices, such as when U.S. President George Bush decided to invade Iraq in 2003.

Though there are multiple agencies involved in the decision-making process, it is the leadership who ultimately decides by examining the cost of available alternatives. As the leadership is the backbone of the policy decision, their course of action and behaviour should be close to reality. The crisis management experience, capacity to study the phenomena, indefatigable attitude during difficult times, and most importantly the cognitive potentiality of the principal players of the decision-making body largely shape the foreign policy outcomes of a country and re-arrange the global political settings at large. This leads us to theoretical conceptualization of national interest.

Since the national interests are paramount, governments design their foreign policies through high-level decision-making processes. Goals may be accomplished by peaceful cooperation with other nations, or through exploitation. Usually, creating foreign policy is the job of the head of government and the foreign minister (or equivalent). Modern states employ hundreds, thousands, or more professional diplomats in their diplomatic service. Much of their work involves implementing and researching the effectiveness of directives toward stated foreign policy goals. They see the task of harmonizing compatible foreign policy goals between partner states and NGO's while also reporting to their agencies on both successes in, and obstacles to their efforts.

Returning to the interstate level of analysis, it is a long-standing fact that the international system consists of big, middle and small power states. The relative level of state power plays an important role in shaping and moulding the foreign policies of those interacting states. The establishment of friendly and cooperative relations between states is the aim of a sound foreign policy. It can be argued that foreign policy is essentially shaped by one's relative power within the international system. The world is continuously changing; new events and personalities create foreign policy problems or challenges to all concerned. Some examples include the impact of the Great October Bolshevik Revolution in 1917; the rise of communist power in People's Republic of China, 1949; the coming to power of De Gaulle in France and Hitler in Germany; and the emergence of new nations in Africa, Asia and Latin America -- all brought significant changes in their power structure and that has impacted the foreign policy of many countries.

The prevailing framework of world politics plays a decisive role in deciding the foreign policy of a country as such foreign policies of states thus change with shifts in the international power structure. In the traditional multi-polar system, it was easier for states to switch sides and gain maximum interests from both sides. During the 1980s, the international system was characterized by a bi-polar system of cold war, and today a unipolar with the USA as the hegemonic power, though they are slowly being challenged by China plus other emerging economies. These events have restructured the power system and have significant effect on the foreign policies of states. During the bipolar world system, it was not easy for states to switch sides effortlessly as the ideological fault lines were clearly marked in spite of the Non-Alignment existence.

The disintegration of the communist bloc at the end of the 20th century, ushering in the Unipolar world under US tyranny, had its own system dynamics such as Bush's 'either with us or against us' rhetoric. This declaration has made many states from the margins of the system to come forward and play effective roles, especially in the so-called Global War on Terror. Thus, we see that, every type of power structure at the international level has its own particular dynamics and impact on the foreign policies of states.

It must be recalled that the last century witnessed two global wars as well as a bipolar bloc after the Bolshevik Revolution in Russia, 1917. Consequently, international relations became a public concern as well as an important field of study and research. After the Second World War and during the 1960s, many researchers in the U.S. particularly and from other countries in general, brought forth a wealth of research work and theory. Most of this work was done for international relations and not for foreign policy as such. Gradually, various theories began to grow around international relations, international systems, and international politics, but the need for a theory of foreign policy (that is, the starting point in each sovereign state) continued to receive negligible attention. The reason was that some of the states used to keep their foreign policies under official secrecy, and unlike today, it was not considered appropriate for the public to know about these policies. This iron-bound secrecy is an essential part for the framework of foreign policy formulation.

In theory, diplomats at any level will not give away their home country or its interests without doing so as part of a calculated strategy hoping to maximize gain and minimize risk. But in practice, incompetence; opportunism; rivalries; bribery; corruption; lapses of sanity; personal grievances; pangs of conscience; dissension from official policy leading to leaks, defections and other acts of internal sabotage; overwhelming despair at a seemingly insurmountable disparity in arms and land, population, and other strategic factors during periods of intense inter-state competition; and unforeseeable flukes of circumstance can all throw the best of intentions off track, and occasionally combine in a perfect storm of what eventually sorts out into world history. World War II and its devastation posed a great threat and challenge for humanity which revealed to everyone the importance of international relations. Though foreign policy formulation continued to remain a closely guarded process at the national level, wider access to governmental records and greater public interest provided more data from which academic work placed international relations in a structured framework of political science.

A theoretical framework of foreign policy is needed to analyse the day-to-day interactions in international relations and to compare individual foreign policies. The focus is primarily on the policies of state actors with defined territories and jurisdictional boundaries, and less on non-state actors, except in the context of how they impact national government decisions and policies. The formal field of study of international relations is itself about 100 years old based on Woodrow Wilson, Chair (1920) and a specific subset of international relations such as foreign policy analysis does not receive wide attention as a field of scientific study. Rather, terms like "foreign policy" and "foreign policy expert" are often used in news media and general discussions about government when such experts may have more extensive backgrounds in fields other than foreign policy analysis. Ben Shapiro (1976), in his comparative study of the foreign policy of different countries, felt that the lack of a basic theory of foreign policy was particularly disabling, and pointed out the harmful effect of the absence of a general theory of foreign policy on foreign policy literature. What we note, therefore, are competing theories at variable levels of analysis.

Suffice it to note that the national interest is adopted as a means or device for analysing fundamental objectives of foreign policy of a nation-state. It is regarded as those purposes which the nation, through its leadership, pursues persistently throughout all time. National interest is also some ideal set of purposes which a nation should seek to realize in the conduct of its foreign relations. Foreign policy is predicated on the national interest of a nation state, and any foreign policy that fails to reflect the country's national interests is doomed to the general disenchantment of the populace. National interest covers three outstanding components of national security: protection and preservation of the welfare of the state, and national prestige. National security relates to the defence of a country's territory integrity and political independence. Foreign policy, on the other hand, is the aspect of national policy that pertains to the external environment and involves the enunciation of principles, and also indicates a country's positions on major international issues; thus, foreign policy is concerned with the substance and conduct of external relations.

National interest is perhaps one of most controversial concepts in International Relations. The controversy is due to several factors. Firstly, the concept has been and continues to be the subject of different interpretation by both analysts and practitioners. Secondly, the concept has been a subject of abuse particularly by politicians and decision-makers all over the world. Thirdly, the concepts are not easily susceptible to analysis. Generally, every nation has the foreign policy which seeks to achieve its national interest. When statesmen and bureaucrats are expected or required to act in the national interest, it means that they are to take action on issues that improve the political situation, the economic and social well-being, and the health and culture of the people as well as their political survival. According to K.J. Holsti (1970), there are three broad categories of interests: core interest, variable interest and complementary interest. The core ones are those interests which are fundamental to the ability of the country to play its role as a sovereign nation within the international system. Often these interests are tied to the survival preservation and continued existence of the state. The implication is that a nation must exist as an actor within the international system before it attempts pursuing or realizing any objective or interest in national terms. Thus, core interest is about the kind of interest or objective to which a nation is prepared to make all possible sacrifices to achieve. The concerns of core interest are the national survival, i.e., protection of the territorial integrity of the state and the lives of all its citizens against external aggression, as well as protection of its political, economic, religious or social institutions. These are objectives for which states are normally prepared to go to war with others. This is why a considerable proportion of the national budget is often committed to national security and defence by all nations.

National welfare is also part of core interest. It is the responsibility of any nation to provide for the socio-economic welfare of its citizens. These necessities compel states to enter into economic intercourse with one another in order to advantageously harness resources to serve domestic needs. No nation, no matter how powerful and richly endowed, has ever achieved economic prosperity and ensured a high standard of living for its citizens without active involvement in the channel of international trade.

A third aspect of core interest is national prestige (e.g., national honour, respect and so forth). The degree of influence a nation can wield on others depend on the extent to which such a state is able to conduct its affairs consistent with a high sense of self-respect, process and national honour. The implication here is that a state that fails to maintain a high degree of acceptable reputation in the international system risks losing respect and even suffering isolation in the community of nations. Apartheid South Africa was a case in point. These interests are not very permanent because interests change more frequently. However, secondary interest does enhance or complement the achievement of core interest objectives. The most easily identifiable secondary interest involves the task that is given to the Mission of the citizen concerned. These are usually national interests, "which a state can apply to a larger geographical area to a larger number of nations, or in several specified fields". General interests are, in most cases, interests that cannot be achieved by any state alone and, by their nature, are long-term objectives.

The interest of a state usually should be defined by its government. The term *national interest* has two broad usages: firstly, it is used by politicians when they seek support for a particular course of action especially in foreign policy. Given the widespread attachment to the nation as a social and political organization, national interest is a powerful device for invoking support. Politicians use the term to seek support for domestic policy objectives, but here it is less persuasive given the normal extent of difference on domestic policy and hence employed less. Secondly, the term evokes anarchic international system where dangers abound and the interests of the nation are at risk. It is used as tool for analysing foreign policy, particularly by political realist. Here, the national interest is used as a foreign policy version of the term "public interest" indicating what is best for the nation in its relation with other states. his use of the term emphasizes not merely the threat to the nation from the international anarchy but also the external constraints, on the freedom of the manoeuvre of the state from treaties, the interests and power of the states, and other factors beyond the control of the nation, such as geographical location and independence on foreign trade. The analytical usage of the term places much emphasis on the role of the state as the embodiment of the nation's interest. The realist usage of the term *national interest* in evaluating foreign policy has focused on national security as the core of national interest. "Interest of state" and "national security interest" are closely allied terms.

The difficulty with the analytical usage of the term is the absence of any agreed methodology by which the best interest of the nation can be tested. Some scholars have argued that the best interests are nevertheless objectively determined by the situation of the state in the international system and can be deduced from a study of history and the success/failure of policies. Other writers concede that national interest is subjectively interpreted by the government of the day. In this version, *national interest* is similar to the politician's rhetorical usage of the term.

If we are to continue Morgenthau's analysis, his "vital objective" is the "national interest sharpening to meet particular inter-national situations" of state's foreign policy vis-a-vis opponents in "the restoration of the balance of power by any means short of war". This kind of analysis by no means clearly defines national interest. In fact, it illustrates rather the temptation to define it in terms of particular theories and of generalizations. National interest does not necessarily exist in abstraction. Indeed, in most cases, the question is not whether, but how, to serve the national interest. That involves the question of what is the national interest in a particular situation. Moreover, there are many national interests, not just one. The difficulties arise in the conflict of one interest with another, for example, in the clash of one interest in peace with the interest in preserving national institutions.

In spite of these difficulties, the concept of national interest is a very useful one which policymakers should never forget. It helps to place foreign as well as domestic policy on the framework of national policy, and it is a much-needed antidote to political short-sightedness and partisanship. However, changed, the meaning can be constraints rather than the variables of international relations. It is likewise true that developments at home or abroad require a continual reassessment of those interests in order to keep pace with unfolding situations in the international system. National interest will have little meaning unless it represents a widespread consensus and it is applied to specific policies. It is also to be remembered that national interest involves not only military security and the nation's economy but also a defence of the nation's values. National security, conceived in military terms alone, involves more than maintenance of a strong defence establishment, it also includes military assistance to other friendly nations and much more.

It is in light of this debate that this book aims to contribute. Its main thrust is revamping of African foreign policies within the context of the continental's Agenda 2063. It is further argued that based on agreed foreign policy benchmarks as stipulated in this continental blueprint, the political and socio-economic development of Africa will, progressively and significantly, change, and therefore, Africa may claim its rightful place in the international community during the 21st century.

In this regard, the book's point of departure is the theoretical and conceptual underpinning of the subject at hand, interrogated in Chapter One. Major theories are critically subjected to scrutiny. Chapter Two focuses on the cumbersome process of decision making, whereby different theories are brought to bear. The difficulties encountered in the evaluation, assessment and ultimate decision are addressed. The nature of the system, whether autocratic or democratic, and the kind of leadership of the day are crucial. The Third chapter addresses the level of analysis. The role of an individual, attitudes, and gender mainstreaming are brought in focus. Both the state and system analysis are discussed in detail. Chapter Four examines different instruments used or applied to implement foreign policy. These tools include: diplomacy, military and security, economy, culture, and diaspora. Their applications are dependent on the material conditions prevailing, and timing. They are not static but rather dynamic. Chapter Five focuses on factors determining foreign policy. These are both domestic and external. Its point of departure is that foreign policy of any country is an extension of domestic policy. The chapter considers domestic factors such as internal politics, geography, form of government, leadership, and public diplomacy. External factors such as regional integration and international organization are also discussed. Chapter Six is devoted to the formulation and conduct of foreign policy. Issues like routine policies, crises of policies, internal policies, appraisal of the external situation, policy objectives, choice and means, preventive diplomacy, soft power, public relations, the presidency, the ministry of foreign relations, embassies, missions, and parliament are extensively examined. To drive the subject home, Chapter Seven is devoted to African foreign policies. This chapter gives the historical background of independent African nations with specific reference to Pan- Africanism, the Great October 1917 Bolshevik Revolution, Non Alignment Movement and the birth of the Organization of African Unity (OAU) in 1963. In this connection, a number of African countries' foreign policies are interrogated. These countries are: Egypt, Ethiopia, Kenya, Nigeria, South Africa, South Sudan, and Sudan. Chapter Eight focuses on the historical development of African diplomacy. It argues that pre-colonial Africa had its diplomacy practiced in different forms. This was nonetheless interrupted and to some extent destroyed by colonialism. While debunking Western view, it however acknowledges the fact that most of this work was not documented, therefore posing intellectual challenges. With the advance of colonialism, this part of African historical development was interrupted and consequently destroyed by very foreign invaders. The debate that ensued between early post-independent African intellectuals and their counterparts in the west, from different disciplines in defence of African history, must be seen within this context. For example, the first generation of African lawyers, the likes of Francis Deng, argued in defence of African jurisprudence. This was in response to Western scholars who contended that the continent had no legal system, an argument that was factually incorrect. In fact, the West had no moral authority to claim this. Chapter Nine reflects on the recently concluded African Continental Free Trade Area. To set the ball rolling, the chapter begins by analysing Trade diplomacy within the context of multilateralism. It contends that at present, multilateralism is under fire by certain nations pursuing nationalistic policies. However, Africa has responded to this situation by establishing AfCFTA. The agreement, signed by 54 countries so far, creates an integrated market of over 1.2 billion people with a combined Gross Domestic Product (GDP) exceeding US $2.5 trillion.[5] It was launched in Nairobi, Kenya on 1st January 2021. This decision has been widely welcomed in Africa and beyond. Chapter Ten, the final chapter, is devoted to the revamping of African foreign policies. The chapter argues that whereas foreign policies of the African states registered some successes in the last century including the OAU's liberation agenda, they need to be revamped in order to meet the challenges of the 21st century which are many and require a new approach. It discusses some of those challenges as being globalisation, terrorism, governance, employment (especially for youth), climate change, poverty, conflicts, infrastructure etc. All these need a collective approach. Fortunately, most of these issues are captured in the agenda 2063, to which all have signed, ratified and domesticated. The chapter concludes with a high sense of optimism given the current appropriate pan–African commitment as well as visionary leadership, together rendering these goals doable and achievable.

---

5   Benedict O. Oramah, (2019).

CHAPTER ONE

THEORETICAL AND CONCEPTUAL FRAMEWORK

This chapter highlights the concept of foreign policy analysis as the basis for comprehending the African experiences. Conceptualizing this involves the systematic identification, location and analysis of documents and articles containing information related to the conceptual framework.[6]

The importance of conceptualization is to discover the trends, dynamics and approaches that have been productive in investigations of similar topics under review. The chapter also demonstrates underlying assumptions and propositions behind foreign policy analysis in the field of international relations.[7] Earlier scholars support these assertions while subsequent ones also concur and add that completing a review of related literature enables authors to revisit the original study idea and define the exact focus of the problem.[8]

Throughout this chapter, several examples of suggested best practices are cited to support, explain or provide advice on various aspects of foreign policy by national governments. This sets the pace to inform foreign policy in African countries in general. Best practices are generally accepted, informally standardized techniques, methods or processes which have proven themselves over time to accomplish given tasks,[9] and can evolve as improvements are discovered.[10]

---

6   Gay, Mills & Airasian, (2006), p.87
7   Boote & Beille, (2005), p.8
8   Hewittt, (2009), p.119
9   Mitchell, Piggott & Kumru,, (2008), p.18
10   Zairi, (2012), p. 94

States cannot remain in isolation due to the anarchical nature of the international system; every state develops their own foreign policies based on its national interest and sphere of influence within the international arena.[11] African countries tend to create foreign policy considered weak, improper and cordial according to international foreign-policy best practices. Foreign policy as a field of study is a subfield of international relations.

1.1 Historical Development of Foreign Policy

This section provides a review of foreign policy in its entirety with specific focus on historical development of foreign policy, the process of formulating foreign policy and the effect of international politics on foreign policy. Additionally, the section provides analysis of foreign policy in general, in the African context. In determining foreign policy formulation in a different context, a comparative analysis is provided.

The history of foreign relations dates back to the early ages as friendships and relations have existed between humans since the beginning of human interaction.[12] As organization developed to promote human affairs, relations between people in terms of the organization advanced. Foreign policy goes back to primitive times.[13] The inception of foreign relations and the need for foreign policy to deal with them has been as old as the organization of human life in groups. Before writing, most of these relations were carried out by word of mouth, leaving little direct archaeological evidence.[14]

In the early days, many countries and states exercised foreign relations that were basically aimed at relating well with neighbours but not getting too involved in the internal affairs of other states. However, globalisation has revolutionized the role of states in other states and happenings in one country are quickly becoming diffused into other states.[15] This has increased the pace and consideration in foreign policy analysis that has been necessitated by increased interdependence among states. Therefore, the making of foreign policy has been inherently difficult in any period.

The conditions of the modern world, however, add greatly to the complexity.[16] The reasons for this were varied. In the first place, there are far more actors on the international stage. Until World War I and even later, international affairs

---

11   Hartmann, (1978), p.6
12   Morgenthau, (1967), p.18
13   Bowie, (1960), p.1
14   Bidabad, (2012), p.183
15   Qavam, (2002), p.66
16   Laura, Neack (2008), Pp.17-25

were largely dominated by a small number of European nations.[17] The Western Hemisphere, including the United States, played only a small role.[18] Asia and Africa were still within the European empires or, like China, too disorganized to be significant.[19] Despite differences, European statesmen were familiar with the history and thinking processes of the nations playing key roles. This assertion has completely changed the interaction of states in today's world where states are involved in complex politics.

Today, over ninety countries are conducting their own foreign affairs, and another score has begun to do so within a relatively short period. These countries differ widely in culture, history, and attitudes. In living conditions and experience, the newer nations are separated by a wide gulf from the developed countries of Europe and North America.[20] Many of them have weak governments that are facing staggering problems. With very limited background, they must decide how to relate themselves to the outside world and should determine their interests as well as priorities.

The sheer number of actors, and especially of new actors, adds enormously to the task of conducting foreign policy for every nation. An added complication is that the relations between nations are far more intimate today than ever before. Further, the domestic affairs of most countries are now closely intertwined with international affairs. Each nation should be concerned to some degree with the internal life of other countries. The progress of growth and change within the newer nations is bound to have profound effects in international relations. Inevitably, other nations have a deep interest in the social, economic, and political evolution of these newer nations. But the same fact is also true among developed countries: Prospects for European nations largely depend on the likely evolution of the political and social order in Germany, France and Britain.[21]

The existence of expansionist powers has often been a feature of international life, but Communist powers have developed sophisticated techniques of pressure, infiltration, and subversion. They show unusual skill in exploiting conditions of instability.[22] However, the existence of other powers such as Russia and China in global politics and trade can be viewed a welcome idea by various developing countries in Africa and Asia, as they have seen traditional powerhouses such as US and Europe as too imperialistic and neo-colonialist.[23] Developments and

17   Krumbein, (2014), p.327
18   Bowie, (1960), p.4
19   Chen, Hsu and Fan, (2014), p.6
20   Petersone, (2013), p.321
21   Qavam, (2002), p.79
22   Chen, Hsu and Fan, (2014), p.11
23   Krumbein, (2014), p.331

relations that African countries in particular are experiencing from China have influenced many African countries to change their foreign policy towards their traditional friends and enemies.[24]

Finally, a pace of change unparalleled in history marks our times. The international environment is not only complicated but is changing with tremendous rapidity. This is the hallmark of our era. Under the pressure of nationalism and the urge for better living conditions, newer countries are actively seeking to modernize their economies as rapidly as possible. They are undergoing social revolution, which will undoubtedly transform the structure of their social order and the attitudes of their people over a relatively short period. Meanwhile, the efforts of Western Europe to transcend ancient rivalries and to draw together in regional groupings seem likely to have a major impact on international relations.[25]

Last, but not least, the revolution occurring in the whole field of military technology in the form of nuclear weapons, missiles, and new space has encouraged states to get into either alliance or counter alliance to comply with new developments. The result is to raise wholly novel questions about the role of force in international affairs. Under the impact of all these forces, international life has become an intricate web of relationships constantly undergoing extreme and rapid change. As a consequence, the effort to appraise this unfolding situation, to disentangle the various forces and to foresee how they will interact, to determine what our interests are and what our goals should be in a world of flux, is far more difficult than in the past.

Our knowledge is very limited about many of these areas of change. Very little is really known about the whole process of accelerated social and economic change or about the effects it may have on institutions and attitudes. Even those best qualified are only beginning to grasp the significance of the revolution in military force and strategy. No one can be very confident about foreseeing the prospects of change in global affairs. These are all new phenomena, bringing the foreign policymaker to face even more uncertainty than usual.[26]

1.2 The Nature, Meaning and Conceptualization

As a sub-field of international relations (IR), the study of foreign policy focuses on external states of the global system through their authorised representatives or governments. The concept of system assumes more than the units enclosed

---

24   Babaci-White, Geo-JaJa and Shizhou, (2013), p.736
25   Krumbein, (2014), p.329
26   Friend and Thayer, (2012), p.114

by a boundary; it also presupposes that there is an interaction between the units. The official relations that take place between the units of the international system constitute the foreign policy. Therefore, below are key the definitions given by scholars to distinguish between foreign policy and foreign policy analysis.

1.2.1 The Meaning of Foreign Policy

Foreign policy analysis (FPA) is the study of foreign policy transactions, the domestic circumstances that produce them, the system's effects on them, and it structures and their influence on them.[27] In brief, FPA is a "bridging discipline" which connects the micro level of politics with the macro level of the international system.[28] By concentrating on the interface between the state and state system, it represents "the continuing erosion of the distinction between domestic and foreign issues, between the socio-political and economic processes that unfold at home and those that transpire abroad."[29]

The term 'foreign policy' has been defined in a number of ways. George Modelski defines it as the system of activities evolved by communities for changing the behaviour of other states and for adjusting those communities' own activities to the international environment.[30] Modelski, in his definition, has emphasized only those aspects of policy which aim at the change in the existing behaviour of states as the primary objectives of foreign policy. In fact, foreign policy includes both change in existing behaviour and continuation of that behaviour at different times. It is concerned with both the change and the status quo insofar as they serve the national interests. Further, Feliks Gross has taken a very liberal view of the term 'foreign policy', opining that if a state decides not to have any relations with some country, it is also a foreign policy. Its concern is both negative and positive. Foreign policy concerns are negative when the foreign policy aims at furthering its interests by not changing behaviour, and positive if it demands a change in the behaviour of other states to adjust its national interests. "Foreign Policy involves the formulation and implementation of a group of principles which shape the behaviour pattern of a state while negotiating with (contacting) other states to protect or further its vital interests."[31] This includes not only the general principles but also those means necessary to implement them. Thus, these principles are those broader

---

27   Margot Light, (1994), " pp. 94.
28   Charles F. Hermann, Charles \V. Kegley Jr., and James N. Rosenau, (1987), p. 1.
29   James N. Rosenau, (1990). p. 3.
30   George Modelski, (1962), pp.6-7.
31   C.C. Rodee, "(1991), p. 571

interests which states strive to achieve in international relations. Others consider foreign policy to be the use of political influence in order to induce other states to exercise their law-making power in a manner desired by the state concerned; it is an interaction between forces originating outside the country's borders and those working within them.[32]

The term 'foreign policy of a nation' can be used to refer to the complex and dynamic political course that a nation follows in relation to other states. The foreign policy of a nation is more than the sum total of its foreign policies, for it also includes the nation's commitments, the current forms of its national interests and objectives, and the principles of right conduct that it professes. 'Foreign policy of a nation' has been defined as "a well-rounded, comprehensive plan, based on knowledge and experience, for conducting the business of government with the rest of the world. It is aimed at promoting and protecting the interests of the nation. This calls for a clear understanding of what, whose Interests are and how far we can help to go with the means at our disposal. Anything less than this falls short of being a national foreign policy."[33] Prof. Gambari Ibrahim defines it as an interaction between identifiable domestic political forces and the dynamics of international political relations, while Dr. Abraham Kuol Nyuon sees it as the process and technique for influencing external states through promotion of the variable national interest in the external milieu.

From Wikipedia, the free encyclopedia, a country's foreign policy, also called foreign relations or foreign affairs policy, consists of self-interest strategies chosen by the state to safeguard its national interests and to achieve goals within its international relations milieu. The approaches are strategically employed to interact with other countries. The study of such strategies is called foreign policy analysis. In recent decades, due to the deepening level of globalisation and transnational activities, states also must interact with non-state actors. These interactions are evaluated and monitored in seeking the benefits of bilateral and multilateral international cooperation. In this regard, foreign policy is a multidimensional concept that lies in the various corners of the state craft and bears different meaning for different people. For some, it is the official and state-to-state relation, both between and among nations, while others focus on the role of non-state actors and non-human factors too in defining foreign policy. Similarly, one school defines foreign policy as the product of internal discourse, another takes as the result of the international environment.

---

32   F.S. Northedge, (1968), pp. 6-7.
33   Hugh Gibson, (1944), p. 9.

According to scholarship from 1968, foreign policy consists of decisions and actions, which involves to some appreciable extent relations between one state and others." By this, foreign policy involves a set of actions that are made within the state's borders, intended towards forces existing outside the country's borders. It comprises the formulation and implantation of a set of ideas that govern the behaviour of states while interacting with other states to defend and enhance their national interests. Scholarship from 1977 asserted, A State's foreign policy is totality of its dealings with the external environment. Foreign policy is the overall result of the process by which a state translates its broadly conceived goals and interests into specific courses of action in order to achieve its objectives and preserve its interests. Two functions and aims of foreign policy can be extracted from this definition: foreign policy is to first attain its conceived goals, and second to pursue its national interests.

In Huge Gibson's (1944) insight, "foreign policy is a well-rounded comprehensive plan based on knowledge and experience for conducting the business of government with rest of the world. It aims at promoting and protecting the interests of the nations. This calls for a clear understanding of what those interests are and how far we hope to go with the means at our disposal. Anything less than this, falls short of being a foreign policy." Thus, Gibson's insight augments the previous definition with discussion of how far states are willing to go with the means at their disposal to achieve their interests.

Such a claim leads us to ask the question, will states be willing to use force when diplomacy fails in achieving their interests? The answer to this is yes. An example of this is the Bush administration's invasion of Iraq in 2003, where the American government turned to military capabilities at her disposal to achieve her national interest.[34] They ultimately removed Sadam Hussein in cold blood. Iraq has, since then, never recovered. More lives have been lost since that time than before.

In Deborah Gerner's dictum, foreign policy is "the intentions, statements, and actions of an actor-often, but not always, a state-directed towards the external world and the response of other actors to these intentions, statements and actions. The definition has drawn criticism as being emphasized on states, ignoring that other actors such as international cause groups, businesses, religions, and the like-in the international system formulate guidelines and goals that direct their actions towards other international actors. Thus, foreign policy can involve both statements and behaviours or actions, and foreign policy "needs to consider more than what states declare to be their goals and how they attempt to achieve them. The study of foreign policy needs to consider how

---

34   John F.Clark, Southern Political Review Vol.23 No.4

certain goals arise and why certain behaviours result. The term 'foreign policy' hardly has any unanimous definition. While one school of thought criticizes its wider scope and multidimensional characteristic, other scholars are not ready to take a narrow approach to define it. "An attempt at an acceptable, and an accepted brief, definition of foreign policy would be to invite ridicule. The nature of foreign policy is not agreed, and one is tempted to believe that in political societies it will never be agreed." surprisingly, most of the literature on foreign policy did not even attempt to define it before debating the issues of foreign policy as a "neglected concept". "This neglect has been the most serious obstacle for providing more adequate and comprehensive explanations of foreign policy." Some scholars surmise that the reason for this neglect is that "most people dealing with the subject have felt confident that they know what foreign policy was;" hence, feel unnecessary to define it. He believes that most people think, "we know it when we see it". However, unlike other concepts of International Relations, Foreign Policy is not confined to one meaning but comprises a range of terms and activities. Based on individual perceptions, it sounds and looks different to different people. Perhaps this is why many, if not most, foreign policy studies did not even attempt to define the term. However, a careful search will reveal that there are dozens of different definitions available, many of which are critically discussed herein.

When analysing and contemplating a definition of foreign policy, it is worthwhile to consider views of previous scholarships attempts to define the concept of foreign policy. Benko (1997) claims that foreign policy is a process and a system of activities performed by a state-organized community of people within the international arena. Its intention is to influence the international arena in line with the aims and objectives of its political activities that are all geared towards its interests. Calvert (1986) understands the concept of foreign policy as decisions and activities which largely concern relations between one State and the others. Frankel's (1963), as seen above, definition of foreign policy is similar in essence. Rosenau (1968), a leading authority on the theory of international relations and foreign policy, defines foreign policy as systematic decision-making by constitutionally authorized officials of individual States. Their intention is to maintain or change the state of affairs in the international system in line with an objective or objectives they or their superiors have chosen.

Vukadinović (1981), in his initial and 'working' definition, outlines foreign policy as an organized activity of a State with which this State tries to maximize its values and interests in relation to other States and subjects who operate within the foreign environment. Crabb (1972), in his definition of foreign policy, sums up its most essential components: 'national objectives' that should be the goal and 'means' that should be used in the process of attaining this goal. For Crabb,

The interaction between objectives and means is the essence of 'statesmanship', and of 'foreign policy'. Kaltefleiter (1982) considers foreign policy as a network of communications which connects other areas of politics and covers a wide span of activities, ranging from summit meetings to informal talks among diplomats at social gatherings. Hill (2003) understands foreign policy as the sum of official (i.e., public; author's note) foreign relations, administered by an independent actor, usually the State, in international relations. Smith, Hadfield, Dunne (2008) define foreign policy as the strategy or approach chosen by the national government to achieve its goals in its relations with external entities.

As for Marxists, Foreign policy is explained as the policy of the ruling class of a State, which is directed towards the outside, i.e., towards the external relations of the State. It comprises the principles, responsibilities and aims of the State in the area of international relations with other States, with groups of States, and with international organizations and movements. It also comprises the means and methods for their achievement.

In their path-breaking classical work, *American Policy: Pattern and Process*, Kegley and Wittkopf (2008) defined foreign policy as "the goals that the nation's officials seek to attain abroad, the values that give rise to those objectives, and the means or instruments through which they are pursued." The definition, while comprehensively defining foreign policy in terms of three concepts – the goals, values, and instruments – limits foreign policy behaviour only to the activities of the state. Stretching the definition further, Robert Jackson and Georg Scorensen observes that foreign policy involves goals, strategies, measures, methods, guidelines, directives, understandings, agreements and so on, by which national governments conduct international relations with each other and with international organizations and non-governmental actors". In *Changing Politics of Foreign Policy*, Christopher Hill has given a comprehensive account of foreign policy: "a brief definition of foreign policy can be given as follows: the sum of official external relations conducted by an independent actor (usually a state) in international relations." Similarly, for Thompson and Mercidis "Foreign policy refers to the way in which policy – making institutions and official actors "define their positions and that of their state vis–á-vis outside […] world over a period of time." "Foreign Policy refers to those decisions made within a country that are affected by and that in turn affect entities outside the country. Therefore, Foreign policy does not and will not have a single agreed-upon definition.

1.2.2 The Nature of Foreign Policy

The actions of a state in the international arena result from individual choices by its citizenry, its political leaders, and its diplomats and bureaucrats aggregated through the state's internal structures. States need the active cooperation, even assistance, of other states in the system to achieve their national objectives. This makes it necessary for the state to be in communication with its external environment. The setting in which foreign policy is made is very important and also to a large extent shapes the resulting policies. A unique characteristic of foreign policy is that it is made in relation to other units or actors in the international system. Unlike domestic policies, the targets of foreign policy decisions are not the home nation but entities external to the state or beyond the state boundary.

A. The Domestic Environment
The primary influence on foreign policy are the objectives the decisionmakers intend to achieve on the international scene. These interests may be short term or long term, and they range from the preservation of the territorial integrity of the state to the welfare of citizens, prestige and even the preservation or promotion of values. The range of a state's objectives and the priority accorded each of these goals will no doubt have a salutary influence on the foreign policy options of a state. Some of the vital influential factors are:

i. **Topography:** A country's topography exercises an important influence on its foreign policy. Topography provides opportunities as it imposes limitations on what is feasible both in domestic and foreign policy programmes. A country's location, topography, terrain, climate, size, population and distribution of natural resources will not only affect the socio-economic development within the country, but also determines the country's needs vis-à-vis other states access to other areas of the world. Whether a country is landlocked, its location in an arid, tropical, or polar region, and whether it has long coastlines or long borders with many neighbouring states all have very important implications for a country's foreign policy. The size of a country also has implications for strategy. Has it got long borders to protect? The small size of Israel explains why Israeli leaders are very sensitive to issues of territorial concessions. It was relatively easier for them to return Sinai to Egypt because Sinai, when demilitarized, is large enough to give the Israelis enough warning both in time and space in the event of a peace violation by Egypt. On the other hand, it has not been possible for Israel to work out similar agreements on the West Bank and Golan Heights because of the small size of the territories involved and their location near Israeli coastal plains, where over 80 percent of Israel's population is concentrated.

ii. **Natural Resources:** The natural resources that a state is endowed with can also be a decisive element in its foreign policy. Is the country endowed with natural resources? Are some of these resources scarce world-wide? However, for these resources to have bearing on policy, the decisionmakers must not only be aware of their existence, they must also have the human, technological and financial capabilities to exploit them. Moreover, whether the economy of a country is a strong or weak one is also crucial. A weak economy can limit the options available in foreign policy. The Arab world is endowed with large quantities of oil and thus provides a large proportion of Western Europe's oil supplies. The Arab nations exerted this power as a conflict strategy during the Arab-Israeli war when they placed embargos on oil supplies to countries that supported Israel. Additionally, the issue of food production can be used as an instrument of foreign policy to achieve certain purposes, particularly during wars. For instance, Nigeria successfully prosecuted the civil war because it had to block the avenues through which Biafra got food relief. The foreign policy of a state is often affected by the extent to which a country's economy is in deficit or surplus in terms of capital, technical skills and finance. What is the level of the country's industrialization? Is the country's degree of industrial capacity adequate to sustain a reasonable high standard of living? Are the military forces and equipment adequate for its defence?

iii. **Population:** The size and socio-economic status of a nation's population constitutes another intangible element of foreign policy. It is a quantitative factor which should be considered in the delineation of a country's foreign policy capacity. The importance of India and China in this regard is becoming evident, especially as countries have shown some measure of deference to them in view of their massive populations. Nigeria is gaining some recognition because of the rate of its population growth. States with smaller populations do not enjoy such attention. Population as an element of foreign policy depends on other related elements, e.g., quality of population, political leadership, level of national morale, and prestige. The Arab nations could not overcome the moral collective of Israel, nor could America's mighty militia subdue the fighting spirit of the Vietnamese forces. In effect, a large population may enable or prevent a state from achieving its foreign policy objectives, depending on a number of other factors. A country's population also indicates the limits and potentials of the country: its size, the level of education and technical skill, its composition, structure and growth rate, and whether it is racially/ethnically homogeneous or heterogoneous will all influence policy options. Internal ethnic diversity may create political difficulties which may consequently weaken a government. It may even create fertile ground for anti-state activities by external enemies.

iv. **Industrial Element:** Since the industrial revolution, nations have come to attach much importance to industrial growth. Countries such as the United States, Russia, Great Britain, France, and Japan have all undergone some form of industrial and military metamorphoses to emerge comparatively stronger in the contemporary global system. It was for instance the industrial potentials of the United States that gave it an edge over others and hence, brought victories to the allied powers in World War II. The balance of power had since then been tilted in favour of America. It is in response to technological advancement that advanced countries are currently acquiring sophistication in their military capabilities. The super-powers are using coercive diplomacy to suppress others from attempting to expand their own military technological capability. This is to ensure their continued dominance in international relations. One example of this is the current face-off between North Korea and the international community for North Korea's nuclear weapon development. A country that depends on external sources for military hardware to defend itself will not only have its foreign policy actions constrained in relation to the "giving states", but it is also bound to have sharp limits imposed on its foreign policy objectives, particularly those concerned with security and strategic issues. The size, quality and mobility of a country's armed forces are important factors when issues with military implications are at stake.

v. **The Internal Structure of Decision Making:** The government structure also plays a role in shaping a country's foreign policy. The structure and the process of decision making vary from system to system and from country to country. The constitution of a state defines and sets limits, for examples, on the role of particular individuals or branches of government in foreign policy-making. The constitutional channels through which the decision-making process flows also affect the nature of those decisions. In the United States, for example, the congress has a coordinating role with the Executive branch on foreign policy matters. In contrast, however, the former Soviet Union did not provide the Supreme Soviet with such a role. In Britain, foreign policy decisions are as a rule taken by the whole cabinet and the role and impact of the legislature is extremely limited. The House of Commons, unlike its American counterpart, does not even have the power to ratify treaties. It only exercises some pressure through "Question Time" and debates. The U.S. Congress, on the other hand, exercises very strong influence especially in such areas as foreign aid and where annual appropriations are required. Congress can even initiate policy on a limited scale through imposing delays and foreign travels by individuals and groups of legislators. In countries with less established constitutional practices, like we find in Africa, the heads of state and government are less hampered by constitutional limitations.

vi. **Public Opinion:** It is difficult to generalize about the specific yet multifaceted relationship between public opinion and a government's foreign policy objectives and diplomatic opinion. It is difficult to ascertain the impact of public opinion on foreign policy development and implementation since it is largely uncrystallised. It is rather cumbersome to be precise about the impact of public opinion on a specific policy in a particular country. Some decision-makers obey the dictates of public opinion, others disregard them. But all decision-makers, even in military dictatorships, strive to mould and re-orient public opinion in their favour.

vii. **Pressure/Interest Groups:** Political parties and pressure groups exercise influence on the foreign policy of a country. However, the influences of such groups vary from country to country and from issue to issue. It also depends upon such variables as general strength or weakness of the government, whether there is a pending election, and the extent to which an unsatisfied group can politically harm leaders who resist it.

B. The External Environment

As stated previously, the very nature and aim of foreign policy makes the process of its decision-making susceptible to influences external to the state.

The international system to which foreign policies are directed is composed of foreign for independent state entities over which the initiating state has no authority or jurisdiction. Decisionmakers must therefore be constantly aware of the interests of other actors in the system. Sufficient account must be taken of what these actors have done, are doing, or are likely to do in the future in response to a particular policy in question.

a. **International Law:** The existence of international law and international ethical norms acts in greater or lesser degree to limit the freedom of states to manoeuvre in the system. It is true that international law is in many respects different from domestic law; it does not flow from the enactment of a body with authority to make laws like legislatures, and it is not enforceable like domestic law. It is mainly constituted by agreements among states on the conventions which are to guide states' mutual relations. Nevertheless, states in their own interests do observe these laws and norms most of the time, despite the absence of an enforcement agency.

b. **International Organisations:** A country's foreign policy option is also often affected by its membership in international organisations. The existence of many of these institutions, which are established for a variety of reasons ranging from cultural to economic and political-strategic, is a major feature of the post 1945 international system. Member states' policies are usually affected by the nature of the particular institution and its policy objectives on the one hand, and the effect of their institutional membership on the policies of other states towards them on the other hand.

1.2.3 The Conceptual Framework:
Policy Analysis Model (PAM)

PAM is one of the wheels with which the process of international politics operates because foreign policy is not separate from national policy; instead it is a part of it. The model consists of national interests that are to be furthered in relation to other states in determining the course of their own foreign policies within the limits of their strengths and the realities of their external environments. The conceptual framework that guides this study shows that the process of foreign policy formulation is affected by both domestic and international factors. These factors are also interrelated. For foreign policy to be effective, the government and policymaking organs need to analyse the situation to formulate foreign policies that adhere to the desired outcome for the state, as illustrated by the theoretical framework model overleaf.

Figure 1: Conceptualization of Foreign Analysis (Authors, 2020)

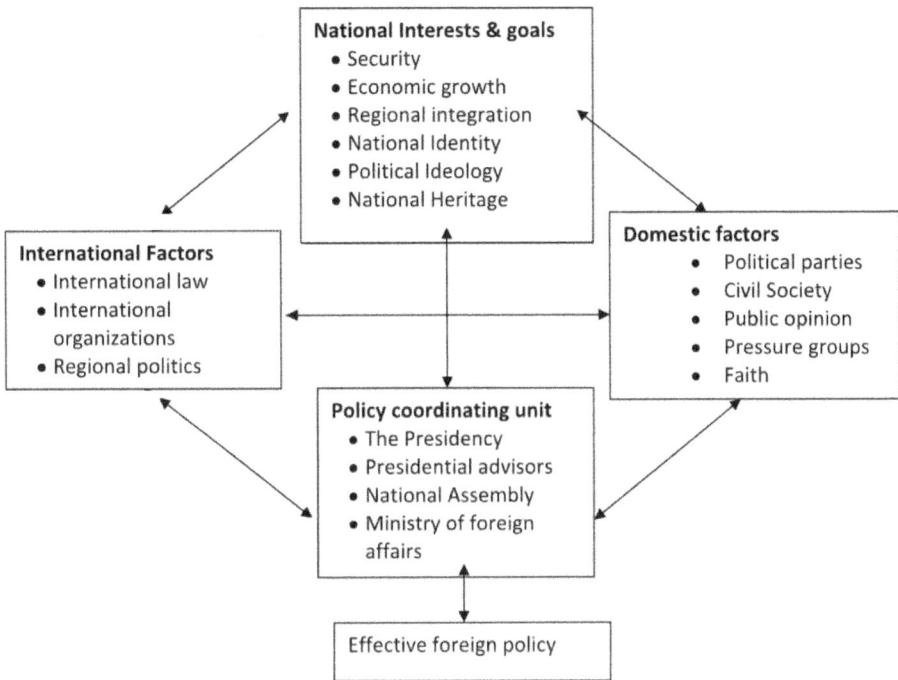

Source: Nyuon, 2017

In the above embedded policy analysis model (PAM) developed by Nyuon, A. K (2017) on formulation and conduct of foreign policy, prioritize national interests as the basis for effective foreign policy influenced by international and domestic factors. The effectiveness of the manipulated international and domestic variables is determined by the nature of foreign policy coordination unit of each African state. In the analysis of the above model, three key variables played a pivotal role. First, the international politics where foreign policies are directed composed of foreign independent states, and entities where the initiating state has no authority or jurisdiction. This means, the decision makers must therefore be constantly aware of the interests of other actors in the international system. Sufficient account is often taken on what these actors have done, or are doing or are likely to do in the future in response to a particular policy in question. Secondly, the domestic politics where; public opinion, national role conceptions, decision making rules and personality traits of the political leaders vary from one state to another. These differences continually affect both foreign policymaking process and execution because the state's final product of the foreign policy is derived from issues of domestic politics as well as foreign relations. The author argued that, the domestic structure is not irrelevant in any historical period. At least, it determines the quantity of social effect which can be keen to foreign policy. Thirdly, both the international and domestic variables are moderated through the policy coordination unit which is the powerhouse for determining the effectiveness and efficiency of the state's foreign policy outcome as illustrated above in the model.

1.2.4 Conceptualizing Foreign Policy Variables

In this conceptualization, a variable is a property that takes on different values. Putting it differently, a variable is something that varies or a symbol to which numerals or values are attached. In order to clearly conceptualize the variables within this study, it was appropriate to first understand the causality between the formulation and conduct of foreign policy in Africa. In this correlation, formulation was the cause while conduct was the effect. In the example below, *the extent of formulating Africa's state's foreign policies* is treated as the independent variable, while *conduct* is treated as the dependent variable. All variables that might affect this relationship, either positively or negatively, are treated as extraneous variables.

Figure 2: Co-relations of Formulation and Conduct of Foreign Policy

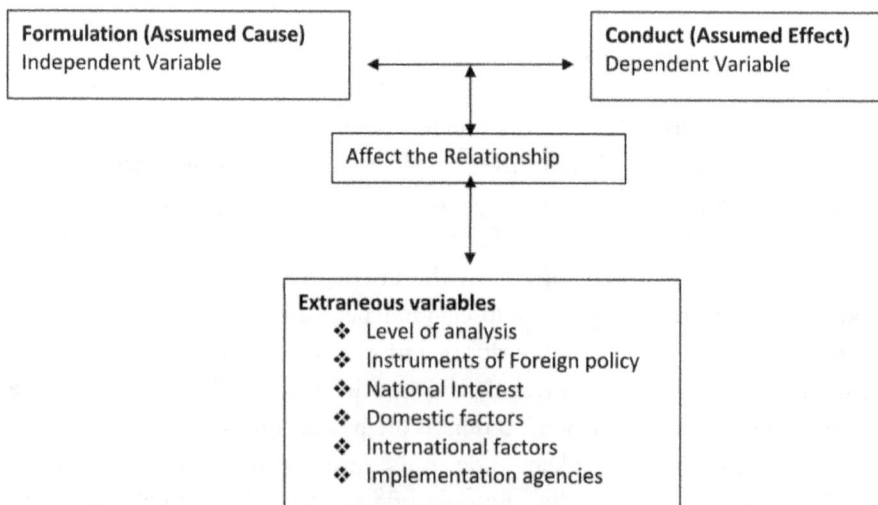

Source: Authors, 2020

In the above diagram, the magnitude or strength of these relationships can be affected, positively or negatively depending on a number of other factors that are not the focus of the study. These extraneous variables were the level of analysis in formulating and conducting Africa's foreign policy by individual leaders. The instruments of foreign policy, national interest, the domestic factors, the international factors and the agencies involved the formulation and conduct of Africa's foreign policy as illustrated above. The aim of the correlation was to explore what happens to conduct when formulation did not follow the appropriate channels. Using specimen correlations, the authors concluded that, there was a strong relation between the formulation and conduct of foreign policy.

1.3 Foreign Policy and International Politics

A state's foreign policy usually specifies the attitudes and confrontations of a state towards other states. In today's world, the foreign policymaking of states is based on their interest necessitation but remains reliant on its current international political environment. As commonly defined, international politics as a field examines the sources of conflict and cooperation between and among states and international actors within the international system.[35] As a distinct branch of international politics, foreign policy analysis (FPA) considers a specific aspect of this larger question by focusing on the processes by which specific international actors, known primarily as state governments and leaders, make choices.

Tracing back to the classic work of Richard Snyder and his collaborators (1962), the resulting scholarship has been enormous on how leaders, groups, and coalitions of international actors can affect the way foreign policy problems are framed, the options that are selected, the choices that are made, and what gets implemented.[36] National interest is an embodiment of the aggregation of a nation's interest (goals/objectives) as a sovereign political entity, while foreign policy is a vehicle for the projection and realization of the national interest as politicians define those interests and keeping in view the external environment. This study has looked at the meaning of the two terms – foreign policy and national interest – especially how national interest has been used either for invoking popular support or for analysing foreign policy.

In the coming years, the challenge for FPA will be to integrate ongoing transformations in international political structures and processes into theories regarding government processes and foreign policy formulation. During this

---

35   Gries, (2004), p.108
36   Hermann, (2001), p. 1

transformative period, new processes are likely to be developed both across and within traditional state boundaries while at the same time the main actors will probably remain the same. As such, FPA will need to develop new understandings regarding the nature of policymaking among the various actors who create foreign policy.

As for the international system, several overarching future visions of world politics have come to dominate popular intellectual discussion. Fukuyama's End of History" view suggests that liberalism, democracy, and the latter's emphasis on individual rights have triumphed ideologically over all competitors.[37] In this vision, the future path of international affairs is an increasingly peaceful coexistence in a slowly enlarging democratic zone with potential conflicts existing between the democratic and non-democratic areas. Kaplan provides an apocalyptic vision when he suggests that societal breakdown in the developing world characterized by poverty, inequality, instability, and strife will eventually spread to the developed world and encompass the entire globe.[38] This vision calls for all nations to have foreign policies that seek to address the global issues of poverty, disease, illiteracy and conflict even though they do not occur within their boundaries. Therefore, this indicates that episodes in the international arena cannot be washed away in a country's foreign policy.

Huntington's expectation of emergence of conflict among various cultural civilizations such as Islamic, Judeo-Christian, Eastern Orthodox and Confucian in a manner that at once potentially supersedes loyalties to the state internally while at the same time provides affiliate motivations among states within a particular civilization seems to be happening.[39] This is illustrated by the emergence of conflicts in various regions such as North Africa, West Africa and the Middle East. The conflicts occurring in these regions have an effect on world peace as these conflicts can influence and overflow to neighbouring countries and regions. With the interconnectedness of globalisation, a conflict in one region is expected to affect other regions directly or indirectly.

Additionally, Friedman identifies the free flow of economic goods and services across the globe as the key international variable to globalisation because nations that embrace globalisation will thrive while those that do not will wither.[40] Traditional balance of power considerations is a continuing foundation for international relations, international politics and internal state dynamics and will increasingly be affected in unpredictable ways by digital

---

37   Fukuyama, (1992), p. 67
38   Kaplan, (2000), p. 112
39   Huntington, (1996), p. 73
40   Friedman, (1999), p. 107

technology's influence on productivity and economies of scale.[41] This is expected to have ripple effects on foreign policy formulation of states. One commonality among these various perspectives is the notion that in the future there will be greater movement of capital, people, ideas, and goods across increasingly porous international borders. The challenge for FPA will be to adapt to these increasingly dynamic processes.[42] Perhaps IPA should be integrated into domestic policies during formulation to expand the state's opportunities in the promotion of national interest through the world's public opinion and globalised citizens.

The changing international context requires that the field emphasize the influence of cross-border foreign policy processes as well as exploit data sets that have not been previously used. Ironically, the barriers to participation by actors outside traditional political systems recede international politics in foreign policy for effectiveness. As a result, FPA needs to become responsive to this chain of events by focusing even more on cross-national bureaucratic public-interest groups and decision-making dynamics. Although scholars and theorists analysing foreign policy-making will probably continue to study decisionmakers in governments, the attention on how these actors perceive and choose to interact with each other should shift, emphasizing the broader context and these expanded processes. Foreign policy formulators, hence, are faced with an ever-increasing array of factors to consider in coming up with effective foreign policy for their states. It is clear from the above analysis that international politics influence the foreign policy of sovereign states through globalisation, human rights considerations, public opinion, conflicts, and advancement of technology.

Extant research in foreign policy analysis (FPA) is vibrant and multi-dimensional, indicated by how it bridges gaps with adjacent disciplines, the policymaking community, and the larger field of international relations. In this section, a review of foreign policy in developed nations is provided. An analysis of foreign policy in the United States of America was given as an example. The major factors considered and the institutions involved in foreign policy analysis in the US are discussed. American foreign relations are determined through a series of complex policymaking decisions. In the analysis preliminary to a policy decision, the external environment, the broad objectives of its foreign policy and the means available for its implementation are usually evaluated, interrelated, and appraised.[43] This analysis is but one of the stages leading to the final conduct of foreign affairs.

---

41   Kupchan, (2002), p. 319
42   Hung, (2000), p.411
43   Bowie, (1960), p.4

In the United States of America foreign policymaking, enlisting the support and resources for a specific policy and the operation or execution of that policy are two further distinguishable stages in the normal order; the analysts follow the policy decision. Moreover, foreign policy expert prediction and appraisal in the original analysis affect the outcome of the actual policy. To cope with the difficult task of formulating foreign policy, several government organizations have been created since World War II. These include the Department of Defense, the National Security Council (NSC), the Central Intelligence Agency (CIA), and the Policy Planning Staff of the Department of State. This policymaking machinery has greatly enhanced the United States' capacity for coping with the complex process of foreign affairs.

The US is observed to have emerged from World War II ill-equipped in its foreign policy machinery. The nation and its leaders misjudged the kind of world which lay ahead and laboured under serious illusions about the country's position and its interests, and the dangers menacing them.[44] The nation has had to develop an understanding of foreign affairs and the techniques for conducting them in a far shorter period than most great powers in Europe. Over the years, it has had to evolve a framework for policymaking during times of unprecedented change and turmoil. In many ways what has been achieved in so short a time is remarkable. However, one could observe that the United States' foreign policy machinery still needs to be strengthened and improved to meet the challenges of the period ahead.

The present United States machinery for making foreign policy dates mainly from 1947.[45] By that time, the Soviet's conduct in occupied Germany, in Eastern Europe, and in the Conferences of Foreign Ministers had dashed the earlier hopes for post-war US-Soviet co-operation. The experience of that period had also shown the serious inadequacy of US instruments for policy formulation. To remedy the defects and fill the gaps, new agencies were created and old ones remodelled. The Defense Department was established to unify – but not to merge – the three military services under the direction of the Secretary of Defense. The Central Intelligence Agency was formed to correlate and evaluate intelligence relating to national security. And the National Security Council was organized to advise the President on the integration of domestic, foreign, and military policies relating to National Security, and to facilitate co-operation among the interested departments. At the same time, General Marshall set up the Policy Planning Staff in the State Department to undertake longer-range analysis.[46]

---

44   Kendall, (2010), p.13
45   Bowie, (1960), p.8
46   Fettweis (2013, p.198)

Currently, these various agencies, and certain additional related ones, have been modified or strengthened in light of experience without changing the basic conceptions undergirding them. The machineries and the modifications that have been done in recent years have improved US policymaking and facilitated the performance of the noble tasks involved in its post-war role. However, the policymaking system can be criticized from various points of view. One common criticism is that the policy papers of the National Security Council are too general. Sometimes this defect is attributed to the tendency of committees to seek the least common denominator as a basis for agreement. This view tends to misconceive the nature of the Council. The National Security Council does not reach any decisions. It is solely an advisory group for the President. It discusses issues before him and makes recommendations, but the only one who can decide is the President.

Members of the National Security Council may espouse divergent views without resolving the issue as a group. Thus, the President has the chance to hear frank expressions of opinion by his principal advisers before deciding on policy issues. The National Security Council papers are often quite general.[47] They seldom prescribe the specific means for handling crises which may arise in different regions across the globe. The machinery does not always produce the right solutions.[48] Entrenched preconceptions may impede or prevent realistic appraisal of some situations. Further, it can be observed that most of US foreign policy is based upon its military power, its economic interest, and human rights. Some have seen this form of foreign policy as the means of the United States trying to impose its values on other states.

1.4 Theoretical Framework

This section explores the relevant theories in comprehending how national interest could be promoted through available paradigms such as role theory, rational choice theory, poliheuristic theory and groupthink theory. While role and rational choice theories serve as broad theoretical frameworks, poliheuristic and groupthink theories should be applied in explaining the key issues that influence formulation and conduct of foreign policy in general.

---

47   Kendall, (2010), p.14
48   Fettweis, (2013), p.261

1.4.1 Role Theory

Kalevi Holsti Originally formulated the concept of role theory as the national role conceptions for policymakers in the definitions for functions of the state, especially what the state should perform on a continuing basis in the international system or in subordinate regional systems.[49] In formulating a foreign policy, a country's policymakers depict the role that the country should play in the international arena; they determine how the country is desired to portray itself towards the world in relation to how it would want to be viewed. Foreign policy is developed with this perspective in mind. In the case of the United States, examples include but are not limited to, hegemon, balancer, tribune and agent of American values, catalyst, integrator, regional leader, regional stabilizer, developer and isolator.[50] Once these variants become salient in elite political discourse, the ideas define the range of acceptable foreign policy options prescribing some actions and encouraging others. It is assumed that role performance – the general foreign policy behaviour of a government – should be consistent with policymakers' role conceptions to a considerable degree.[51] Role theory can be applied to determine the factors that influence a country's foreign policy because it integrates both domestic and international levels of analysis. Previous studies have, for example, put much effort into explaining how and why Chinese foreign policy makers hesitantly but succinctly subscribed to the idea of China as a responsible stakeholder in international affairs, even though their country is still predominantly viewed as a developing nation domestically.[52] The main driving factor of this role adaptation is growing international expectations with respect to Chinese crisis management, economic aid and the way in which China is becoming a driving force in the development of countries mostly in Africa.[53] A few words on the relationship between social roles and other immaterial factors such as culture or identity may help at this point. Some authors interpret the link between roles and identity as one of reciprocity or co-constitution.[54] However, the view taken in the current study was that roles imply a positioning or functioning in the international system that is in relation to other states, regimes or actors more generally. Identity or culture does not accept that the former usually requires social construction. The identity or culture of a country would not therefore have a major impact on

---

49　　　Holsti (1970), p.245.
50　　　Le Prestre (1997), p. 69.
51　　　Holsti (1970), p. 245.
52　　　Zoellick (2005), p.6.
53　　　Gottwald & Duggan (2011), p.241.
54　　　Nabers (2011), Pp. 82 -83.

the relationship between a country and other states.[55] Yet unlike roles, notions of identity do not imply structurally diverse and multifaceted social relations. For instance, consider the developed and developing nations, protector and prestige or liberator and defender, that could not have been created by the simple working of a mere inclusion or exclusion dynamic.

A second difference between roles and other ideational factors, such as identity and culture, relates back to the levels of analysis. Foreign policy roles, according to newer theoretical role research, are mutually constituted by domestic variables such as an ego expectations and foreign states' expectations.[56] Thus, social roles have an inherent conflict, a potential that is twofold: There are conflicts within a role known as intra-role conflicts and conflicts between roles referred to inter-role conflicts.[57] The former refers to conflicts between domestic and foreign expectations, or between several more or less incompatible domestic expectations. This happens when some roles that are portrayed in foreign policy are contested domestically.[58] Contesting roles domestically is due to the fact that state leaders are often guided by more than one role conception at the same time.[59]

Depending on circumstances, leaders can therefore find themselves in a position that requires contradictory role performances through enactments of foreign policies.[60] Both intra-state and inter-state role conflicts might lead to reinterpretation efforts that alter the substance of national role conceptions in order to meet diverging expectations and to accommodate conflicting role conceptions. Therefore, role theory indicates that foreign policy comes into being after several consultations and bargaining both within a country and external to it, with other international actors and states.

Although role theory has been widely used in the field of foreign policy analysis, it has had very few applications to studies in African foreign policy. It has, however, been applied in a study of India's China policy since 1988[61] and another historical study in which the evolution of the Indian conception of great power status is delineated.[62] The theory has been previously applied in a study of American foreign policy[63] and also in Chinese foreign policy.[64]

55   Reinke de Buitrago, (2012), p. 17.
56   Harnisch (2011, p. 8).
57   Harnisch (2011), p. 8, Thies (2010), p. 6337.
58   Brummer & Thies (2014, p.27), Cantir & Kaarbo (2012, p.19).
59   Holsti (1970, p. 277).
60   Thies (2010, p. 6337).
61   Vogel (2010, p.6).
62   Wagner (2005, p67).
63   Le Prestre (1997, p. 69).
64   Zoellick (2005, p.101).

In the current study, role theory should provide guidelines for identifying the most salient role conceptions that have been expressed by contemporary foreign policy decisionmakers in any country globally. The theory highlighted was developed as a result of some divisions between egos and alter expectations. Thus, it entails an analysis in evolution of national role conceptions over time such as unravelling the causes and constitutive factors of those national role conceptions.

1.4.2 Rational Choice Theory

Rational choice theory depicts the decisionmaker as a rational actor. The term "rational actor, broadly defined, refers to an individual who makes choices by taking the following steps: searching for relevant information regarding the conditions of choice; integrating that information so as to discover existing alternatives for action; drawing upon empirical generalizations to deduce the likely results each alternative yielded by judging the best choice that satisfy his or her wants and choosing a course of action accordingly."[65]

Rational choice theory is parsimonious and elegant in explaining foreign policy decisions. This is because few straightforward assumptions explain a wide range of policy decisions. Perhaps the simplest conceptualization of decision-making according to rational choice theory is that it proceeds from a simple and intuitive idea. If one can establish what people want, one can hence be able to explain and predict what they do. Rational choice theory assumes merely that people are cognitively competent to match means to ends and to rank options accordingly. In standard formulations, a rational analysis simply needs information about what people want, what alternatives are open to them, and what they know or can reasonably be expected to figure out about the likely costs and benefits of alternatives.[66]

The key assumption of the rational choice school of thought in international relations is that nations are led by rational, forward-looking, expected-utility-maximizing leaders.[67] Scholars distinguish between thin and thick rationality. Thin rationality refers to the strategic pursuit of stable and ordered preferences whereas thick rationality assumes, in contrast, that actors have specific preferences. Thus, in politics, the preference for most politicians is typically perpetuation in office.[68] The downside to this rationality is that some foreign policy decisions will not always be for the common good of the citizens. This therefore indicates that selfish interest of leaders in any country can inform

---

65   Rosenberg (1995, p. 111).
66   Stein & Welch (1997, p. 52)
67   Bueno de Mesquita & Lalman (1990, p. 751).
68   Mintz & DeRouen (2010, p. 59).

policy decisions. Rational choice approaches in foreign policy analysis and international relations have centered on several important contributions.[69] A review of this literature shows that these authors use the rational choice approach to explain and predict outcomes in foreign policy and international conflict. In general, the analytic, rational model should lead to better decisions, although not always to better outcomes.[70]

Rational choice theory should be used to analyse many different historical foreign policy and national security choices. Rational choice theory was more persuasive in explaining domestic leaders' decisions pertinent to the Sino-Indian War and the Seven Weeks' War.[71] The theory was also applied to examine the creation and evolution of the U.S. nuclear defense policy in the 1940s.[72] A study of European Union politics including decision-making with respect to integration, legislative, executive, and judicial politics within the context of the European Union and public opinion as well as Europeanization showed they all applied rational choice theory.[73] Further, the study aimed at assessing how decisionmakers take situational perceptions into account in war and peace decisions through the application of rational choice theory. More specifically, the study was able to specify the conditions under which differences in perception were more or less likely to lead to war.[74]

However, rational choice theory has limitations, which leads to criticism. Perhaps the chief critique of rational choice theory was the notion of bounded or procedural rationality, which states that decisionmakers are still rational, only bound.[75] Specifically, rational choice models have been depicted as insensitive to the cognitive limitations of individuals and organizations.[76] The theory claimed that individuals are bounded rational beings who have limitations in information-processing capacities relative to decision-making.[77] Thus, this indicates that foreign policy decisions are not always rational and are bound to be affected by limitations of policymakers in gathering and interpreting information.

In the above review, rational choice theory has been applied in assessing how political leaders in Africa searched for relevant information regarding conditions of choice, how the policy could be integrated or existing alternatives for action

---

69   Bueno de Mesquita (1989, p.53), Wittman (1979, p.65).
70   Mintz & DeRouen (2010, p. 58).
71   Bueno de Mesquita and Lalman (1992, p.67).
72   Szalai (2008, p.41).
73   Pollack (2007, p.98).
74   Kim & Bueno de Mesquita (1995, p.9)
75   Simon (1957, p.115).
76   Simon (1992, p.37).
77   Simon (1990, p.198).

discovered, how they draw upon empirical generalizations to deduce the likely results each alternative will yield, and how this informs the policy decisions of the country. The forces behind foreign policy decisions in the country have been analysed to identify the main factors influencing foreign policy decisions in Africa.

1.4.3 Poliheuristic Theory

Poliheuristic theory concentrates on the why and how of decision making, which makes the theory relevant to both the contents and the processes of foreign policy decision-making. The term poliheuristic can be deconstructed into the prefix *poly,* meaning many, and the root *heuristic,* meaning shortcuts, together referring to the cognitive mechanisms decisionmakers utilize in attempts to simplify complex decision tasks.[78]

The poliheuristic theory of decision-making proposes that foreign policymakers employ a two-stage decision process. In the first stage, decisionmakers screen available alternatives utilizing cognitive-based heuristic strategies. In the second stage, when the decision matrix has been reduced to a more manageable number of alternatives and dimensions, policymakers resort to analytic, expected utility, or lexicographic rules of choice in an effort to minimize risks and maximize rewards. The first phase in the decision-making process typically involves a non-exhaustive search where decisionmakers process information across dimensions in an attempt to select surviving alternatives before completing the consideration of all alternatives along all dimensions. The second phase, then, consists of a lexicographic or maximizing decision rule used in selecting an alternative from the subset of surviving alternatives.

Another key premise of poliheuristic theory is the reference to the political aspects of decision making in a foreign policy context. The assumption is that the policymaker measures costs and benefits, risks and rewards, gains and losses, and success and failure in terms of political ramifications above all else. Furthermore, politicians are concerned about challenges to their leadership, their prospects of political survival, and their level of public support. Domestic politics is the essence of decision. Because loss aversion outweighs all other considerations, avoiding failure rather than attaining success drives leaders more.[79] The political dimension is important in foreign policy decisions not so much because politicians are driven by public support, but because they are averse to loss and would reject alternatives that may hurt them politically.

---

78   Geva, Redd, & Mintz (2000), p.20.
79   Anderson (1983, p.369).

The theory, then, suggests procedures for eliminating alternatives by adopting or rejecting courses of action based on this political heuristic in the decision process.

The theory also posits that different decision heuristics may be employed in response to different decision tasks as a function of environmental and personal variations. This premise implies that these decision heuristics and strategies may be suboptimal. Again, decisionmakers not only use different strategies depending on various environmental and cognitive constraints, but they also resort to the use of different strategies en route to a single choice.

There have been various studies conducted based on poliheuristic theory. In a study of the Persian Gulf crisis of 1990-1991, Iraqi president Saddam Hussein rejected outright the option of withdrawing from Kuwait because there was an absolute certainty in his mind of what could not be sacrificed, such as his political survival.[80] This description fits poliheuristic theory which asserts that policymakers will use an attribute, or dimension-based process instead of an alternative-based approach for processing information. A dimension-based or intra-dimensional strategy signifies that an individual focus on a given dimension and then reviews information within that dimension across alternatives and then continues the process for another dimension.[81] An intra-dimensional, or attribute based, processing is cognitively easier and hence more likely to be employed in cognitively demanding conditions.[82]

This theory was applied in the examination of Clinton's decision-making in the Kosovo crisis, which found that President Clinton's decision was influenced by non-compensatory domestic political calculations through the strong influence of his Secretary of State, Madeleine Albright.[83] More specifically, President Clinton's decision was heavily influenced by his concern over how Congress and the public would react to his initial decision not to act because of possible casualties from the use of force. He greatly feared the loss of American lives and how such losses would influence his political fortunes. On the same note, Carter's decision making with respect to the Iran hostage rescue decision was examined and it was found that Carter eliminated, in a non-compensatory fashion, all options that threatened his chances of re-election. He narrowed the choice set down to a few politically palatable alternatives by engaging in more maximizing processes that focused on military and strategic concerns.[84]

---

80   Freedman and Karsh (1991, p. 35)
81   Payne (1976, p.372).
82   Russo and Dosher (1983, p.684).
83   Redd (2005, p. 129).
84   James & Oneal (1991, p.326)

Moreover, poliheuristic theory was applied to examine how Latin American leaders processed information with respect to ratifying the Kyoto Protocol.[85] Leaders used cognitive heuristics that eliminated various policy options en route to the choice, and their choices surrounding this environmental treaty were often not motivated by environmental concerns but by domestic political calculations. Moreover, in application of the theory globally, crisis decision-making in China,[86] comparatively in China and Turkey,[87] were assessed using poliheuristic theory, with researchers finding that it does quite well in explaining leaders' crisis decision-making. Poliheuristic theory should be applied to depict how leaders use information and circumstances to make foreign policy decisions that involve critical aspects of security, economy and regional integration. It should be used to assess whether political survival acts as a key factor that leaders consider when making foreign policy decisions.

1.4.4 Groupthink Theory

Groupthink is a theory of defective decision-making.[88] More specifically, groupthink addresses defective decision-making on the part of a cohesive decision-making group in which loyalty to real or perceived group norms takes precedence over independent, critical judgment.[89] Conformity is the result of two possible factors: conformity from group pressure on the individual that directs group pressure against dissenters, usually from the emergence of self-appointed mind-guards, and conformity from stress-induced cohesion. Time pressure may cause members of the group to withhold dissenting opinions for the sake of reaching consensus.

Consequences of groupthink and its resulting defective decision-making include an incomplete survey of alternatives and objects such as failure to examine the risks of preferred alternatives and failure to reappraise initially rejected alternatives. Other consequences include poor information search, selective bias in processing information and failure to work out contingency plans.[90] The most famous example of groupthink documented is the U.S. Bay of Pigs invasion that has been referred to as a fiasco by the John F. Kennedy Administration in 1961.[91] The Bay of Pigs invasion was labelled a

---

85   Below (2008, p.25).
86   James and Zhang (2005, p.43).
87   Sandal, Zhang, James, and James (2011, p.38).
88   Janis (1982, p.96).
89   Charles , F, H (2012), Pp.11-23
90   Janis (1982, p.281).
91   Badie (2010, p.281).

perfect failure.[92] Kennedy and his advisory group suffered from illusions of invulnerability, illusions of unanimity, suppression of personal doubts among the advisers themselves, and the presence of self-appointed mind-guards.

Groupthink theory is used to examine the Iran–Contra scandal during the Reagan administration,[93] and helped in explaining the flawed decision-making of British leaders during the Munich crisis.[94] Moreover, the G.W. Bush Administration's decision to attack Iraq was the result of groupthink, resulting from an incomplete survey of the alternatives to war, a failure to re-examine previously rejected alternatives, and existence of a selective bias in the manner in which intelligence information was interpreted.[95] For better comprehension on the role of theory in decision making, three crises facing the John F Kennedy Administration were examined for evidence of groupthink: the Bay of Pigs, the Cuban Missile Crisis, and the Vietnam conflict; findings showed that a higher level of groupthink led to poorer quality decision processes.[96]

In spite of these different theories, each can be applied by a country depending on specific historical and material circumstances in that state. The major aim is to secure optimal realization of the country's national interests. The national interest, as discussed in our introduction to this book, is always the bedrock for any nation's survival. In this respect, the choice of leadership a country takes and consequences of those decisions are critical.

1.5 Features of the Revamped African Foreign Policy

1.5.1 Vision-Based Strategy

Africa should adopt a visionary approach in formulation and conduct of foreign policy. It should develop an appropriate mechanism for mitigating crisis rather than responding to foreign policy crisis as it occurs. This premise shows that international politics is a very dynamic process, thus necessitating vision-based strategies in foreign policymaking instead of line-based or crisis-based strategies which are reactive or defensive.

Moreover, if Africa wants to have an effective and vibrant foreign policy with international impact, the Ministry of Foreign Affairs should develop value-oriented visionary policy with a strategic vision rather than short-termed interest in foreign policy formulation since visions with strategic targets prevent

---

92   Janis (1982, p. 14).
93   Hart (1994, p.83).
94   Walker and Watson (1989, p.211).
95   McQueen (2005), p.76.
96   Beckner (2012, p.88).

probable deflections in strategy and provide strategic continuity and accession to defined foreign policy goals. Visions also unify short-term tactics with long-term strategies. Otherwise, policies remain for the day and could not be carried to the future.

1.5.2 Development of Consistent and Systematic Framework

Another essential aspect for improving Africa's Foreign policy is the development of a consistent and systematic framework with which to work. African policy should have a coherent policy framework that should address the interest of different actors in its international relations. In order for Africa to have a systematic foreign policy framework, the Ministry of Foreign Affairs should develop a true and consistent unified mindset, strategic planning, and political will for formulation and implementation of foreign policy. This framework will enable all the policymakers to ensure coherency in foreign policy formation among policy stakeholders.

1.5.3 Capacity Building Initiative

The conduct of diplomacy is transforming in the 21st century because of various actors vying for space in the international arena. In revamping African foreign policies in the 21st century, it is vital for the African states to exert effort in building the capacity of diplomats to present their case well in the international forums or the diplomatic missions abroad in promoting the national interest to effect a positive change. Moreover, the Ministry of Foreign Affairs should take charge in training the diplomats on negotiation, mediation, lobbying and advocacy strategies as well as key performance indicators for diplomats.

In African diplomatic perspective, capacity development should be geared toward empowering diplomats with skill and knowledge to create, unleash, maintain, strengthen and adapt capacity over time for effective performance and sustainability. To Illustrate this in the context of South Sudan, studies have shown that lack of skill and knowledge led to poor coordination of the attempted coup between 2014 and 2015, though it was a policy of the government of the Republic of South Sudan to inform the international community on what transpired on 15th December, 2013. The lack of enough capacity among the government diplomats and envoys empowered the opposition to triumphed in convincing the international community to buy-in their position of no coup attempt. Therefore, empowering diplomats is paramount because the capacity-building process strengthen the performance and abilities of African diplomats through relevant skill training and organizational support. The quality of design and execution of the diplomatic mission programs determine the quality of African foreign policies abroad. The capacity-building strategy for the Ministry of Foreign Affairs in Africa should comprise the collection and analysis of baseline information about the existing capacity gap in the diplomatic mission, calling for consulate and embassies abroad to design effective and efficient institutional development programs. The same thing must apply to regional and continental African organizations.

1.5.4 Merit-Based Appointment

The merit system is the process of promoting and hiring foreign service employees based on their ability to perform a job rather than on their political connections, which is the opposite of the spoils system.

The recruitment and selection processes that result in merit-based appointments include these essential elements: structured process that is transparent and fair; assessments that are objective and relevant to the job; and decisions that are reasonable. Merit-based hiring takes into consideration both legislation and recruitment policy. Where applicable, requirements of collective agreements are also considered. These elements support a merit-based approach to hiring and are considered part of the audit and review of appointment decisions undertaken by the Ministry of Foreign Affairs of every African state. Sadly, Foreign Affairs ministries are always under-resourced and, in most cases, they are perceived to be spenders rather than producers. This is a misconception particularly in the era of economic diplomacy. Apart from projecting the national image abroad, they are heavily involved in promoting the sending country's products and managing potential investors, markets, and prestige.

1.5.5 Alignment of National Interest

National interest is perhaps one of most controversial concepts in International Relations. The controversy is due to several factors. Firstly, the concept has been and continues to be the subject of different interpretation by both analysts and practitioners. Secondly, the concept has been a subject of abuse particularly by politicians and decision-makers all over the world. Thirdly, the concepts are not easily susceptible to analysis. Generally, every nation has a foreign policy which seeks to achieve its national interest. When statesmen and bureaucrats are expected or required to act in the national interest, it means that they are to take action on issues that improve the political situation, the economic and social well-being, the health and culture of the people as well as their political survival.

National interest is adopted as a means or device for analysing fundamental objectives of foreign policy of a nation-state. It is regarded as those purposes which the nation, through its leadership pursues persistently through time. National interest is also some ideal set of purposes which a nation should seek to realize in the conduct of its foreign relations.

Foreign policy is predicated on the national interest of a nation state, and any foreign policy that fails to reflect the country's national interests is doomed to the general disenchantment of the populace. National interest covers three outstanding components of national security; protection and preservation of the welfare of the state, and national prestige. National security relates to the defense of a country's territory integrity and political independence. Foreign policy on the other hand is the aspect of national policy that pertains to the external environment and involves the enunciation of principles and also indicates a country's positions on major international issues thus foreign policy is concerned with the substance and conduct of external relations.

According to K.J. Holsti, there are three broad categories of interests, namely: core interest, variable interest and complementary interest.

1.5.5.1 Core Interests

Core interests are those interests which are fundamental to the ability of the nation to play its role as a sovereign nation within the international system. Often these interests are tied to the survival preservation and continued existence of the state. The implication is that a nation must exist as an actor within the international system before it attempts pursuing or realizing any objective or interest in national terms. Thus, core interest is about the kind of interest or objective to which a nation is prepared to make all possible sacrifices to achieve. The concern of core interest is the national survival, i.e., protection of the territorial integrity of the state and the lives of all its citizens against external aggression as well as protection of its political, economic, religious or social institutions. These are objectives for which states are normally prepared to war with others. This is why a considerable proportion of the national budget is often committed to national security and defence by all nations.

National welfare is also part of core interest. It is the responsibility of any nation to provide for the socio-economic welfare of its citizens. These necessities compel states to enter into economic intercourse with one another in order to advantageously harness resources to serve domestic needs. No nation, no matter how powerful and richly endowed, has ever achieved economic prosperity and ensured a high standard of living for its citizens without active involvement in channels of international trade.

Another aspect of core interest is national prestige, e.g., national honour, respect and so forth. The degree of influence a nation can wield on others depends on the extent to which such a state is able to conduct its affairs consistent with a high sense of self-respect, appropriate process and national honour. The implication here is that a state that fails to maintain a high degree of acceptable reputation in the international system risks disrespect and even isolation in the comity of nations.

The state has to girdle itself to realize these objectives directly, quickly, forcefully and effectively; it has no luxury of time in case of fulfilling these core objectives. They are usually stated in the form of basic principles of foreign policy and become articles of faith that a society accepts uncritically. These objectives include:

i.   **National security:** It is the primary goal of a foreign policy. The concept of national security is not confined to territorial integrity or security of national borders. It may include the security of cultural and political institutions and beliefs and values. States also have the primary objective of maintaining their political independence i.e. the ability to play their prestigious role in the international arena at their own will.

ii. **Economic Development:** The promotion of economic interests of a nation is the fundamental goal in foreign policy as it is directly associated with state's existence. Contemporarily, national interests are more economic than political and foreign policy is more guided by economic factors than political ones.

1.5.5.2 Variable Interest

Variable interests are not very permanent because interests change frequently. However, secondary interest does enhance or complement the achievement of core interest objectives. The most easily identifiable secondary interest involves the task that is given to the citizen concerned.

The objectives are sought to be achieved within a specific time period, implying that after the expiration of the term, the objectives even if attained would have lost their real value. Here the targets are more than one or two states. A state has to carry out trade with a number of states and trade blocks. It has to deal with multiple sources while pursuing these objectives. The rationale of the objective includes:

i.   **Non-Political Cooperation:** In the field of international relations mutual cooperation is more than necessary today. So, the objectives of a foreign policy inevitably include economic, cultural and social cooperation. It is usually the keen desire of each state to establish, strengthen and widen its economic ties with other states. Status and prestige of a state can be secured only if the state is economically stable and prosperous. In the process, the state has to diversify its trade and economy in order to make it resilient enough to come up to the challenges of the competitive world. It has to export its goods, commodities and raw material to more than one destinations/state; it has to strengthen its export base in more than one commodity or good, so that no state, MNC, or group could exploit its vulnerability in this regard.

ii. **Promotion of National Prestige:** This policy of states which are meant to develop an impressive image on the states abroad. In the past, this was done primarily through diplomatic ceremonial and displays of military capabilities. However, in today's world, prestige is increasingly measured by levels of industrial development and scientific and technological skills. Industrialized countries and major powers can increase their international prestige through a number of policies and actions, including expansion of military capabilities, distribution of foreign aid, diplomatic ceremonies, industrial and scientific exhibition, and particularly through development of nuclear weapons and the capacity to explore outer space.

iii. **Territorial Expansion:** The policy of territorial expansion includes imperialism and colonialism which the states adhere to meet their economic and political aspirations. From 18th to 20th century the European States had adopted the policy of imperialism to capture the markets, raw materials and to claim superiority in European affairs. Territorial expansion becomes an end in itself, whether or not it fulfils any strategic, economic or social needs. Others do not occupy foreign territory but seek advantages, including access to raw materials, markets and trade routes, which they cannot achieve through ordinary trade or diplomacy. In modern times, the traditional imperialist policy has undergone a change and this can be explained by illustrating its two prevalent forms. The first is a policy which aims at the increase of areas of influence or ideology, such as the Russian policy of imperialism. The second is a policy that seeks to capture the economic resources by reducing the other state to the status of dependency, such as the economic/dollar imperialism of the USA and the Western European Countries.

1.5.5.3 Universal Interest

These are objectives aiming at restructuring the international system. Unlike, the primary and middle range goals, the long-range goals are the ambitions which the states may achieve in distant future and/or the states never press them too much in the present. These distant goals of foreign policy are the plans and dreams of a state which an ideology forms to establish the international system of its own liking. They have no time restrictions, as time limit is usually employed in pursuit of core and middle range objectives. Long Range Objective are not only time consuming, but are also indefinite and vague i.e. nothing can be ascertained regarding the outcome of the pursuit, so they are unpredictable as well.

They are usually interests which a state can apply to a larger geographical area ₁to a larger number of nations, or in several specified fields. General interests are in most cases interests that cannot be achieved by any state alone, and they are, by their nature, long-terms objectives. An example of a general interest is the foreign policy of Nigeria which seeks to influence the course of development within the international system. After the Communist Revolution of 1917 the Russian communist leaders, Lenin and Stalin reiterated that they would endeavour to expand communist ideology through every nook and corner of the Globe, as to them the capitalist system was defective and exploitative in its very nature. It was the Long-Range Objective of Communist Russia, because by doing so they did not set any time limit for the realization of these objectives.

1.5.6 Identification of the Essence of National Interest

The national interest of a state usually should be defined by its government. The term *national interest* has been subjected to two broad usages. It is used by politicians when they seek support for a particular course of action especially in foreign policy. Given the widespread attachment to the nation as a social and political organization, national interest is a powerful device for invoking support. Politicians use the term to seek support for domestic policy objectives, but here it is less persuasive given the normal extent of difference on domestic policy, and hence employ it less. In foreign policy, in contrast, the term evokes an anarchic international system where dangers abound and the interests of the nation are at risk.

'National interest' is used as tool for analysing foreign policy, particularly by political realists. Here, national interest is used as a foreign-policy version of the term "public interest" indicating what is best for the nation in its relation with other states. This use of the term emphasizes not merely the threat to the nation from international anarchy but also external constraints on the state's freedom of manoeuvre from treaties, the interests and power of the states, and other factors beyond the control of the nation such as geographical location and independence of foreign trade. The analytical usage of the term places much emphasis on the role of the state as the embodiment of the nation's interest. The realist's use of the term 'national interest' in evaluating foreign policy has focused on national security as the core of national interest. "Interest of state" and "national security interest" are closely allied terms.

Again, difficulty with analytical usage of the term is the absence of any agreed methodology by which the best interest of the nation can be tested. Some scholars have argued that the best interests are nevertheless objectively determined by the situation of the state in the international system and can be deduced from a study of history and the success/failure of policies. Other writers concede that national interest is subjectively interpreted by the government of the day. In this version, national interest is similar to the politician's rhetorical usage of the term – national interest is merely what politicians say the national interest is.

Here, if we are to continue Morgenthau's analysis, his "vital objective" that is, the national interest [requires] sharpening to meet particular inter-national situations" of a state's foreign policy vis-a-vis opponents in "the restoration of the balance of power by means short or war. This kind of analysis by no means clearly defines national interest. Rather, it illustrates the temptation to define it in terms of particular theories and of generalizations. National interest does not necessarily exsist in abstraction. Indeed, in most cases, the question is not whether, but how, to serve the national interest. That involves the question of what is the national interest in a particular situation. Moreover, there are many a national interests, not just one. Difficulties arise in the conflict of one interest with another; for example, in the clash of one interest in peace with the interest in preserving national institutions.

In spite of these difficulties, the concept of national interest is a very useful one which policymakers should always keep in mind. It helps to place foreign as well as domestic policy on the framework of a national policy, and it is a much-needed antidote to political short-sightedness and partisanship. However, changed, the meaning of national interest can be the constraints rather the variables of international relations. It is likewise true that development at home or abroad requires a continual reassessment of those interests in order to keep pace with unfolding situations in the international system. National will has little meaning unless it represents a widespread consensus and unless it is applied to specific policies. It is also to be remembered that national interest involves not only military security and the nation's economy but also a defence of the nation's values. National security, conceived in military terms alone, involves more than maintenance of a strong defence establishment; it also includes military assistance to other friendly nations and much more. In doing so, the state should decide on her foreign policy orientation. Orientation refers to the general policies, strategies and obligations of a state. The foreign policy orientation of a state can only be understood by a continuous observation of the state's moves in the field of international politics. There are three types of foreign policy orientation, namely, isolation, nonalignment, and coalition making and alliance construction.

1.5.6.1 Isolation

It is often based on the assumption that the state can best gain security and independence by reducing transactions with other units in the system. The policy of isolation is not the policy of isolating oneself from the rest of the world; it only means to avoid the pitfalls of international interest. It is a strategy which aims at avoiding transactions that may be detrimental to the security, liberty and welfare of the nation. States generally adopt the policy of isolation in view of their geographic and topographical characteristics, freedom of action, freedom from international complication and tension, and economic necessity. Logically, an isolationist orientation would be adopted or could succeed only in a system with a reasonably diffuse structure of power; where military, economic or ideological threats do not persist; and where other states are regularly shifting alliances.

1.5.6.2 Nonalignment

This is an independent policy which does not associate itself with the so called communist and non-communist blocs. It is a policy of keeping out of alliances because the alliances and counter-alliances may breed tension and ultimately lead to disaster. Nonalignment may be explained by perception of external threat as well as by domestic economic and political variables. To be non-aligned is to maximize opportunities to meet domestic economic needs, while minimizing dependencies. In contemporary international politics, the policy of nonalignment is very popular with the newly independent states. Successful strategies of non-alignment require many conditions including; favourable structure of power and influence in the system, national capacity to defend independence and territorial integrity against those who do not honour a neutral position, the benevolent attitude or indifference of the great powers, reasonable remoteness from the main centers of international conflicts, and reasonable amount of internal political stability.

1.5.6.3 Coalition Making and Alliance Construction

Governments that seek to construct permanent diplomatic coalitions or military alliances assume that they cannot achieve their objectives, defend their interests or deter perceived threats by mobilizing their own capabilities. Thus, they rely upon and make commitments to other states that face similar external problems or share similar objectives. The states with common problems and common enemies generally make diplomatic and military alliances. The diplomatic pacts are made to achieve economic and cultural interests while military alliances are purely for collective defense.

CHAPTER TWO

DECISION-MAKING IN FOREIGN POLICY: A THEORETICAL EXPLORATION

Interactions between the internal and the external environments of states require protection of national goals and interests. There are competitive and collaborative actions in the pursuit of those goals and interests which form the core of decisions in foreign policies and international relations. The international environment may be cordial or hostile depending on the methods and styles of pursuing national goals. In other words, the behaviour of a particular or several states triggers the necessity of taking decisions. Decision making of foreign policy is the key to protection of national interests. Hence, decision-making in foreign policy is the process by which governments analyse existing problems, evaluate alternatives and take appropriate actions to overcome sticky issues in their relations. In this respect, MacKenzia argues that decision is a real choice to meet the end and all approaches to attain the end. In other words, a decision consists of the cumulative sequence of stages of choices rather than the choice to arrive at a conclusion.[97] In addition, other scholars provide similar meanings of decision-making. In a similar way, Allen states decision-making is the work, which a manager performs to arrive at a conclusion and judgement."[98]

---

97   MacKenzie, W.J.M, (1975). pp. 176-179.
98   Allen, Louis A., (1964), p. 70

Decision-making is a process in individual life and collective interactions, and a tool of institutional actions which involve choice. It occupies a peculiar aspect in foreign policy and manifestation in the international system. The process implies action depending on the information available to the person or group of individuals intending to take action on a specific foreign policy issue. In general, a decision is the commitment based on the analysis of available information and capabilities to take action in response to the environment of the event necessitating such an action. In 1954, three scholars – Richard Snyder, H.W. Bruck and Burton Sapin published a famous monograph concerning the framework of decision-making.[99] One of its assumptions was that the study of state behaviour should address the role of people involved in influencing state actions. Snyder went further to suggest that rational analyses of decisions should be built on the environment of decision-making.

2.1 International Relations and Foreign Policy Decisions

International relations is the study of behaviour of and interactions among states and the concept is as old as the state's existence in history. The state's behaviour is affected by the relationships or interactions between states and other bodies acting on the international stage. Political Scientists like James N. Rosenau, Harold and Margaret Sprout have examined interactions, their nature, how they change and why change takes place over a period of time.[100] The word "interactions" suggests a "system". A system in its rudimentary definition is a set of interacting parts. These parts may be material or immaterial. They may also be biological, e.g., a human being. There are many systems in the world. Some of them are real and material while others are abstract or conceptual. Their components act together to serve a purpose. Each part has a vital function, which operates to make the whole body or structure work. It must be understood that the concepts of dependence and interdependence intervene in systems. Several types of interactions consist of parts of a whole functioning within the framework of harmony. When there are problems in the way parts operate, there is bound to be dysfunction and the system finds itself in trouble.

Most analysts who have applied systems analysis to the study of international relations have tried to identify interactions that take place among states and other bodies in the global system. The existence of the international system is associated with states and international organizations that involve relations and interactions requiring decisions. States are the significant units that constitute

---

99   Snyder, Richard, C., H.W. Bruck, and Burton Sapin (1954). Pp.25-30
100   Hudson, Valerie M. and Christopher S. Vore, (1995), Pp. 212-214.

the international system in the field of political science. The pioneering application of systems analysis made by Martin Kaplan in his "System and process in International Politics" resulted from the idea that the state is central in the International system.[101] Sometimes political scientists consider the international system as something absolutely concerning the state. They assume that there is no other international system other than a system of states. This way of conceiving of the international system is not always true. There are other forms of international systems. One might observe that many interactions that take place relate to or arise from production and distribution of wealth. These interactions are economic transactions in the international economic system. Thus, one could identify the international cultural (Olympic) ideological and political aspects of the international system.

It is from the concept of international system that other sub-concepts stem. Frequent references are made today about concepts such as international community, which is closely linked with the community of states and the entities they create for cooperation to achieve defined objectives. It is assumed that when interactions are not regulated, there is disorder that may lead to anarchy. States are affected by conflicts, wars and anarchy. This is the demonstration of disorder among and within states. The situation of anarchy could be best avoided by interactions that would lead to maintaining stability. However, there is no agreement on how the international system could exist in an orderly manner. This is why states contemplate decision-making to address foreign policy incompatibilities. History shows that states strive to establish stability or harmony by organizing themselves and negotiating their primary national interests. Since their national goals differ considerably, states go for basic norms, which maintain some kind of order that undergoes transformation depending on the circumstances under which those norms exist. The form of organization states adopt leads to an international order where their national goals prosper. In the past, alliances and balances of power constituted an ideal international order to maintain peace and security.

2.2 Systems Theory and Decision-Making Modelling

Systems theory dominated social science investigation since its emergence in the 1950s. It strives to build relationships between various theories in social sciences. The theory is associated with T. Parsons and his associates at Harvard University. Later works of Parsons provide a general theory of social systems, which aims at the integration of sociological theory with other developments in

---

101   Kaplan, Martin F, and Charles E. Miller, (1987). Pp. 306-313.

social sciences such as psychology, economics and politics. Systems theory applies to various studies and is widely influential in the study of political processes, which includes international relations. This theory is also relevant to intra-state and inter-state interactions. Policy directives at national and international levels lend themselves to various reactions or responses with varying consequences. The behaviour of actors in a political system is the concern of political science especially in the field of international relations.[102]

In international politics, systems theory approaches have been used mainly to analyse foreign policy at the level of the international system. Many definitions of *system* are available. In the broadest sense, a system is "a set of interrelated elements of complex entities". These entities include states, government, political parties, organizations and interest groups.[103] Scholars are less interested in precise definitions of a system; they are more concerned with elements which constitute a system. For example, John Lovell tries to define a system by citing the core elements, which are as follows:

a. A set of component parts which together can perform some purposeful activity.

b. Functional interrelationship of the parts in a system. In other words, the various components are necessary if the system is to work properly.

c. An on-going interrelationship between these parts and the environment. This means that the parts monitor the environment, respond to it and influence it.

d. In international politics, the concept of a system might be applied at any level of analysis. Any groups of individuals are a system and so is a state, a government or an organization. All these entities interact in the international system.

There are different kinds of systems approaches that have been influential in the study of international politics. Among them is the input-output analysis, which is particularly useful in the study of foreign policy.[104] Consequently, those concepts relating to a systems approach in the process of decision-making require further definitions:

a. *Input.* An input is the injection into the system of some information or any other resource that provides knowledge concerning an issue that demands a decision.

b. *Memory.* Memory consists of the facilities and processes by which information is stored and recalled for use when need arises.

---

102   Morgan, Patrick M. (1977), pp.146-148.

103   Reynolds, P. A., (1980), Pp. 156-196

104   Morgan, Patrick M. (1977), pp. 146-148.

c. *Decision.* A decision is a commitment based on an analysis of available information and capabilities to take some action vis-à-vis the environment of the decision-making processes.

d. *Output.* Output is the system's action which is taken by decisionmakers.

e. *Goal.* A goal is whatever objective sought by the action of decisionmakers.

f. *Feedback.* Feedback is the new information about the results of the previous action on which the decision-maker can start a new cycle all over again.

The setting of decision-making emanated from domestic politics. Mathews and Mushi like many political scientists preceding them, accept that foreign policy of a country reflects its internal policy and that foreign policy is the extension of the internal policy. The substance of decision-making lies in abstract elements such as ideology and markets.[105] The idea of decision-making in foreign policy rotates around the need for choice among alternatives. Decisions in foreign policy are understood to be the sum totals of decisions governments take to guide their national interests. Such decisions comprise a process to reach a desirable conclusion to address outstanding foreign policy complexities. Baumann and Deber defined decision-making as the situation in which a choice is made among a number of possible alternatives often involving a trade-off among values given to different outcomes.[106] Making a decision on one or more policy issues in an area that affects national interests requires an amount of information on the subject in question. It is a complex process to choose the best among analyses that offer constructive conclusions. In short, foreign policy decision-making refers to the choices policymakers make with the assistance of relevant domestic actors that affects or defines a nation's action on the international stage.[107] It has to be understood that there are many institutions besides the Ministry of Foreign Affairs which are involved in processes of decision-making to enable leadership to make the ultimate decision by assessing the values of available alternatives.

So many factors shape patterns and trends of foreign policy decision-making. The most frequent factor that determines decision-making is the crisis in the international system. It compels policymakers and leadership to always engage in the process of searching for the best alternative costs and consequences and choosing the best course of action to take. Crisis management experience involves the capacity to study the phenomenon, the socio-political and economic environment, and the attitude during difficult times and characters of principal players of the decision-making body. For better understanding

---

105   Mushi, S.S. and Mathews, K., (1981), pp. xii-xvii.

106   Baumann, A., and Deber, R., (1989), Pp. 69-71.

107   Mintz, Alex and DeRouen , Karl Jr., (2010)., p. 3.

of the world of decision-making, policymakers examine certain attributes that contribute to rational decision-making, which requires rearrangement of the global political setting. Scholars refer to this situation as the search for an ideal perfect decision-making.[108] It involves what should be happening in the process of state behaviour. The state should make perfect choices among alternatives based on rational attitude. John Lovell developed the concept of perfect decision-making in his book *Foreign Policy Perspectives*. He identified several variables of perfect decision-making, which he called an "Imaginary Ideal Machine for Making Policy" (IIMMP). The variables are as follows:

a. *Scanning.* Finding out what is going on in the world. This function is assigned to diplomatic missions, think tanks and intelligence agencies.

b. *Coding.* Sorting and labelling all resulting information. In other words, there are bodies in the state including specialised bodies of academia involved in processes of analysing data and information collected internally and externally by relevant agencies.

c. *Transmission.* Circulating all information collected within the government. This process involves sharing of information with relevant sectors and institutions.

d. *Storage and recall.* This function requires the storage of useful information and instant recall whenever they are needed. Governments keep coded information which can be used immediately or stored for future whenever the need arises.

e. *Recognition of alternatives.* Providing the decisionmaker with options based on a wide range of alternatives. The information coded and analysed are organised in such a way that the government has wider alternatives and multiple options.

f. *Decision-making and implementation.* These activities involve choosing one of the alternatives and executing it. It implies that the results of the whole process can be communicated in the system and be included in making the next decision.

However, realities of decision-making are different in state behaviour. In international politics, a system is composed of states which undertake processes of policymaking. They invest considerable resources for processes of policymaking such as gathering various types of information around the world. All types of information collected are stored to be used later when any situation requires a decision. Intelligence services supply the state with information from within the state or from embassies. Actions such as laying an embargo or a

---

108   Stein, Janice Gross, (2002), pp. 292-308.

blockade on a certain state and going to war are based on accurate information and rational behaviour of states involved.[109] Analysts using communication theory emphasize input – output analysis in evaluating the role of governments in the conduct of their foreign relations. Decision-making is the process of asserting a priority of values, selecting and some alternatives among others. A decision constitutes the course of action that the decision-maker will cope with in the immediate situation. Most decisions, whether made by an individual, a group of individuals or an organization, are concerned with the discovery and selection of satisfactory alternatives.

Concerning Lovell's framework, it should be noted that perfect decision-making is an imaginary perception of decisional processes in the international system. For example, scanning is fragmentary in detection and spotty in coverage. Coding may be biased, and the transmission may be delayed and distorted. In crisis management, time may be too limited for exploiting information available in memories (stores) of states. Further, alternatives recommended for decision-making may provide limited options and limited problem-solving capacity. Such a situation can lead to an irrational decision.[110] The implementation of the decision may be subject to faulty coordination. In real life, the feedback can be imperfect. All information concerning responses to a state's action could be inaccurate, thus making the correction of an error more difficult and complicated. Therefore, the process of decision-making spreads within the political system. The head of state or government is central in this process. The other components of decision-making fall to various branches of the state and the opposition is considered the alternative decision-maker.

2.3 Models of Decision-Making in Foreign Policy

Decisions are part of human life. They constitute daily activities in society and institutions or organs of the state that are particularly involved in making important decisions. In this respect, the analysis of decision-making needs to be considered under a broad heading in the field of international relations. Scholars have identified several main types of decision-making. In a study conducted by Roger Hilsman, it was found out that there are three major types of decision-making. They are crisis decision-making, declaratory decision-making and program decision-making.[111] While decision-making is a complex and ever-changing process, it is important to highlight the evolving nature and types of foreign policy decision-making.

---

109   Reynolds, P. A., (1980), pp. 156-196.
110   Lovell, John P. 1970 in Morgan Patrick M. (1977), p. 148.
111   Hilsman, Roger (1987), p.58

However, all types of decision-making are declaratory in nature. As a result, this chapter examines the other types of decision-making. Crisis decisions imply a confrontation between two or more states while declaratory decisions refer to statements concerning intentions and objectives of states which are parties to a particular conflict. In democratic countries, the executive branch of the government usually handles crisis and declaratory decisions. Programme decision-making is a process which falls under shared responsibilities of the executive and the legislative branches of government.

2.3.1 Crisis Decision-Making Model

The treatment of crisis decision-making would be useful if we could provide a definition of the term 'crisis'. A crisis is "the action of the state that policymakers of a nation considered as a threat to their vital and security interests". The crisis implies an unexpected threat and a rapid counteraction. In moments of crises, a few individuals make decisions: the head of state, selected official advisers, trusted friends, and counsellors from outside the government. There is the tendency of isolating a considerable portion of bureaucracies from the process of decision-making.

Crisis decision-makers feel enormous pressure because crises tend to be short-lasting phenomena. This time pressure increases the level of tension. Under circumstances of crisis, inaction is a defect, which can lead to the deterioration of the situation. Thus, decision-makers are compelled to act promptly.

Another feature of crisis decision-making is that non-violent responses are minimized while much emphasis is placed on effects of potential and real violent actions. Policymakers tend to base their actions on relatively scarce information at their disposal. The less information they have, the greater their reliance on a broad emotional image of the enemy. Under such a situation, decisionmakers consider themselves as having few alternative courses of action. However, they assume that the opponent is holding a number of more options than those at their own disposal. It follows that policymakers usually seek an urgent legislative approval because prolonged debates may demoralize domestic morale. This process is important because crises easily develop into wars. For example, during the Cuban Missile crisis of 1962, deliberations took the Kennedy Administration a short time to decide the naval and air blockade of Cuba.[112] The duration was short because intelligence photos of the Soviet Missile construction were received before the installation was completed.[113]

---

112   Ray, James Lee (1979), pp. 72-75.
113   Allison and Zelikow, (1999), p. 18.

Supposing that the installation was accomplished, the USSR would have declared its missile strength in Cuba, a declaration that would have resulted in the eruption of a nuclear war.

2.3.2 Programme Decision-Making Model

The programme decision-making model of decision-making involves a large number of participants and requires a long period to reach a decision. Actors in the programme decision-making process include foreign policy bureaucracies, members of national security, members of the legislature, political parties and several interest groups. At the level of the legislature, decision-making powers are highly dispersed among specialized committees. For this reason, reaching a decision and having it adopted requires the mobilization of various groups. The process of making a decision may prove to be time-consuming and frustrating. Interest groups may also attempt to influence decisions concerning the specific programme under discussion. When a programme draws the attention of the public, the decision-makers tend to take public opinion seriously in order to avoid reactions such as demonstrations and industrial action (civil disobedience or strike). Therefore, programme decision-making requires considerable time to enable decision-makers to formulate policies that could harmonize contradictory interests.

Programme decision-making is also referred to the *Organization Process Model (OPM)*. It addresses the emerging complexity in the process of decision-making that the leadership on its own is incapable of dealing with. The reality in this regard requires an efficient and multidimensional organization to make appropriate decisions. Hence, scholars offered two more different models of decision-making. One of the models is the OPM. According to Greg Cashman, the government is a conglomerate of large autonomous semi-feudal loosely allied organizations where policy decisions are not the result of rationality but an outcome of large organizational discourse which is continuously involved in formulating policies within a standard operating procedure. The process of decision-making in the government involves inter-branch organizations that are linked with each other and function under a well-established procedure of discharging their duties.[114] The OPM is a top-down approach where agencies usually function as the result of government demand or the top leadership and vice versa.[115]

Bureaucracy plays an important role in the decision-making process. Political scientists refer to the roles of bureaucrats as Bureaucratic Political

114   Cashman, Greg, (2000), p. 86
115   Hollis, Martin and Steve Smith, (1991), pp. 196-202.

model. The question is how does it function differently from the OPM. Under this model, the structure of decision-making is divided into several sub-agencies that are eventually arranged as a top-down line of command. In most practices, the leader dismantles the whole problem and assigns sub parts among small specialised agencies. The concerned authority of that particular section has to resolve the given task within the stipulated time frame. Considering the limitation of time and resources during times of crisis, leaders usually settle on the first alternative to address the crisis issue rather than exploring the best option. With regard to the sequential goal preference, the problem of control, and coordination of various stakeholders and fixed ground rules of decision-making units, the outcome seems to be satisfactory rather than rational.[116] The OPM approach to addressing emerging problems is highly beneficial during times of war or war-like crises where leaders have to take decisions quickly with limited information. Tanzania espoused this model during the Tanzania-Uganda limited war in 1978 as described in the document "Tanzania and the War Against Amin's Uganda[117] The OPM process is based on the shared responsibility and shared organisational goals and procedure.

2.3.3 Snyder Model as an Analytical Framework

An analytical scheme is also known as a framework necessary for making analysis of a situation. It consists of a list of factors and events that are relevant for understanding a particular subject. Such factors are also referred to as interactive variables. The Snyder model analyses the complex structure of input-output models and is comprised of three pillars. They are the internal environment and the external environment, with decision-making processes and an action box in the middle. This section explores also other models of foreign policy analytical decision-making frameworks that are susceptible to further explanation.

In 1954, three scholars – Richard Snyder, H.W. Bruck and Burton Sapin – published a famous monograph setting forth a decision-making framework. This work was based on three assumptions. The first assumption was that research in international relations lacked a clear target and rigorous concepts. Some systematic framework was needed within which the concepts and their interrelationships could be effectively studied. The second assumption was that the best way to study the behaviour of states was to develop an approach applicable to any state. The goal is to generalize about them all, but not to

---

116   Simon, Herbert A., (1956), pp. 129-138.
117   Mushi, S.S. and K. Mathews, (1981), pp.305-312.

emphasize peculiarities of each. The third assumption was that for purposes of research, the nation is at any given time its decision-maker. In this respect, analyses should focus on those officials involved, not those officials supposed to be involved by law or the constitution. Snyder et al went further by suggesting that rational analysis be built on the decision-makers of the world. The external environment would only be relevant to this extent and the ways it is perceived. [118]

Figure 3: The Complexity of Snyder's Model of Decision-Making.

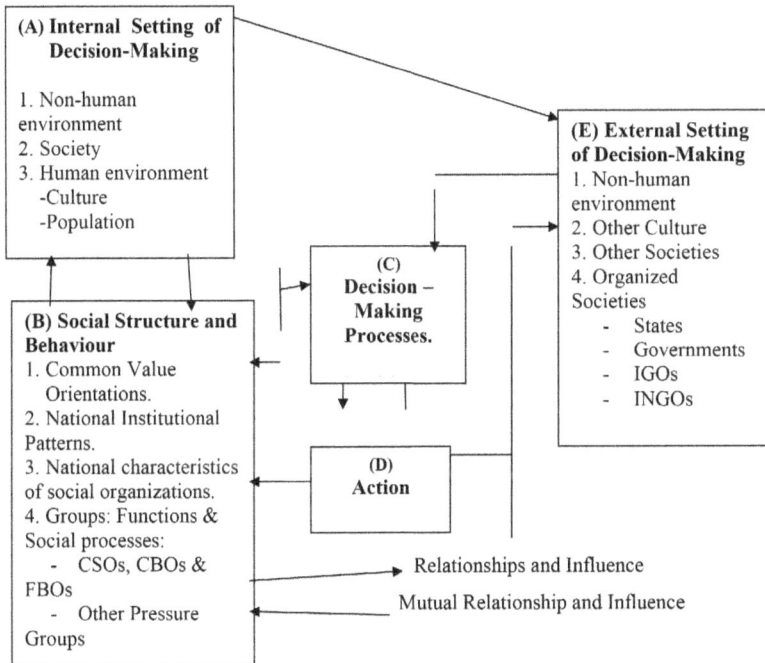

Source: Morgan, Patrick M., 1975

Considering the assumptions concerning the process of decision-making, Snyder constructed a model in order to facilitate an analytical framework. His framework is rather more complex. He listed many variables that could influence the behaviour of decision-makers. The framework includes clusters of relevant factors and, by means of arrows, suggests likely relationships among them. According to this model, there are three major groups of factors constituting the environment which influences decision-making processes. Factors are relating to the internal setting, social structure and behaviour, and the external setting (A, B, C, D & E). The C represents the effective decision-

118   Morgan, Patrick M. (1977), pp.144-145.

making processes and the role of decision-makers. Finally, D represents actions taken by decision-makers because of decisions based on the analysis of factors we refer to as outputs.

Snyder's model is dynamic because there are several responses between the internal and external environments, and decision processes between components of the environment themselves. This framework was designed to pull together many levels of analysis into a coherent work. Personal qualities of political leaders and diplomats can be covered in C. Boxes A and B are internal factors, which cover issues like public opinion, interest groups, national culture and institutions. Box E takes into consideration to the external environment and D represents outputs and feedback.

2.3.4 The Rational Actor Model (RAM)

Who is the rational actor in this model? The rational actor is the leader who makes decisions the way they should have been made, without bias or influence. It is normal to consider rationality as the best way to solve conflicts in society. Rationality refers to the behavioural attitude having its very purpose. According to Allison Graham, rationality refers to consistent value maximizing choice with special constraints.[119] Other scholars like Duncan and collaborators consider rational actor models of decision-making as the process to choose the right options to achieve national goals by analysing all possible alternatives and consequences. The leadership in this model is open to receive new input and analyse the information that the decision-maker chooses gives the best results.[120]

Many scholars consider the idea of rational actors as an ideal because rationality is a complex phenomenon which is hard to identify and define. It is an ideal approach of foreign policy decision-making, which is a highly politicized business. Like other models, the Rational Actor Model involves several stages of decision-making. It identifies and defines the goal, analyses the problem, prioritizes the goal, develops alternatives, evaluates alternatives, selects the best options and executes the best option.[121] Above all, the Rational Actor Decision-Making Model demonstrates several other characteristics such as:

  a. **Open to new information and evidence.** Under the Rational Model, the state is the only player and non-state actors and interest groups are side lined. The decision-maker is heavily provided with flow of

---

119   Allison and Zelikow, (1999), p. 18.
120   Duncan, W. Raymond, Barbara Jancar-Webster and Bob Switky, (2009), pp. 130-158
121   Geva, Nehemia and Alex Mintz ,(1997), p. 143.

information from advisors and other reliable sources. Under this model the leader is not bound to go along with advice or input information.

b. **Open to discussion and believe in transparency**. The Rational Actor model allows the participants to discuss the cause and consequences of each available option in the decision-making process. The decision-maker acquires more and detailed information by initiating discussion. Most policymaking mechanisms do allow more debate before coming to conclusion, though the decision of the leader is considered supreme and reliable information.

c. **Other principles of the RAM practices.** This model believes in rationality and selection of options based purely on merit and probability. As mentioned earlier, the state is the only actor and ignores non-state actors. The state is the supreme and perhaps the only actor in the decision-making process. There is no place for actors like NGOs, IGOs, pressure groups, interest groups and terror organisations. Also, there is no place for emotions. The foremost feature of RAM is that it is purely based on the rational choice of available alternatives without any presumptions or emotion. Decision-making according to this model should be free from values, notions and emotions for the proper decision.

There is no ideal model for decision-making in the international system. Therefore, there are limitations to RAM. Some of the most frequent concerns political and social scientists count against this model are the following:

- The model ignores the importance of the individuals involved in decision-making as individuals espouse their beliefs, values, emotions, perceptions, ideologies and hosts of other traits, which might affect decisions.[122]

- As information is key to decision outcomes there is a possibility that the leader may not evaluate the situation correctly, may be misinformed and may choose the inappropriate policy, which may hinder the national goal. Further, the leader or advisor may tend to block out information that does not agree with what they have already believed to be accurate. This was the case of Iraqi war during the Bush administration.

- Sometimes emotion plays an important role in the pride of nations. RAM ignores national emotion, namely nationalism. Ignoring it in favour of highly logical decision-making may discourage policymakers from radicalising the population whenever there will be the need to galvanise action in the future.[123]

---

122   Duncan, W. Raymond, Jancar-Webster, Barbara and Bob Switky, (2008), pp. 145-146.
123   Morrow, James D., (1997), pp. 12-33.

- Often the state faces multiple problems and in a globalised world the decision-making bodies are usually pushed to deal with multiple and highly complicated issues at the same time. As a result, the decisionmaker may not find enough time to study the problem and to calculate the available options to select from.
- Finally, foreign policy decision-making occurs at two levels: international and domestic. Along with the international environment, domestic politics is also considered an important factor while making policies on external relations, but in RAM, this domestic aspect is neglected.

Overall, RAM is one of the most effective decision-making models for foreign policy due to its logical policy preference. It opts for the appropriate policy to deal with any issue. Some rational actor literature states that decision-makers including the central decision-makers do not have complete freedom of action and they are not in full control of their rationality. In due process, decision-makers are often forced to abandon the preferred and most effective alternative and end up with least preferred outcome even though they choose rationally at every step along the way.

2.3.5 Foreign Policy Analytical Model (FPAM)

Foreign policy analysis takes a foreign policy decision-making approach to study international relations. The question is how do international relations look when viewed through the lens of FPAM? First and foremost, the decision-making approach of this model breaks apart the monolithic view of nation-states as unitary actors. It focuses on the people and units that comprise the state. From its inception, the FPAM model asserts that there are correlations between how foreign policy decisions and the source of individual and collective human behaviour change in international politics. This model builds on what social sciences (e.g., psychology, economics, sociology, anthropology, geography) are learning about human decision-making.[124] There are shifts in paradigms of foreign policy decisions within evolving thoughts in the international system. Walt identifies ideologies that determine foreign policy decisions under the question "Where Are We Coming from? he asserts the study of international affairs is best understood as a protracted competition between the realist, liberal and radical traditions.

Policymakers contemptuous of "theory" cannot avoid ideas about how the world works in order to decide what to do. Walt argues that it is hard to

---

124   Hudson,Valerie M. and Christopher S. Vore, (1995), pp. 210-214.

make good policy if one's organizing principles are flawed, just as it is hard to construct good theories without knowing a lot about the real world. A number of important works focused on the characteristics of states, government organizations, or individual leaders. Most of the literature in the field of international relations and foreign policy are complements to the three main paradigms. The opposite table summarises the evolution of foreign policy analysis across the competing paradigms.[125]

Several actors and factors influence the process of foreign policy. These elements are similar to those which constitute the process of decision-making. Although the main actor is the state, the other actors are the government, political parties, interest groups and individuals. These factors constitute the domestic environment of a foreign policy process.[126] Similarly, other nations constitute the most important factor because they are the direct targets of foreign policies. Responses of foreign policy actors to patterns of policies can be analysed through input-output analysis and the circulation of feedback. Inputs are those responses which result from reactions of other nations and from the systematic change in the external environment. These responses do influence the behaviour of actors in domestic politics, which in turn influence the government.

Outputs are the policies made by the state which determine foreign policy patterns. For example, military expansion could be an output emanation from decisions of a government; conversely, protection of local industries could be a policy output. Outputs of a particular foreign policy actor do influence the behaviour of other nations. In other words, outputs of other nations become inputs of the actor while outputs of this actor become inputs of other nations. This is a circular process in international relations. Foreign policy patterns consist of policies a government makes which are injected into the environment.

Results of foreign policy decisions are communicated back to the government through a process known as feedback. This is comprised of information collected concerning other nations' behaviour with respect to a particular foreign policy decision. Feedback does affect internal factors such as individuals, elites, political parties and several others. Therefore, the foreign policy behaviour of actors is an outgrowth of past behaviour. It must be seen as dynamic rather than a set of isolated or status events.

---

125   Walt, Stephen M. (1998), pp. 30-40.
126   Mushi, SS., (1981), pp. 4-15.

Table 1: Evolving Theories and Foreign Policy Decisions

Competing Paradigms	Realism	Liberalism	Constructivism
Main Theoretical Proposition	Self-Interested States compete constantly for power or security	Concern for power overridden by economic/political considerations	State behaviour shaped by elite beliefs, collective norms and social identities.
Main Units of Analysis	States	States	Individuals (especially elites)
Main Instruments	Economic and especially military power	Varies (International institutions, economic exchange, Promotion of democracy)	Ideas and discourse
Modern Theorists	Hans Morgenthau, Kenneth Walter	Michel Doyle, Robert Keohane	Alexander Wendt, John Ruggue
Representative Modern Works	Waltz, Theory of International Politics Mearsheimer, "Back to the Future: Instability in Europe after the Cold War"	Keohane, After Hegemony Fukuyoma "The End of History" (National Interest 1989)	Wendt, "Anarchy is What States Make of It" (International Organisation, 1992), Kolowski & Kratochwil, "Understanding Changes in International Politics" International Organization, 1994
Post-Cold war Prediction	Resurgence of overt great power competition	Increased cooperation as liberal values, free markets & international institutions spread	Agnostic because of it cannot predict the contend of ideas
Main Limitation	Does not account for international change	Tends to ignore the role of power	Better at describing the past than anticipating the future

Source: Walt, p. 38

2.4 Conclusion

Foreign policy is one of the fundamental concepts in the theory of interactions in the international system. It consists of a range of actions taken by a state corresponding to actions of other states or international actors. Each nation determines and defines its foreign policy. Although definitions of this concept may vary from one nation to another, scholars define foreign policy as the set of directives formulated by a legitimate structure of a political authority (state), which is characterized as manifestly directed to any aspect of targets lying beyond its sphere of territorial legitimacy. The process of foreign policymaking involves the government, political parties and other interest groups. These actors define goals which have to be included in the foreign policy. The whole process consists of a systematic formulation of national goals that must conform to targets a nation is seeking to achieve. However, goals that nations seek are many and they also differ in importance. Similarly, the importance of certain goals tends to fluctuate with situation and time. That is why the formulation of foreign policy should be flexible. Consequently, goals of foreign policy are classified into two categories, namely, vital goals and secondary goals.

Foreign policy decision-making is a process based on individual life, collective interactions and a tool of institutional action that involves choice. The process implies action depending on the information available to the person or group of individuals intending to take action on a specific issue. In general terms, a decision is the commitment based on the analysis of available information and capabilities to take action in response to the environment of the event necessitating such an action. Decision-making is the process of asserting a priority of values, and selecting some alternatives among others. A decision constitutes the course of action that the decision-maker will cope with in the immediate situation. Most decisions, whether made by an individual, a group of individuals or an organization, are concerned with the discovery and selection of satisfactory alternatives.

This chapter has therefore shed light on different aspects and the practice of foreign policy decision-making in the international system. As stated above, foreign policy decision-making consists of types and models. Foreign policymaking consists of many decisions which are sequential and involve a series of interrelated and interactive decisions. In all analysis of decision-making in foreign policies, there are levels where policymakers, especially leaders, take individual decisions. There are also situations where group-level decisions are preferred and taken at an appropriate time. All efforts have been invested to provide explanation and linkages between domestic politics and its extension into regional and international environments.

CHAPTER THREE

FOREIGN POLICY TRAITS: LEVEL OF ANALYSIS

The foreign policy formulation process is depicted as very complex. It is therefore necessary to untangle the intricacies by studying foreign policymaking from three perspectives termed levels of analysis. These include individual-level analysis, state-level analysis and system-level analysis.

3.1 Individual-Level Analysis

This level of analysis assesses the impact of people as individuals or as a species on policy. As technology progresses, the power in the hands of individual citizens to react to the foreign policies of nation-states could influence traditional state leaders to alter their policies accordingly. Although much attention recently has focused on the role that domestic politics play in shaping foreign policy, most of the work outside of FPA has emphasized the importance of domestic structure and society at the expense of the policymaker. Further, in many countries there is disconnect between public opinion and the foreign policy that political leaders follow. For example, George W. Bush went on to engage in the US-Iraq war in 2003 despite public opinion in United States and the rest of the world being against the war.[127]

An increasingly globalised international environment provides foreign policy leaders with a new set of individual and institutional actors that

---

127   Gordon, (2003), p. 1

they need to consider. Although it is now common to argue that domestic political calculations influence foreign policy choices, these analyses currently tend to assume that leaders react in an undifferentiated manner to domestic pressures.[128] However, even though these pressures are likely to be experienced by all policymakers, leaders should not be expected to react in the same manner to such pressures. For instance, when scholars argue that foreign policy leaders consider electoral factors in their choices, it is often assumed that all foreign policy officials calculate and react to these pressures in the same way.

However, research on the influence of public opinion on the foreign policy decisions of US presidents suggests that even though all presidents are generally aware of public interest groups and electoral incentives and the costs involved in a foreign policy choice, systematic and predictable variation in responses to these pressures exists across individuals. In short, a large body of literature indicates that we need to factor in how individual leaders perceive, interpret, and react to pressures from society across states with similar and varying institutional structures and within a single state.[129]

With increasing globalisation, FPA will be critical in sorting out the interactions among the international, domestic, and individual levels of analysis and their effect on policy. Just as some business leaders have proven to be adept at seizing the implications of the new opportunities provided by shifts in technology and some political leaders embrace avenues to enhance their political fortunes, others try and fail, and still others sense no opportunity at all.[130] For these reasons, FPA needs to become increasingly attentive to the cross-national nature of domestic political influences. More research needs to be done on foreign policy in diverse countries, not just the US. The empirical review indicates that most studies on foreign policy are within the US and very few focus on the other countries. However, this is somehow understandable given the position that US occupies in global politics.[131] Individual level analysis focuses on people. People make decisions within nation states and therefore people make foreign policy. Scholars might look at the roles of different leaders. This level of analysis might explain World War II by examining the role of Hitler. What about Woodrow Wilson 14 points statement of principles for peace that was to be used for peace negotiations in order to end World War I. This is a focus on perception, misperception, and communication. Individual level analysis might ask questions such as these: Are there aspects of Donald Trump's character and belief systems that have defined the US response to

128   Byman and Pollack, (2001), p. 124
129   Rosati, (2000), p. 56
130   Hagan ,(1994), p. 197
131   Stern and Sundelius, (2002), p. 79

climate change or global affairs? Would Obama or Joe Biden have behaved any differently in a similar situation? How do Biden and his senior decision makers perceive the world and their role in it?

In addition, the radical change in technology associated with computers and the internet, rather than undermining the role of leaders in formulating foreign policy, might just enhance their ability to ascertain, anticipate, and respond to world opinion if they can creatively marshal new technologies to their ends. The response of business leaders to the internet might be instructive. Unlike the dot-com failures, many established companies combined traditional business methods with new technologies to enhance their connections with customers and expand their businesses.[132] Similarly, the US military employed the Internet in its information warfare plan in the 2003 war against Iraq, albeit with limited results.[133]

In the future, perceptive leaders might use the internet as a diplomatic tool in yet unforeseen ways to enhance their connections to their citizens and the citizens of other nations.[134] Although government websites that provide both information and opportunities to e-mail the leader exist, none have employed the web as an additional force in governance on the scale adopted in business. As the speed and complexity of international politics increases, leaders could find that traditional methods of assessing citizen sentiment (polling, elections, letters, press, and so on) do not adequately address their needs in determining the intensity and nuance of public attitudes. Emerging evidence suggests that within global politics, leaders already employing these tools to measure public opinion are doing so in a different manner.[135]

Just as some businesses have successfully seized upon the internet as a means to enhance their traditional functions, the web could serve such a purpose for leaders in a globalised future. Although some have claimed that the increasing speed of media communications hamstrings policymakers, the data suggest that the media's need for instant news allows savvy politicians to shape the message in a manner previously unthinkable. Similarly, the Internet provides an opportunity for creative politicians to interact with world opinion in ways limited only by their imagination.

Individual level analysis can provide important assistance to the strategic interaction literature by assessing where foreign policy preferences come from and how these preferences are translated into policies.[136] Strategic interaction

---

132   Kurtzman and Rifkin, (2001), p. 190
133   Shanker and Schmitt, (2003), p. 1
134   Dizard, (2001), p. 87
135   Wang and Chang, (2004), p. 15
136   Stern and Sundelius , (2002), p. 79

research at the international level largely takes preference as given and assumes that the institutional environment, the configuration of the actors' preferences, and their strategic behaviour given these factors mediate the transmission from preferences into outcomes. When domestic politics are included in these models, assumptions are made about the preferences of various domestic actors. Outcomes are then analysed by examining how the preferences of the various actors interact within a specified domestic institutional environment.

Individual decision-making not only has differing values and beliefs but unique personality, experiences, intellect, capabilities and personal style which shape national foreign policy negatively or positively.

3.1.1 Leader's Personality

The personality of a country's leader plays a significant role rather than systematic and national attribute factors because foreign policy decision-making involves the existence of alternative courses of action which require judgment in terms of one's values. The personality of those tasked with making decisions of Africa's – or any – foreign policy determines the choices based on limited or bounded rationality.

People should make decisions in accordance with their personal intuitions about the situation, which may not conform to everything they know. Perceived images and personal characteristics of the decision-makers, such as cautiousness vs rashness, anger vs prudence, pragmatism vs ideological crusades, superiority vs inferiority, creativeness vs destructiveness, paranoia vs confidence and so on influence the decision. These factors are generally known as "Idiosyncratic variables" and these variables are concerned with the perceptions, images and personal characteristics of decision-makers generally.

3.1.2 Personal Attitudes

This section deals with linking the personal characteristics of political leaders to their country's foreign policy. The assumption is that Africa has high-level policymakers such as heads of state and government. Given such individuals and situations, how will we have expected that foreign policymaker's personal characteristics and their general interest will affect the foreign policy of his/her country? The more general interest the head of the government has in foreign policy, the more likely his/her personal characteristics should affect foreign policy behaviour.

The importance of interest in foreign policy will be of paramount attention to the foreign policymaking process. The head of government wants to be kept informed about what is going on in foreign affairs. The major purpose behind this is to remain informed about foreign affairs of his country. These reasons can include placing value on good foreign relations, fearing of an enemy takeover, and seeing foreign affairs as a way of gaining re-elections.

If the president has an interest in foreign affairs, or has trained or studied the subjects of foreign affairs, then this secondary personal characteristic will affect the foreign policy of his country. If the head of government has little training but has some knowledge about the success and failure in international relations, then he will try to match the strategy with specific issues. On the other hand, if the head of government has not trained or does not have previous experience or no special skills to face the problems, this suggests the possible plans of actions for how to solve the problem pertaining to the effectiveness of the country's foreign policy.

The third personal characteristic, general-sensitivity to one's environment, also affects his relationship between other characteristics and foreign relations. Sensitivity to the environment shows the reach of an individual's reaction to incoming stimuli from objects in the social surroundings in which he works.

3.1.3 Organizational Behaviour

The organizational behaviour approach studies role factors that is, how people act in certain personal or professional positions. The approach is also concerned with how groups behave and how the interactions affect decisions. Group/think is one is one possible outcome of organizational behaviour, and can lead to bad decisions. Ignoring or suppressing dissidents, discordant information and policy options are all causes of groupthink. Another is the reluctance subordinates to offer discordant.

The individual-level analysis is concerned here with identifying the characteristics of the complex process of human decision-making. This includes gathering information, analyzing that information, establishing goals, pondering options, and making policy choices. The individual – level analysis would include: the human element, organizational behaviour, and leaders and their idiosyncrasies.

3.2 State-level analysis

Policymaking is significantly influenced by the fact that it occurs within the context of a political structure.[137] Countries are the most important of these structures. By analysing the impact of structures on policymaking, state-level analysis improves our understanding of policy. This level of analysis emphasizes the characteristics of states and how they make foreign policy choices and implement them. What is important from this perspective, then, is how a country's political structure and the political forces and subnational actors within the country cause its government to decide to adopt one or another foreign policy.

One variable that affects the foreign policy process is the type of government a country has.[138] These types range along a scale with absolute authoritarian governments on one end and pure democratic governments on the other. The more authoritarian a government is, the more likely it is that foreign policy will be centred in a narrow segment of the government, even in the hands of the president or whoever the leader is. It is important to realize, though, that no government is absolutely under the control of any individual. States are too big and complex for that to happen, and thus secondary leaders (such as foreign ministers), bureaucrats, interest groups, and other domestic elements play a role even in very authoritarian political systems.

At the other end of the scale, foreign policymaking in democracies is much more open, with input from legislators, the media, public opinion, and opposition parties, as well as those foreign policymaking actors that influence authoritarian government policy.[139] However, it is not always true that in a democracy, a group does foreign policy formulation. Even in the most democratic states, foreign policy tends to be dominated by the country's top leadership.

The policymaking process also varies within countries. A country's situation is one variable. For example, policy is made differently during crisis and non-crisis situations.[140] The crisis situation occurs when decisionmakers are surprised by an event, feel threatened (especially militarily), and believe that they have only a short time to react. The more intense each of the three factors is, the more acute the sense of crisis. Whereas non-crisis situations often involve a broad array of domestic actors trying to shape policy, crisis policymaking is likely to be dominated by the political leader and a small group of advisers. One

---

137   Dizard, (2001), p.79
138   Kurtzman and Rifkin, (2001), p. 207
139   Hagan, (1994), p.199
140   Gordon, (2003), p. 1

reason this occurs involves the rally effect. This is the propensity of the public and other domestic political actors to support the leader during times of crisis.

How foreign policy is decided also varies according to the nature of the issue involved.[141] Issues that have little immediate or obvious impact on citizens can be termed pure foreign policy. A narrow range of decisionmakers usually makes such decisions in the executive branch with little or no domestic opposition or even notice to the general public. By contrast, foreign policy that has an immediate and obvious domestic impact on citizens is called intermestic policy. This type of policy is apt to foster substantial activity by legislators, interest groups, and other foreign policymaking actors and thereby diminish the ability of the executive leaders to fashion policy to their liking. Foreign trade is a classic example of an intermestic issue because it affects both international relations and the domestic economy in terms of jobs, prices, and other factors.[142] This domestic connection activates business, labour, and consumer groups who, in turn, bring legislature into the mix. Therefore, national leaders, such as presidents, usually have much greater say over pure foreign policy than they do over intermestic policy.

This is another approach to understanding world politics, which emphasizes national states and their internal processes as the primary determinants of the course of world affairs. This approach focuses on mid-range factors that are less general than the macro analysis of the international milieu but less individualistic than the micro analytical focus of idiosyncratic level analysis as explored.

3.2.1 Conceptualization of State-Level Analysis

This system-level of analysis believes that states have long been and continue to be the most powerful actors on the world stage. The two approaches differ, however, on how much freedom of action states have over the regulators of the international system. Unlike a systemic level of analysis, which believes that the international system pressures states to behave in certain ways, the state level of analysis contends that states are relatively free to decide what policies to follow, what to do, and how to decide which policies to follow.

Studying what the state does is based on the view that much of what goes on in world politics revolves around interactions between governments of two or more states trying to gauge the rationales behind the other's actions and

---

141   Byman and Pollack, (2001), p. 138
142   Hocking. (2004), p.22

anticipate its next move.[143] These interactions are called events studied through event data analysis. This approach is useful for analysing matters such as reciprocity between countries. For example, if country A upgrades its military (event), how will country B respond (event)? This could result in an arms race.

The second concern deals with investigating how countries make policy choices to determine decision making. Once again to contrast systemic and state level of analysis, a systemic level of analysis would contend that a military response to invasion of any country should be inevitable given the realities of benefit derived from the system. A state level of analysis would differ strongly and insist that the state response depended on the presidential and executive relations, the strength of public opinion, and other factors internal to the national interest. Therefore, state-level analysts would conclude that to understand the foreign policy of any country, it is necessary to understand that country's domestic factors and its foreign policymaking processes. These factors, state level of analysis, may combine a determination on how states act and by extension, how the international system works as a sum of these actions.

3.2.2 The Government Policy Framework

Most people do not think much about how foreign policy is made, and when they do, many imagine that presidents or prime ministers decide, and it is done. In reality, decision making is usually a complex process. Sometimes the national leader may be pivotal, but more often the leader does not play a decisive role.

The point is that all foreign policy decisionmakers, whether in democratic or dictatorial states, are limited by an intricate web of governmental and societal restraints. To understand this web, we will explore three general aspects of foreign policymaking: how differences in the type of government, the type of policy, or the type of situation influence the policy process; the impact of political culture on foreign policy; and the roles of the various political actors in making foreign policy.

3.2.2.1 Types of Government

One variable that affects the foreign policy process is a country's type of domestic political system. Classifying political systems, such as democratic and authoritarian governments, is an important preliminary step to studying how they vary in policy and process because there is strong evidence that differences

---

143   Hermann &. Hagan, (1998), p.133

in the process will result in differences in policy substance. The line between democratic governments and authoritarian governments is not precise. One standard that differentiates the two types, however, is how many and what types of people can participate in making political decisions.

3.2.2.2 Types of Situations

Whatever the form of government, the policymaking process is not always the same. Situation is one variable that determines the exact nature of the foreign policy process. There are a number of ways that political scientists have classified situations to try to study variations in the foreign policy process. Of these classifications, the most widely studied are the differences in policymaking that can be observed in crisis situations compared to non-crisis situations. A crisis is a circumstance in which decisionmakers are surprised by an event, feel threatened and believe that they have only a short time in which to make a decision. The more terrorism-intense each of the three factors is, the more acute the sense of crisis.

3.2.2.3 Types of Policy

How foreign policy is decided also varies according to the nature of the issue area involved. This type of analysis rests on the idea that different subject areas will be decided by different decisionmakers and by different processes. One theory about policymaking holds that presidents and other leaders have greater power to decide foreign policy than they do to determine domestic policy. The latter area, however, is one in which legislatures, interest groups, and even public opinion play a greater role.

3.2.3 The National Political Culture

To recap an important point, the state is not a unitary structure. Even authoritarian states are complex political organisms. Therefore, All foreign policy decisions occur in a particular domestic context. This environment includes the political culture of a society. Political culture refers to a society's general, long-held, fundamental practices and attitudes that are slow to change. It has two main sources: one is the national historical experience, the sum of events and practices that have shaped a country and its citizens. The fact that the United States has been invaded only once, in 1812, while China has been invaded many times makes American and Chinese attitudes about the world very different. The second source of political culture is the national belief system: the ideas and ideologies that people hold, whether it is capitalism in the United States, Shiism in Iran, Sino centrism in China, Zionism in Israel, or Russia's sense of its greatness, these intellectual orientations are important determinants of how a country defines itself and decides its policy.

Before proceeding, some comments should be made. First, political culture does not usually create specific policy. Instead, political culture is apt to pressure leaders or allow them to move or not move in a general direction. In this sense, political culture is important in establishing a country's broad sense of its national interest. Second, political culture changes; shifts are usually evolutionary, though, because much of a country's political culture is rooted far back in its history and is resistant to change. Third, a society's political culture is not monolithic. American political culture, for example, includes both liberal humanitarian and isolationist impulses.

3.2.4 The Essence of Actors

No national actor is a unitary structure, a so-called black box. Instead, the state is more of a "shell" that encapsulates a foreign policy process in which a variety of subnational actors take part. These subnational actors include political executives, bureaucracies, legislatures, political opposition, interest groups, and the people. It is the pattern of cooperation and conflict among these subnational actors that constitutes the internal foreign policymaking process.

3.2.4.1 Political Executives

The beginning of this section showed President Franklin Roosevelt's frustrations with the limitations on his authority. Yet it can also be said that political executives (officials whose tenure is variable and dependent on the political contest for power in their country) are normally the strongest subnational actors in the foreign policy ·process. These leaders are located in the executive branch and are called president, prime minister, premier, chancellor, or perhaps king or emir.

Whatever their specific title, political executives have important formal powers, granted by statutory law or the constitution. Most chief executives are, for example, designated as the commanders in chief of their countries' armed forces. This gives them important and often unilateral authority to use the military. Political executives also frequently possess important informal power. Their personal prestige is often immense and skillful leaders can use public standing to win political support for their policies.

While the chief executives in most democratic countries hold formal and informal foreign policy powers that are greater than their domestic authority, presidents and premiers are not absolute monarchs. The spread of democracy and the increasingly intermestic nature of policy in an independent world mean that political leaders must often engage in a two-level game in which each national leader plays both the international and domestic games simultaneously.

3.2.4.2 Bureaucracies

Every state, whatever its strength or type of government, is heavily influenced by its bureaucracy. The dividing line between decisionmakers and bureaucrats is often hazy, but we can say that bureaucrats are career governmental personnel as distinguished from those who are political appointees or elected officials. Although political leaders legally command the bureaucracy, they find it difficult to control the vast understructures of their governments. Bureaucracies often favour one policy option over another based on their general sense of their unit's mission and how they should conduct themselves. However, many given policies will affect the organization and are also important factors in creating bureaucratic perspectives. Bureaucrats would often engage in filtering information recommendations of policy options and their implementation.

3.2.4.3 Legislatures

In all countries, the policy role of legislatures is less than that of executive branch decisionmakers and bureaucrats. This does not mean that all legislatures are powerless. But their exact influence varies greatly among countries. The foreign policy making process in Africa should officially begin with either the drafting of a Bill, the drafting of a cabinet paper or the drafting of a private members motion and presenting the same to parliament.

Parliamentary diplomacy refers to a wide range of activities undertaken by members of parliament, or parliament as an institution, to increase mutual understanding between countries and to improve scrutiny of government.[144] Its objective is, as in other fields of parliamentary policy-making, to influence government decisions on behalf of the citizens.[145] It is often, but not exclusively, referred to in the framework of open and multilateral diplomacy. In a broad sense, parliamentary diplomacy is about the construction of state actors, about

---

144   Weisglas and de Boer (2007): p. 93
145   Squarcialopi quoted in Sabic (2013), p. 26

the pooling of power and about common ideals.[146] If so, what sort of state actor other than government is parliament? With democratisation expanding around the globe, the number of regional and other parliamentary organisations has been steadily increasing and the intensity of inter-parliamentary contacts growing. They vary greatly as to the scope and content of their activities, their mandates and statutes according to which they operate, their formal or informal ambition, authority and abilities, their size and financial/institutional resources, and, in general, as to their role/involvement in foreign policy and international relations. They primarily engage in inter-parliamentary cooperation on the international scene by debating and adopting non-binding recommendations on pressing regional and international issues of common concern with the expectation to be able to influence related government policies and international developments. However, what 'unites' all parliamentary organs is that they do not operate in a vacuum but each in relation (whatever form it may take) to their government, the main body administering policies in this domain. Their role as new players in the international arena is not to duplicate, replace or compete with governments but to complement, enrich and stimulate policies with wider implications to provide impulses, direction and follow- up.

3.2.4.4 Political Opposition

In every political system, those who are in power face rivals who would replace them, either to change policy or to gain power. In democratic systems, this opposition is legitimate and is organized into political parties. Rival politicians may also exist in the leader's own party. Opposition is less overt and less peaceful in non-democratic systems, but it exists nonetheless and in many varied forms. One distinction divides opposition between those who merely want to change policy and those who want to gain control or the government. A second division is between those who are located inside and outside of the government.

3.2.4.5 Interest Groups

Interest groups are private or nongovernmental associations of people who have similar policy views and who pressure the government to adopt those views as policy. The increasingly intermestic nature of policy is changing that, and interest groups are becoming an important part of the foreign policymaking process. We can see this by looking at several types of interest groups. These groups have long been active in international politics because the level

---

146   Götz (2005), p. 276

of their involvement in formulation and conduct of foreign policies have increased significantly since World War II. A confluence of factors accounts for the explosion in international lobbying groups activities. These include the increasing importance of international organizations, such as the United Nations (UN), its various agencies, and regional organizations, such as the European Union (EU), with jurisdictions that extend beyond national borders; the fact that many issues such as environmental protection, wildlife management, and the fight against global pandemic like Covid 19 require an international approach and increasing awareness of issues because of advances in communications and the adoption of many international connectedness.

3.3 Systemic Level Analysis

Countries may be theoretically free to make any foreign policy decision they want, but as a practical matter, achieving a successful foreign policy requires that they make choices that are reasonable within the context of the realities of the international system.[147] These factors are roughly divided into those related to the system's structural characteristic, its power relationships, its economic realities, and its norms. All systems, whether it is the international system, the country's system, or the immediate, local system have identifiable structural characteristics.

The relevance of domestic and international environments to foreign policy analysis determines how authority should be organized in the international system and scope as well as the level of interaction among actors in the system.[148] The structure of authority for making and enforcing rules, for allocating assets, and for conducting other authoritative tasks in a system can range from hierarchical (vertical) to anarchical (horizontal). The international system is a mostly horizontal authority structure. It is based on the sovereignty of states. Sovereignty means that countries are not legally answerable to any higher authority for their international or domestic conduct. As such, the international system is a state-centric system that is largely anarchic; it has no overarching authority to make rules, settle disputes, and provide protection.

The anarchical nature of the international system has numerous impacts on national policy.[149] However, though all states are sovereign, in practice, some states have more power and they coerce others into making some foreign policy decisions. Moreover, one could observe that while the authority structure in

---

147   Stern and Sundelius, (2002), p. 83
148   Hagan, (1994), p. 189
149   Wang and Chang, (2004), p. 21

the international system remains decidedly horizontal, change is underway. Sovereignty is declining and that even the most powerful states are subject to a growing number of authoritative rules made by international organizations and by international law. Countries still resist and often even reject international law, but increasingly, they also comply with it.

Another structural characteristic of any political system is the scope, frequency, and level of interactions among actors.[150] At the international system level, the scope, frequency, and level of interaction among actors has grown extensively during the last half century. Economic interdependence provides the most obvious example. Countries trade more than they did not do so long ago, and each of them, even the most powerful United States, is heavily dependent on others for sources of products that it needs and markets for the products that it sells. The level of interdependence in the world today is high and thus, states need to have strong ties for sustainability. Additionally, countries are restrained by the realities of power in the international system, much like individuals are limited by the distribution of power in more local systems. The conduct of the international system is heavily influenced by power considerations such as the number of powerful actors and the context of power. In the current system, there is one powerful polar, the US. Though some see the US as playing an important role in global relations, some scholars view it as imperialistic. Needless to say, there is considerable debate over such views.

Some scholars contend that a reduced US presence in the world would not destabilize the system.[151] Yet other analysts debate the motives behind and the implications of the US conducting itself as a hegemonic power. Some condemn it as a destructive imperialistic impulse.[152] This level adopted a top-bottom approach to the study of world politics. It starts with the view that countries and other international actors operate in a global socio-economic, political and geographic environment that has specific characteristics of the system to help in determining the patterns of interaction among the actors. Any expert of international politics interested in serving as a systems analyst knows that any system operates in somewhat predictable ways with behavioural tendencies that the actor countries usually follow.

Most people do not think much about systems, but they are an ever-present part of our lives. Although each of us has free will, each of us is also part of many overlapping systems that influence our behaviour and make it reasonably predictable. These systems range from very local ones like your family and the school you attended, to much larger systems like your community, state, the

---

150   Axworthy. (2003), p.87
151   Buthe and Milner, (2008), p.751
152   Buckley, Clegg, Liu, Voss and Zheng, (2007), p.512

country and the world at large. Whatever its size or how each of these systems operates is based on four factors: structural characteristics, power relationships, economic realities, and norms. All systems have identifiable structural features that determine the outcome of interaction. These features include how authority has been organized, the key actors and the scope of interaction among the actors, as follows.

3.3.1 The Establishment of Authority

The authority structure of a system for making and enforcing rules, allocating assets and conducting other authoritative tasks can range from very hierarchical to anarchical. Most systems in Africa, like South Sudan, have hierarchical systems starting with the president to the subordinate working in the government institution like a cleaner or private in the army. They have a vertical authority structure in which subordinate units answer to higher levels of authority. Vertical systems have central authorities that are responsible for making, enforcing, and adjudicating rules that restrain subordinate actors. Other systems have a horizontal authority structure in which authority is fragmented. The international system is one such system with a mostly horizontal authority structure. It is based on the sovereignty of states. In this context, *sovereignty* means that states should not be legally answerable to any higher authority for their international and domestic conduct, especially the promotion of national interest abroad. The only issue hindering the ability or capacity of state sovereignty is that the international system is anarchic, which means it has no overarching authority to make rules, settle disputes, and provide protection. This notion has been solved somehow through establishment of intergovernmental organizations or international institutions like the United Nations. To see how horizontal and vertical structures operate differently, ask yourself why all countries are armed and only few countries could enforce their interest successfully. The reason is that states in the international system depend on themselves for protection. If a state is threatened, there is no international body that regulates the behaviour of the states. Given this self-help system, each state feels compelled to be armed.

Many analysts believe that sovereignty is declining and that even the most powerful states are subject to an increasing number of authoritative rules made by intergovernmental organizations (lGOs) and by international law. This is the language African countries should know in dealing with superpower like United States of America because the world is currently unipolar in nature.

3.3.2 The Actors

Another characteristic of any system is its actors. What organizations operate in the system, and what impact do they have on the course of international interaction? We can answer these questions by dividing actors into three general categories: nations actors (Tanzania, South Africa, Egypt, Cameroon), international actors (IGAD, AU, UN), and transnational actors (Apple, Samsung, Ford).

3.3.3 The Range of Interaction

A third structural characteristic of any political system is the range of areas in which the actors interact and the frequency and intensity of those interactions. One key to understanding the evolution of the international system is to see that the level of international interaction is very much higher now than during the 1800s or even in the first half of the 1900s.

Economic interdependence provides the most obvious example of the escalating level of interaction. It is nonsense today to imagine that any country can go it alone in splendid isolation. Even for a powerful country like the United States, a fortress America policy is impossible without foreign oil, to pick one obvious illustration, without which the entire U.S. transportation industry would literally come to a halt soon.

3.3.4 Norms of behaviour

The widely accepted standards that help regulate behaviour are the fourth major element of any system. These standards of behaviour, or values, constitute the norms of a system. Norms must be generally recognized and followed but need not be either accepted or practiced universally. Systems develop norms for two reasons. First, various psychological and social factors prompt humans to adopt values to define what is ethical and moral. Second, humans tend to favour regularized patterns of behaviour because of the pragmatic need to interact and to avoid the anxiety and disruption caused by the random or unwanted behaviour of others. Over the centuries, pragmatism led to norms about how countries treat each other's diplomats even in times of war. Changes that occur in the norms of the international system arc an important aspect of how the system evolves. What is evident in the current system is that norms are becoming more universal while they are simultaneously being challenged.

CHAPTER FOUR

FOREIGN POLICY TRENDS: TOOLS AND INSTRUMENTS

This chapter highlights key tools applied by any country in making their foreign policy realistic with considerations such as diplomacy, economy, diaspora, security and military strategy among others to promote her national interest within the international arena. The application of these tools (instruments) largely depends on the situation on the ground.

4.1 Diplomacy

Diplomacy is a set of norms and rules regulating relations between states. As such it is embedded in organizational structures, procedures, routines and habits of foreign ministries.[153] Diplomats traditionally carry out diplomacy according to institutionalized professional standards and habits. Diplomatic negotiations and other diplomatic interactions are therefore conducted with strong emphasis on the professional norms of the diplomatic community with all its peculiarities including protocol and secrecy. For centuries, diplomacy has also had a public face. Public ceremonies organized whenever an ambassador arrived at a capital in the late Middle Ages communicated a great deal to the assembled crowds about the sovereignty that the ambassador represented.[154] Diplomatic relations occur between states, but diplomacy is not achievable

---

153   Faizullaev, (2013), p.21
154   Hamilton and Langhorne, (1995), p.121

without the activity of organizations and individuals. Authorized organizations such as governments, parliaments, ministries of foreign affairs, and embassies, missions and official individuals such as heads of state and governments, ministers, ambassadors, and others play important roles in conducting international diplomacy. Scholars have extensively examined both the role of states as unitary actors as well as the roles of state institutions and individual representatives in diplomacy and diplomatic negotiations.

Diplomacy and diplomatic negotiators widely use symbols and symbolic actions and interactions, including rituals and ceremonies.[155] The most important symbolic attachment of diplomatic negotiations is state flags. To create fair conditions for the parties involved, diplomatic protocol suggests rules regarding the use of flags during official meetings and negotiations. The equality of national flags, both in number and size, is one of the symbolic expressions of parties' equality around the negotiation table. Official visits, the exchange of gifts, the recall of ambassadors, the increase or reduction of diplomatic presence in a foreign country, and other aspects of diplomatic practice are full of symbolism.[156] Often, states with conflicting interests enter into indirect bargaining through symbolic interactionism. The significance of indirect bargaining increases when states cannot negotiate directly or arrange negotiations through a third party. They may use different kinds of symbolic gestures and actions, including ambiguous body language signalling, demonstrations of military might, contact with the other side's enemies or friends, public statements, publications related to the disputed issue, abuse of the opponent's identity symbols, and many others. These actions, though not instruments of direct or mediated negotiations, may serve as tools of negotiation positioning and bargaining between states. To interact effectively, diplomatic negotiators need to organize their interactions, including symbolic interactionism, by paying attention to social norms, procedures, decision-making mechanisms, and the physical arrangements of the negotiation. Even food and cuisine can be used as instruments for "cross-cultural understanding in the hopes of improving interactions and cooperation."[157] Because sharing food can have symbolic significance and can foster affinity between people in every culture, gastronomic diplomacy, or diplomacy at the dining table or culinary diplomacy, has always had its role in diplomatic interactions.[158]

Aggregations of state and non-state players are playing growing roles in international relations and politics. These actors negotiate together or form

---

155   Faizullaev, (2013), p.18
156   (Biswaro, (2000).
157   Chapple-Sokol, (2013), p.161
158   Neumann, (2013), p.87

supranational bodies for dealing with a particular issue. Different kinds of contact groups could include states, including international governmental and nongovernmental organizations, political and donor groups, and representatives of civil society. For example, the International Contact Group for the Mindanao peace process in the Philippines was established in 2009 by the government of the Philippines and the Moro Islamic Liberation Front (MILF). It was comprised of four states (the United Kingdom, Japan, Turkey, and Saudi Arabia) and four international nongovernmental organizations such as Conciliation Resources, Muhammadiyah, The Asia Foundation, and the Center for Humanitarian Dialogue.[159] Nonetheless, states remain the main actors of international diplomacy. States, not organizations or individuals, establish diplomatic relations. Such global or regional international organizations as the UN and the Organization of American States have diplomatic missions and staffs with diplomatic status, but no international institution has any power other than the power conferred upon it by States.[160]

As a fundamental instrument of foreign policy, international diplomacy serves the political or other objectives of states in a civilized manner. These objectives may be related not only to the political and economic interests of the state in a narrow sense but also to the protection of human rights and the interests of the civil society, poverty reduction, health and environmental safety in the world, and maintaining international peace and security. Though diplomacy has been defined as the organized conduct of relations between states and diplomatic negotiation as an organized form of interaction between states aimed at a favourable agreement, states are the principal actors of international relations and diplomatic affairs and they do not act on their own in the international arena but rather through their organizational agencies and individual agents.[161] One of the most important aspects of diplomatic effectiveness is the ability to coordinate efforts and activities at three levels: state–actor, organization–agency, and individual–agent.

Negotiation is a key instrument of diplomacy based on organized interactions between states through their official representatives. With its culture, rules, and traditions, diplomacy provides states, their organizational agencies, and individual agents a way of organizing interactions in order to manage interstate relations and make joint decisions. International law and such peculiarities of diplomatic practice as diplomatic immunity and diplomatic passports, diplomatic correspondence, conferences, protocols, symbols, ceremonies, and specific languages play a significant role in organizing diplomatic intercourse

---

159   Conciliation Resources, (2013), p.3
160   Plantey, (2007), p.308
161   Henrikson, (2013), p.118

as a whole and negotiations in particular.[162] Negotiation is a joint decision-making process that occurs as parties act on each other. Interaction is a condition and means of negotiation.[163] No diplomatic negotiation happens without the participation of all three acting entities of diplomacy: state–actors, organization–agencies, and individual agents. No individual diplomat can act without the backing of his or her organization agency; no foreign ministry or embassy can function without individual agents and the state; and no state–actors can interact without agencies and agents who represent them.

In diplomacy, the state–actor, organization–agency, and individual agent reinforce and constrain each other.[164] The efficiency of diplomatic negotiations depends on the organization and quality of both interstate and intrastate interactions. In diplomatic negotiations, the organization–agency's strength is derived to some extent from the state's resources, structure, decision-making mechanisms, communication capacities, and legal foundation; the individual agent's strengths are powered by his or her knowledge, skills, status/rank, personal relations, and political backing. Each part of the actor–agency–agent system can strengthen or weaken the others. Although in international diplomacy the state–actor and its authorized organization–agencies and individual agents form inseparable tripartite acting bodies, all three parts of the system may have a particular autonomy from each other: the state as actor, organizations as agencies, and individuals as agents can sometimes differ in their stances and disagree.[165] Such relative autonomy presents both risks and opportunities for the diplomatic actor. On the one hand, any inconsistency between its parts can harm the state's foreign policy, but on the other, that might give the actor and its agencies and agents some flexibility and complementarity. Dynamic equilibrium and congruence among diplomatic actors, agencies, and agents contribute to the negotiation efficacy of the state.

The state's self is one of the sources of diplomatic negotiating power.[166] States with well-defined and stable selves have certain advantages in diplomatic negotiations over states that have a weak comprehension of their selves. A strong sense of self – a clear awareness of identity, values, and interests – makes a state–actor, organization–agency, and individual–agent stronger. This does not mean that states with strong selves always prevail in diplomatic negotiations because the outcome of a given negotiation is determined by various factors. The state's ability to negotiate with others depends not only on its enduring

162   Faizullaev , (2013), p.94
163   Faizullaev, (2014), p.295
164   Henrikson, (2013), p.118
165   Faizullaev, (2014), p.277
166   O'Neill, (2002), p.81

self, on effective diplomatic agencies, and on competent diplomatic agents, but also on how it can organize internal and external interactions as well as its relative bargaining power which, in its turn, depends on both the capabilities and relationships of the state.[167]

The organization, process, and outcomes of diplomatic negotiations are affected by state–actors' selves, structures, and resources; by organization–agencies' policies and attitudes which are based on their installations, functions, and goals; and by individual-agents' knowledge and skills, which are based on their information, education, training, and understanding of the state's aspirations and organizations' guidelines.[168] The way diplomatic negotiation is managed, however, depends not only on the top-down connections between state–actors, organization–agencies, and individual–agents but also on bottom-up forces within this triad: individuals can make a difference in organizations, and organizations and individuals can greatly affect states' international behaviour. Further analysis of the relationships between the state and its diplomatic agencies and agents and the impact of that relationship on interstate interactions and negotiations could particularly focus on studying the factors that help or hamper synchronism between these three entities and create cohesion among them, the social and political forces that promote or inhibit coordination at these three levels, and the influences of the set of competing discourses and practices that define the state's self in international interactional and relational contexts.[169]

4.2 Security and Military Strategy

Military diplomacy entails the military of one country aspiring to expand its cooperation with foreign militaries in order to maintain peace and contribute to international development.[170] Moreover, military diplomacy has been termed as the use of the military by a state to advance diplomacy and its engagement in bilateral and multilateral security arrangements.[171] It has long been one of the essential constituents of international diplomacy. In the range of acceptable nation-to-nation contacts, military diplomacy is increasingly being accepted as an effective method in fostering bilateral and regional relationships. As a component of foreign policy, it aims to bring in greater transparency and confidence in the military sphere and contribute to closer relations with

---

167   Adler-Nissen and Pouliot, (2014), p.9
168   Shell, (2006), p.150
169   Faizullaev, (2014), p.290
170   Singh, (2011), p.800
171   Sachar, (2004), p.296

countries. It is essential to strike the right balance between foreign policy and security interests through foreign policy tools like arms transfers, participation in joint military exercises, military training programmes, security dialogues, and military confidence-building measures. Peacetime military diplomacy is an important constituent of the five basic channels of nation-to-nation contact between friendly governments, i.e., political, diplomatic, economic, cultural, social, and last but not least, military. While it is true that diplomacy is the first line of defence, it can be reasoned that one can have military diplomacy whereby the military is seen as an additional channel and avenue by which conflicts could be averted, if not resolved.[172]

Rather than viewing diplomacy and force as opposing ends of the spectrum of national policy – where one is used when the other fails – it is important to recognize that each must seamlessly support the other. This entails striking the right balance between foreign policy and security interests and strengthening military relations through foreign policy tools like military training programmes, arms transfers, security dialogues and confidence-building measures. These efforts pay off with stronger security relationships with other countries. Military diplomacy does not in any way develop outside the diplomacy of the state and the scope and scale of military relations are influenced by the tenor of overall relations. The government spells out the broad parameters of foreign policy and military diplomacy in an essential component of her foreign policy. Peacetime military diplomacy can help to build the foundation for regional cooperation, which is based on mutual trust and confidence.[173] Upgrading military ties by looking at various alternatives of peacetime military diplomacy in a sustained manner can reduce the security concerns in the region and assist in the fulfilment of the foreign policy objectives.[174] International Military Training Cooperation (IMTC) and participating in peacekeeping efforts in the region is an essential component of peacetime military diplomacy and can prove vital in furthering the state's strategic interests. However, to be able to participate in regional peacekeeping and cooperation efforts, it is important for the young state to have peace and tranquillity locally.[175] It would prove a challenge to engage in regional peacekeeping efforts when there is no peace in Africa.

Peacetime military diplomacy has been recognized as an instrument of state policy by a number of countries. Great Britain and China are two countries that have institutionalized peacetime military diplomacy and are conducting it in a

---

172   Sachar, (2003), p.405
173   Sachar, (2003), p.407
174   Singh, (2011), p.796
175   Sachar ,(2003), p.415

coordinated and sustained manner.[176] The establishment of military diplomacy as a defence mission by Britain has provided better coherence and renewed impetus to peacetime activities by its armed forces. China has been active in developing an omni-directional and multi-level form of military diplomacy. Chinese armed forces have been active in participating in multilateral military diplomatic activities to bring the positive role of the Chinese armed forces into full play in the sphere of international military affairs.[177] Closer to home, participation of the regional military in peacekeeping efforts can be a critical consideration in Africa's foreign policy.

In the region, African Union Mission in Somalia (AMISOM) is, by definition, an active regional peacekeeping mission. In practice, it is a peace enforcement mission mandated by the African Union with the approval of the United Nations. The AMISOM is mandated to support governmental structures, implement a national security plan, support Somali security forces, and assist in creating a secure environment for the delivery of humanitarian aid.[178] It includes forces from various East African countries including Kenya, Rwanda and Uganda. As part of its duties, AMISOM also supports the Federal Government of Somalia's forces in their battle against the al-Shabaab militants. The AMISOM was established by the African Union's Peace and Security Council on 19 January 2007, and on 21 February 2007 the United Nations Security Council approved the mission's mandate.[179]

This involves the use of force, terrorist attack and military coercion in conducting foreign policy objective of states. The most important role of military instrument is that of providing a background of assurance and stability for diplomacy. This means that military power is a major accompaniment of diplomacy or the ability to attain policy objectives. Because of its violent nature, it is often used as a last resort when, for instance, diplomacy and other mechanisms of achieving peaceful settlement of disputes failed. On the basis of whether or not military force is actually used, there are two types of military instruments:

A. Military Pressure: It is defined as the threat of use of military force by a foreign policy actor against another actor in order to achieve certain foreign policy objectives and without having to use actual military force. The use of military pressure has proved quite efficient in reaching foreign policy objectives, avoiding more damaging conflict and maintaining peace at large. It nevertheless entails high risks, such as that of escalating a conflict and ending

---

176   Singh, (2011), p.814
177   Sachar ,(2003), p.406
178   Nduwimana, (2013), p.3
179   Nduwiman, (2013), p.4

up in a situation of actual warfare. Additionally, the use of military threat as a foreign policy instrument must infer indeed the possibility of actual warfare in order to be efficient.

B. Warfare: Whereas war has been classically considered as one of the main instruments of foreign policy, such position has gone under pressure in recent times. The use of war as an instrument of foreign policy intends to achieve foreign policy objectives by the coercion or the use of military force on other actors. War may be divided into conventional (open warfare with the use of conventional weapons), unconventional (covert warfare or with the use of non-conventional weapons, such as nuclear, biological or chemical) and asymmetric (where the parties in conflict differ greatly in their military capabilities).

Unlike other instruments, the use of war as a foreign policy instrument entails an enormous amount of risk and cost. Risks include the possibility of a military defeat which would render impossible the achievement of the pursued foreign policy objectives, compromises and even put the vital interests at stake. Another possible risk is the lack of public support for the war effort, ultimately leading to the demise of a government. Under international law, war is a legitimate course of action, only if it is confined to self- defense (Article 51 of the UN Charter). This international law is aimed at the reduction of the human and economic costs of war

4.3 Diaspora Diplomacy

Africa has a great diaspora potential to influence events abroad. The concept of Diaspora Africa diplomatic practice demands innovative interrogation to bring out its diverse aspects, dynamics and potential. In its narrow sense, this concept should refer to Africans living and working abroad. The Statutes of the Economic, Social and Cultural Council of the African Union (ECOSOC, 2004), provides for the participation of the diaspora in all its activities (Article 2(2)). Africa is also beginning to draw huge investments, technology transfer, cultural linkages and even diplomatic engagements from this diaspora. Indeed, the African Union recognizes the African Diaspora as the sixth region of its components.

4.4 Economic Diplomacy

Many countries use several institutions and activities, such as export promotion agencies, economic departments at embassies and foreign trade offices known as business support offices and trade missions, to promote exports.[180] This is generally referred to as economic diplomacy. Diplomatic activity is an important aspect of international relations. The friendly diplomatic interaction may lead to a good investment environment for multinational corporations (MNC) and hence influence MNCs' location decisions. Thus, any country should seek to create a good external environment for economic development and to improve international economic cooperation through economic diplomacy.[181]

Public interest is the set of private interest, and diplomatic activities are driven by both national and private interest.[182] Traditional diplomatic systems emphasize political exchange but neglect economic exchange, while modern diplomatic systems regard business diplomacy as a main goal. Governments have re-allocated diplomatic activities to concentrate more on business activities and extend the diplomatic business scope.[183] Governments are likely to become business co-operators. To some degree, senior political visits are spatial extensions of the political power of overseas investors from the home country to the host country. The home country's political influence on the host country is an important way for overseas enterprises to gain business advantages in the host country.[184]

Multinational corporeations also enforce contracts and protect the property rights of foreigner investors. Therefore, the home government provides a good institutional arrangement for its MNCs through bilateral political visits which originate from bilateral political negotiations or pressure. Bilateral senior visits are friendly signals that help investors in the home country trust the host country. MNCs always follow the flag of bilateral political relations to avoid political risks, and they prefer to invest or increase investment in host countries that have good relations with their own country. Moreover, MNCs from emerging economies tend to be more attuned to government priorities and preferences.[185] This implies that the governments' political preference can influence MNCs' investment decisions. Put concretely, when a government prefers a country, bilateral visits increase, which in turn sends an encouraging signal to investors, leading MNCs to invest in the country. With respect to the host country, bilateral senior visits improve the awareness of, or foster a positive sentiment toward, the investing country, creating a friendlier investment environment for foreign companies to overcome the liability of foreignness.

---

180   Head and Ries, (2010), p.760
181   Zhang, Jiang and Zhou, (2014), p.221
182   Lee and Hudson, (2004), p.351
183   Ibid, (2004), p.356
184   Transparency International, (2002), p.67
185   Gammeltoft et al, (2010), p.96

This friendly environment is also favourable for MNCs to invest in the host country.

Overseas MNCs face two types of political risks: domestic systematic risk and risk related to political ideology. The former is due to the poor quality of domestic institutions, which affects all MNCs in the host country equally; the latter scenario is related to the bilateral diplomatic risk between host and home countries.[186] Host country officials do not distinguish foreign investors from their government, and foreign investors are regarded as extensions of the home government or informal agents of their home country.[187] Meanwhile, foreign direct investment (FDI) is a long-term investment, and it is less likely to escape evacuation. Host countries can easily penalize the home country for political conflicts by shifting the cost of political conflicts to MNCs.

The host government can capture investors' surplus by outright expropriation, strict regulation, heavy taxation, rigorous entry barriers, visa requirements, or selective law enforcement.[188] Rising political tensions lead governments to adopt policies that reduce investment interdependence and encourage investors to transfer investment to other partners. In addition, MNCs' products are constrained by the host consumers' public choices. Consumers' cognition and demand propensity toward different countries may be different. Consumers express goodwill or solidarity toward those they identify as friends, but nationalist feelings lead them to shun, punish or boycott those they perceive as foes.[189] Therefore, bilateral political conflicts result in reduced expected return of ex ante investors, and lower the probability of re-investment due to damage in ex post investors' property rights. As a consequence, MNCs are reluctant to invest in countries with diplomatic conflicts with their home country. In other words, bilateral diplomatic risks lead to lower investment.

Additionally, the institution-based view suggests good institutions promote economic activity, since good institutions are associated with a favourable business environment as well as lower uncertainty and complexity. In line with many empirical results from developed countries, countries with good institutions are more likely to attract foreign investment.[190] However, that does not mean foreign investment is less likely to flow toward host countries with poor institutions. In the empirical literature on MNCs from emerging economies, poor institution in a host country seems not to be a barrier, and some authors even regard it as an environmental advantage for MNCs from emerging economies.[191]

---

186   Desbordes, (2010), p.94
187   Cuervo-Cazurra et al, (2007), p.719
188   Buthe and Milner, (2008), p.754
189   Davis and Meunier, (2011), p.639
190   Garcia-Canal and Guillen, (2008), p.1104
191   Quer et al , (2012), p.1096

In the case of China, evidence indicates that Chinese firms are investing in countries with poor institutions, endowed with natural resources.[192] In fact, political influence strongly impacts economic activities of countries where laws, rules, and market mechanisms are lacking. Investing firms can thus maintain their economic benefits through political power. The institutional gap can be remedied by friendly bilateral diplomatic activities. A host country's political preference toward firms from certain countries is enhanced by friendly bilateral diplomatic relations. Firms from these countries are given more investing priorities and supplied with favourable obligatory institutional arrangements. This arrangement is also selective and exclusive, only being offered to MNCs from preferred countries. Firms from preferred countries can access economic resources and gain more contracts and developing opportunities. Friendly bilateral diplomatic relations between investing and host countries therefore create a new institutional advantage for foreign firms.[193] This new institutional ownership advantage may substitute or complement the existing institutional advantage. In many cases, political leaders are more influential in countries with weak institutions than those with strong institutions. One can expect that the weaker the institution, the stronger the influence of the politician's diplomatic activities.

It can be used almost simultaneously to reward one state and punish another. A state may be given preferential trade terms by another state in order to encourage friendship and support while other may be deliberately excluded from such suppliers of preferential treatments in order to create problems for their economy and domestic interest capable of altering the policies of states or in fact bringing about a change of government. The economic instrument is also useful in war situation as states at war known to engage in activities which are intended to undermine the economic capacities of their enemies and hence reduce the enemy's ability to fight back. Example is Iraq war, where each country targeted areas such as oil field and petroleum refinery tanks, was intended to undermine the economic base of military power. The main economic instruments are trade, foreign aid and economic sanctions.

i.   **Trade:** Trade is the most noticeable and the most widely used instrument of an economic nature. It is defined as the exchange of goods and services between foreign policy actors. The world today is an interdependent world in which hardly any nation can be said to be totally independent of others in respect to its national needs. The inter-dependence puts in the hands of state a major weapon with which they can manipulate other

---

192   Kolstad and Wiig, (2012), p.30
193   Quer et al, (2012), p.1098

states to attain desired policy objectives. The normal processes of trade encourage friendship among states; hence, states are perpetually involved in promoting trade and sorting out motions arising from such exchanges. While trade policy was in the past a typically bilateral instrument, it has become increasingly multilateral in the recent years, with the creation of trade blocks such as the European Economic Community (now the European Union), and WTO.

ii. **Foreign Aid:** It refers to the voluntary and intentioned transfer of resources, typically, although not always, from one State (donor) to another (recipient). However, foreign aid has been often used to support ideologically closed regimes which have then used that aid to repress their population or enter into aggressive militarist policies towards other States. Additionally, there has been widespread criticism as to the efficiency of aid to achieve its pursued objectives. Foreign Aid is in itself divided into different categories depending on the objective pursued by the use of the transferred resources and which include:

- *Humanitarian Aid* - to relieve human suffering during and after man-made or natural disasters, without tackling the original causes of the vulnerability;
- *Development Aid* - to contribute to the economic and social development of the recipient in the long term without necessarily alleviating immediate suffering; and
- *Military Aid* - dedicated to the strengthening of the military capabilities of the recipient.

iii. **Economic Sanctions**: Economic sanctions are a typically coercive measure intended by an actor of Foreign Policy (imposer, the sanctioning actor) to cause economic damage to another actor of Foreign Policy (target, the sanctioned actor) and thus force it to pursue a certain course of action. They may include tools such as embargoes, boycotts, freezing of funds and assets and other trade or economic restrictions and may be bilateral or multilateral. The use of sanctions has been refined with the use of the so-called 'smart' sanctions, targeted at specific sectors of the economy or specific persons. The objective of these smart sanctions is to force compliance on the target without unnecessarily damaging the society as a whole, including those parts which may have nothing to do with the policies that the sanctions aim to prevent. The European Union follows sanctioning regimes imposed by the UN and complements them with further sanctions. It also imposes its own sanctioning regimes. The European Union has imposed sanctions, among others, on Iran, Syria, Ivory Coast, Congo, Egypt, Tunisia, Libya, etc.

4.5 Declaration of War

Whereas war has been classically considered as one of the main instruments of foreign policy, such position has undergone pressure in recent times. The use of war as an instrument of foreign policy intends to achieve foreign policy objectives by the coercion of other foreign policy actors, achieved by the use of military force upon them. It is important to bear in mind that, unlike other foreign policy instruments, the use of war as a foreign policy instrument entails an enormous amount of risk and cost. Risks include the possibility of a military defeat which would render impossible the achievement of the pursued foreign policy objectives, compromise other foreign policy interests and objectives and even put vital interests at stake. Another possible risk is the lack of public support for the war effort, ultimately leading to the demise of a government. It is important to bear in mind that, under international law, war is a legitimate course of action, even if it is confined to self-defence (Article 51 of the UN Charter). International law has aimed at the reduction of the human and economic costs of war.

War is thought to involve armed conflict between two or more parties usually fought for political ends. The main focus of the idea of war is on the use of force between large-scale political units such as states or empires, usually over control of territory. It is all about power. War makes anything resembling normal existence impossible. It destroys and ruins lives, it imposes immense burdens on national economies and imperils the freedom of everyone, and it endangers man's very existence on this planet. It is the great curse of an international society, the endemic disease of the nation-state system. Today, the term "war" is used in many different ways, as for example, cold war, hot war, limited war, total war, conventional war, unconventional war, civil war, guerilla war, preventive war, political warfare, propaganda war, psychological warfare, race war and tribal war.

4.6 Propaganda as Psychological Instrument

Psychological instruments comprise the various attempts and means by which the government agitates the minds and emotions of people in other states. Essentially, psychological instruments are used to appeal to people rather than to the government, although the ultimate intent is to get an image of policy on the part of the government by using their people as the pressure point. One of the most used psychological instruments is propaganda. Propaganda is basically a verbal instrument, i.e., articulated in word, and it is a systemic method of influencing minds and emotions for a specific purpose. In its simple term, propaganda refers to the manipulation and distortion of information in order to achieve one's interest and defeat the interest of an opponent. It is used to make a favourable image of one self and unfavourable image of others. Some countries can be painted as bad in the international milieu. It is also used to persuade others to see things in one's way. Propaganda is often selfish to attain its policy objective. This can be done through radio, film, pamphlets, social media and other instruments for creating a favorable image for a country's foreign policy objectives. It involves extensive use of mass media. Iraq used propaganda to project a bad image of the U.S. in the hostage issue and Reagan also used it to damage the prestige of Libya. Also, past and present governments in Nigeria have often resorted to this means whenever they wanted to justify their actions on certain sensitive issues that have ramifying effects on other states or the international community. Internal propaganda is done within a nation-state on issues that are domestic in nature or that deals with domestic policy and decisions. Propaganda techniques include:

- *Name Calling:* This is projecting bad names onto individuals or individual states. For example, Gaddafi of Libya was once named the "mad man of Middle East" by the United States in an effort to curb its excesses.
- *Glittering Generality:* This is done to describe policies and ideas. It is a way of putting across one's policies and ideas to the outside world in such a way as to make them attractive. It is acceptable and commands both sympathy and respect.
- *Systematic dismantling:* This means elimination or obstruction of rival sources of news and information through the process of condemning and banning publication from a rival group or actor.

4.7 Foreign Aid

Foreign aid refers to the voluntary and intentional transfer of resources, typically, although not always, from one state (donor) to another (recipient). Foreign aid is in itself divided into different categories depending on the objective pursued by the use of the transferred resources, and which include Humanitarian Aid (to relieve human suffering during and after man-made or natural disasters, without tackling the original causes of the vulnerability), Development Aid (to contribute to the economic and social development of the recipient in the long term without necessarily alleviating immediate suffering), and Military Aid (dedicated to strengthening the military capabilities of the recipient). As argued elsewhere, although foreign aid is sometimes considered as a non-coercive instrument of foreign policy, it is mostly dedicated to human, economic and social development. However, the instrument may be, and is often, used in a coercive manner by the establishment of the link between the receiver of aid and certain policy objectives of the donor. Conditionality becomes the order of the day.[194] Foreign aid has often been used to support ideologically closed regimes that have then used that aid to repress their population or enter into aggressive militarist policies towards other States. Additionally, there has been widespread criticism as to the efficiency of aid to achieve its pursued objectives. In Africa, the provision of foreign aid by western countries and China has made some African countries compromise on the execution of their own national interest against the countries providing aid.

---

194   Biswaro, op.cit..

CHAPTER FIVE

VARIABLES
OF FOREIGN POLICY

This chapter reviews various factors that influence the foreign policy of any country around the globe. States' foreign policies are premised on certain domestic and external situations, circumstances and developments, also known as variables. These variables shape the foreign policies of states. Domestic factors include character of the state, geography, demographics, political system/ structure, leadership, economy, military capability, historical values, national interest, media and public opinion, pressure groups, and others. External variables include intentions of other states, consideration regarding immediate neighbours, national security, membership of international institutions, international law, opinions and actions of great powers, and so on. These factors could be domestic or international.

5.1 Domestic Factors Influencing Foreign Policy

Various factors have been found to influence foreign policy of any nation. These include political factors, geography, public opinion, social groups, form of government and political leaders. The domestic environment refers essentially to features, factors and forces peculiar to the states' foreign policy being made. The domestic environment includes geographical location of the state, its peculiarity, natural and human resources, the nature of the political system, quality of leadership, and the nature of the interaction among groups in society. This section highlights key domestic factors that affect the formulation of South Sudan foreign policy.

5.1.1 Internal Politics

Each country's foreign policy tends to reflect its political culture. This concept represents a society's widely held traditional values and its fundamental practices that are slow to change. Leaders tend to formulate policies compatible with their society's political culture because the leaders share many or all of those values. Also, even if they do not share a particular value, leaders want to avoid the backlash that adopting policies counter to the political culture might cause. To analyse any country's political culture, one needs to look into such things as how the people feel about themselves and their country, how they view others, what role they think their country should play in the world, and what they see as morally acceptable.

Examples are how Americans and Chinese feel about themselves and about projecting their values to others. Both Americans and Chinese are persuaded that their own cultures are superior. In Americans, this is called American exceptionalism, an attitude that, for instance, led 81% of Americans to agree in a poll that the spread of their values would have a positive effect on other parts of the world. A similar sense of superiority among the Chinese is called Sino-centrism. This tendency of the Chinese to see themselves as the political and cultural centre of the world is expressed, among other ways, in their word for their country: "Zhong Guó" meaning "middle place" and symbolising the Chinese image of society.[195] Where Americans and Chinese differ is in their beliefs about trying to impose it on others. Americans are sometimes described as having a missionary impulse that possesses zeal to reshape the world in the American image. For example, it is this aspect of American political culture that has led the United States to try not only to defeat hostile regimes in Afghanistan, Iraq, Libya and elsewhere, but additionally, to replace them with democratic governments. There is also evidence that the United States makes other decisions, such as foreign aid allocations, based in part on how closely countries adhere to American conceptions of human rights.

Chinese attitudes about projecting values are very different. Despite China's immense pride in its culture, there is no history of trying to impose it on others, even when China dominated much of the world that it knew. The orientation is based in part on Confucianism's tenet of leading by example rather than by forceful conversion. This is the influence that China wants to portray in

---

195   Gries, (2004), p.321

Africa as foreign relations between China and Africa improve. It also has to do with the Sino-centric attitude that the "barbarians" are not well suited to aspire to the heights of Chinese culture and are best left to themselves as much as possible.[196]

Among other current ramifications, China's non-missionary attitude makes it very hard for the Chinese to understand why Americans and some others try to insist that China adopt what it sees as foreign values and standards of behaviour on human rights and other issues. Instead of taking these pressures at face value, the Chinese see them as interference or worse, as part of a campaign to subvert them. A question that arises for FPA is how important domestic factors, such as internal politics, remain relative to international or systemic factors in determining foreign policies. The importance of these factors in the different contexts and states is also a significant subject of debate. In foreign policy analysis, the role of internal politics in foreign policy established that China's internal experiences ongoing fragility and its democratic base is rather tenuous, yet it exercises tremendous power and influence in its sub-region, in Africa and on the global stage.[197]

One of the greatest lessons the Nigerian civil war had for its foreign policy was the futility of relying almost exclusively on its traditional friends and allies in the west, especially Great Britain and the US. Right from independence, Nigeria had come to see Britain as an external friend. Nothing encapsulates this notion better than Sir Abubakar's independence speech in which he spoke of the British "whom we know always as friends."[198]

Nigeria was rapidly Pro-British in its foreign policy orientations. It was with this confident perspective that the British were always friendly that the Nigeria Federal authority approached the British for military assistance to prosecute the war. Nigeria's expectation and requests were turned down.[199] Nigeria learnt a significant lesson that in foreign relations, there are no permanent friends or foes, only permanent interests. In the face of this unbelievable and painful British disappointment, Nigeria's turn to America also proved unproductive. Embattled at home and betrayed by her traditional friends in the west at a most crucial hour of need, the federal government had to approach the Soviets for military assistance.[200] This move was really a significant one compelled by the circumstances of the times.

---

196   Ibid, (2004), p.327
197   Adebajo and Mustapha, (2008), p. 132
198   Fawole, (2003), p. 62
199   Ibid, (2003), p. 2
200   Ibid, (2002), p. 12

Prior to that time, Nigeria had been so fanatically anti-communist that it banned the importation, sale and circulation of any type of communist literature in Nigeria in the 1960s. While the freedom of movement of British and American diplomats was unfettered, those of the Soviets were monitored.[201] This was largely the situation when Nigeria became compelled by the circumstance of the civil war to change her policy towards the Soviet Union. A seller-buyer symbolic relationship immediately developed between the two countries. The supply of weapons was accompanied by deployment of soviet military and other technical personnel to train Nigerians in the handling and use of these weapons. Consequently, Nigeria's landscape began to experience the influx of Soviet nationals. The restrictions on the number of their embassy personnel no longer held and neither could their movement be curtailed anywhere. Put simply, domestic politics are seen in this case to matter either by causing states to pursue suboptimal foreign policies, or when the differences in states, political institutions, cultures, economic structures, or leadership goals unrelated to relative power are causally relevant to explaining different foreign policy choices.[202]

5.1.2 Geography

A country's topography exercises an important influence on its foreign policy.[203] It provides opportunities as it imposes limitations on what is feasible both in domestic and foreign policy programmes. Its location, topography, terrain, climate, size, population and distribution of natural resources will not only affect the socio-economic development within the country, but also determine the country's needs in relation to other states as well as access to other areas of the world. Whether a country is landlocked, located in an arid, tropical or polar region, or has long coastlines or long borders with many neighbouring states signals an important implication for a country's foreign policy.

It determines the national goals and aspirations and hence is one of the most potent factors influencing the formulation of the foreign policy. Geographical factors, like the size and the location of a country and its natural resources contributes to the power of the nation, which in turn shapes its foreign policy. Although geography was and remains to be an important factor in foreign policy yet in recent years, owing to scientific and technological advancement its importance is receding. However, it does not mean that geography has

---

201   Fawole, (2003), p. 3
202   Fearon, (1998), p. 302
203   Partowazar, Jawan & Soltani, (2014), p.338

lost its importance altogether, it still plays a significant role. Soviet Union's historic concern about the East European countries is because of geography and the USA's deep involvement in South American States is again because of geographical proximity.

5.1.3 Form of Government

Foreign policy formulation in a democratic country is different and involves different democratic entities and actors than in other types of governments. Democratic leaders have to respond to the public and political parties and build a foreign policy based on their input. According to liberal theory, because of differences in the government organization, the behaviour of a democratic state is more peaceful than authoritarian systems.[204]

In a democracy, even if a leader is leaning towards a certain foreign policy, he has to convince other role players and justify the military and economic consequences. Democratic institutions create a political culture that is built on finding a peaceful solution for problems.[205] In a democratic system, citizens know that they can solve their disagreements peacefully. On the other hand, authoritarian leaders are the sole decisionmakers. They make their decisions without any constraints. Both democracies and authoritarian governments can involve and initiate the conflict. Democracies seldom fight other democracies. Scholars follow this idea that democratic cultural values and institutional constraints make democratic foreign policy different. However, the evidence does not support the theory that democracies are more peaceful in their foreign policies.[206] On the other hand, it is not always true that authoritarian leaders act without any limitations. These leaders also have to deal with groups or entities such as military that might disagree. In authoritarian systems, citizens cannot remove their leaders from office through voting processes. However, they can use alternative measures such as supporting non-governmental opposition groups, military coups, assassinations, and revolutions.

Newly formed authoritarian regimes encounter opposition and do not have enough control.[207] They therefore have to take public opinion into consideration. Some countries have serious economic, religious, and ethnic domestic diversities that can reduce the state's legitimacy. The leaders of these states may utilize foreign policy to make statements on national identity, show strong leadership, or distract attention away from domestic issues. In some

204   Henrikson, (2013), p.122
205   Ibid, (2013), p.126
206   Kotur, (2010), p.22
207   Henrikson, (2013), p.131

authoritarian states, foreign policy decisions are made based on mutual opinion of a group and no single leader controls it. Significant differences exist between the organizations of democratic and authoritarian governments. However, it is possible that the differences between the foreign policy of democratic and authoritarian states have been exaggerated. Actual decision-making authority in democracies may be not as diverse as it is assumed. Citizens in a democracy are not usually well rehearsed on political issues and cannot affect foreign policy.[208] Foreign policy decisions typically are centralized at the top of the government's hierarchy. The second feature of government organizations that affect foreign policy is bureaucracy. Bureaucracy includes collecting information, forming proposals, providing consults, reinforcing policy, and making foreign policy decisions. In international politics, because of the complexities in many problems, governments are organized bureaucratically, assigning responsibility to various areas or jurisdictions of policy to different agencies or departments. Separate agencies are responsible for diplomatic relationships and various parts of the military.

Dealing with a complex world requires bureaucratic organization that can also cause problems.[209] Different parts of the system may have disparity in the application of the same opinion. Departments might be acting on their own which may create inconsistencies in the execution of national foreign policy. It could also affect decision-making processes that may not be well considered for destruction or benefit of the state. These kinds of issues might be rooted in bureaucratic organization of the government, which occurs less frequently in certain circumstances. However, bureaucracy exists in all states. Moreover, sometimes a single leader or single unifying force can ratify the decision-making of the system. On some matters there is a common ground between all entities that overrules the differences and unifies the system. In some critical situations, top leaders mostly override the system and lower the effects of bureaucratic politics.

The kind of organization that should determine Africa governmental foreign policymaking and decision-making process domestically as well as internationally should have competent human resources. In execution of these processes, two characteristics are particularly important for the formulation and execution of national foreign policy: democratization and bureaucratization. The foreign policy process is quite different for democracies' decision-making authority because it tends to be diffused across democratic institutions, and thus more actors are involved. In contrast, authoritarian leaders often make decisions by themselves. Democratic leaders are also directly accountable to

---

208   Glenn and Susskind, (2010), p.212
209   Berridge, (2005), p.81

political parties; the public and must therefore build a consensus for foreign policy. Authoritarian leaders do not face these constraints and may enjoy considerable latitude in choosing their own policies.

These leaders are accountable to a public that is often more concerned with economic than military issues. Furthermore, democratic institutions are built on and create a political culture that is likely to emphasize the value of peaceful resolution. In a democracy, citizens learn that conflicts of interest can be resolved non-violently through elections, peaceful means of influence, or in the courts. They transfer that value to their relations with other states. The differences between making foreign policy in democratic and authoritarian governments may be exaggerated. Actually, the decision-making authority may not be as diffuse or constrained in authoritarian regimes because citizens are often not well informed, and their influence over foreign policy is debatable. Furthermore, foreign policy decisions, unlike most domestic policy decisions, are often highly centralized at the top of a government's hierarchy.

Although citizens in Africa cannot vote their leaders out of office, they do have other means of holding leaders accountable, including forming or pledging allegiance to non- governmental groups who oppose the authoritarian leader and espouse a change of government, as well as starting a non-violent revolution. The leaders of South Sudan have a great opportunity to use foreign policy as a reagent of building national identity, demonstrating strong leadership, or diverting attention away from internal problems. African's foreign policy systems should not be left to few elites from the Presidency or the Ministry of Foreign Affairs and Parliamentary Group to control foreign policy. Decisions should be made collectively to promote South Sudan's image regionally and globally.

5.1.4 Leadership

The person or individuals who are the head of government have the ability to make decisions on foreign policy.[210] A leader's characteristics become more a focus of attention when they have more power in forming foreign policy and performing in unpredictable situations. In these situations, the personality and value system of the leader plays an important role in forming the state's behaviour. In other words, the leader's uprising and personal life experiences play an important role in their political behaviour.[211] We assert that since every leader has a unique personal background, in coping with foreign policy problems they use their values, beliefs and experiences.

---

210   Partowazar, Jawan & Soltani, (2014), p.351
211   Marikje, B (2007), Pp.27-35

In spite of differences, different people prefer to ignore facts in order to sustain consistency in their beliefs. When leaders see another country as their enemy, their opinion gets biased about the information they gather about that country. As a result, changes in images and impressions of the enemy are very difficult even with changes in the enemy's behaviour. According to their images and behaviours, leaders can be subtyped in different groups. The first group looks for conflict and domination. The second group looks for acceptance and cooperation. The third type can be nationalist, with lack of trust and belief in the use of power to solve their issues. The last group considers their state as a part of the world community and tries to solve the problems with trust. The style of a leader's decision-making and how they handle information and the people around them is important. Some leaders try to be active in foreign policy decision-making; others authorize other centres of power to make foreign policy decisions. Additionally, some leaders come with an agenda for foreign policy and show lack of flexibility to any changes or accepting others' opinions.[212] Others try to maintain their power and are selfish in their foreign policy formulation. They pay attention to advice and do not make any decision without consultation and consensus. A leader may belong to one of these groups but that does not mean that a leader cannot change the group he belongs to. Change in the type of leadership can be due to experience.

A top leader who directs affairs of the country and leads the nation and Africa is not an exception. At the top of every government sits a leader who has the authority to make foreign policy. Characteristics of leaders are generally more important when they have significant latitude in shaping foreign policy especially when the situation is uncertain, ambiguous, or complex. Under these conditions, which occur frequently in foreign policymaking, a leader's personality and beliefs may shape what the state does. The decision may be shaped by his personal history, childhood or early political experiences, or teachings that certain values and ways of handling problems are important. Since every leader's personal history is unique, one might expect each individual to draw on a particular set of beliefs, values, and experiences in coping with foreign policy issues. Despite their individual differences, all humans prefer to be consistent in their beliefs, and studies show we often ignore or distort information that contradicts what we already believe. This is especially likely when we have strongly held stereotypes or "images" of other countries. Leaders who see another country as their enemy, for example, will often selectively attend to or perceive information about that country in a way that confirms their original belief. We can categorize leaders into types of personalities. Some

---

212   Partowazar, Jawan & Soltani, (2014), p.344

leaders may be motivated by a need to dominate others and may thus be more conflict-focused in foreign policy; others may be more concerned with being accepted, and may therefore be more cooperative. Some leaders are more nationalistic, more distrustful, and believe that the world is a place of conflict that can only be solved by force, whereas others see themselves and their state as part of the world community that can be trusted and believe that problems are best solved multilaterally/collectively.

Leaders' decision-making styles and how they manage information and the people around them can be important. Some leaders are crusaders who come to office with a foreign policy goal/agenda. They tend not to compromise on their vision and are less open to advice. Others are interested in keeping power or bridging conflicts. They tend to be sensitive to advice and are reluctant to make decisions without consultation and consensus.

5.1.5 Public Opinion

Public opinion refers to the citizenry's attitudes especially about the problems in foreign policy. Society may agree or have different opinions on an issue. The average individual is usually not too interested in foreign affairs. Leaders usually do not pay attention to public opinion on foreign policy. Leaders try to shape public opinion towards their own desired form or dismiss opinion altogether. Evidence shows that leaders who do not consider public opinion usually do not suffer in polls because in elections, domestic policy takes priority to foreign policy. The media have a significant effect on the public-state relationship. It can affect public opinion on foreign policy. There is a correlation between changes in public opinion and changes in foreign policy. In some special cases of foreign policy decisions, leaders are paying attention to public reactions. Although in foreign policy the public does not formulate specific stable opinions, they have more long-lasting core values or opinion moods.[213] A country's identity and its perception of its role in the world in relations with other countries form strong opinions in society. Leaders must stay within these expectations or face public opposition. Similar to public opinion, identity and role of a specific policy can be shaped by elites and utilized to support specific foreign policy positions. In reality, most research on public opinion focuses on promotion of democratic values.[214]

Democracies have established mechanisms for the public opinion's influence on leaders. In authoritarian political systems, the public does not have any

---

213   Partowazar, Jawan & Soltani, (2014), p.349
214   Ibid, p.351

influence on foreign policy. In this system, the core values held by the public may set boundaries. Authoritarian systems might be built on foreign policy orientations. Therefore, basic values and character of a society are rooted in traditions and common opinions of that society. These draw the big picture of foreign policy. These values can be individualism, collectivism, pragmatism, or moralism. Cultures with high moral values can be judgmental in internal and foreign policies. Cultures also influence the mechanism through which foreign policy decisions are made. This sometimes might prolong the decision-making process, for example by the process of public consultation. In spite of the usual opinion that cultural characteristics do not affect policies, it is difficult to measure the influence of culture on foreign policy.[215] A good foreign policy for a country should be shaped by public opinion. However, not many countries in the world put emphasis on public opinion when formulating foreign policy.

In this book, public opinion has been defined as the attitudes citizens have about particular foreign policy issues. The citizens of any country in Africa have rights and privileges to agree on an issue or be deeply divided over foreign policy issues affecting them internally and externally. For example, the public may be for or against their state intervening militarily in another country or signing a particular trade agreement such as joining the East Africa Community. Scholars have continued to debate the impact of public opinion on foreign policy, even in highly democratized states in which policy supposedly reflects the will of the people.

Based on findings of this study, the conventional wisdom is that the public simply does not influence foreign policy in Africa. The average person tends to know little and care little about his or her country's foreign affairs. Even if the public were knowledgeable about foreign policy issues, it is not clear that leaders would follow their opinion. They may instead try to lead the public opinions that are in line with their preferences or ignore their opinion altogether. The media also play a role in the relationship between the public and the state, as they, too, may influence public opinion on foreign policy.

However, the question of public opinion and foreign policy may be more complicated than this conventional wisdom implies. Some researchers have revealed that there is more congruence than sceptic assumption between changes in public opinion and changes in foreign policy. For example, research on African foreign policy decision-making showed that leaders were not sensitive to public reactions. As with public opinion on a specific policy, identity and role may be constructed by elites and used to support particular foreign

---

215   Ibid, p.350

policy positions.[216] The government of South Sudan should take core values and national identity as a society's political culture by promoting the values, norms, and traditions that are widely shared by its people and are relatively endured over time. These enduring cultural features may also set parameters for foreign policy. A country's culture may value individualism, collectivism, pragmatism, or moralism, and these culturally based values may affect foreign policy. Cultures that place a premium on morality over practicality may be more likely to pass moral judgment over the internal affairs and foreign policy behaviours of others. Culture also affects the way foreign policy is determined. Cultures where consensual decision-making is the norm, for example, may take longer to make policy, because the process of consultation with many people may be just as important as the final decision.

5.1.6 Social Groups

Leaders focus on societal group inputs more than the whole society because societal groups can connect the society to the state and could oppose or compete with the state. Interest groups represent a particular sector of society and are able to activate that sector on demand. Interest groups have different forms built on a single objective such as ethnicity, religion or economics. Economic interest groups can be a significant societal source of foreign policy because these groups produce wealth and economic welfare, which is the primary function of modern states. In order to promote their foreign business adventures abroad or to protect markets from competitors internally, economic groups have an interest in foreign relations.

An interest group's leverage on a foreign policy depends on the level of that group's organization.[217] Relationships between the state and the interest groups can have an influence on foreign policy. Interest groups struggle to influence the government when the government is not in agreement with them. The government has more ability to affect the problem and control public awareness of the issue. By depending on the political system, the government has political support from the public. Both globalisation and liberalization have increased the number of economic groups which have an interest in foreign policy of states.[218] This increases the capability of these groups to influence foreign policy.

Political parties, as a part of the government, are able to communicate societal opinion to political leadership. The function of parties in many ways

---

216   Abraham, Ph.D. Thesis, (2017)
217   Berridge, (2005), p.56
218   Partowazar, Jawan & Soltani, (2014), p.353

is similar to interest groups. In some countries, only one party can dominate the political system, and the ideology of that party can be important in setting limitations to debate over foreign policy stands and in forming rhetoric for leaders' speeches.[219] In such countries, some sections of parties enjoy a more important role. In political systems, factions can be important when a party has the majority of parliament and rules alone. Party factions try to dominate each other or they have to make compromises for party unity. Even when in a party, and there is agreement over an issue, foreign policy can be influenced by differences inside the party.

In a fragmented multi-party-political system, factions remain important.[220] However, competition between the parties becomes important too. Parties try to distinguish themselves from each other ideologically in vying for the public's support, thereby polarizing the debate over foreign policy. Or, in order to capture the moderates, they try to move toward the centre of the political spectrum that often decides elections. In some multiparty systems, parties must enter into coalitions and share power to make policy because the political scene is fragmented. For example, policy leaders are more likely to pay attention to, and react to, the opinions of specific, organized societal groups than to society at large, as they play the role of linking society to the state or of opposing and competing with the state. Interest groups articulate a particular societal sector's position, mobilize that sector to pressure, and persuade the government. Interest groups come in a variety of forms. An interest group's influence on foreign policy often depends on the particular issue, how organized the group is, and the relationship between the interest group and the government.

5.1.7 Public Diplomacy

There are many ways Africa should utilize public opinion in promotion of foreign policy regionally and globally. The fact that the world is politically, economically as well as socially competitive and complex makes public diplomacy an essential tool for actively promoting African image, values and culture abroad. The African states' foreign policies approach therefore should embrace use of available technologies and platforms, especially social media networks to communicate with stakeholders on the country's foreign policy. Africa also should continue to provide institutional support and capacity-building in the region through regional technical cooperation programs by establishing a Regional Technical Cooperation Fund to be managed by the Ministries of Foreign Affairs.

---

219   Melissen, (2005), p.68
220   Partowazar, Jawan & Soltani, (2014), p.347

5.1.8 National Capacity

It refers to the military strength/preparedness of the state, its technological advancement and modern means of communication. The economic development and enlightened political institutions are also associated with the national capacity. National capacity is a significant factor that determines and implements foreign policy. In fact, the foreign policy of states is directly associated with their national capacity. If the state increases its national capacity, it will strive to achieve a status of distinction in international relations; if it decreases the state will have to compromise with its poor status. For example, at the end of Second World War Britain became a less powerful state in Europe as well as in the world. This change in national capacity has brought overwhelming diversions in British Foreign Policy.

5.1.9 The Political Organization

The internal political structure of a country has an important impact upon the country's approach to international affairs, as is evident from a comparison of the decision-making processes in an absolute monarchy or a dictatorship on the one hand and in a parliamentary democracy on the other. A despotic government has greater power, through censorship and the promulgation of regulations, to prevent the expression of undesirable opinions than a free government does. Indeed, the distinguishing mark of a free government is the very freedom allowed the citizens to express their options on public policy, domestic or foreign. The quality of government depends upon a number of factors, such as support extended to it by the population, the organization of the government, the quality of persons serving the government, willingness of the government to take the aspirations of the general people into account.

5.2 International Factors Influencing Foreign Policy

The foreign policy of a country becomes very critical when leaders are willing to make alliance with another independent country to enhance the security of both countries. For effectiveness of Africa's foreign policy conduct, the following factors are vital.

The very nature and aim of foreign policy make the process of its decision making susceptible to influences external to the state. The international system to which foreign policies are directed is composed of foreign independent states, entities over which the initiating state has no authority or jurisdiction.

Decisionmakers must therefore be constantly aware of interests of other actors in the system. Sufficient account must be taken of what these actors have done, are doing, or are likely to do in the future in response to a particular policy in question.

Account also has to be taken of the relative capabilities of interacting entities. Changes in the international power structure could bring about fundamental changes in the objectives and actions of states.[221] Apart from international power configuration, the structures of international economic relations also affect the options available to states.

The first major factor that affects foreign policy internationally is international law. The existence of international law and international ethical norms acts in greater or lesser degree to limit the freedom of states to manoeuvre within the system. It is true that international law is in many respects different from domestic law: It does not flow from the enactment of a body with authority to make laws like legislatures, and it is not enforceable like domestic law. It is mainly constituted by agreements among states on the conventions that are to guide states' mutual relations. Nevertheless, states in their own interests do observe these laws and norms most of the time, despite the absence of an enforcement agency.

Another factor on the international front that affects foreign policy is international organizations. A country's foreign policy option is also often affected by its membership in international organizations. The existence of many of these institutions, which are established for a variety of reasons ranging from cultural to economic and political-strategic, is a major feature of the post-1945 international system.[222] Member states' policies are usually affected by the nature of the particular institution and its policy objectives on the one hand, and the effect of their institutional membership on the policies of other states towards them on the other hand. However, the degree to which member states' policies are affected by their membership is a function of value attached to a particular membership of the organization. But if it is a military alliance, member states' policies are generally affected and even determined by the constitution of the alliance.

5.2.1 Regional integration

Regional integration has become a major avenue for enhancing foreign policy of any country all over the world and South Sudan is not an exception. It is

---

221   Partowazar, Jawan & Soltani, (2014), p.329
222   Garrison, (2001), p.793

an advantage for South Sudan to be a member of regional institutions such as the East African Community (EAC), Inter Governmental Authority on Development (IGAD), Common Market for Eastern and Southern Africa (COMESA) and the African Union (AU) as a principal avenue for pursuing its foreign policy goals. Therefore, regional integration should continue to be one of the cornerstones of South Sudan Foreign Policy for stability and increase of trade among others. Below is the highlight on few regional organizations associated with South Sudan in promotion of her foreign policy.

5.2.2 International Organizations

The issue of human rights abuses by the government of South Sudan beginning from its assumption of power had been raised as a great concern by various humanitarian and other international organizations locally, regionally and globally. The repeated accusations directed against government for indiscriminate civilian targets in the country, recruiting minors for military service especially the local militias against the backing of government, disbanding organizations and purging individuals opposed to it, and interfering with the delivery of food relief shipments has resulted in discrediting the regime. This contributed to the isolation of the country. The imprisonment without justice by the government on the civil population was also raised by these international organizations as a grave violation of human rights.

In addition to this, Amnesty International together with African Rights, a London based-humanitarian organization, launched a campaign against human rights violations and severely criticized the Government of South Sudan for these violations. Since this western international organization's campaign against the South Sudan government has been damaging her international image, it could be difficult for the government, which was seriously seeking the support of the West to establish sustainable close relations when the criticism was at its height.

Thus, while relations between international organizations, both MNCs and humanitarians, have been mainly determining factors related to national interests of western countries, the assessment of international organizations regarding the situations in South Sudan had impacts on the relations with home countries.

The international organizations have started playing important role in foreign policy formulation. The states have to take a note of international law, treaties and contracts so that their violation may not jeopardize the policies. The Communist China, for a long time, showed utter disregard of these factors and consequently could not secure its due position in the field of international relations. Only after 1971 she recognized their importance and that move on the part of Communist China have introduced new dimensions in international politics.

5.2.3 The Nature of the International System

Policymakers of different nations perceive major structural changes in the international political system in almost the same way, and through a series of gathered information tend to modify their states' foreign policies to fit that structure. For instance, in a "polar" structure, policymakers of some newly independent countries have calculated that their security can best be achieved by alliance with one military bloc leader or other, without an option of neutrality. Thus, they are compelled by conditions in the international political system to either be on the side of the US or the USSR to safeguard their national security interest in order to survive as nations.

Margaret G. Hermann, Charles F. Hermann and Joe D. Hagan (1987)[223] in "How Decision Units shape foreign policy Behaviour have observed that "although we recognize that numerous domestic and international factors can and do influence foreign policy behaviour, these influences must be channeled through the political apparatus of a government which identifies, decides and implements foreign policy. This political apparatus of a government is the foreign policy decision making system. Thus, the foreign policy decision making systems of a state requires understanding about its foreign policy dynamics."

The nature of the decision structures affects the nature of the decision process, which in turn affects foreign policy conclusions. Decision structures can provide a predominant leader with a small subordinate and pliable staff; an authoritative leader with individuals who have some autonomy and independence; an authoritative leader with individuals who represent the views of some bureaus or groups; and a small or large group of individuals who represents the views of some outside entities to which the belong. In an African context, it should be noted that these different decision structures result in different decision processes in terms of independence of decisions and speed to reach decisions.

The establishments of friendly and cooperative relations between nations are the aims of a sound foreign policy; the complexity of task arises from the very nature of international politics. The multiplicity of attitudes and their interactions apart the difficulty of conducting foreign policy arise from the fact that a state has no sure means of controlling the behaviour of other

---

223   Margaret G. Hermann, Charles F. Hermann and Joe D. Hagan, p. 309

sovereign states. It can persuade, promise or deny economic and military aid, it can threaten another state with the use of force and, nevertheless, it cannot be certain the state will act in the way it desires. There is another source of difficulty. The world is continuously changing, new events and personalities create fresh foreign policy problems for all concerned. To select instances at random, the impact of the October Revolution of 1917, the rise of Communist Power in China in 1949, the rise of De Gaulle to power in France in the fifties and the emergence of new states in Asia and Africa since Foreign Ministers of the time. Yet it has been rightly said that there is both continuity and change in the foreign policies of all states, for every nation also has its history and its traditions.

5.2.4 Reactions of Other States

The states have to take notice of the interests of other states while formulating their policies. They will never endeavour to pursue those interests which are totally opposed to the fundamental interests of other states. Hitler in 1939 committed a blunder when he refused to be guided by the British reactions and events ahead with his Polish invasion. The result is well known. Japan's failure in assessing American reactions in Pearl Harbour incident again brought disaster to Japanese policy which had intelligently avoided offending the USA up to that period.

5.2.5 World Public Opinion

World public opinion is very dynamic element. Like a flicker of light it influences the foreign policies only too occasionally. Only if the domestic public opinion supports the world public opinion it becomes an important determinant of foreign policy. The establishment of democratic institutions, the increase in the standard of living, the scourge of First World War and expansion of education have made the world public opinion a significant factor in foreign policy. The States never dare pursue the interests contrary to world public opinion. At least they will pursue only those interests which are not opposed to world public opinion.

CHAPTER SIX

FOREIGN POLICY INGREDIENTS: FORMULATION AND CONDUCT

This chapter explores how states formulate and execute foreign policy to suit national interest. Scholars have described foreign policy as a pattern of behaviour that one state adopts in relation with other states, an idea that other scholars consider as the strategy and tactics employed by the state in its relation with other states in the international system. Foreign policy is thus a plan or program of actions of a state, which determines the sum-total of the state's objectives in the international system. Put differently, they are the actions of a state toward the external environment and the conditions under which such actions are formulated. This seems to agree with Henry Kissinger's often quoted submission that in foreign policy analysis, the domestic structure is taken as given, as foreign policy begins where domestic policy ends. Simply, foreign policy could mean the external attitude of a state. The ultimate goal is to maximize greater advantage for the country. To this end, the foreign policy of developing countries like Africa should be geared towards national economic development to gain better leverage in international politics.

6.1 Formulation of Foreign Policy

The foreign policy of a state is what it actually does in its relations with other states. That end product, however, is shaped by various factors. There is the initial task of deciding what to do and how to do it. The analysis and judgment required for this purpose are considered herein. Then there is the job of marshalling the necessary support and resources to carry out the selected course.[224] The proposed policy may require appropriations, legislation, or other action by authorities in a state that have been mandated to sanction such policies. It may depend on allied approval, co-operation and stage of executing the policy.[225] In its own way, each of the phases has a part in shaping the eventual policy. Proposals as initially framed may take into account anticipated responses of different state authorities, public opinion, or support from stakeholder nations, but they may have to be modified in the course of obtaining the requisite support and co-operation.

It is important to indicate that the process of foreign policy formulation is complex and dynamic.[226] This is observed by the fact that the process has many actors that need to be considered and the factors continually change over time. It is therefore important to point out the reasons which make the formulation of foreign policy such a difficult and complex task. The fundamental reason is that it must deal primarily with external conditions that will prevail in an uncertain future, and over which, at best, any one nation has limited control or influence. The basic task of any nation is to decide how to use its resources and influence to modify and shape her foreign policy. The process of foreign policy formulation involves at least three factors which influence and act upon each other.

6.1.1 Policy Establishment

The process taken in formulation of Africa's foreign policy, therefore, should determine the execution technique. The best practice in the field of foreign policy shows poor policymaking resulted into uncoordinated foreign policy conduct. This section examines some key approaches in Africa's foreign policymaking process such as routine policies, crisis policies, and intermestic policies as herein.

---

224   Krumbein, (2014), p.325
225   Bidabad, (2012), p.191
226   Mintz and DeRouen, (2010), p.453

6.1.1.1 Routine Policies

This aspect of policy is of concurrent nature. According to this kind of role conception in foreign policymaking, Africa should resolve routine issues through diplomatic channels. In contrast with the previously mentioned crisis policy, such policies give Africa an opportunity to confront other states diplomatically for compromise to be reached in achieving both states' national interest. No state can ignore altogether the demands and desires of its own neighbour. These national demands, when aggregated, should be given weightage while formulating policies.

6.1.1.2 Crisis Policies

These kinds of policies are formulated by the state because of an unanticipated situation in which one's interests are threatened. There is little time to decide what to do. States confront crisis in their relations when they misperceive each other's self-interest and tend to be hardliners in conflict resolution. To illustrate the African context, in 2015, the government of South Sudan succumbed to international pressure to sign the agreement on resolution of conflict in South Sudan. This made the government accept the conditions set in the peace agreement with some reservation.

Their policies in such an environment may be either of standoff or of coercion. Pressures and the policies of the adversaries also influence the foreign policy at large are similar. A state today is not immune from environmental pressures, whether emanating from within or thrust upon it from the external orbit. While fixing its options or priorities, the policymaker in South Sudan should therefore try to convince or accommodate his adversaries.

6.1.1.3 Intermestic Policies

The role of intermestic policies in the formulation and conduct of Africa's foreign policy is the intermingling of domestic and inter-state interests. Policies need to be designed for mutual confidence-building by developing a conducive domestic environment. Regardless, the state gives response either in crisis or routine situations. It is, therefore, important to analyse the concept of national interests. The basic objective of any state's foreign policy is to secure its national interests because the national interest is the key concept in foreign policy. National interest is the general and continuing end for which the nation or state acts, and South Sudan is not an exception in the conduct of foreign policy within the international system.

6.1.2 Appraisal of the Present External Situation

This first factor deals with situation analysis and appraisal of the present external situation as well as the course of its development.[227] Formulators of the policy should scrutinize the environment in which foreign policy is conducted. In large part, this estimation involves both effort to predict the interests, purposes, and actions of other states and the impact of their differing motivations and actions on them and on each other.

However, the ability of policymakers to competently predict and analyse the external situation varied. Some leaders are very capable in monitoring and scanning the external environment and hence having policies that are effectively placed towards enhancing the state's interest in the international arena. On the contrary, it is expected that some policymakers will have deficiencies in both gathering and analysing external information and hence will be very incompetent in predicting future outcome and reactions of other states. This therefore explains why various leaders will follow very different policy directions when faced with similar circumstances. Consequently, in assessing the environment, the policymakers must start with some conceptions of national interests and purposes in order to consider how they may be threatened or impeded.[228] Similarly, the appraisal must seek to determine the ways in which the situation is subject to influence both by national actions and by the actions of friendly or hostile powers. The effort to determine the basic direction of policy of countries in Africa involves a comparable analysis. The broadest aims of policy, like security and prosperity, may be treated as given. But practical objectives must be chosen in the light of external conditions and the means available to the nation.[229] The policymaker must be concerned both with what is necessary and what is feasible.

6.1.3 Policy Objective

The second factor relates to objectives that should guide the policy.[230] In its broadest sense, the aim of a state's foreign policy is to create and maintain external conditions congenial to the state's way of life and values. To provide a basis for action, however, this general purpose must be made more specific in terms of security, economic activities, and other such values held by the state. Also, relative priorities must be established among these interests. On

---

227   Damodaran, (1987), p.56
228   Fettweis, (2013), p.171
229   Mintz and DeRouen, (2010), p.461
230   Fettweis, (2013), p.112

this factor, it is expected that some leaders will follow priorities that have the welfare of the state in mind while others will follow selfish interest that have their own welfare and survival in mind. This explains why some leaders make sub-optimal policy decisions even when information and future states were more or less evident.

6.1.4 Choice of Means

Finally, there is the choice of means.[231] There are many instruments which a nation can conceivably use to influence the outside world such as the military, political activities, economic measures, propaganda, and various other ways. The state should decide which of these are most suitable for attaining a specific purpose and how best they could be used. Resources are seldom large enough to allow the use of all possible means in an indiscriminate way. In deciding on the means, policymakers have various factors to consider and a lot of factors come into play. These factors cannot be treated separately; they are all interrelated and influence each other.[232] It is not feasible to study them one at a time. For instance, when considering the question of appraising the external situation, there must be objective analysis for it to be useful. The assessment must be objective, but it cannot be passive. The policymaker should not look at conditions as a bystander, but as one of the actors. The purpose therefore, is not merely to anticipate history but to assess how future forces and events may affect the interests and purposes of the nation. The situation is similar with respect to means. In deciding what instruments to create and utilize, the policymaker must take into account both what objectives he wishes to accomplish and what methods he deems most likely to be effective in influencing the external environment. However, this does not always happen and that is the reason why many countries, mostly developing ones, have foreign policies that do not perpetuate their national interest.

The task of any foreign policy analyst is to solve an equation with three variables, which affect each other. Moreover, none of these factors is neat or precise: They all involve large elements of prediction, appraisal, judgment, and choice. Anyone who has been charged with trying to cope with such analysis cannot fail to be impressed with the uncertainty inherent in the process. In evaluating future policies, the decisions regarding conditions, purposes, and means pose many baffling dilemmas and alternatives.[233] As historians and

---

231   Mintz and DeRouen , (2010), p.186
232   Clinton, (2014), p.87
233   Mintz and DeRouen, (2010), p.76

columnists have discovered, second-guessing on foreign policy is much easier and less risky than its initial formulation. Time and events remove most of the uncertainties and foreclose many of the alternatives which the policymaker had to face and choose between.

6.2 Conduct of Foreign Policy

This section reviews the practices and systems that are applied by states to promote diplomatic relations. Discussed herein include small state diplomacy, public relations, soft power and monetary diplomacy.

6.2.1 Small State Diplomacy

For small and medium-sized states, public diplomacy represents an opportunity to gain influence and shape international agenda in ways that go beyond their limits. Resources in relation to size, military and economic strength shape national foreign policy. Despite such a potential of public diplomacy for small and medium-sized states, the literature on public diplomacy has been dominated by accounts on major powers.[234]

A major challenge for small and medium-sized states is receiving recognition by the rest of the world for who they claim to be. Foreign perceptions of small and medium-sized states are usually characterized by lack of information and at best by long-established stereotypes. This applies not only to the perceptions of small states by societies of major powers or to perceptions of small states by societies on the other side of the globe, but also to perceptions by societies immediately neighbouring each other. In their conduct of public diplomacy, small and medium-sized states face a different set of challenges than major powers. One U.S. practitioner of public diplomacy reflected upon the issue indicating that a major power is going to be the subject of discussion and controversy no matter what it does.[235]

Generally, the smaller powers do not enter the global public discussion unless a crisis or scandal envelops them.[236] However, it may seem to be the events that attract the global media and interest the mass audiences to which they catered. Perhaps it is for this very reason that small powers need public diplomacy programs just as major powers do. The task for the smaller powers is to be heard on the stories that matter to them, to explain their positions

---

234   Nye, (2008), p. 105
235   Leonard and Small , (2003), p.1
236   Nye, (2004), p.22

and aspirations during the non-crisis moments, and to do so in a way that captures attention.[237] For large countries like the United States, the United Kingdom or China, public diplomacy is mainly focused on changing images and re-branding. However, public diplomacy of small states should be focused on invisibility.

A further difference between the public diplomacy of major powers and that of small and medium-sized states is related to the volume or breadth of messages and images used in public diplomacy. While major powers usually have a broader cultural impact and a larger reservoir of messages and images that they represent and that represent them, the smaller countries, those who have been successful in getting an international profile, usually focus their public diplomacy efforts at a few niche-areas. Norway is a case in point with its strongly promoted profile as an international peace-broker.[238] While such orientation on a few niche messages and values enables small states to capture attention, it also has to do with the more general foreign policy tendency of small and medium-sized states to concentrate their scarce resources on a few niche areas which provide them with comparative advantages in international affairs.[239]

Finally, another difference is related to what might be termed outset legitimacy. While major powers usually dispose considerable hard power resources and their national interests are therefore among other features also defined in military terms, a number of small and medium-sized countries have managed to define their national interest to include attractive causes such as attracting foreign direct investments, attracting tourists, peace-making or developmental aid.[240] Hence, some conceptualizations, for instance the concept of human security as a foreign policy priority, enabled the Ghanaian government to gain the support of numerous international NGOs and other small and medium-sized governments.[241] It is observed that Africa only appears in the global landscape when something bad like conflict happens. It is therefore important for foreign policymakers to ensure that the country is heard even during times that there was no conflict. This may portray the country in a positive light to the world. We observe that the first difference between the foreign policy of major powers and small states is related to its mission. Thus, while the efforts of the former are first and foremost focused on explaining, advocacy, and possibly re-branding, those of the latter are focused on capturing

---

237　　　Egeland, (1988), p.76
238　　　Nye. (2004), p.112
239　　　Cooper, (1997), p.44
240　　　Nye, (2004), p.9
241　　　Ibid, (2004), p.10

attention. However, elements of explaining and advocacy are present in the public diplomacy of small and medium-sized states, especially in times of crises.

6.2.2 Preventive Diplomacy

Preventive diplomacy is a term generally associated with specific functions of the United Nations (UN), as well as similar functions carried out by regional organizations associated with the UN and nongovernmental organizations.[242] Preventive diplomacy refers to a range of peaceful, problem-solving activities that aim to prevent violent conflict or to de-escalate emerging violence. Preventive diplomacy takes place prior to a dispute developing into armed conflict, at either an early stage in the process through early prevention, or through late prevention.[243] Prevention work involves both early warning mechanisms and early action. Early warning ensures that disputes are detected, analysed, and brought to the attention of those who will take useful action. Early action involves efforts to offer suggestions and support for averting violent conflict. Parties can be offered assistance with dispute resolution, encouragement to de-escalate tensions, new perspectives and successful models for resolving disputes, advice and support on methods for negotiating with the other party, referrals to a third-party mediator or facilitator, assistance with organizing meetings with technical experts or potential sources of economic assistance, and arranging arbitration or adjudication.[244] Preventive diplomacy can also involve directly mediation or facilitation between parties.[245]

Another preventive approach is to encourage and support parties in putting into practice confidence-building measures. These are often preliminary actions of one or more disputing parties that aim to break down the cycle of mistrust and lay a foundation for achieving more substantive agreements. In prevention efforts an important distinction is made between addressing proximal causes of conflict which may reduce violence in the short term, and addressing root causes of the conflict. Root causes are seen as the underlying structures and systems, or denial of basic human needs or rights, which lay the foundations for disputes and armed conflict to emerge repeatedly over time. These root causes can include unfair political systems, lack of good governance, weak states, discriminatory legal or economic processes, corruption, lack of voice, and marginalization of particular subgroups in society.

---

242   Peck, (1996), p.5
243   Jentleson, (2000), p.321
244   Peck, (1996), p.52
245   Biswaro, (2013).

However, though preventive diplomacy can be crucial for peaceful coexistence, one of the challenges of preventive diplomacy has been to develop early warning and early action mechanisms which do not raise Member State fears that they will receive unwanted attention or interference in their internal affairs.[246] Mechanisms need to exist which can allow preventive diplomacy to take place without eliciting these concerns. Moreover, there is the concern of regional bodies in preventive diplomacy.

6.2.3 Public Relations

This section links two developments in the public relations discipline. The first pertains to ways that public relations can help governments reach their foreign policy goals. The public relations scholarship has identified similarities between public relations and international relations bodies of knowledge.[247] Vujnovic and Kruckeberg provided theoretical suggestions about the role of public relations in foreign policy settings while Zhang and Benoit empirically investigated the link between public relations and the management of foreign affairs by governments. The second development that this work addresses is the conceptualization of public relations as a strategic management function by states.[248] According to the relational perspective, public relations add value to a country when this function strategically manages mutually beneficial relationships between an organization and its key constituencies.

The public relations scholarship has acknowledged that the function of public relations can help governments reach their foreign policy goals.[249] Similarities between public relations and foreign affairs have been discussed. For example, Signitzer and Coombs[250] compared the four models of public relations to the goals of cultural diplomacy. They suggested that public relations practitioners and diplomats perform similar functions: representation of their governments, negotiation and peace-making on behalf of their governments, counselling of the senior government officials, intelligence gathering, and environmental scanning in contexts that their governments operate. However, this traditional understanding of public relations does not sync with the context of Africa where public relations officials are seen as non-communicators and lack vital information on government decision making boards.[251]

---

246   Biswaro,(2000).
247   Signitzer and Wamser, (2006), p. 443
248   Ledingham. (2006), p. 476
249   Signitzer and Wamser, (2006), p. 439
250   Signitzer and Coombs, (1992), p. 140
251   Zhang, (2006), p. 41

Nevertheless, public relations literature has provided conceptual insights into ways that public relations can help governments reach their foreign policy goals.[252] It has been proposed that governments should practice public relations in a symmetrical manner. Governments can reach their goals through dialogue, collaboration and compromise.[253] However, to be able to apply public relations as a practice aimed at promoting diplomacy and foreign relations, governments must practice international public relations as a strategic management function that is an integral part of the overall governmental processes. Governments should use the situational theory of publics to learn about a country's strategic constituencies abroad. Signitzer and Wamser supported this view[254] by acknowledging that governments could employ public relations as a boundary-spanning function in order to understand their international environments. The two scholars believed that the public relations discipline could also provide governments with knowledge about the most effective channels of communication and ways that relationships can be built with publics of different nations.

However, in our view, public relations functions should exceed the publics who have direct consequences on the government, and include society at large. This is supported by a few empirical investigations into the link between public relations and foreign policy settings that have been conducted. Research on foreign embassies in Washington applied the excellence principles to policy advocacy function, finding that excellent policy advocacy is characterized by two-way communication, formative and evaluative research, symmetrical internal information exchanges, ethical communication, and involvement in a government's strategic management of foreign affairs.[255]

A significant portion of empirical studies has explored the media coverage of various foreign governments' publicity campaigns. The findings of these studies suggested that the mass media influences and mobilizes foreign public opinion. Zhang and Cameron[256] conducted a content analysis of several US national print media sources to measure the success of the Chinese government's image campaign in the USA. Wang and Chang[257] conducted a similar study to explore the local and national coverage of a Chinese head of state's visits to the USA. Zhang and Benoit [258] explored the Saudi government's image campaign and

252   Peterson, (2013), p.315
253   Grunig, (1993), p. 150
254   Signitzer and Wamser , (2006), p. 438
255   Yun, (2006), p. 301
256   Zhang and Cameron, (2003), p. 19
257   Wang and Chang , (2004), p. 23
258   Zhang and Benoit, (2004), p. 164

its effects on the US media after September 11. Zhang,[259] who studied the US media after the 2005 tsunami in Southeast Asia, suggested that countries around the world used international relief aid as a symbol that helped them to cultivate and maintain national identity and to facilitate state policy agendas.

The above-discussed empirical works on public relations contributions to the attainment of foreign policy goals has mostly approached public relations as a publicity function whose goal is to ensure media coverage abroad. These empirical studies differ from the conceptual scholarship that views public relations as a strategic management function that helps governments manage international affairs by facilitating dialogue and collaboration, scanning environments and spanning boundaries, identifying international publics, and building communities.[260] In our view, public relations as a practice by government is more important to a developing nation in Africa than it is for developed nations. This is because developing nations require not just support but even funding for their local and international policies. On the national level, public relations should seek the public's support for national policies.[261]

Further, the nation should extend public relations to the international level to indicate their accountability for the state's activities. To reach the goal of the public's support for foreign policies, public relations practitioners should produce press releases, videos and photos about developing countries for reporters, organize press conferences, commission programs for public television channels and create an update information about the state's foreign policies and projects for governmental web sites. It may be more important for a young country like Africa to develop its presence in several media houses where its policies are communicated.

6.2.4 Soft Power

The idea of soft power, developed by Joseph Nye,[262] was initially applied to US foreign policy. Its key premise can be defined as the ability to obtain what you want through co-option and attraction rather than the hard power of coercion and payment. In international politics, the soft power of a country rests primarily on its culture and its foreign policies when they are seen as legitimate and having moral authority. Political values are also significant, and in the case of the US, promotion of democracy could be considered as such.[263] However,

259   Zhang, (2006), p. 26
260   Vujnovic and Kruckeberg,, (2005), p. 340
261   Peterson, (2013), p.312
262   Nye (1990), p.15
263   Nye, (2004), p.76

there are various criticisms regarding legitimacy of the US in promoting its form of democracy to the world. Some critics see it as imperialism and trying to impose its ideologies on the rest of the world. The Capitol Hill events of 4th January, 2021, whereby the pro-President Trump supporters stormed into the House in order to stop certification of Joe Biden's victory, dealt a big blow to liberal democracy. Lives were lost, scores of people wounded and the House damaged.

The means by which this soft power is communicated is also important, as states look to integrate the notion of soft power into their diplomatic manoeuvrings, particularly those that are targeted towards a wider international audience beyond the confines of high-level deliberations between governments. Thus, public diplomacy becomes an important outlet for such propagation. Leonard, Stead and Smewing, define three distinct purposes, or areas of public diplomacy namely political/military, economic and societal/cultural. The latter is particularly important as public diplomacy plays an important role in acting as the means by which a country can promote its soft power. Public diplomacy can be seen as an instrument that mobilizes a country's soft power resources.[264] These can be mobilized through numerous channels, be they through broadcast media or cultural and information exchange, or at high-level discussions between heads of states/governments and political speeches/statements.

States have arguably become more image-conscious and seek to appropriate the benefits of advances in communication and technology to promote themselves on the international stage. The speeches and statements from leaders and officials that help form the image of a state remain important as a means of promoting a certain image, and can act as a useful soft power tool itself. The notion of soft power is also a good exemplar of the importance of ideas in foreign policy. It is a concept that straddles both theory and practice, and its utility is evidenced in the widespread currency that it has among a range of governments. Scholars have written widely on China's harnessing of soft power.[265]

These are important contributions in light of China's increasing importance on the world stage. They highlight the importance placed by Beijing on utilizing soft power resources, be it through its successful hosting of the 2008 Olympics, or its recent expansion of Confucius Institutes throughout the world. Soft power has also featured as an analytical tool in studies of Turkish foreign policy and formed a key plank of its foreign policy discourse.[266] There are trends that

---

264   Nye, (2008), p. 95
265   Ding, (2010), p.270
266   Onis and Yilmaz, (2009), p.12

have entered policymaking circles in developing countries too.[267] However, with the exception of China and Brazil, few thus far have attempted to explore the soft power ambitions of states that are perceived as emerging and authoritarian.

The African case is particularly instructive as it demonstrates how new states practice a form of soft power projection that is markedly state-led. This is because developing nations have very little soft power and hence primarily rely on soft power to build their diplomatic relations.[268] Moreover, the top-down approach that is likely to be used by developing nations is in contrast to considerations of grassroots cultural exchange through non-state actors. One can therefore draw some similarities from Africa's approach with those of China and Russia in terms of the state's role in seeking an improvement in their public image on the world stage while maintaining strict authority in their respective domestic policies. Up to this point, the term 'soft power' has been presented as a given. Many scholars who have applied the concept have focused on states increasing their attractiveness through cultural exchange and public diplomacy.[269] However, the concept itself is not without its critics. Lukes[270] third face of power explores the ability to shape the wishes and desires of others too, but that does not mean a confluence with Nye[271]. On the contrary, Lukes sees the notion of soft power as blunt because it fails to distinguish between the 'different ways in which people's interests can be influenced and the battle for their hearts and minds engaged'.[272] Hence, there is a lack of distinction between processes that are disempowering and those that are empowering in their effects. There are myriad different ways in which such preferences can be shaped, and because power is a potentiality rather than an actuality, it is difficult to measure and may indeed never be actualized.[273]

Therefore, soft power should not be understood purely in terms of its juxtaposition with hard power, but it can actually be seen as one and the same. This is explained through focusing on the idea of representational force, which posits that a certain degree of coercion is inherent in the means utilized to deploy soft power, as "its success will ultimately depend on knowing how exactly to make their idea and themselves attractive to a target population."[274] This could certainly be seen as relevant when one examines states' international media operations.

---

267   Gomes-Saraiva, (2014), p. 65
268   Courmont, (2013), p.349
269   Ding, (2008), p.193
270   Lukes, (2007), p. 95
271   Nye, (1990), p.15
272   Lukes, (2007), p. 95
273   Ibid, (2007), p. 84
274   Mattern (2005, p. 584).

There are two major stages of foreign policy formulation that start with formulation and end in conduct. The previous section has outlined the process of making foreign policy in the context of Africa while this section would present the process of conducting foreign policy in the context of Africa. This section looks at the structures and institutions involved in foreign policy implementation such as the Presidency, the Parliament, the Ministry of Foreign Affairs, embassies and missions abroad and Matrix on institutions engaged in implementation of foreign policy.

6.2.5 The Presidency

The President of the Republic is the Chief Executive Officer in charge of foreign policy and has the mandate to ensure that all policies are executed according to the Constitution by promoting unity and activities that will enhance the Republic. The Presidency, through considered planning, co-ordination, oversight, mobilization, and support, functions to facilitate a common programme that aids the fulfilment of the electoral mandate and the enhanced integrity of state. Furthermore, the Presidency aims to facilitate an integrated and coordinated approach to governance through the alignment of sectorial priorities with the national strategic foreign policy framework.

According to the Constitution, the president appoints the Ministers and assigns their powers and functions. The president is also responsible for the development and implementation of a national foreign policy framework. The president is always diplomat number one in the country, while the foreign minister is number two. The appointment of ambassadors, diplomats and consular representatives is within the jurisdiction of the president. Therefore, any default in the conduct and execution of Africa's foreign policy should be definitely associated with the presidency. The president should avoid the concept of appointing diplomats for tribal representation and accommodation of political elites who do not have the capacity to promote national interest regionally and globally.

6.2.6 Parliament

The legislative branch of government has a broad role in foreign policy decision-making processes such as the ratification of treaties, evaluation of policy documents, allocation and appropriation of funds to the ministry of foreign affairs, and international co-optations. In this way, legislature has the opportunity to play a central role in defining, shaping and directing foreign policy. The Parliament should play and give hints by debating important issues affecting the country. The Speaker of the National Legislative Assembly should provide oversight and accountability for the formulation and conduct of foreign policy through the Parliamentary Portfolio Committee on International Relations and Cooperation. Critics have raised concerns that most parliamentarians in Africa do not give due attention to foreign matters. Their contributions are always limited.

6.2.7 Ministry of Foreign Affairs
and International Cooperation

This ministry is the primary actor in conducting, coordinating and promoting international relations and foreign policy objectives or goals. It also monitors international developments and advises government on foreign policy issues and related domestic matters. Therefore, the aims of the Ministry of Foreign Affairs are to protect and promote national interests and values through bilateral and multilateral interactions. However, in most cases they suffer from budgetary constraint.

6.2.8 Embassies and Missions Abroad

This is an important institution for the implementation of foreign policy abroad through promotion of domestic policies. It is made up of ambassadors, high commissioners, military attaches, national security attaches, immigration personnel, as well as other staff with clerical tasks. The assignment of these workers at foreign missions is mainly to pass information from their home government to the host government and vice-versa as relating to decisions taken at home that affect the host government and its citizens.

It is vital to note that missions abroad do not just pass information from home to the host country, but explain and educate the government and people of their host countries regarding the policies of their home government. They do this in many ways with the ultimate aim of projecting a positive image of their home governments. The missions abroad failed the test of time and profession in 2014 when the entire diplomatic corps failed to convince the African region and the entire international community on the fouled attempted coup on 15th December 2013, which led to conflict between the government and SPLM/A in opposition. It can also be stated that some embassies and high commissions do more than just exchange information between governments; some are fully involved in espionage activities as well as economic diplomacy.

CHAPTER SEVEN

FOREIGN POLICY DYNAMICS: THE AFRICAN EXPERIENCES

Foreign policy is one of the fundamental concepts in the theory of interactions in the international system. It consists of a wide range of actions taken individually by a state or collectively by intergovernmental organizations corresponding to actions of other states or international actors. Theorists argue that each nation determines and defines its foreign policy, but in practicality, collective policy directives do prevail. In the case of Africa, a history of oppression, exploitation, deprivation, humiliation, injustice and subjugation heavily influenced and determined the direction as well as trends of foreign policy adopted at independence. Africa suffered the humiliation of slavery and the subjugation of European colonialism and neo-colonialism after independence. Africa and its diaspora embarked on the search for unity under the ideologies of Pan-Africanism particularly after its Fifth Congress in Manchester, 1945.

Decolonized countries sought ideas about continental unity in different platforms like the Monrovia group, the Brazzaville group and the Casablanca Group as expressions of Pan-Africanism. The latter is such a complex set of ideas that Tim Murithi referred to it as having no single definition. There are as many ideas about Pan-Africanism as there are many thinkers who had their perceptions of the ideology. Rather than being a unified school of thought, Pan-Africanism is more of a movement which has as its common underlying theme: the struggle for social and political equality, and freedom from economic exploitation and racial discrimination.[275] African countries expressed social and economic emancipation through philosophies like "Ubuntu" in South Africa which underscores solidarity. The Tanzanian philosophy of "Ujamaa" emphasizes collective work or cooperative movement, and Kenya's "Harambee" meaning pulling together, etc.

Following the wind of independence that blew across Africa, the new states took, adopted and sharpened those ideas of Pan-Africanism to forge them into ingredients of foreign policy suitable for African countries. As mentioned earlier, differences arose about the form of unity. During the 25 May 1963 summit in Addis Ababa, the idea of immediate continental unity was substituted with that of gradual continental unity. This was a compromising document that garnered consensus of the 32 member states. In this regard, African states established the Organization of African Unity (OAU) on the basis of gradual unity.

The foundation of African foreign policy lay in the struggle for social and political equality and freedom from economic exploitations and racial discrimination. The cornerstone of African foreign policy was the liberation of African territories still under colonial rule and apartheid in South Africa as well as struggle against neo-colonialism.[276]African countries got their independence during the period of Cold War. Politics of the Cold War divided nations between supporters of the Western imperialism and the Soviet communism. The newly independent African Countries in the 1960s became active members of the Non-Aligned Movement (NAM) born at the 1955 Bandung Conference in Indonesia, which developed into a Third World Movement.

Although in practice African foreign policy varied from one country to another, scholars found a consistent set of directives and guidelines formulated by states which targeted foreign policies and issues lying beyond African territorial legitimacy. The OAU encouraged its members to support liberation movements in Africa in countries like South Africa, Zimbabwe, Namibia, Angola, Mozambique Guinea Bisau, Cape Varde, Sao Tome and Principe, and Western Sahara. African countries coordinated their foreign policy actions in international organizations like the United Nations to secure independence of colonial territories, and impose sanctions against apartheid South Africa and its isolation from the international system. They also used Alliances like the Commonwealth. They succeeded in the liberation struggle by dismantling apartheid South Africa in 1994.

The African Union (AU) succeeded the OAU in July 2002 in Durban.

---

275   Murithi, Tim, (2015), pp. 217-233.
276   Young, Crawford, (2017), pp. 11-22.

The new Organization institutionalized Pan-Africanism in its structures. The organization has instituted principles of peace in the Protocol on Peace and Security Council, Principle of Post-Conflict Reconstruction and principles of development by establishing the New Partnership for Africa's Development (NEPAD). The AU has introduced principles in the area of governance which have implications for African foreign policy. They include the African Peer Review Mechanism and Unconstitutional Change of Government. African countries are careful about their policy directives outside their territorial boundaries. This was partly a response to changes in a world that witnessed the disintegration of the eastern bloc, therefore paving the way for Unipolar system, globalisation, climate change, terrorism, WTO etc. Overall, this analysis (background) serves even today as the overarching foreign policy, explaining how African states interact in the continent and beyond. The study has chosen seven countries, Egypt, Ethiopia, Kenya, Nigeria, South Sudan, South Africa and Sudan as examples, and in a nutshell, to understand how foreign policy has been formulated and conducted in Africa as indicated in this chapter, bearing in mind specific historical and cultural developments.

7.1 Egypt's Foreign Policy

Geopolitics play a great role in understanding the dynamics of Egypt's foreign policy. This is due to the fact that Egypt occupies a strategic position as a land-bridge between two continents and a link between two principal waterways, the Mediterranean Sea and the Indian Ocean. Thus, it must be strong enough to dominate its environment or risk becoming the victim of outside powers. Its security is also linked to control of the Nile, on whose waters its survival depends.

7.1.1 Origin and Development

This section offers an overview of the major events in Egypt's foreign policy in the period from 1952-1991. Major foreign policy decisions taken by Presidents Nasser, Sadat and Mubarak are highlighted and the driving force behind them is explained. The objectives and style of the three presidents' foreign policy is analysed. Furthermore, the foreign policy decision-making process in the three eras is discussed. The concluding section summarizes the major findings of the chapter.

Egypt had historical ties with Sudan and has sought satisfactory relations with the states on Sudan's southern borders, currently the Republic of

South Sudan, Uganda and Zaire. The land-bridge to Asia, route of potential conquerors, had also to be secured, and Egyptian rulers traditionally tried to project their power into Syria and Arabia, often in contest with other powers in Anatolia (Turkey), or the Euphrates River Valley (Iraq). In contemporary times, Israel, backed by a superpower located on Egypt's border and blocking its access to the East, was perceived as the greatest threat to Egyptian security. In this section, we explore the origin and development of Egyptian Foreign policy and the key determinants of the foreign policy:

7.1.1.1 The Pre-Revolutionary Epoch 1945-1951

During this period, most analysts agree that an independent, concrete and fully-fledged Egyptian foreign policy did not emerge before the Free Officers' revolution of July 1952. Egypt under the monarchy, militarily occupied and politically preoccupied with the internal power struggle among the ruling parties under the King, the British and political parties did not have a well-defined or active foreign policy. The totality of foreign policy was limited to two issues: the desired withdrawal of British occupation from Egyptian territory and the unity of Egypt and Sudan. In a letter to his British counterpart, the Egyptian Foreign Minister in 1950 asserted: "Our foreign policy is a very limited one, and can almost be resolved in these two questions now under discussion, the question of evacuation and that of the unity of Egypt and the Sudan under the Egyptian crown. Obviously, both issues required dealing with the British but since progress on both tracks – due to the huge asymmetry of power – was slow, even absent, the Anglo-Egyptian relationship often turned conflictual. In fact, that conflict "was so central to political life in Cairo that it informed all aspects of Egyptian foreign policy in the post-war era. Cairo's regional policies were thus driven in part by its deep animosity towards British schemes but were constrained at the same time by its status as an occupied state. Naturally, Egypt was in no position to determine its own foreign relations as long as the British army occupied Egypt. In the period between 1943 to 1945, for example, Egypt led the diplomatic efforts aimed at founding a regional political organization that would assert its supremacy in the Arab World. Those efforts culminated in the establishment of the Arab League in March 1945 with Cairo chosen as its permanent headquarters and an Egyptian (Abdul-Rahman Azzam) serving as its first Secretary-General.

Egypt's prime objective in founding the League lay in hampering Britain's plans for a new Middle Eastern order favouring Cairo's Hashemite rivals. The decision to participate in the 1948 Arab-Israeli confrontation is another case in point. Driven by fierce competition with other Arab monarchs (Abdullah of

Jordan, Faisal of Iraq and Abdul-Aziz al-Saud of Saudi Arabia) and pressured by a heated public opinion that was disturbed by the establishment of the state of Israel and the loss of Palestine, the Egyptian King, after an initial period of hesitation, took a last-minute decision to engage (along with other Arab armies) with the nascent Jewish state. In 1950, and to frustrate a potential Iraqi-Syrian union that would have weakened Egypt's influence in the region, Cairo proposed the creation of an Arab security arrangement: The Arab League Collective Security Pact (ALCSP). The pact also sought to undermine the British military presence as it implied the replacement of the order underpinned by the network of British military bases with a new indigenous Arab order.

In brief, Egypt's external relations before the 1952 revolution were predominantly hostage to its problematic relationship with Britain. Yet, Egypt's centrality in the region propelled it at times to take major political initiatives to protect its supreme position from challenges posed by regional powers. These efforts, however, were seriously constrained by its dependence on London. An independent foreign policy had to wait for the year 1952 when a group of army officers, led by Colonel Gamal Abdel Nasser, indignant at their country's occupation and the corrupt political system, waged their coup d'état that overthrew the monarchy and established Egypt Arab Republic.

7.1.1.2 The Revolutionary Epoch 1952-1956

The 1952 takeover was not a regular, Latin American-type coup, nor was Nasser a regular military officer; the foreign policy of the new regime did not reveal itself before the years 1954-55. The first two years of the revolution were marked by intense competition among the free officers themselves as well as with other political forces. In 1952, the constitution was abrogated and political parties were banned and in early 1954, General Mohamed Naguib, the façade leader Nasser used to give the new regime a popular face, was side-lined. The power of the leaders of the 'ancient regime' was further weakened by the agrarian reforms implemented as early as September 1952. After consolidating his power at home, Nasser paid attention to the challenges of foreign policy. Nasser's personality and ideas imprinted Egypt's foreign policy from the very start. In fact, if the psychological school needs a proof of the impact of idiosyncrasies on policy outcomes, then Nasser would be its best example in the Middle East. He envisaged, for example, a leading role for Egypt in the Arab world. An often-cited paragraph in his manifesto, *The Philosophy of the Revolution*, went as follows: "History is…charged with great heroic roles which do not find actors to play them on the stage. I do not know why I always imagine that in this region in which we live, there is a role wandering aimlessly about seeking an actor to play it. I do not know why this role…should at last settle down, weary and worn out, on our frontiers beckoning us to move, to dress up for it and to perform it since there is nobody else who could do so…We and only we are impelled by our environment and are capable of performing this role.

After signing the Anglo-Egyptian treaty in 1954 that laid down a speedy timetable for the evacuation of British forces from the Suez Canal area, Nasser became released of a major source of pressure and was free to pursue a dynamic independence-oriented foreign policy. Egypt's interaction with, and creation of, the dramatic events of the year 1955 represented the pillars of the new Egyptian foreign policy that was to last for more than a decade: The political battle with the Baghdad Pact, the Bandung Conference, and the Czech arms deal were the first real signs of 'change' in Egypt's post-revolution foreign policy, the policy that is often dubbed as 'revolutionary'.

In April 1955, Nasser attended the Afro-Asian conference in Bandung, another significant landmark in Egypt's quest for a leading regional role. The gathering was a chance for Nasser to project Egypt's influence outside the conventional borders of the Arab World and into the wider arena of the then expanding developing world. The convention was the nucleus of a wide assembly of Third World states who were gravely concerned about protecting their embryonic independence from great powers' games and avoiding getting caught in the Cold War confrontation. Out of Bandung did Nasser, along with Tito of Yugoslavia and Nehru of India, articulate the notion of "positive neutrality" adopted by the non-aligned movement, a grouping that constituted a substantial political force in world politics till the end of the Cold War.

The new foreign policy was injected with an inspiring ideology: Pan-Arabism, the ideology that was deeply-rooted in a country like Syria was somehow new to Egypt. As Nasser frankly admitted to the Syrian and Iraqi delegations during the 1963 tripartite unity talks, "the nationalist feeling in Syria has been clear for a long time. In Syria when an infant is born, he utters the words Arab nationalism and Arab unity. Here in Egypt, this feeling emerged only in 1955 or 1956." The use of Arabism started with the Baghdad Pact battle. In the words of Dawisha: "It was soon realized that the most effective method was to appeal directly to the fermenting nationalist and anti-West sentiment by using Nasser's personality and his rhetorical ability […] the principle of Arabism was espoused by the decision-making elite primarily as a response to political and strategic factors."[277] The change in Egypt's external relations was paralleled internally by a similar transformation of Egyptian politics and society. Politically, the

---

277   Bahgat Korany, (1986), p.51.

liberal experiment of the period from 1922 to 1952 was shunned and power became centralized in the hands of the revolutionary council (later on the central government controlled by Nasser himself). Measures to realize social justice (e.g., agrarian reforms) were implemented and rushed efforts towards industrialization and self-sufficiency were embarked on. In that new setting, a public sector geared towards economic growth was to become the backbone of the economy.

The turbulent events of the years 1955 and 1956 illustrated a number of points with regards to Nasser's foreign policy.

- First, they highlighted Nasser's determination to pursue an independent course of development at all costs, including sustaining a strained relationship with the US and inviting communist influence to the region. Independence was a key feature of Nasser's political blueprint.

- Second, all four events – Baghdad Pact, Bandung, the arms deal and nationalizing the Suez Canal Company – highlighted Nasser's genuine desire in assuming the mantle of leadership in the Arab world. Along with strategic and political considerations, the pursuit of leadership was partially driven by economic considerations. Nasser knew that Egypt "the regional leader" would be in a better position to extract resources from superpowers than Egypt "the ordinary state".

- Third, the previous two elements (independence and leadership) stemmed from Nasser's political beliefs, in particular his perceptions of how Egypt's foreign policy should be run. Also, it could be argued that both objectives were the cause and consequence of Nasser's charismatic leadership. A charismatic leader, Nasser could not afford to be perceived as a puppet of Western powers and had to constantly prove his credentials to maintain security and order at home. At the same time, showing the ability to lead the Arab world and maintain national independence despite the plots of superpowers lent him additional popularity and support in Egypt and beyond, which further solidified his stature as a 'charismatic' national leader.

- Fourth, they revealed a key feature of Nasser's personality: his reluctance to submit to threats and readiness to take risks, albeit calculated, and defy great powers when the stakes are high. This trait had a direct impact on the conduct of his foreign policy. As Dawisha pointed out: "Nasser's courage, coupled with an almost uncanny confidence in his own tactical skill, made him take decisions and formulate policies that were both unorthodox and unexpected. Many of these decisions were rapid responses to international stimuli but were naturally risky, yet cannot be considered as reckless.

7.1.1.3 The Response to the Suez Crisis 1957-1967

The response to the Suez crisis of 1957-67 was a turning point in the modern history of the Middle East and a milestone in the development of Egypt's post-revolution foreign policy. By the time the last Israeli soldier left the Sinai in March 1957, Egypt, turning a military defeat into a political victory, fully established its hegemony in inter-Arab politics and its centrality in the Third World at large. Nasser's popularity skyrocketed and his political ideology "Arab Nationalism" gained new ground. Thus, it was the thrust the Pan-Arab movement received from Egypt's rising power in the Arab world after the Suez crisis that helped to pave the way for the merger of Egypt and Syria in February 1958 in what came to be known as the United Arab Republic (UAR). In particular, Syria's Arab nationalists, represented by the Arab Socialist Ba'th Party (ASBP), found in Nasser a formidable ally that could be relied upon to outbid their local political rivals. "An alliance with Nasser was their ticket to power and stardom."[278] Relations between both countries had actually been fostered since the year 1955 by the conclusion of a number of military and economic treaties. A mutual defence pact was signed in 1955 followed in 1956 with an agreement for industrial cooperation.

In 1957, an agreement aimed at the unification of the economies of both states was concluded too. The Syrian stand of solidarity with Egypt during the 1956 tripartite aggression was reciprocated with the support Egypt gave in the following year to Syria against Turkish border provocations. Syria, a hotbed of Arab national sentiment, was at the time ripe for union. Unrest prevailed in 1957 with, on one hand, growing communist influence at home and, on the other, an American outcry about the prospects of Syria turning into a Soviet satellite. In January 1958, a group of nationalist and Bathi Syrian officers rushed to Cairo and demanded an immediate union with Egypt. Nasser, who had previously announced more than once that a constitutional unity should take at least five years of steady preparation, first rejected then accepted the offer. Yet, by accepting the risky venture under the pressure of circumstances, he took what turned out to be the first of a series of miscalculations.

Why Nasser changed his mind at the eleventh hour is a controversial question. Strategic considerations may have influenced his thinking. Nasser always acknowledged the importance of Syria for Egypt's foreign policy in the Arab world; no hostile regime shall take over Damascus and threaten Egyptian interests in the Levant. He was therefore weary of the red tide in Syrian politics and the mounting possibility thus of two unfavourable scenarios: a

---

278   Walter Lippmann, (1943), p. 51.

radical communist coup or an American intervention to abort it. Moreover, he recognized the leverage the new state would give on the regional and international arenas as well as the influence and prestige he would personally enjoy in the Arab world. Also, by extending his control to Syria, Nasser would be in a position to exercise control over Middle Eastern oil transported to Europe. The power of the new state and the repercussions its instatement created was evident in the anxious comment made by the Turkish Prime Minister Adnan Mandreis in a letter sent on the eve of the union to the US Secretary of State: "I slept last night with a state of six million people to the South of my country. I woke up today to find a state of thirty-six million on my Southern borders.[279]

Nasser's decision to decline the Syrian offer then accept it showed how much foreign policy decisions in Egypt are centralized and personalized. As Hinnebusch explains: "the president is supreme commander, declares war, concludes treaties, proposes and vetoes legislation, and may rule through decree under emergency power. The extent of the president's consultation with the top elite and with foreign policy professionals in the policy process is, therefore, very much a matter of his personal taste, while the relative influence of such elites depends more on their personal relations with the president than their official position. In brief, politics under Nasser "was one-man rule" and the realm of foreign policy was no exception. Centralization of foreign policy to a large extent continued to be the norm under Presidents Sadat and Mubarak.

7.1.1.4 The Six Day War: 1967-1970

In the mid-1960s, the Arab world was virtually divided into two contrasting camps: the 'progressive' or revolutionary camp encompassing countries like Egypt, Syria, Iraq and Yemen and the reactionary camp comprised of the monarchies of Jordan and Saudi Arabia as well as the 'moderate' regimes of Lebanon and Tunisia. The Arab 'Cold War' between both camps shaped inter-Arab relations in the 1960s and up to the 1967 war. In May 1967, reports spread of Israeli military concentrations on the Syrian border in response to Syria's support for Palestinian; an attack against Damascus seemed imminent. Nasser was meanwhile exposed to a vicious propaganda campaign emanating from reactionaries' radio stations accusing him of "hiding behind the blue skirts of the UN," (The UNEF had been positioned in the Sinai as part of the conclusion of the Suez war) and of fighting the brethren in Yemen instead of the enemies in Israel. Again, Nasser's legitimacy was threatened and his primacy in the Arab world challenged. To regain his legitimacy at home and re-establish

---

279   Stephen Walt, (1987), Pp. 21-22

his hegemony in the region, the daring Nasser took a number of dramatic steps: he asked the UN peacekeeping troops to leave, ordered the blockade of the Gulf of Aqaba to Israeli shipping, and remilitarized Sinai (which had been de-militarized at the end of the Suez war). Israel claimed the closure of Aqaba meant suffocation and could not be tolerated. On the 5th of June 1967, Israel launched a massive military strike against Egypt, Syria and Jordan and defeated them in less than six days. The Arab loss was huge: The Sinai of Egypt, the Golan Heights of Syria and the West Bank of Jordan, including East Jerusalem.

Throughout his political career, fighting Israel was never a high priority on Nasser's agenda. He was aware of the acute disparity in military power and Egypt's inevitable vulnerability in any would-be military confrontation with Israel. He "hoped to succeed where Muhammad Ali had failed, namely, to bring the Arabs under Egyptian control without firing a single shot and without outside interference. Thus, exerted effort to contain and isolate the impulsive Syrian regime whose dangerous policies could drag him into an unwanted war with Israel. Heikal, for example, wrote that Nasser told King Hassan of Morocco in 1965 that his priority lay in settling the conflict in Yemen and not in embattling Israel. He added that some Arab leaders cannot differentiate between "dreams" and "actions". King Hassan concurred and expressed to Nasser his fears that the attitude of the Syrians would play into the hands of Israel's hawks. Nasser was obviously attentive to the dangers involved in an unprepared for conflict with Israel. Hence, the measures he took in May 1967 that escalated the crisis did not mean he intended to go into battle with Israel, but rather to maintain his legitimacy in Egypt and the Arab world by appearing tough vis-à-vis Israel.

7.1.1.5 Reframing the Policy Course: 1970-1990

The then-shadowy Sadat could not at first depart from the policies he had inherited from his predecessor. The Nasserite line in foreign policy thus continued to guide Sadat's international behaviour until October 1973. Sadat, however, was not as compliant as his local opponents envisaged. On May 15th, 1971, he launched a pre-emptive strike against the Nasserist old guards who continued to interfere in his foreign policy and had, in effect, the power of disrupting his plans. Having his opponents in jail (1971) and doing well against Israel (1973), Sadat established his legitimacy and had a free hand in running Egypt's foreign relations. In a few years, Sadat changed Egypt's official name (from the United Arab Republic to the Arab Republic of Egypt) as well as its national anthem and flag. Those trivial changes preceded a more profound structural change in the second half of the seventies. The main objectives of Egypt's foreign policy under Sadat were the following: restoring the Egyptian occupied territories, ending the state of war with Israel as the economic burden resulting of it became unbearable, improving Egypt's relations with Washington, and modernizing Egypt's economy by attracting foreign investment and Western technology.[280] Knowing the dangers inherent in a military confrontation with Israel, Sadat pursued a diplomatic solution to the occupied Sinai territory problem. A number of diplomatic initiatives were taken in the years 1971 and 1972 but failed on the rock of Israeli intransigence and American indifference. Sadat realized that the standoff could not be broken without military action. On the 6th of October, 1973, Egypt and Syria launched a well-coordinated surprise offense against Israel. The two-week war heralded a substantial change in the foreign policy of Egypt.

Hosni Mubarak was nominated by the People's Assembly for the Presidency on the 7th of October, one day after Sadat's assassination. A referendum was held on the 13th and the following day he was proclaimed President. In his first statements, Mubarak declared Egypt's full commitment to its obligations and emphasized that it will honour the Camp David Accords and the peace treaty with Israel. Meanwhile, Mubarak, with an eye on easing tensions with regional and international powers, made various conciliatory gestures towards the Soviet Union and Arab states. In a speech given in November, he announced that Egypt was ready to deal with anyone "without complexes" as long as he did not interfere in Egypt's internal affairs. By the end of the year, "it was clear that Egypt was set on a more balanced course in her relations with the superpowers and the Arab states."[281] One of Mubarak's primary objectives was to break Egypt's isolation in the region ensuing from the Camp David Accords without having to jeopardize its peace with Israel and its special relationship with Washington. Hostile propaganda campaigns against Arab regimes were thus stopped. In contrast to Sadat's depiction of Arabs as dwarfs or kids, Mubarak used a balanced and friendly discourse towards other Arab states and heads of state. Furthermore, he repeatedly announced that Egypt's peace with Israel was not hindering its Arab commitments. An early test came in June 1982 with the massive Israeli invasion of Lebanon.

Mubarak seized the opportunity of the escalation of the Iraq-Iran war to prove Egypt's Arab commitments by extending excessive military aid to Iraq. More importantly, Mubarak intensified his efforts, in coordination with the Jordanians and consultancy with the Americans and Europeans, to find a political solution for the Palestinian problem. As Egypt spoke on behalf of

---

280   Ayoob, Mohamed. (2003), p. 13.
281   Hans Morgenthau, (1985), p.5.

Palestinian rights, "states like Algeria and Syria could no longer condemn Egypt for betraying the Palestinian cause."[282] Egypt's diplomatic efforts bore fruit in September 1984 with the restoration of full diplomatic relations with Jordan. The circle of isolation was broken and it became clear that it was only a matter of time before Egypt would be fully readmitted into the Arab state system. Egypt under Mubarak was keen on playing an active role in Arab affairs, but the level of involvement of the Nasserist era was abandoned, so as not to provoke the Americans too much. The rapprochement with the Arab world was not paralleled by any major change of attitude towards Israel. Though a freeze on normalization went into effect as a result of Israel's provocative actions (annexing the Golan Heights, invading Lebanon and the collapse of Palestinian autonomy talks) and relations between both countries were since then dubbed "cold peace", Egypt's policy towards Israel as a whole remained unchanged. For example, Mubarak's response to the annexation of the Golan Heights in December 1981 was no different from that of his predecessor to Israel's bombing of the Iraqi nuclear reactor a few months earlier. In short, Mubarak followed in the footsteps of Sadat to attain security.[283]

The economic challenge was closely linked to the other fundamental challenge the Egyptian President could not escape facing, namely the rise of political Islam groups on the political landscape and the threat these groups directed to the legitimacy and survival of his regime. Mubarak's ascendance to power was the direct result of the assassination of his forerunner, the first Egyptian ruler in ages. The violent clashes that broke out the following day in the Upper Egyptian city of Assuit between Islamic militants and security forces was just an example of what was to become a characteristic of Egyptian internal politics in the 1980s and 1990s. Islamic extremists aimed at infiltrating all major institutions to advance their cause. The loyalty of the army, the chief instrument of political change in authoritarian states, was, thus, "a major preoccupation" of Mubarak. He realized that the economic crisis was sowing the seeds of fanaticism and violence in Egyptian society and polity.

The instability that rose again to the surface in 1986 with the bloody riots of the Central Security Forces reinforced Mubarak's convictions. His approach to ameliorate the twin problem of economic misery and Islamic extremism was likewise twofold. First, the security apparatus was given the green light to launch a massive crackdown on Islamic activists, including those who never resorted to violent means. Accordingly, the security apparatus was conferred a greater role in dealing with the 'enemies of the regime' which, ultimately, led

---

282   Robert Osgood, (1953), Pp. 5-7.
283   Raymond Aron, (1966), Pp. 73-76.

to a greater input in the decision-making process. Second, priority was given to means of mitigating the negative sides of the acute economic crisis. What was proposed entailed a greater dependence on the private sector. Businessmen were invited to help breathe life into the ailing economy, an approach that increased their influence and bolstered their alliance with the regime.

From one perspective, Mubarak's path in the 1980s can be seen as a qualified success; Egypt under his leadership managed to correct many of the deviations resulting from the frantic years of Sadat's presidency. Back to the Arab world, friendly with the Soviet Union and other major powers as well as experimenting with democracy domestically, Egypt, it seemed, produced a major positive change in its foreign and domestic orientation. From another perspective, Mubarak's achievements were limited and the changes he introduced were more cosmetic than real. Egypt's dependence on the US, for example, was not altered. Egypt continues to maintain a "special" relationship with one superpower and normalized relations with the other, calling it balanced relations. Moreover, the political system he ran, despite all improvements, remained for the most part authoritarian. Additionally, the economy was still in shambles and on the decline.

In its broad lines, Hosni Mubarak remained faithful to the general policies of Anwar Sadat. The relationship with Washington, peace with Israel and some kind of commitment to economic liberalization and political liberalization (combined with repression of the opposition when it became threatening) at home all followed the path designed and initiated by Sadat in the mid-seventies. In other words, in the quest for security, Mubarak continued to appease outside threats and balance internal ones. The change had more to do with style than essence. Still pragmatic and realist, Mubarak was more moderate and less dramatic. Mubarak, described as a cautious man with "no grand idea that would land him in trouble" and "has neither worldwide vision nor a sense of historical processes is not the type of leader that would embark on major policy change plans. Instead, politics of the status quo gained the upper hand and dominated political life. Generally speaking, Egypt's foreign policy under Mubarak had been stagnant and motionless compared to the activity and dynamism it experienced during his energetic predecessors. Moreover, Mubarak seemed more overwhelmed with domestic issues than foreign policy matters.[284] He rarely attended the OAU/AU Summits. The economic challenge and the urge to preserve power had taken precedence over regional and international ambitions. In fact, foreign policy was employed to improve the critical economic standing at home.

---

284   Steven David, (1991), Pp.236-247

7.1.1.6 The Dominance of the Status Quo: 1991-2001

Everything in Mubarak's foreign policy in the 1990s resembled his policies of the 1980s. Regionally, Egypt tried to take advantage of the momentum the peace conference held in Madrid had generated to promote direct negotiations between Israelis and both Palestinians and Syrians. Even though Egypt was not directly involved in the Oslo negotiations (and was believed not to be informed of it in the first place), one cannot deny that its efforts in advocating reconciliation and bridging gaps between belligerent parties bore fruit. The signing of the Palestinian-Israeli Declaration of Principles (1993) and the Jordan-Israel Peace Treaty (1994), as well as the crucial progress materialized with the Syrians before the death of Israel's Prime Minister Yitzhak Rabin would, most probably, not have taken place had Egypt been aloof. And when later negotiations stumbled or violence resurrected, it was Cairo and Sharm ElShiekh that hosted gatherings whose mission was to 'rescue faltering peace'. Egypt's peace strategy aimed at achieving a number of objectives.

- First, peace nurtured the stability and order needed badly for economic development at home.
- Second, Egypt's services, on that front, augmented Egyptian-American relations and ensured that no cut in financial and military assistance would take place. Indeed, in the face of recurrent attempts made by Congressmen to cut or reduce the level of financial assistance, US administrations' uniform reply was that Egypt's contribution is vital to America's interest in the strategic Middle East; and
- Third, with a diminishing regional role and a shrinking of resources, the Arab-Israeli conflict became the last arena where Egypt could play a leading role in the Arab world. The demise of the Soviet Union in the early 1990s intensified Egypt's dependence on the United States.

The triumphant US asserted its political and military supremacy worldwide (and specifically in the Middle East), and that appeared difficult to contest by regional players. Egypt's manoeuvrability space shrank and its options became limited. The availability of allies plays into the choice of strategy. Egypt opted for solidifying its alliance with the US after the downfall of the Soviet Union. Domestically, economic and political liberalization were not abandoned, but were not unconditionally embraced, either. In reality, the 'one step forward, one step back' idiom best describes the oscillating fashion with which the state dealt with these two issues. Various measures (e.g., privatization, cutting subsidies, controlling budget deficits, etc) were taken to appease international creditors and local capitalists, but they stopped the moment the state, by sheer instinct, felt that it was losing control of the economic sector, or that measures proposed were potentially lethal to its stability. Likewise, in order to appear 'democratic', various cosmetic changes were introduced into the political system: longevity of the regime, naturally, needed extra legitimacy at home, and good reputation abroad. But, in essence, the authoritarian regime established in 1952 endured, in fact, exhibited a remarkable ability to reproduce itself against all odds.

Apparently, the crucial battle against militant Islamists was won by the end of the 1990s through repression; thousands of suspects were jailed, hundreds executed and human rights were abused day after day. In tandem, political life remained strictly controlled. The activities of political parties and professional guilds continued to be restricted, elections were rigged as regular as a Swiss watch, and rubber-stamp parliaments faithfully served the regime instead of monitoring the performance of the Executive. And, needless to say, maximal control of security agencies, the chief bulwark of the regime against dissidents, was exercised. In short, the primacy of balancing against internal threats to the regime lived on. The second decade of Mubarak's presidency seemed less successful than the first. By the new millennium, three major crises faced the Egyptian leadership, in the face of all of which it seemed helpless and incompetent. The first was related to Egypt's economy. After a few years of improvement in economic indicators, a cash shortage crisis emerged in the year 2000. All measures designed to contain it failed, including the decision to float the Egyptian Pound in January 2003. With the rise of prices, inevitably, discontent and frustration rose too. Regionally, the collapse of the peace process and the eruption of the second Palestinian 'Intifada' dealt a severe blow to Egypt's peace efforts. This coincided with a conspicuous decline in Egypt's regional standing and its ability to control events in the Arab world, including in Sudan whose Mashakus agreement took the Egyptian government by surprise. On the international level, Egypt's 'special' relationship with the United States was put to a new test because of the events of September, the newly-elected administration, led by the inexperienced George W. Bush, considered reform of the Middle East's dictatorships to be the panacea for the threat of Islamic terrorism. Accordingly, it pressured its Arab allies to democratize and introduce political reform.

7.1.2 The Determinants of Foreign Policy

Ever since the Egyptian Revolution of 1952, Egypt has been playing an important role in the Middle East, Africa and international politics, featuring rather active foreign relations. To understand and perceive the foreign relations of contemporary Egypt at a macro level, focus should be placed on the following four points.

7.1.2.1 Geo-Strategic Location

Egypt was politically strategic. As Nasser saw it, with considerable justice, Egypt was potentially at the centre of three "circles:" the African, the Arab, and the Islamic. Egypt viewed itself as playing a major role in Africa and beyond that, was long a leading mover in the wider Third World camp and a major advocate of neutralism and nonalignment. This geopolitical importance made the country the object of interest to the great powers, when Egypt's strength enabled it to play the great powers against each other and win political, economic and military aid from all sides across the three circles.[285] Even the weakened Egypt of Mubarak was able to parlay its strategic importance in the Arab Israeli conflict and as a bulwark against Islamic political activism into political support and economic aid from both the West and the Arab world. The unique geographic position determines fundamental directions of Egypt's foreign relations.

7.1.2.2 The Arab World

Geographically, Egypt is a bridge that connects the eastern and western parts of the Arab world, making Egypt the centre of the Arab world. The unchangeable geographic and historical factors of Egypt, reiterated Nasser, predetermined that Egypt is not only part of the Arab world but also the centre of the Arab world, the hero and leader who must undertake the mission of Arab unity.[286] Therefore, what Nasser pursued throughout his political life was Arab nationalism. Prior to the Yom Kippur War in 1973, President Sadat fought for the lost land of the Arab world under the banner of Arab nationalism. However, ignoring the opposition of the Arab world, President Sadat made a separate peace with Israel, which isolated Egypt from the Arab family.[287] In history, Egypt has been playing two roles in the Arab world, i.e., unification and innovation. Now Egypt, isolated from the Arab family, has lost its ideals for the future and its activities also come to a standstill in its limited political and geographic spheres in this area, a situation similar to that in the Balkan area took shape here.[288] After taking office, President Mubarak fully realized the important position of Egypt in the Arab world. He made great efforts so as to enhance the relations between Egypt and other Arab states, finally bringing Egypt back to the Arab family. Among the relations between Egypt and other Arab states, Egypt cares most about the following three states.

---

285   CHEN, Tianshe , (2011), p. 84
286   Chen, (2005) p.9
287   CHEN, Tianshe , (2011), p. 85
288   Heikal, & Guan, (1992), p. 371

- The first country is Sudan. For one thing, Sudan has close ties with Egypt in history; the former has always been regarded by the latter as its strategic backyard. For another, Sudan, an upstream country on the Nile, bears on the water security of Egypt.

- The second country is Palestine. Palestine bears on Egypt's security in the east wing. In addition, as Palestine is a key entity at the core of the Arab-Israeli conflict, it is an important stage for Egypt to bring into play its influence in this area.

- The third country is Saudi Arabia. Due to the unique religious position and abundant oil dollars of Saudi Arabia, Egypt, on the one hand, longs for its support when it comes to Middle East affairs and more economic aid from Saudi Arabia, but, on the other hand, tries its best to avoid possible unrest.

7.1.2.3 The Israel

As a powerful neighbour in the east, Israel is an important factor concerning the national security of Egypt. All previous Egyptian governments deemed that Israel is a major country to be alert against, always paying close attention to the situation in Israel. Even after peace was made between the two countries, Egypt still keeps an eye on Israel, unwilling to develop further relations with the latter. What is more, the fact that Israel is the only Middle Eastern country in possession of nuclear weapons makes Egypt upset. Former Egyptian foreign minister Amr Moussa once said, "As long as Israel possesses any weapons of mass destruction that pose a threat to its neighbour's, it's unthinkable for Israel to integrate into this area."[289] Of course, Israel has no complete trust in Egypt, either, which remains an important factor for the appearance and continuation of Egypt's "cold peace" with Israel.

7.1.2.4 Europe and Africa

Geographically, Egypt is close to Europe. Actually, both sides had close ties in history. In modern times, Egypt was deeply influenced by Europe and later, under the invasion and control of European powers, finally became a semi-colony and protectorate of the UK. After the Suez War of 1956, the influence of the UK and France on Egypt was actually not worth mentioning. After the 1973 Yom Kippur War, Egypt's relation with Europe, especially with the European Union, underwent substantial changes. Egypt and the European Union began bilateral cooperation and political talks.

---

289   Dowek, (2001), p.267

The first decade of the 21st century saw rapid development of bilateral relations between Egypt and Europe. In May 2004, Egypt and Europe signed a partnership agreement, followed by frequent visits of state leaders. By the end of 2006, President Mubarak had paid 46 visits to France, 24 visits to Germany and 18 visits to Italy.[290] At the same time, state leaders of European Union countries also paid numerous visits to Egypt. In recent years, the European Union has become the largest trade partner of Egypt. For example, in 2005, Egypt's imports from France and Germany reached €1.418 billion and €1.35 billion respectively. Its imports from Italy, the second biggest trade partner after the US, reached €2.6 billion. Additionally, the European Union was one of Egypt's main donors. Between 2004 and 2005, assistance from the EU to Egypt amounted to $522 million.[291] Egypt has traditional relations with Africa. One ring in Nasser's Three Ring Theory is Africa. When Nasser was still in office, Egypt supported the national liberation movements in Africa and Egypt had rather close ties with Africa. As most African countries opposed Sadat's decision of making separate peace with Israel, the relationship between Egypt and Africa cooled down. Today this has changed significantly. Egypt remains a strong member of the African Union.

7.1.2.5 The Influence of International Politics

The influence of international politics has been a difficult problem for Egypt to tackle with its relations with great powers especially the US and the Soviet Union in the international community. In terms of its relations with other countries, argued critics, "Egypt's relationship with the Arab world affects its foreign relations within the region as a whole while its relations with the UK, the US and the Soviet Union are of great significance outside this region."[292] The interference of these three powers is one root reason for the long-term disturbance in the Middle East. Egypt's relations with these three powers stand out among all its foreign relations. To be more specific, Egypt's relationship with the US and the Soviet Union, the two superpowers, seem particularly important for it affects the overall situation of Egypt's foreign relations.[293] As a result, Egypt has to be rather cautious to survive the fighting between world powers. For instance, during Nasser's reign, although Egypt was in close ties with the Soviet Union, it also kept a relationship with the US for a long time. Later on, during Mubarak's reign, although Egypt was on good terms with the

---

290   Wang, (2006), p.86
291   Chen, (2005), p. 133
292   CHEN, Tianshe , (2011), p. 86
293   Chen, (2005), p.34

US, it also developed a relationship with the Soviet Union (Russia) so as to seek some kind of balance. This was non-Aligned policy at its best.

The Cold War was an important factor affecting international relations from the end of World War II to the early 1990s. After World War II, Egypt became a focus of the competition between the two superpowers, the US and the Soviet Union. As early as the 1950s, the US attempted to include Egypt in its Middle East defence plan so as to contain the Soviet Union, but was rejected by Egypt. During the Suez Crisis, the US put great pressure on Egypt instead of supporting this strategic ally. The main reason was that the US feared that the Soviet Union might take advantage of this opportunity to get in the Middle East. Former American president Dwight Eisenhower said," We should put forward the best thinking for problems likely to be solved; in particular, the rescue mission of helping Egypt, Saudi Arabia and Syria out of their failure under the control of the Soviet Union [...] Since Britain and France have lost their influence in the Middle East, to save these countries and make them turn to the West, we must dare to be the leader."[294] However, the US failed to render Egypt much real help. Meanwhile, the Soviet Union opened the Egyptian gate through economic and military aid, making Egypt a tower of strength of the Soviet Union in the Middle East. In contrast, Egypt and the US fell apart and finally broke off their diplomatic relationship in 1967. Although the relationship between Egypt and the Soviet Union developed rapidly after the Six-Day War, the role of the US played in tackling the Palestine-Israeli conflict reduced Egypt's confidence in the Soviet Union. Therefore, it was no surprise that Nasser improved the Egyptian-US relations in his late years.

In the 1990s, under the influence of the Cold War, the foreign relations of Egypt had been in the shadow of US-Soviet confrontation. The US and the Soviet Union were rather active during the Suez War of 1956. During the Yemeni Civil War, the republicans and the royalists were at daggers drawn; the two sides were supported by Egypt and Saudi Arabia respectively. It happened that Egypt and Saudi Arabia were supported by the Soviet Union and the US respectively. The Six-Day War of 1967 and the Yom Kippur War appeared to be the confrontation between the Arab world and Israel, which actually was the confrontation between the US and the Soviet Union. The Soviet Union backed Egypt while the US supported Israel. The Yom Kippur War was actually a grand contest of Soviet weapons versus American weapons. The failure of Arab countries led by Egypt during the two wars indicated that the US had the upper hand in its contest against the Soviet Union in the Middle East.

---

294   Warner, (1991), p.316

Although Egypt had been consistent in its neutral and non-aligned policy, Egypt had to rely on one side against the background of the Cold War. "In the global political zero-sum game played by the two superpowers in the 1950s, Washington believed that Egypt's non-aligned policy diminished the strength of the West in a key strategic region [the Middle East], calling Egypt a traitor. In contrast, Egypt considered the Baghdad Pact, which included Britain and Iraq, to be Egypt's adversary and be an alliance against Egypt. Due to its objection to the West Camp which supported the establishment of the military advantage of Israel, Egypt turned to the East Camp for weapons."[295] The evolution of the Egyptian-US relationship had an impact on the evolution of the Egyptian-Soviet Union relationship and vice versa. "At that time [during Nasser's reign], to make any change in Egyptian policies was considered to be undermining the position of the US because the starting point of the American position was to ensure the relations between Egypt and the West stay as they used to be. Therefore, the policy changes of Egypt always led to mutual estrangement between Egypt and the US. Meanwhile, this would always push Egypt toward the Soviet Union a little bit more, which then led to more contacts between Egypt and the Soviet Union. It was said that Egypt had become a gateway through which the Soviet Union could easily get into the Middle East.

7.1.2.6 Arab-Islamic Character

The Arab-Islamic character is another variable that shaped Egypt's foreign policy in the international milieu. To be sure, Egypt had a long pre-Islamic heritage that gave it a distinct identity, and in periods such as the British occupation it developed apart from the Arab world. Egypt's national identity was never merged in an undifferentiated Arabism because they were shaped by their own distinct geography, history, dialect, and customs. The content of Egyptian identity was indisputably Arab-Islamic. Egypt was inextricably a part of the Arab world. It was the largest Arabic-speaking country and the intellectual and political centre to which the whole Arab world looked in modern times. It was also a centre of Islamic civilization, its Al Azhar University one of Islam's major religious institutions and its popular culture profoundly Islamic. Although a portion of the most Westernized upper class at times saw Egypt as Mediterranean or pharaonic, for the overwhelming majority, Egypt's identity was Arab-Islamic. Indeed, Egypt saw itself as the leader of the Arab world, entitled to pre-eminence in proportion to the heavy burdens it bore in defence of the Arab cause.

---

295   Lefebvre, (1993), p.325

This Arab-Islamic identity was a great asset for Egyptian leaders. To the extent that Egyptian leadership was acknowledged in the Arab world, this prestige bolstered the stature of the ruler at home, entitled Egypt to a portion of Arab oil wealth, and gave credence to Egypt's ability to define a common Arab policy, hence increasing the country's strategic weight in world affairs. This leadership position also meant that Egypt was a natural part of the inter-Arab power balance, typically embroiled in the rivalries that split the Arab world and a part of the solidarities that united it. In the 1950s, modernizing, nationalist Egypt's rivals were traditional pro-Western Iraq and Saudi Arabia, and its main ally was Syria. In the 1970s, an alliance of Egypt, Syria, and Saudi Arabia led the Arab world in its search for peace with honour; when Sadat made a separate peace, Syria became Egypt's main rival. The country's Arab-Islamic identity also put certain constraints on foreign-policy decisionmakers: to violate it risked the legitimacy of the whole regime.

7.1.3 Ideals of Anti-Imperialist Nonalignment

Lastly, Egypt's foreign policy was pulled in contrary directions by the ideals of anti-imperialist nonalignment and the webs of dependency in which the country was increasingly enmeshed. Egypt's long history of subordination to foreign rulers, especially European imperialism, produced an inferiority complex, an intense anti-imperialism, a quest for dignity, and, particularly under Nasser, a powerful national pride among Egyptians. Egypt's national ideal was to be independent of both East and West, to be a strong prosperous state, to stand up to Israel, and to lead the Arab world. Yet, as a poverty-stricken developing country and a new state actor in the international power game, Egypt could not do without large amounts of economic aid and military assistance from the advanced economies and the great powers. Such dependency, of course, carried heavy costs and threats to national independence. The problem of dependency could be minimized by diversifying aid sources, and Nasser initially pursued a policy of balance between East and West, which won aid from both sides and minimized dependence on any one.

7.1.3.1 Interests as the Fundamental Starting Point

National interests are "pivotal factors that determine and affect the behaviours of a state in international relations and inter-state relations reflect the interest interaction between different political and economic entities."[296] National

---

296   Zhang, (1989), p.54

interests are a comprehensive concept, mainly including security, economic and political interests.[297] The foreign relations of Egypt are no exception; their starting point and purpose is to safeguard the national interests of Egypt.

However, different tasks encountered by Egypt at different times meant its national interests had different priorities, which correspondingly affected the foreign relations of Egypt. When Nasser first took office, the primary task for Egypt was to realize and consolidate the national independence of Egypt and the most urgent problem was how Egypt could obtain enough weapons and economic aid to defend the newly-born regime. As Egypt's efforts of calling for help from Western countries failed, Egypt had to turn to the Soviet Union. The relationship between Egypt and the Soviet Union developed rapidly for the generous Soviet aid made Egypt almost completely dependent on the Soviet Union. After the Yom Kippur War in 1973, the primary task of Egypt was to recover the Sinai Peninsula occupied by Israel and save its collapsing economy.

The US became what Egypt could rely on because of its unique influence on Israel and enormous amount of foreign aid. The following years saw rapid recovery and development between Egypt and the US. The Egyptian-Israeli relationship also briefly improved. The Soviet Union was ignored because it could not help Egypt as the US did. Then the relationship between Egypt and the Soviet Union went from bad to worse and finally the two countries fell apart. Former American Secretary of State Kissinger said, "Russians can only offer Egypt weapons but we can offer you peace."[298] During Mubarak's reign, the primary task faced with Egypt was to develop the economy and increase its regional influence. The first difficulty Mubarak faced was how to return to the Arab family. For this purpose, Egypt decided to freeze its relationship with Israel so as to win approbation from Arab countries step by step. Egypt gradually improved its relations with Arab countries and finally recovered diplomatic relationships with these countries. In May 1989, Egypt returned to the Arab League. Since the 1990s, Egypt has been improving its relations with Arab countries seriously and engaged itself in resolving big issues of the Arab world. Since then Egypt has been playing an important role in the Arab world. Meanwhile, considering the leading position of the US in the Middle East and its enormous aid to Egypt, Egypt continued to attach importance to its relationship with the US.

Although Egypt placed its relations with great powers in the centre of its foreign strategy, Egypt tried to protect its national interest instead of simply catering for great powers. In its relation with the Soviet Union, Nasser insisted

---

297   Ibid, Pp.55-56
298   Heikal, & Xing, (1979), p.4

not approving the military base eagerly needed by the Soviet Union in spite that the Soviet Union offered Egypt a large amount of military and economic aid. When the "neither war nor peace" strategy of the Soviet Union hindered Egypt's preparation for its war against Israel, President Sadat made up his mind to drive out the military experts of the Soviet Union from Egypt.

During Mubarak's reign, the US, as an ally of Egypt, continued to provide Egypt with a lot of military and economic aid, which, however, did not prevent Egypt from criticizing the US. Egypt made strong criticism of the US with regard to many issues. For instance, Egypt and the US had constant disputes over issues like the US-led global counterterrorism war and democratization and the peace process in the Middle East. Statistics of the US Congress show that 80% of Egypt's votes on the general assembly of the UN were against the US.[299]

Besides its national interests, Egypt, as an Arab country, also bears the mission of safeguarding the interests of the Arab nation. The Palestine-Israeli conflict is mainly concerned with the interests of the Arab nation. Egypt was a main force of the Arab camp in the Palestine-Israeli conflict. It has been working hard for the resolution of the Palestine issue. During the peace talks between Palestine and Israel, Egypt always worked as a supporter of Palestine, pressuring Israel all along.[300]

When the Arab nation was faced with challenges, Egypt was rather active in mediating all parties, fighting for unity of the whole Arab nation. To some extent, Egypt's attitude was a symbol of the attitude of the Arab world. Nevertheless, the national interests of Egypt were often in discord with that of the Arab nation. On such occasions Egypt would sacrifice the interests of the Arab nation so as to protect its own interests. For example, to recover the Sinai Peninsula, Egypt sought for separate peace with Israel in breach of its policy of "no recognition, no peace, no negotiation" against Israel. This badly damaged the interests of the Arab nation, which was also the root cause that Egypt was isolated by Arab countries after Egypt had made peace with Israel.

In addition, the heavy debts and responsibilities that Egypt bears caused much negative influence on itself. For instance, Egypt's involvement with the Palestine-Israeli conflict caused severe human resource, economic and military losses to itself. Egypt's economic losses in the four Arab-Israeli wars reached $100 billion.[301] Nasser's keen support to Arab revolutions, especially its involvement in the Yemeni Civil War, brought more losses than gains. During Mubarak's administration, however, Egypt paid great attention to the balance

299   Wu, Chen, & Wang, (2004), p.128
300   Chen, Tianshe, (2011), p. 88-92
301   Wang, (2006), p.32

between its national interests and the interests of the Arab nation. For example, before most Arab countries recognized Israel, Egypt insisted that Egypt should maintain peace with Israel but the Egyptian-Israeli relationship must be kept at a reasonably low level.

The worst case occurred during the Yemeni Civil War in the 1960s. The two countries once broke off their diplomatic relations because of their different opinions on making peace with Israel. Moreover, the two countries were in discord because they both wanted to be the leader of the Arab and the Islamic world. For instance, when making security arrangements in the Gulf area after the Gulf War, Saudi Arabia rejected the proposal of rebuilding its security forces out of Egyptian troops; instead, Saudi Arabia relied on Western countries for its safety. The imbalance between the interests of Arab countries and the interests of the Arab nation influenced the unity and cooperation in the Arab world badly. "All Arab nationalists require, consciously or subconsciously, the interests of Arab nationalism to be subordinated to their national interests, class interests and personal interests, which is the very reason why Arab nationalism cannot lead the Arab nation to unification."[302]

7.1.3.2 Leaders' Personal Traits

According to the 1956, 1958, 1964 Constitutions and the 1971 permanent Constitution as well as its amendments, Egypt is a presidential republic where the president has been dominating the political life of the country. When making foreign policies, the president has nearly absolute decision-making power.

During Nasser's reign, Egypt gave extensive support to the national liberation movements in Asia and Africa because Nasser himself hated colonialism and imperialism. He took part in the Palestine War of 1948. The humiliation of the defeat of Arab countries made up his mind to fight against Zionism and devote himself to the Palestine-Israeli conflict. Out of his sense of responsibility for the Arab nation, He was keen about the Arab unification. He precipitated the union of Egypt and Syria in 1958, also known as the United Arab Republic. He also worked hard to expand Egypt's influence in the Arab world and supported Arab revolutions. Taking Egypt as an example, many other Arab countries organized free officers' movements and launched revolutions. Egypt was hailed as the source of Arab revolutions.

When Sadat took office, he had no confidence in developing a relationship with the Soviet Union because he distrusted it. The relationship between Egypt

---

302   Yang & Zhu, (1996), p. 82

and the Soviet Union worsened steadily. Ismail Fahmy, once Foreign Minister of Egypt, said that Sadat, "never understood, liked or trusted Russians and Russians treated him the same way."[303] In contrast, Sadat liked the American leaders; he had full confidence in President Carter, regarding him as a friend of the Egyptian people who could be relied on. Therefore, he welcomed Carter's mediation in the Egyptian-Israeli peace talks with open arms, which led to big breakthroughs in and rapid development of the Egyptian-US relationship.

Sadat liked to act in an arbitrary fashion and discriminated against those with different views. He often made big decisions by himself. It was said "when faced with important problems, he would return to his place and stay there for a couple of days. He did not like to read memos or reports. He liked to surprise his assistants. His advisors called him a Pharaoh in private."[304] Former American President Nixon once described him as a person who liked to think, and to be alone. He seldom exchanged views with his ministers. Many important decisions were made when he was walking alone along the Nile after lunch.[305] Sadat often made unexpected decisions which he called "lightening shock strategy."[306] This made many foreign policies that he decided during his tenure often surprising.[307] For instance, in 1971 he made the decision to join the Libyan-Syrian Federation. Only two people knew about his decision of driving out the Soviet experts, which was only made several hours before the Soviet ambassador got the notice. The personality and the position in foreign policy decision-making of Sadat played an enormous role in Egypt's foreign relations especially in the breakthroughs of the Egyptian-Israeli relationship. Ephraim Dowek, former Israeli ambassador to Cairo, commented, "No doubt, he is a major peace maker. Without his vision, determination, willingness of risking himself and the nation and his evaluation of the short-term and long-term historical process, it would be unthinkable for our generation to realize peace with Egypt."[308]

Mubarak also held in hand the power of foreign policy decision-making. After he became president of Egypt, the Egyptian National Security Council seldom held meetings. Interestingly, the Council was responsible for making relevant national security strategy and handling important problems concerning national security. Mubarak preferred to consult the courtiers and associates around him. After serving the army for a long time, Mubarak developed a

---

303   Fahmy, (1983), p.11
304   Karawan, (1994), p. 257
305   Nixon, (1983), p. 340
306   Karawan, (1994), p.256
307   Chen, Tianshe , (2011), Pp. 93-95
308   Dowek, (2001), p.282

character of determination and following orders. After the assassination of Sadat, the Egyptian-Israeli peace process was fragile. Mubarak did not hesitate to let the peace process continue. However, he did not think well of most Israeli leaders. For example, he disliked Israeli Prime Minister Shamir, whom he took to be "uncompromising and dogmatic [...] an enemy of peace and an obstacle of Egypt's goals in this region."[309] Therefore, he insisted on not meeting with Shamir at any place and waited for the change of the Israeli administration. Later on, he strongly condemned Israeli Prime Ministers Netanyahu and Sharon. He distrusted them so he met with them as seldom as possible. For instance, Mubarak did not invite Sharon to visit Egypt until a long time after the latter took office in 2001.

Even during the Rabin administration and the Barak administration when the Egyptian-Israeli relationship improved, Egypt did not hold back its criticism on Israeli leaders. Mubarak always refused to visit Israel (the only exception was his participation in the funeral of Prime Minister Rabin). To sum up, the Egyptian-Israeli relationship stayed in a cold peace situation for quite a long time. During president Al-Sisi reign, the foreign policy that conflicts with the U.S and its allies' interests was his surprising interest in Iran. After ousting the Muslim Brotherhood from Egypt's government, Al-Sisi invited Iranian President Hassan Rouhani to attend his inauguration ceremony. This trip made him only the second Iranian president to visit Egypt since the countries severed diplomatic ties in 1980. Conversely, a major objective of United States foreign policy in the Middle East has been the containment of Iranian influence. Since the days of the Clinton administration and its "dual containment" policy in the Gulf, the United States has been in the business of calling Iran to "cease its support of international terrorism and subversion, end its violent opposition to the Arab-Israeli peace talks, and halt efforts to acquire weapons of mass destruction. However, the United States unintentionally allowed Iran to initially leap over this containment hurdle and spread its influence, which created a new security architecture dominated by Russia and Iran in the region. Contrary to al-Sisi's welcoming attitude towards Iran, al-Sisi has vowed to maintain and support Saudi Arabia, Bahrain, and the UAE in blockading Qatar, partly for Qatar's ties with Iran. Additionally, al-Sisi decided to intervene in the War in Yemen at a minimal scale. Later, Egypt asserted that it supports a political settlement and dialogue in Yemen to end the conflict. This decision was contrary to Saudi Arabia's goal in Yemen and it indirectly supported Iran because it backed the Houthi rebels and their cause. Consequently, al-Sisi's future with Iran was somewhat unpredictable. For example, in February of 2011 Egypt

---

309   Ibid, p. 290

allowed an Iranian frigate and replenishment ship to transit the Suez Canal en-route to Syria, marking the first Iranian Navy transit through the Suez in three decades. Israel viewed this Iranian transit as a provocation. Though this transit occurred under al-Sisi's predecessor, the potential for another similar transit is likely due to al-Sisi's welcoming attitude toward Iran. This decision would place the Iranian navy in Israel's backyard, which will in turn put pressure on the United States to interject on some level.

President Morsi inherited a state that lacked political stability following the revolution in 2011. After assuming office, Morsi took drastic changes to purge Mubarak's security and political institutions and to regain his legislative powers. Morsi dismissed a number of senior military leaders, issued a new constitution which gave him full legislative authority, and reinstated the parliament. Additionally, Morsi sought to create a healthy alliance with the army, Egypt's strongest institution. This attempt would help prevent future challenges to his authority as president. Like Mubarak, President Morsi strived to maintain positive relations with the United States and Israel. This could be attributed to ensuring that economic and military aid continued to flow into Egypt.

Additionally, as President Morsi succeeded Mubarak, he found himself bound to the Camp David agreements established by Mubarak's predecessor President Sadat. With the backing of the Muslim Brotherhood party, President Morsi initially adopted a different foreign policy from Mubarak towards the Gaza Strip and Hamas. Though Morsi never supported Hamas openly, he took actions to ensure his relationship with the organization was positive. At his first U.N. General Assembly speech on September 26, 2012, Morsi characterized Israel as an illegal occupier and denounced its presumed nuclear weapon stockpile being fabricated outside international institutions. There was an apparent setback in Egypt-Israeli relationship as the Muslim Brotherhood assumed power in Egypt. This setback originated because Muslim Brotherhood leaders claimed that the struggle between Palestinians and Israel in the Gaza Strip is a wider pan-Islamic issue with Zionists as the enemy.

Morsi's heavy support for Hamas and its political aim began to throttle back as conflict in the Gaza Strip escalated. Initially, Morsi relaxed Egypt's control over the divided border city of Rafah. Essentially, this allowed the increase of goods to be traded and moved in and out of the Gaza Strip through Egypt. This support also included the implementation of a relaxed policy over the smuggling tunnels. However, his relaxation of the border crossing came to a halt after Hamas launched over 100 rockets into Israel in a 24-hour period in November of 2012. In response, Israel launched operation "Pillar of Defense," and Morsi took on an aggressive role in controlling the underground smuggling tunnels into the Gaza Strip.

The Muslim Brotherhood's shift in political posture provides a secondary explanation for Morsi negotiating a truce and upholding positive Israeli relations. After the revolution, the Muslim Brotherhood became more interested in domestic competitive politics and less concerned with implementing any drastic revolutionary changes in Egypt. The Muslim Brotherhood began to view Israel and the complexity of the Gaza Strip from the lens of the Egyptian state rather from a religious movement. Consequently, Morsi in conjunction with the Muslim Brotherhood party was unable to fundamentally alter Egyptian foreign policy toward the Gaza Strip from the Mubarak era.

It is thus clear that the presidential system and the unique decision-making mechanism of Egypt stamped Egypt's foreign relations with a brand of Egyptian leaders. The personality traits of the leaders influenced the development of Egypt's foreign relations to some extent. However, it must be pointed out that despite the influence of the sentiment of Egyptian leaders, what determines the essence of Egypt's foreign relations is still the national interests of Egypt.

7.1.4 Conclusion

In summary, geography, interests, international politics and Egyptian leaders are four fundamental starting points toward understanding Egypt's foreign relations. Geography is the basis of Egypt's foreign relations; it sets the fundamental directions on Egypt's foreign relations: The Arab world, Israel, great powers, Europe and Africa. Although safeguarding its national interests is a fundamental starting point in Egypt's foreign relations, its national interests have shown different points of emphasis at different stages. Additionally, Egypt still bears the mission of protecting the interests of the Arab nation. The Cold War had great influences on many aspects of Egypt's foreign relations; the United States and the Soviet Union were top priority in its foreign relations before the 1990s. Under the unique political mechanism of Egypt, the Egyptian leaders have supreme power in foreign policy decision-making thus Egypt's foreign relations were stamped with a brand of Egyptian leaders.

However, it is believed that geography, interests and leaders are the basic focus of external relations of Egypt, so the Egyptian foreign relations pattern is unlikely to have dramatic changes. First, the Egyptian-US relations will continue to develop. The United States has provided substantial long-term economic and military aid. During the political changes in Egypt, the Egyptian military had close cooperation with the US and had also got its support. Meanwhile, the Middle East strategy of the United States also needs help from Egypt. Therefore, the development of Egyptian-US relations is a mutual request. Secondly, peaceful relations with Israel will not change. This kind of peace is critical not only for Egypt, but also for Israel as well as the United States. The three countries have been in line with the fundamental interests.

7.2 Ethiopia's Foreign Policy

The capacity of the state to influence other states in the relationship is also an important factor to be considered in the adoption of foreign policy because the implementation of the latter is dependent upon the power to exert pressure on others. The power of enforcing pressure is in turn dependent upon different sub factors which include economic strength, internal stability and political unity, the size of the population as significant market potential and defence base, technological development and military strength, the government's capacity of organization and mobilization, and the potential for alliance formation. The evaluation of the power of the states in its relative sense with due consideration of the possible involvement of other states, in one way or another, lie in the adoption of foreign policy that determines its content. This is because the relations of states are mainly governed by the power they possess.

7.2.1 Origin and Development

Generally, in order to understand the changes and continuities in the foreign policy and diplomacy of the regimes of modern Ethiopia, it is necessary to place this discussion in a historical perspective.[310]

7.2.1.1 The Emperor Tewodros II

Emperor Tewodros designed a foreign policy that would help him unify his domain and consolidate his power in relation to others. Throughout his reign, Tewodros tried to develop a dynamic foreign policy that reached out beyond the Horn of Africa region. He distinguished Christians and Muslims, i.e. he considered Christians as friends and Muslims as enemies. He perceived the Turkish and Egyptians as the basic enemies and he wanted to have positive relationships with Russia, France and Britain because these countries are Christians. Sovereignty and reciprocity in diplomacy become fundamental principles of his foreign policy.

---

310   Fasil Solomon (2020), Pp. 29-45

Tewodros attempted to have his regime recognized on an equal footing with the great powers of Europe. He appealed specifically to Britain, France, and Russia as fellow Christian nations to assist him in whatever ways possible in his fight against the Turks, Egyptians, and Islam. He also wanted these powers to keep produce local military weapons and wanted to be independent. His strong desire was not to import weapons but to produce locally. Regardless of his ambitions, Tewodros was not successful because Britain and France were not ready to help Tewodros in many respects.

7.2.1.2 The Emperor Yohannes IV

As a personality and as a ruler, Yohannes highly differed from Tewodros. He was more patient and less impulsive than his predecessor. Although both envisioned a united, Christian Ethiopia, their approaches were in contrast. Yohannes valued order more highly than the rigid centralization that had characterized Tewodros's rule.

Yohannes's most outstanding accomplishments were in the field of foreign policy. He pursued an active and cunning foreign policy similar to Tewodros II and even more acute than Tewodros. Whereas Tewodros had attempted brazenly to demand respect and the recognition of Ethiopia by European powers, Yohannes followed a course of prudent, practical and patient diplomacy. Yohannes concluded treaties and agreements externally with the British and Egyptians. The *Hewett Treaty* (1884) with Anglo-Egyptians was one of the eminent treaties concluded during his reign.

Yohannes faced strong external challenges from Mahdists and Italians. It was a period when Sudanese Mahdists challenged Ethiopia on its western border. It was also a time of heightened European interest in Africa as a base for colonial expansion.

Although Yohannes considered Islam a threat, he saw European expansionism as an even greater threat to Ethiopia's political survival. At one point, Yohannes even made an abortive attempt to form an alliance with the Mahdists against a potential European incursion. When these countries were not ready to solve their differences peacefully with Yohannes, he conducted wars and won at the battle of Dogali, Saiti, Gundet and Gura. In 1889, the battle with Mahdists in Metema culminated his life.

7.2.1.3 The Emperor Menelik II

Menelik started conducting relations with the European powers especially the Italians when he was king of Shewa, Emperor Yohannes's serious competitor.

In 1889, after the death of Yohannes, Menelik II and the Italians concluded the *Wuchale Treaty* in the small town of Wuchale, what is now Wollo Province. The treaty generally guaranteed a measure of security and trading privileges to both Ethiopia and Italy. However, Article XVII in the Italian version of the treaty, which essentially implied that Ethiopia was a protectorate of Italy, created disagreements between Menelik and the Italians.Menelik's diplomatic efforts to solve this problem failed and the battle of Adowa erupted in 1896. The Italians were resoundingly defeated at the battle with more than 35 percent of their troops being killed.

The Ethiopian victory at Adowa sent shock waves throughout Europe and caused the reigning Italian government to fall. For the first time, the European powers realized that Ethiopia was an African power to be reckoned with. Britain, France, Russia, and Italy flocked to Menelik's court in order to arrange the exchange of ambassadors and to conclude diplomatic agreements. Britain, France and Italy signed treaties with Menelik to demarcate the frontiers between their colonial possessions and Ethiopia. The treaties established Menelik's exclusive rights to the territories bordering the colonial possessions claimed by these powers. Even Sudanese Mahdists sought to stabilize relations with Ethiopia at this time. Thus, it was clear that the emperor was gifted with considerable diplomatic expertise, playing off one power against the other as pawns in an effort to secure the sovereignty of his country.

Furthermore, Menelik established modern institutions of administration after the battle of Adwa. In 1900, he established a council of ministers composed of nine ministries, including the Ministry of Commerce and Foreign Affairs, as an institution to execute the country's foreign relations. Ethiopia's foreign relations at that time were more of foreign trade and this might have influenced the emperor's decision of combining the two ministries together. Naggadras Haile Giyorgis, a traditional person with no modern education, was appointed as the first Minister of Commerce and Foreign Affairs.

The main task of the ministry was to deal with guests, to talk with other states and ministers. Yet, it did not have the power to enter into agreement with its counterparts. The duties of the ministry were divided into four categories;
•   To talk about consular relations with other countries,
•   To talk about relations with other states and ministers,
•   To deliver passport to foreigners who live in Ethiopia, and
•   To translate books, newspapers and journals into Amharic.

The level of development of diplomacy during the reign of Menelik was limited due to lack of educated manpower and lack of understanding about the role of foreign policy. Ethiopia's Diplomatic representation abroad was limited during the time. Though the first and only consul was opened in Djibouti in 1897, there were neither permanent legations nor embassies established abroad. At that time, foreign relations were conducted through a delegation system of representations. Different delegations were sent to various countries to negotiate on various issues and to promote the country's national interest. For instance, a delegation led by Fitawurari Damtew Ketema was sent to Russia in 1895, presented Menelik's letter to the Czar of Russia and discussed on bilateral issues. Besides, there was no written foreign policy document that guide the country's relations with other countries. The Emperor made foreign policy decision in a pragmatic way according to the need of the time in consultation with close advisors. He followed "largely defensive and survivalist foreign policy".

Emperor Menelik II fell ill in 1906 and very soon he was totally incapacitated. His illness and the anticipated death alarmed a bitter struggle among different factions for succession domestically. The situation created internally soon affected relations with the powers ruling the adjacent territories. Britain, Italy and France agreed to cooperate in the event of Ethiopia's disintegration and possible territorial rearrangement in their own interests.

7.2.1.4 The Emperor Haileselassie I

A. Pre-Italian Occupation Period

Menelik II died in 1913, it was not until 1930 that the next strong emperor, Haileselassie I, assumed the throne. Ethiopia's foreign relations began to take modern shape under Haileselassie I. It is during his period that permanent representations have begun and diplomatic missions were opened in many countries. He was dedicated to the creation of a stronger, more modern bureaucratic empire with unquestioned respect in the world community.

When he was the heir to the throne from 1917-1930, Teferi vastly utilized diplomacy for building his image abroad, and in related matters of prestige and foreign affairs. In 1923, Teferi engineered Ethiopia's entry into the League of Nations. He wrote to the League for reconsideration of Ethiopia's membership and after lots of deliberations, the country was admitted to membership, by unanimous vote at the General Assembly. Ethiopia's admission to the League had three advantages:

- It helped Teferi to pursue energetically his policy of domestic reforms, raised his popularity nationally and internationally and increased his power base;
- It exposed the country to world politics as peace loving and committed to collective security as a guiding foreign policy principle; and

- At least in relative sense, it protected the country from colonization that could have been pursued by the neighbouring colonial powers.

Teferi also undertook a grand tour in 1924 accompanied by large retinue of noblemen, and visited Palestine, Egypt, France, Belgium, Holland, Sweden, Italy, England, Switzerland and Greece. Although he did not attain his objective of an outlet to the sea, he came back with his and the country's international stature increased and his commitment to introduce European way of administration strengthened.

Though Teferi was interested in European civilization, he was cautious of maintaining the traditional values intact. He reshuffled the ministerial system - he dismissed all ministers except the war minister, added new ministries and assigned a secretary general as his aid. Foreign advisers were recruited to organize the ministries and advise the appointees. This has enabledhim to run foreign relations personally and manipulate the benefits of foreign policy to his own ends.

Following his accession to the throne in October 1930, Emperor Haileselassie I began in earnest to lay the ground work for the development of a modern foreign service. In the 1931, Haileselassie I promulgated the first written constitution by which in Art. 14 he took into his hands all power of diplomacy and foreign policy. Furthermore, the decree that was published on Negarit Gazeta No.5 order 1/1935 stipulated the duties and powers of the Minister of Foreign Affairs. None of the Articles and Sub-articles provided the Ministry with real power to conduct foreign relations. The Ministry remained important but vested with residuary power to coordinate minor foreign activities such as financial and administrative issues with the consent of the Emperor.

Foreign policy was an important area where the Emperor was concerned to put his personal control. He went to the extent of controlling very minor activities. He regulated foreign activities by requiring entry visas for visitors, registration for commercial firms operating in Ethiopia, and the licensing of all lawyers appearing in the special court that handle cases between nationals and aliens. The Emperor was controlling not only the foreign relations of the ministry but also the routine management of day-to-day activities of the ministry.

B. Post-Liberation Period

In 1936, the fascist occupation of Ethiopia aborted the peaceful development of the country's foreign policy. However, the country's diplomacy continued as the patriotic war of the people continued within the country against the fascist force. The Emperor's continued diplomatic struggle in bilateral and multilateral forums coupled with the patriotic struggle waged by the people enabled the country to be liberated in 1941.

Following the liberation of the country, Ethiopia's foreign relations has expanded and started taking better shape. The organizational structure of the ministry has expanded and its duties increased. Many embassies, consulates, liaison offices and legations were opened in different countries. Nevertheless, the professional qualification as well as the number of workers with the necessary skill and knowledge were greatly lacking in contrast to the structure.

Though liberated from the shackles of fascism, Ethiopia remained under the protectorate of Britain not to pursue an independent foreign policy. The British government that allied with Ethiopia in the common struggle against fascist Italy dominated the aftermath of the country's political independence. British imperialism in Ethiopia completely controlled and embezzled the country's economic, financial and industrial resources. Britain totally controlled Ethiopia's import and export; the railway from Djibouti to Addis Ababa; and Ethiopian access to shipping.

Therefore, the priority of Haileselassie's foreign policy objective of the time was to guarantee the independence of the county and to oust the British out of the country. Haileselassie continued to elicit American interest in every aspect of Ethiopia's development. Gradually America's strategic interest in Ethiopia grew. On the other hand, Britain had to address its internal economic problems and social discontent that forced the labour government to give precedence to social security at home over the needs of imperial security abroad. It was not even in a position to cover the cost of the British Military Mission in Ethiopia (BMME). Hence, the British hegemony in Ethiopia came to an end in 1950 giving way to the ascendancy of Ethio-American relations.

In 1945, Haileselassie met with President Roosevelt of USA in Egypt. They discussed on the strategy of their future foreign policies. USA's foreign policy was mainly interested in the containment of communism in Europe and its possible expansion to Africa. Thus, Ethiopia was treated as a significant ally of US because of its proximity to the Middle East, Persian Gulf, the Gulf of Aden, the Indian Ocean and the Red Sea. The Ethio-US relations were based on Ethiopia providing America with communication base - the issue of strategy. The Kagnew Station, a military base located in Eritrea served as a center for all US air and space operations. Since then, the US government showed greater interest in Ethiopia and continued to provide the government with increased economic and technical assistance.

The Emperor also had a keen interest to see a strong army of his own, and he wanted a strong military relation with the US to achieve his goal. In 1953, the two countries signed mutual defense agreement, which attached the

US Military Assistance Advisory Group (MAAG) to the Ethiopian Ministry of Defense. The MAAG heralded that the US took the responsibility to establish and strengthen the Ethiopia military establishment. The assistance enabled the Emperor to suppress the internal rebel groups.

The period from 1950s to 1960s was witnessed as a period where the Ethiopia's foreign policy was mainly targeted at gaining access to the sea and restoration of Eritrea. To achieve this goal, the government used the US as one of the world super powers to play the game on its behalf. The US played a determining role in the multilateral and bilateral forums in order to enable Ethiopia get Eritrea and have an access to the sea. The US tried to influence the General Assembly of the United Nations; it employed every possible means of diplomatic maneuver to satisfy the interest of Ethiopia in having Eritrea. The amicable Ethio-US relations began to deteriorate in the 1960s due to the following reasons;

- With the development of satellite technology, Ethiopia's strategic importance to America began to be less important.
- USA's reluctance with regard to supporting Haileselassie on the conflict with Somalia because it feared that supporting Ethiopia means losing Somalia to the Soviet bloc.
- Ethiopia's visit to Moscow; in 1959, the Emperor was visiting Moscow for about two weeks and got some assistance and USSR pledged to construct the Assab refinery. This event was a headache for the US.
- The 1960 coup d'état attempt against Haileselassie that indicated the weakening of the Emperor.

The above highlight policies resulted into the following principles:

i. **The principle of collective security:** was one of the first guiding principles of the Ethiopian foreign policy enunciated by Haileselassie at the League of Nations. Despite the unjust treatment of Ethiopia by the League of Nations during the fascist aggression, the Emperor remained ever loyal to the principle of collective security. He actively participated and supported the establishment and the collective security actions of the United Nations. Ethiopia was the only African country that sent troops and participated in the UN's collective security duties in Korea and Congo.

ii. **Peaceful co-existence:** this involve good relations with neighbors and peaceful resolution of international conflicts were also the guiding principles of Haileselassie's foreign policy.

iii. **Building strong defense capacity:** The Emperor had strong interest to maintain strong military power. He organized modern armed forces that were observed to be the best in Africa where the Ethiopians handled the maintenance of the military machines dominantly. He devoted about 20 percent of the country's budget for military modernization.

iv. **Non-alignment:** The basic objective of this principle was to diversify aid, and to change the country's image of being identified with the western world, in particular with the USA.

v.   **Pan-Africanism:** Ethiopia has been the "silent servant of the leaders of African liberation movement". The repeated victory of the Ethiopia over the colonial powers has boosted the moral of the colonized African people. Ethiopia not only served the African cause, it also overtly identified itself with the continent.

7.2.1.5 The Dergue Regime

The reign of Emperor Haileselassie I came to an end in September 1974 by a military coup d'état. The military regime that took control of state power in 1974 adopted a foreign policy largely oriented to socialist ideology. The primary objectives of the foreign policy were survival of the regime and maintaining the territorial integrity of the country. Apart from these, restructuring the society along socialist lines was also considered as the foundation for the foreign policy motives at home. The major strategy to achieve the stated objectives heavily focused on building the military capability of the country. And force had been employed as the best strategy to silence dissent at home and deter the perceived external enemies of the country.

Since socialism was the guiding philosophy of the country, friendship and alliance with socialist countries of the world was considered as a viable strategy for realizing socialism at home and perhaps in the world. However, since the regime did not have the necessary economic and military capabilities to achieve its objectives, the country was very much dependent on economic and military aid on the others. In this regard, the country was heavily dependent on military aid on the Soviet Union which prevented it from securing any kind of military and technical assistance from the US and other European countries. The regime was condemned by the west for its human rights record, especially its treatment of former government officials. This resulted in declining Ethio-US relations marking its lowest point with the closure of the US military base and operation of military assistance within 72 hours (Keller). Following such problems, internal and external enemies began to take action to hasten the demise of the regime.

Internally Eritrean Liberation Front (ELF) launched military attack on the Ethiopian Army. Many external actors were involved in sponsoring the rebel group, including; Saudi Arabia, Egypt, Sudan, Somalia and later USA itself.

Moreover, Somalia's invasion of the Ethiopian region of Ogaden was one of the serious external challenges of the Ethiopian Government at the time. The government did not have enough capacity to calm the Eritrean Rebels and the Somali irredentist invasion. However, the regime managed to reverse the Somali aggression with the help of the new powerful patron, USSR. The involvement of USSR in the region only heightened the superpower rivalry between the USA and USSR during the cold war era (Schwab).

The corner stone of Ethiopia's foreign policy at the time was maintaining continuing friendship with the Soviet Union and other socialist countries. Apart from the Dergue's near total dependence on the leaders in Moscow and their Warsaw Pact allies for military and logistical support during the war with Somalia and in the Eritrean conflict, several others factors have facilitated the consolidation of this new special relationship. These include: the immediate and unhesitant recognition of Mengistu's government by the Soviet Union; the quick and generous support they offered when the military regime needed assistance and guidance to address problems inherited from the past and related to the new socio-economic and political order.

Indicative of the magnitude of its foreign relations, the Dergue has signed numerous economic, social, political, trade, cultural, educational, consular, and administrative agreements and protocols with almost all socialist countries. The Soviet Union and its allies were thus able to exert immense influence in both domestic and foreign affairs of Ethiopia. Experts from the German Democratic Republic assisted the military regime in its struggle against domestic guerilla movements and external opponents, and in training cadres for the completely reorganized security services, later consolidated in to a full-fledged ministry with the biggest budget in the country. The Dergue had sent hundreds of Ethiopians for training to the Soviet Union, Eastern Europe and Cuba while employing many of their administrators and technicians.

Apart from socialism, Ethiopia's strategic locations and other questions, such as; Eritrea, Somalia, and the issue of the Nile, had also shaped the foreign policy orientation and behavior of military government. Ethiopia being located in the Horn of Africa is at the cross roads to the oil rich middle East region and Indian Ocean. As a result of this the U.S.S.R was keen to have stronghold over the area, replacing the United States. U.S.S.R came at the right time when the Dergue called for military aid to reverse the aggression from Somalia in the East and quell the Eritrean nationalists in the north part of the country. It should be noted that U.S.S.R was used to be a friend of Somalia, yet all of a sudden, it made a swift change of policy when it came to Ethiopian side; while the U.S.A piped in to Somalia. That was a time of cold war whereby the two super powers, U.S.S.R and U.S.A were pitting each other to have a sphere of influence in the region.

Ethiopia shares the Nile and its longest border with Sudan, yet the relation between the two had been strained for decades. Sudan was one of the host countries for Ethiopian opposition forces. In turn Ethiopia had been supporting the dissent groups in southern Sudan, including the Sudan's People's Liberation Army/SPLA (Amare Tekle). Amare argues that Ethiopia's foreign policy towards Sudan was based in part on the mistrust of the Arab Northerners as well. Similarly, Amare contends that, "Ethiopia's relation with any third state in the Nile Valley have been shaped as much by Egypt's attitude and action as regards to Somalia, Eritrea and the Sudan and by its close association with Arab and Muslim States".

With regard to Africa's broader issues of decolonization and anti-Apartheid struggle, Ethiopia played significant role. The regime had extended its military and technical support to Freedom fighters in Angola and Rhodesia. The regime had also showed its solidarity to Palestine's cause by condemning Israel and sought political allegiance with the Arab world, however the negative perception that most Arab countries have towards Ethiopia remained unchanged. Finally, the regime collapsed following the end of cold war unable to survive in the absence of military aid from the socialist blocs, USSR, Cuba.

In general, the adoption of socialism and its subsequent impact on the foreign policy of the country could be considered as a departure from its predecessors; however, the policy objective of the country remained unchanged. The country's policy towards its neighbors, the region, and the Arab world remained unchanged. Such continuity of in the era of dynamic world teaches us the determining role of geography in the making and implementation of foreign policy of Ethiopia. The issue of Nile River, boundary issues, the strategic location of the country, unique culture (Christianity) amid the Islam religion and Arab culture had cumulative effect in shaping the foreign policy the country.

7.2.1.6 The Ethiopian Peoples' Revolutionary Democratic Front (EPRDF) Government.

During this time, various changes occurred both internally in Ethiopia and externally at the global level.

i.   **Domestic changes: there were political, economic and social changes in the country.**
* *At the political level: There was an ideological change in association with global political changes. Socialism ceased to be a state ideology and the most important institutions of the Dergue regime such as the Worker Party of*

Ethiopia and the National Shengo were dismantled. Ethiopia transformed from one party system to multi-party system. The centralized and unitary form of state structure also changed to decentralized and federal one.

- **Economically:** *The market economy philosophy replaced the command economy of the previous regime. Liberalization and privatization are adopted as economic policies of the new regime.*

- **Socially:** *The class-based analysis of social relations during the Dergue period changed with the coming to power of EPRDF. Instead of classes, ethnic lines for analysis of social relations become dominant. This becomes prevalent with the regime's recognition of Eritrea's self-determination.*

ii. **External changes**

- ***The promotion of the Western ideologies:*** With the end of the Cold War in 1991, the New World Order emerged, manifested by the west's promotion of the ideas of democracy, free market economy and human rights particularly in the Third World. The policy of containing communism was replaced by supporting democratization, peaceful ways of conflict resolution and fight against terrorism as important policy of the Third World.

- ***The promotion of international institutions:*** The west also raised the role of international institutions such as the UN, World Bank and the International Monetary Fund (IMF) in the New World Order. They are given significant role in the international relations and also affected the foreign policy of Third World Countries.

The EPRDF government had to respond to the domestic and international changes to stay in power. The democratization process of the new regime was unique in the sense that it is ethnic based. The neighboring countries, for fear that it would have some implications for their domestic politics did not accept ethnicization of politics. Thus, the foreign policy concerns of EPRDF right up on coming to power were:

- Peace and security at the domestic scene and sub-regional levels particularly with the neighboring countries; and

- The need to change the attitudes of neighbors towards the new policy measures taken by EPRDF. Accordingly, the regime pursued the following diplomatic measures to change the attitude of neighboring countries:

- The issue of Eritrea was also the foreign policy concern of EPRDF. The issue of Eritrea was not only the issue of Ethiopians but also for African diplomacy. Eritrea's departure from Ethiopia was not in line with the OAU Charter for the Charter declares that boundaries are not subject to changes in accord with the Cairo declaration.

Furthermore, the positive relation that existed between Eastern and Southern African countries with the previous military regime created another challenge to the EPRDF government. Therefore, the new regime was endeavoring to make its relation good with these countries especially with Zimbabwe. West Africa region especially Nigeria which is very vocal in the region also presented a challenge for the government. It was believed that the policy of the new regime was dissatisfying the policy makers of Nigeria because of the ongoing internal problem with the Biafra Secessionist Movement. Thus, changing the attitude of Nigerian policy makers was one of the tasks of the regime.

Generally, the post-1991 Ethiopian foreign policy has been characterized by active involvement in various African affairs such as the African common market, the OAU/AU conflict prevention and management mechanisms, the African peace keeping issues, the anti-apartheid struggle in South Africa, and the issues in the Horn of Africa. The foreign policy has also been characterized by the effort to diversify the country's foreign relation partners. The EPRDF's foreign policy identified both western as well as non-western powers as Ethiopia's external relation partners. It provided special attention to the particular significance of the rising powers in accelerating the country's socio-economic and political development.

7.2.2 Basic Features of the Relations

The relations between South Sudan and Ethiopia cannot be explored without examining the relations between Ethiopia and Sudan generally since South Sudan was part of its territory. The existing Sudanese regime which came to power through a military coup on 30th June, 1989 did not have good relations with the Ethiopian government for various reasons.

Firstly, since the *Derg* was ideologically communist, while the National Islamic Front (NIF) which encouraged and backed the 1989 coup in Sudan was anti-Communist, they had become ideological competitors in the region. Secondly, mutual and reciprocal harbouring and supporting of opposition groups known as Sudan People Liberation Army/movement (SPLA/M) fighting to overthrow their respective regimes had been seriously affecting the relations between Sudan and Ethiopia. Thirdly, the apparent gradual decline in the power of the *Derg* regime led the government in Sudan to believe that it was wise to contribute towards the downfall of the regime. Sudan acted by extending strong support to the Eritrean People's Liberation Front (EPLF) and the Tigray People's Liberation Front (TPLF) because the fall of the Derg regime was synonymous with the fall of SPLM/A. In countering this move, the Ethiopian government of the day was supporting the Sudan People's Liberation

Army (SPLA) and its political wing the Sudan People's Liberation Movement (SPLM) during the same period.

Two years after General Omar Hassan al-Bashir assumed power in Sudan with the support of the NIF, the Ethiopian People's Revolutionary Democratic Front (EPRDF) came to power in Ethiopia on May 28, 1991 and established the Transitional Government. This important event in Ethiopia had coincided with the end of the Cold War, the downfall of Said Barre in Somalia on 26 January 1991 and the establishment of a de facto government in Eritrea which eventually seceded from Ethiopia.[311] EPRDF's seizure of power was warmly welcomed by the Sudanese regime.

This was highly expected given the previous close relations of the government of Sudan with the TPLF and the EPLF. In this connection, Woodward (1996) underlined that when Mengistu finally fell in 1991 Sudanese forces were evidently present in Addis Ababa, apparently keen to capture the SPLA leaders in the capital.[312] Hence, the 1991 assumption of power by the EPRDF appeared something of a victory for the Sudanese rulers rather than their rivals in Ethiopia (SPLM/SPLA). One has to note here that General Al Bashir was the first Head of state to visit Ethiopia after the EPRDF seized power.[313]

It is widely believed that the TPLF had strong backing from Khartoum, during the period of its struggle against the Derg, as a counter balance for the support the Derg was extending to the SPLA/SPLM. This seems to have made the Sudanese Government believe that greater opportunity would be created in the event where the EPRDF is in power for driving out the SPLA and its Sudanese supporters from Ethiopia. In addition to this it is believed that Sudan was trying to create close relations to implement its long-term policies in Ethiopia, and through it, to other neighbouring countries.[314] The EPRDF on its part was enthusiastic to create friendly relations with Sudan as a means of paying what it owed to the former.

On the basis of these background contacts and conviction between the government of Sudan and the EPRDF, Ethiopia and Sudan started their relations anew in 1991 by concluding various agreements with the view of promoting friendly relations.

311   Woodward, (1996), p.72
312   Ibid, p.124
313   Kinfe, (1994), p.43
314   Smith, (1996), p.907

7.2.3 Approaches and Principles of the Foreign Policy

Thus given, the Ethiopian foreign policy has an approach of what some calls *"inside –out"*. Accordingly, the bases for the policy are: -

i. **Promoting development and building democratic system:** this is to refer that the key interest of the Ethiopian people is eradicating poverty, diseases, and illiteracy. In other words, having accelerated development is not only a question of improving the living standards of the people but also of existence as a nation. Therefore, the government has already issued the development policy and strategy to achieve this. On the other hand, democracy is the key instrument to ensure citizen's rights, good governance that enables the people to have a peaceful life and focus on their development activities. It also ensures the peaceful co- existence of the diversified Ethiopian people. Hence, development and democratization are the basis of the foreign policy.

ii. **National Pride:** National pride is nowadays very much related to development and democracy. Ethiopians are proud of their civilization and the good things done by the previous generation. But the present generation is also humiliated due to poverty, backwardness, and lack of democracy and good governance. Ethiopians are now known as beggars due to the atrocious famine that claims thousands of life every year. What this in turn means is that the civilization and good things recorded by the previous generation, though we are proud of it, cannot rectify the humiliation of the present generation as Ethiopians are losing their national pride for the humiliation of poverty and backwardness which force them to look for help every year in saving the life of the people. Thus, from this perspective; national pride must be the base for the Ethiopian foreign policy.

iii. **Globalization:** The efforts that Ethiopia is making to bring about development, democracy and good governance cannot be separated from the regional and global situations. The world economy is highly influenced by the process of globalization. No country (poor or rich) can be free from the influence of globalization. Globalization, with both its opportunity and challenges, has become, a reality, whether we like it or not. Therefore, the foreign policy makes globalization the base for the country's relation with other nations with the view to protect the damages and to make use of the opportunities of globalization.

Accordingly, the foreign and security policy established the following foreign policy strategies that should be employed:

a. **Devoting the prime focus to activities at home:** The strategy based on the "domestic first, external second" approach, that focuses on what can be done in the country and to meet the need of its domestic requirements.

b. **Strategy centered on the economy:** The country's relations of friendship or otherwise should be based first of all on economic matters. Accordingly, its diplomacy should be mainly centered on economic diplomatic activity. Also, the country's defense capability should not be built in a way that would have a detrimental influence on its economy.

c. **Full utilization of benefits based on proper analysis:** We should be able to maximize what we can receive and utilize any assistance in the appropriate manner. Possible avenues of cooperation and access to them need to be thoroughly assessed and studied. It is important to know in detail the development cooperation policy of each country.

d. **Minimizing threats on the basis of proper analysis:** Strategies to forestall the threats of Ethiopia's national interests and security should be developed. It is necessary to carry out detailed and accurate studies as a first key step of a strategy to reduce threats and dangers.

e. **Reducing vulnerability to threats:** A strategy correctly identifying the sources of the country's vulnerability and then dealing with the problem should be employed. The principal sources of the country's vulnerability, i.e. poverty and political problems should be reduced.

f. **Building a reliable defense capability:** Strength in military power is a necessary pre- condition for deterrence, effective diplomatic action, and to acquire military victory with minimal damage. Therefore, it is proper that the institution of an intelligence capacity and the strengthening of defense capabilities must be the basic strategy.

7.2.4 Foreign Policy Formulation in Ethiopia

On May 28, 1991, a change of government had taken place in Ethiopia resulting in the overthrow of the Derg regime and its replacement by a Transitional Government dominated by the Ethiopian People's Revolutionary Democratic Front (EPRDF). The Transitional Period Charter of Ethiopia which was the legal basis for the establishment of the new government had not specifically and clearly vested the power of directing the foreign policy of the country in a particular authority.

This can be understood from article 9(c) of the Charter which entitles the President of the Transitional Government, who is the Head of State, to nominate the Prime Minister subject to the approval of the Council of Representatives. From this, one can gather that the Prime Minister had been accountable to both the Council of Representatives and the president. Moreover, the Prime Minister had not been specifically given the power of heading the foreign relations of the country. Besides, Article 19(1) of Proclamation No 41/1993 has clearly limited the power of the Ministry of Foreign Affairs to formulating foreign policy guidelines and submitting them to the Council of Representatives for approval. This clarifies that the power of adopting the foreign policy of the country was vested in the Council of Representatives.

It is also equally true to say that the president, as the chairman of the Council of Representatives and the head of state, had the power of initiating and submitting the draft foreign policy of Ethiopia to the Council of Representatives for approval and to make overall supervision over its implementation. It must be noted, however, that no systematically formulated written policy document was issued to govern the foreign relations of Ethiopia during the Transition Period.

The adoption of the FDRE Constitution on December 8, 1994 had reserved the conduct of foreign policy within the exclusive power of the Federal government. Moreover, the Constitution had shifted the responsibility of heading the foreign relations of Ethiopia from the president to the Prime Minister. This did not bring any significant change in institutional responsibility since both the president and the Prime Minister have been the chief executives at different times. From the point of view of the power of the legislative organ, however, there is a great shift in power of adopting foreign policy from the legislature to executive organ.

Furthermore, the Constitution under Art. 77(8), has assigned the power of formulating Ethiopia's foreign policy, and the responsibility to exercise overall supervision over its implementation, to the Council of Ministers. The power vested in the Prime Minister under Article 73 (6) to exercise overall supervision over the implementation of the Ethiopia's foreign policy.

The Ministry of Foreign Affairs, which is responsible for the foreign relations of the Ethiopia has the power of coordinating the relations of other government organs with foreign states, plays determinant role in the formulation of the Ethiopia's foreign policy because it is legally vested with the task of conducting studies on the Ethiopian foreign relations and preparing draft policy guidelines on foreign affairs.

This enables the Ministry to evaluate current internal and external situations based on suggestions from its departments and diplomats as well as proposing an appropriate policy which will give it great opportunity to influence the Council of Ministers in making its decisions on foreign policy matters. More importantly, the Minister of Foreign Affairs can influence the Prime Minister due to his sufficient exposure to current international situations and his frequent contacts with the latter to discuss issues of foreign relations. This is not, however, to undermine the role of other branches of the executive organ in contributing policy issues related to their respective sectors, and the regional governments particularly in providing information related to concrete facts on the activities of neighbouring states.

Direct contribution of public opinion influences foreign policy formulation, as evidenced from past practices. Generally, it should be understood that Ethiopia's foreign policy was initially, mainly devoted to internal stability and establishing international support for its newly enshrined government.

7.2.5 Execution of Foreign Policy

The responsibility of administering the effective implementation of Ethiopia's policies regarding its foreign relations is vested in the Ministry of Foreign Affairs. This is to say that the day-to-day activities of the country's international relations are discharged by this institution while the ultimate power of control over the implementation of the country's foreign policy is specifically designated to the Prime Minister under Article 73(6) of the Federal Constitution. It is thus important to stress here that the powers granted to the Council of Ministers to exercise overall supervision over the implementation of the foreign policy of the country under Article 77(8), and the power of the Ministry of Foreign Affairs to follow up the implementation of guidelines on foreign affairs enshrined in Article 25(1) of proclamation No. 4/1995, are subject to the control of the Prime Minister.

The relations of power between the Prime Minister and the Council of Ministers warrants this conclusion because, firstly, the Prime Minister is the Chief Executive. Secondly, the Council of Ministers is responsible to him pursuant to Article 76(2) of the Constitution. Thirdly, the power of exercising overall supervision is clearly vested in the Prime Minister. The power of the Prime Minister to negotiate on issues involving the interests of the country, his power as commander-in-chief of the national armed forces and his power of nominating ambassadors and other envoys give him effective authority with respect to the execution of the foreign policy of the country. The important instruments for the implementation of the policy are the diplomats of the country.

Assigning capable diplomats is thus no doubt a prerequisite for a policy's efficient and effective implementation. Satisfactory success does not, however, seem to have been registered in this regard in the last ten years as has been shown during the Ethiopian-Eritrean War. This had mainly been caused due to lack of diplomatic experience resulting from the absence of maintaining continuity by retaining experienced diplomats. This was coupled with the weaknesses of the country stated, which made the achievement of objectives such as the attraction of foreign investment capital to the country inadequate.

In this connection, it is very much relevant to consider the role of the House of the Peoples Representations and the president of the country. Since the former is entrusted with the power of declaring war and ratifying international treaties signed by the Council of Ministers, it is not difficult to understand the strong power position this organ occupies. These are substantive powers which enable the legislative organ to control the activities of the executive organ in connection with foreign policy execution. The control is meaningful particularly on issues of entering into war and concluding binding international agreements, which can significantly affect the interests of the country.

The power of the president, on the other hand, is limited to the appointment of ambassadors and other envoys to represent the country abroad. But he can appoint these representatives only when their list is submitted to him based on the recommendation of the Prime Minister. In addition to this, the president receives the credentials of foreign ambassadors and special envoys assigned in Ethiopia. In both cases, the power of the president is only ceremonial as per of Article 71(3,4) of the Constitution. The article rejects the discretion of any recommendation of the Prime Minister for assignment, nor dismisses any representative of the country abroad. This Article does not also imply that the declaration of persona non grata is within the power of the president. Thus, it can be underlined that the power of the president in the execution of foreign policy, like that of its formulation, is insignificant.

7.2.6 Ethiopia's Relations with South Sudan

In the international aspect, the new government of Ethiopia was busy looking for both political and economic support from different countries. Since the new government was not initially stable in its domestic political base and nor did it have a dependable international ally, its foreign policy was devised mainly with the view of creating peaceful relations with its neighbours and securing political and diplomatic support. Consequently, Ethiopia declared an open-door policy with respect to its relations with neighbouring countries.[315]

This unilateral move taken by Ethiopia made its boundary wide open for the free movement of people without the requirement of an entry visa and resulted in the uncontrolled flow of people and goods from neighbouring countries in which Southern Sudan was inclusive.[316] There was not, however,

315   Kinfe, (1994), p. 42
316   Ibid, p.47

immediate reciprocal response on the part of the neighbouring states except that a friendship agreement was signed between Sudan and Ethiopia, which included the opening up of their respective boundaries to allow the movement of people and goods freely.

More importantly, the two countries reached mutual understanding for expelling opposition groups operating in their territories against the regime in their homeland.[317] This was important to both governments because the SPLA/M could not get any form of support from Ethiopia, which would give Sudan the opportunity of taking the upper hand in its fighting in its Southern part. Regarding Ethiopia too, this could avoid the involvement of Sudan in assisting any guerrilla movement that might threaten the EPRDF dominated fragile new regime. It is clear from the above assertion that South Sudan relations with Ethiopia were pegged entirely on Ethiopia's relations with Sudan generally after the fall of the Derg regime. Therefore, the following phases of relations were examined in the context of Sudan in which the South was part of it.

7.2.6.1 Phase One: The Short-Lived Friendship

The political environment created in Ethiopia was duly noted by the NIF National Islamic Front (NIF)-led government of Sudan, which had clear foreign policy objectives of expanding political Islam in North East Africa.[318] Ethiopia with its large Muslim population had thus been found to be ideal as the NIF target for its major operation of expanding Islam in the Horn of Africa. With this conviction, Sudan had taken two significant moves, which were meant to facilitate the situation for its primary target of promoting political Islam.

Consequently, first, it expanded the Sudan Embassy in Addis Ababa under Ambassador Osman El-Seed and established Sudanese Consulate in Gambella. Second, immediate actions were alleged to have been taken to create conditions in Ethiopia for the rapid proliferation of Islamic NGOs which were affiliated to the NIF.[319] These diversified moves of Sudan designed to spread the ideology of Political Islam through means ranging from government representatives to international NGOs had been taking place at the time when Sudan was at a comparatively advantageous position.

According to Girma (1999), there were three reasons for Sudan foreign policy success such as: firstly, Ethiopia and Eritrea were close friends which were favourable towards Sudan so that the latter did not have to worry about

---

317   Girma, (1999), Pp.37-38
318   Woodward, (1996), p.125
319   Ibid, p.142

the issue of balancing its relations with these states so long as it maintained good relations with both. Secondly, since the Transitional Government of Ethiopia was mainly engaged in restructuring its internal administration and in ensuring sustainable peace and stability, it can be argued that Sudan did not encounter any check and control in its political activities in Ethiopia due to the open-door policy of the latter. Thirdly, the government of Sudan had been undertaking its clandestine activities in Ethiopia with great optimism for the achievement of objectives due to the emergence of a lawless situation in Somalia as a result of the absence of government in the country.[320]

In addition to this, the internal situation in Sudan relating to its conflict in the Southern part had been showing substantial change in favour of the central government. This was mainly because of the occurrence of a major contradiction and splits within the SPLA, as a result of a coup attempt staged on 28 August 1991 by three SPLA Commanders, Riak Machar, Lam Akol and Gordon Kong, to overthrow Colonel Garang from his leadership position.[321] Continuous fighting between the two factions in 1991 and 1992, and intermittent clashes in 1993 and 1994 eventually followed this line.

It thus seems tenable to argue that the fall of Mengistu in Ethiopia created shock within the SPLA and resulted in the split, given that Addis Ababa, the friendliest capital in Africa to the Southern Sudanese, had been transformed overnight into the friend of their worst enemy, the regime in Khartoum.[322] During this time the Sudanese government was claiming military victory against the SPLA/M main stream in the South.

7.2.6.2 Phase Two: The Fading Friendship

Ethiopian-Sudanese relations had reached a point of crisis when Islamic terrorists attempted an assassination on the life of Egyptian President Hosni Mubarak on 26 June 1995 in Addis Ababa during the OAU Summit. Even though five of the terrorists were killed, three were captured, one was declared to have managed to escape and fled to Sudan to join two others, members of the group who were alleged to have been planning and directing the attempted assassination were from Sudan. Consequently, the Ministry of Foreign Affairs of Ethiopia formally accused the government of Sudan, on the 1st September 1995, for providing sanctuary to the perpetrators of the crime and furnishing them with travel facilities to and from Addis Ababa.[323] This situation brought

---

320   Girma, (1999), P.49
321   Ibid, p.53
322   Gurdon, (1994), Pp.92-93
323   The Ethiopian Herald, (1995), p.1

about the end of the first phase of the relations between the two countries, which lasted from May 1991 to June 1995.

On 1ˢᵗ August 1995, the Ministry of Internal Affairs of Ethiopia declared the identity of the members of the group involved in the assassination attempt, who all happened to be Egyptians, but news was reserved for publicizing the country alleged to have been behind the action. Together with this, undeclared diplomatic means were said to have been attempted by the Ethiopian government for the handover of the alleged criminals to Ethiopia by Sudan.[324]

As a result of Sudanese non-compliance, the Ethiopian government took measures against the activities of the Sudanese government in Khartoum. Accordingly, the Ministry of Foreign Affairs issued a declaration on the 1ˢᵗ September, 1995 regarding the following measures: first, the Sudanese Consular Office in Gambella was closed, and its Sudanese personnel were ordered to leave Ethiopia within seven days. Second, the number of diplomats working in the Sudanese Embassy in Addis Ababa was reduced not to exceed four including the ambassador, and the rest were ordered to leave Ethiopia within seven days. Third, organizations directly or indirectly linked with Sudan operating in Ethiopia as non-governmental relief agencies were ordered to cease activities, close their offices and their Sudanese personnel to leave Ethiopia within seven days. Fourth, Sudanese Airways was prohibited from flying to Ethiopia and its Sudanese staff working in Addis Ababa were to leave within seven days, and the Ethiopian Airlines also ceased its flight to Sudan. Fifth, an entry visa requirement was reimposed on Sudanese nationals seeking to enter Ethiopia, and sixth, Ethiopia reduced its diplomatic staff in Khartoum.

These measures secured immediate Egyptian favour and as a result its Foreign Minister Amr Moussa expressed his country's support for the result of Ethiopia's investigation in the failed assassination attempt during his talk with Prime Minister Meles Zenawi on the 4ᵗʰ September 1995.[325] During this period, Sudanese internal opposition forces started gaining strength in different fronts, registering major victories against government forces. This strength could be the result of various factors, frst and foremost, the attitude of suspicion Ethiopia, Eritrea, Uganda and Kenya developed towards Sudan on the basis of its alleged involvement in terrorist activities which had created a conducive situation for Sudanese opposition forces to secure direct and indirect political as well as material assistance from these countries. Secondly, the revival of the National Democratic Alliance (NDA)in 1996 spread the war to the northern front which enabled the NDA forces to take successive attacks in 1997 forcing government forces to withdraw from Kassala.[326]

---

324   Ibid, p.6
325   Ibid, p.1
326   Girma, (1999), p.40

Uganda also cut off diplomatic relations with Sudan in April 1995 accusing Sudan of supporting the rebels opposing the government in Kampala. The relations between the two countries deteriorated particularly when they exchanged artillery fires in 1996 and 1997.[327] On the other hand, at the beginning of the second phase of its relations with Sudan, Ethiopia was relatively stable in adopting its Federal Constitution and conducting the election of deputies to the Federal and Regional Assemblies on 7th May, 1995. Since Sudan continued with its refusal to comply with the demand of the OAU Ministerial Committee meeting to handover the suspects, the matter was submitted to the UN Security Council on the basis of Ethiopia's appeal lodged on 21st December 1995. The Council considered the matter on 31st January 1996 and passed Resolution No 1044/1996 calling the Sudanese government to be bound by the OAU Resolution to handover the alleged criminals and to act in accordance with the OAU and the UN Charters. The Security Council again convened on 11th March 1996 to consider the implementation of its previous resolution and passed Resolution No. 1054/1996 expressing its regret on the failure of Sudan to comply.

The decision of the Council stated that all member countries reduce the number of their diplomats in Khartoum and imposed diplomatic and travel sanctions.[328] Even though the resolution had little practical impact on Sudan, it had damaging political effects on its foreign relations while Ethiopia gained significant political and diplomatic support. The SPLA forces also launched anti-government attacks beginning from October 1995, and by mid-1997 controlled the major part of southern Sudan.[329] The government of Sudan, on the other hand, had been attempting to reverse the domestic situation in its favour by presenting the war as an international plot staged against Islam implicating Ethiopia as one of the perpetrators. This was undertaken with the view of mobilizing the Muslim population of the country. It also appealed to the UN Security Council on 12th January 1996 accusing Ethiopia for invading its territory.

The US had already cut off aid to Sudan and severed its diplomatic relations with the country. It was supporting Sudan's neighbours and the opposition forces of Southern Sudan with the view of overthrowing the NIF-led government. US Embassies in Kenya and Tanzania were bombed by terrorist attacks on 7th August, 1998 killing 12 Americans and more than 258 Kenyans and Tanzanians.[330] The new phenomenon in the Ethiopia and Eritrea relations

327   Ibid, p.39
328   Ibid, p.30
329   Ibid, p.50
330   Woodward, (1996), p.123

is believed to have become a turning point in easing and ultimately normalizing the hostile Ethiopia and Sudan relations. Accordingly, their relations shifted to its third phase which can be categorized as friendly. Ethiopia's flexibility in its relations with Sudan would help it to follow a new foreign policy which could protect its national interests.

7.2.6.3 Phase Three: Improvement of Relations

It is relevant to underline, at the outset, the fact that various important events and actions that could influence the relations of the two countries took place after the Ethiopia and Eritrean relations started to deteriorate. Sudan, which had been suffering from continuous internal conflicts in its southern part since 1983, came to a point where its government and the SPLA/M agreed in principle to hold a referendum on the issue of self-determination for Southern Sudan at IGAD Ministerial sub-committee peace talks in Kenya in May 1998.[331]

Since the sub-committee of the IGAD Mediation Committee, which consisted of Ethiopia, Eritrea, Kenya, and Uganda, played a significant role in bringing this result, it is possible to infer the realization of the Sudanese government of the contribution of its neighbours in bringing peace to Sudan. Ensuring Ethiopia's severance of support to the Sudanese opposition movements could be taken by the NIF regime as an important element for the success of the peace process to resolve the outstanding issues regarding the extent of the area of southern Sudan and the relationship between state and religion.

This is of mutual national interest which would attract both governments to improve their relations and derive mutual benefits thereof. The completion of the oil export pipeline laid down from the southern part of Sudan to the export terminal near Port Sudan with a distance of 1,600 km in August 1999 could be considered as one of the important factors in influencing the two countries to improve their relations. This was expressed in concluding an oil sale agreement, which later proved to be the desire of both parties.[332] The Sudanese government, which was declaring its commitment to resolve the conflict in the Southern part of the country, enacted a constitution in June 1998 endorsing a referendum for the South. The possibility of ending Sudanese internal problems by constitutional means had, however, appeared unlikely due to the embodiment of the Sharia law in the Constitution as the guiding principle of the Country. The continuation of the conflict in southern Sudan had thus enabled Ethiopia to have an important political card to secure Sudan's neutrality in its future

---

331   The Ethiopian Herald, (1998), p.1-2
332   (Country Profile, Sudan (2000), p.12

military engagement against Eritrea in return for Ethiopia's severance of its relations with the Sudanese opposition movements.

The efforts made on the part of the governments of Ethiopia and Sudan since 1998 to improve the relations of the two countries have eventually come into fruition and resulted in the conclusion of different bilateral treaties. These treaties include trade, industry, investment, telecommunication, oil sale to Ethiopia and port use agreements. To facilitate the implementation of these agreements, and to strengthen their friendly relations a Joint Border Development Commission headed by Regional Administrators of adjacent Regions of the two countries was established with the responsibility of handling border development issues.

7.2.6.4 Phase Four: Ethiopia and South Sudan Relations

The relations between South Sudan and Ethiopia has a long history if taken in a wider context. The peace agreement signed in 1972, brokered by the World Council of Churches, contributes to South Sudanese trust of Ethiopia as a peaceful and concerned neighbour. The relations between the two countries was pegged on the following premises: First, Ethiopia and South Sudan seem to have realized that the internal political stability of one is dependent upon the stability of the other, the realization of which necessitates their cooperation. Secondly, the end of the Ethio-Eritrean war in favour of Ethiopia gave the latter a strong power image in the Horn of Africa which South Sudan cannot ignore in the formulation and conduct of its foreign policy.

In nutshell, the basis of the current Ethio-South Sudan friendly relations and the conclusion of cooperation agreements has been compatible with their national interests, which include the enhancement of economic development and establishing internal peace and stability. The friendly relations between these countries have undoubtedly contributed to the improvement of relations among the Horn and IGAD countries. The hosting of Sudan People's Liberation Army/Movement (SPLA/M) has given the current government in South Sudan and the people great faith in developing a cordial relation with Ethiopia.

7.3 Kenya's Foreign Policy

The Kenyan foreign policy is depicted to provide a broad framework on Kenya's foreign relations and diplomatic engagements within a contemporary globalised environment. The policy further seeks to provide a direction to ensure the achievement of the collective aspirations of Kenyans, bearing in mind the critical role of foreign policy in meeting national priorities.[333] Kenya's foreign policy is informed by the constitution of Kenya, Kenya vision 2030 and its medium-term plans, sessional papers, manifestos of the ruling political parties and executive pronouncements and circulars, among others. Kenya's foreign policy aims to achieve several national objectives. These include protecting Kenya's sovereignty and territorial integrity, promoting integration, enhancing regional peace and security and advancing the economic prosperity of Kenya and her people. Other objectives of Kenya's foreign policy include projecting Kenya's image and prestige, promoting multilateralism, promoting the interests of Kenyan diaspora and partnering with the Kenyans abroad.

Kenya's foreign policy is informed by five key areas: peace, economy, diaspora, environment and culture. In regard to peace, the foreign policy seeks to consolidate Kenya's legacy in cultivating peace and stability as necessary conditions for development and prosperity. The economic focus aims to achieve robust economic engagement in order to secure Kenya's socio-economic development and prosperity that ensures that the nation becomes a middle income and industrialized economy by the year 2030. In regard to diaspora, the foreign policy aims to harness the diverse skills, expertise and potential of Kenyans living abroad, and facilitate their integration into the national development agenda. Moreover, environment factors in the foreign policy underscore Kenya's commitment to sustainable management of the environment and shared natural resources while the cultural aspect seeks to use culture as a vital tool to promote a favourable image and prestige for the country globally.

The institutions involved in Kenya's foreign policy formulation include the executive comprising the presidency, cabinet, ministry of foreign affairs and international trade, relevant ministries, departments and agencies. Parliament is also included in Kenya's foreign policy formulation. Other Kenyan institutions informing foreign policy include county governments, offices of retired heads of state and other statesmen, civil society organizations, corporate entities and the people through their elected representatives. The above analysis indicates how Kenya uses her pillars of foreign policy such as trade, the economy, peace and security, diaspora and the culture to promote her interest in the international arena. The study has examined South Sudan's foreign policy based on the variables provided in the analysis of Kenya's foreign policy to come up with key pillars that should guide South Sudan foreign policy.

---

333   Republic of Kenya, (2014), p.5

7.3.1 Foreign Policy Framework

The benchmarks guiding the country's relations with the world were set by the imperative to re-align its goals at the international level to the turbulent and shifting dynamics of a divided world during the Cold War era (1945-1989). Even though Kenya's liberation struggle enhanced the country's international image and stature, paradoxically, this heroic history also risked playing into the East-West ideological divide.

In order to strategically place the country in the international arena, the architects of Kenya's foreign policy charted a pragmatic approach, informed by several principles, which have stood the test of time. This approach has ensured that Kenya successfully forges mutually beneficial alliances with the West while constructively engaging the East through its policy of positive economic and political non-alignment. In pursuing its national interests in the international arena, Kenya continues to enjoy a favourable international profile arising from its strategic location, sustained stability, strong political institutions, sound economic policies, dynamic environmental strategies, and highly educated and skilled human resources. Other positive attributes are outstanding performance by Kenya's sports persons and the increasing involvement of Kenyans abroad in national development.[334]

7.3.1.1 Policy Objectives

Kenya's foreign policy seeks to protect Kenya's sovereignty and territorial integrity, promote sub-regional and regional integration and co-operation, enhance regional and global peace and security, advance the economic prosperity of Kenya and her people, project Kenya's image and prestige, promote international cooperation and multilateralism, promote and protect the interests of Kenyans abroad, and enhance partnership with the Kenya Diaspora and descendants. These objectives are pursued through five key inter-linked pillars of Kenya's foreign policy.[335]

7.3.1.2 Guiding Principles

The execution of Kenya's foreign policy and the conduct of her international relations are guided by the following principles:[336]
• Sanctity of sovereignty and territorial integrity of the Republic of Kenya;

---

334   Kenya Foreign Policy strategy, (2014), Pp.14-15
335   Ibid, p.19
336   Ibid, p.19

- Peaceful co-existence with neighbours and other nations;
- Resolution of conflicts by peaceful means;
- Promotion of regional integration;
- Respect for the equality, sovereignty and territorial integrity of states; and
- Respect for international norms, customs and laws.

7.3.1.3 Philosophy and Values

Kenya's foreign policy is guided and driven by a vision of "a peaceful, prosperous and globally competitive Kenya" while the mission is "To project, promote and protect Kenya's interests and image globally through innovative diplomacy, and contribute towards a just, peaceful and equitable world." The policy is inspired and guided by the following national values and aspirations of the Kenyan people as enshrined in the Constitution of Kenya:[337]
- Unity in Diversity;
- Honour and Patriotism;
- Peace and Liberty;
- Justice and Equity;
- Quest for Prosperity; and
- Harambee Spirit (pulling together).

7.3.1.4 Sources Informing the Kenya Foreign Policy

Though Kenya has in the past not had a single written foreign policy framework document, the conduct of Kenya's foreign relations has been informed by various official documents, and executive pronouncements and circulars, including the following:[338]
- The Constitution of Kenya;
- The Sessional Paper No. 10/1965 on African Socialism and its Application to Planning in Kenya;
- The Sessional Paper No. 1/1986 on Economic Management for Renewed Growth;
- Manifestos of the ruling political parties;
- National Development Plans;
- Kenya Environmental Policy, 2013
- Kenya Vision 2030 and its Medium-Term Plans; and
- International Treaties, Conventions, Agreements and Charters.

---

337   Ibid, p.20
338   Ibid, p.20

7.3.2 Pillars of Foreign Policy

Kenya's foreign policy rests on five interlinked pillars: Peace diplomacy pillar; Economic diplomacy pillar; Diaspora diplomacy pillar, Environment diplomacy pillar and Cultural diplomacy pillar.

7.3.2.1 Peace Diplomacy

Underlying Kenya's peace and security diplomacy is the recognition of peace and stability as necessary pre-conditions for development and prosperity. Linked to this is Kenya's conviction that its own stability and economic wellbeing are dependent on the stability of the sub-region, Africa and the rest of the world.

The objectives of this pillar are to promote the resolution of conflicts by peaceful means; collaborate with other African countries to strengthen the conflict prevention, management and resolution capacity of regional institutions, including the East African Community (EAC), Intergovernmental Authority on Development (IGAD), Common Market for Eastern and Southern Africa (COMESA) and the African Union (AU with the aim of promoting sustainable peace and development; support peace efforts by the African Union and the United Nations through contributing troops and providing leadership in peacekeeping missions within the continent and globally; and create conflict analysis and prevention capacity nationally and in the region through the Foreign Service Academy.[339]

In pursuing these objectives, Kenya's foreign peace diplomacy continues to draw on Kenya's experiences in mediation, conflict resolution and peacekeeping. Further, Kenya will continue to support institutions that are involved in peace keeping in the Continent which include International Peace Support Training Centre and East African Standby Force Command among others.

7.3.2.2 Economic Diplomacy

Kenya's quest for a peaceful and stable environment is linked to its socio-economic development and prosperity and that of the region. A robust economic engagement is necessary to secure Kenya's regional and overall economic objectives in line with the Kenya Vision 2030.

The objectives of this pillar are to increase capital flows to Kenya and the East African region; support export promotion and investment by Kenyan

---

339   Ibid, p.22-23

enterprises within the region and beyond; promote the country as a favourite destination for foreign direct investment, tourism, and conferencing; expand access to traditional markets and explore new destinations for Kenya's exports; enhance technological advancement by exploring new sources of affordable and appropriate technology; support the exploration of alternative sources of traditional and renewable energy; strengthen regional economic communities and organizations to serve as competitive springboards to emerging and global markets; and promote fair trade and equitable bilateral, regional and multilateral trade agreements.[340]

7.3.2.3 Diaspora Diplomacy

The Government of Kenya recognizes the huge and untapped potential of Kenyans abroad which can contribute to the country's national development agenda. The Diaspora pillar aims to harness the diverse skills, knowledge, expertise and resources of Kenyans living abroad, and facilitating their integration into the national development agenda. This informs the Diaspora Pillar which seeks to harness the contribution of Kenyans living abroad through the implementation of the National Diaspora policy. The objectives of this pillar are to provide effective and responsive consular services, facilitate Kenyans Abroad to participate in national development, promote the access by Kenyans to the international labour market, utilize outstanding Kenyans, and tap into the skills and resources of the Kenyans Abroad for national development.[341]

7.3.2.4 Environmental Diplomacy

The Kenya Environmental Policy 2013 underscores that environment and natural resources are valuable national assets upon which the country's sustainable development is anchored. Kenya recognizes its enormous stake in the sustainable management of its own natural resources, as well as those of the region and the world. The strong orientation towards environmental issues is therefore a distinct feature of Kenya's foreign policy. Among key issues underlined by the environment pillar is the effective implementation of the Multilateral Environmental Agreements (MEAs) such as the Convention on International Trade of Endangered Species (CITES). Kenya takes its obligation to transmit humanity's inheritance to posterity seriously. Underlying this commitment is the urgency to confront the impact of contemporary environmental problems

---

340   Ibid, p.23
341   Ibid, p.24-25

such as global climate change, ozone depletion, ocean and air pollution, and resource degradation compounded by the increasing world population.

The objectives of this pillar are to champion the strengthening of United Nations Environmental Programme (UNEP) and United Nations Human Settlements Programme in (UN HABITAT) in prioritizing the global sustainable development agenda; promote compliance with the relevant national, regional and international environmental legislation, regulations, standards, and other appropriate operational procedures and guidelines; promote the integration of environmental management into national and regional economic activities, including agriculture and tourism to minimize negative impact on the environment; promote research as a mechanism to encourage innovation and reduce adverse environmental impacts; and encourage public dialogue, awareness and knowledge creation on environmental matters through national, regional and international forums.

7.3.2.5 Cultural Diplomacy

The potential of Kenya's cultural heritage is enormous and there is a need for its exploitation for the development of the country. Over the years, Kenya has continuously placed emphasis on cultural recognition and understanding as the basis for dialogue. It is through cultural activities that a nation's idea of itself is best represented. Kenya's cultural diplomacy aims to increase awareness of her cultural richness and to generate interests in the country's cultural heritage.

The objectives of this pillar are to respect and recognize cultural diversity and heritage; promote cultural exchanges and partnerships; promote global intercultural dialogue; promote sports and art diplomacy by recognizing the role of Kenyan artist, athletes and other sportsmen and women; and promote the recognition of Kiswahili as a continental and global language. The implementation of these pillars will provide a guiding framework for diplomatic engagements. This will further guide the country as it pursues its vision of becoming peaceful, prosperous and globally competitive while promoting sustainable development.[342]

7.3.3 Execution Determinants

In the modern globalised world, interconnectedness and interdependence are a reality. Kenya therefore recognizes the importance of strengthened bilateral relations, regional cooperation and enhanced multilateral engagement as

---

342   Ibid, p. 27

fundamental components of its foreign policy and entry points for achieving its national interests.

7.3.3.1 Bilateral Relations

Kenya continues to embrace bilateralism in pursuing its foreign policy objectives through bilateral trade, and political, environmental and cultural agreements with other countries. Among priority countries are East Africa Community member states which are Kenya's strategic trading partners. These countries host a significant number of Kenyans expatriates and remain the focus of the Kenyan business community. Kenya will also seek to enter into bilateral partnership with countries in other African sub-regions within the context of its afro-centric foreign policy.

The implementation of bilateral arrangements with foreign countries beyond Africa forms a critical component of Kenya's foreign policy agenda which lays emphasis on emerging economies and economic zones. Kenya will further strengthen its bilateral diplomacy through establishment of diplomatic missions in countries of strategic importance and exchange of high-level visits. Further the promotion and protection of the interests of the large number of Kenyans abroad will continue to inform the strengthening of bilateral relations with other countries.

7.3.3.2 Regional Integration

Regional integration has a key of advantages to Kenya which include regional stability and increase in trade among others. Therefore, regional integration will continue to be one of the cornerstones of Kenya's foreign policy. The East African Community (EAC), Intergovernmental Authority on Development (IGAD), Common Market for Eastern and Southern Africa (COMESA) and the African Union (AU) are Kenya's principal avenues for pursuing its foreign policy goals.[343]

7.3.3.3 Multilateralism

Kenya continues to promote the principles of the United Nations (UN) Charter and play its rightful role in supporting the work of the United Nations system in the promotion of international peace and security, trade, human

---

343   Ibid, p.29

rights and democracy, refugees, sustainable development and the reform of the UN system. In this regard, Kenya will forge greater collaboration with the United Nations system and other international institutions and bodies. Kenya's foreign policy also supports the reform of the United Nations system to make the world body more responsive to all countries and regions of the world with equal representation in its organs and institutions as a top priority.

Kenya continues to effectively engage with the Commonwealth, South-South Cooperation, Indian Ocean Rim-Association for Regional Cooperation (IOR-ARC) and other multilateral organizations to promote international cooperation and collaboration in finding lasting solutions to global challenges and in helping transformation of the multilateral system to reflect the diversity of our nations, and to ensure its centrality in global governance. In addition, Kenya will continue to defend and advance her overall international policy goals through robust engagement at the World Trade Organization (WTO) to create a predictable, transparent and enabling environment for fair multilateral trading system.[344]

7.3.3.4 Public Diplomacy

In a competitive and complex world, public diplomacy is essential to actively promote Kenya's image, values and culture abroad. The Kenya foreign policy approach therefore embraces use of available technologies and platforms, especially social media networks to communicate with stakeholders on the country's foreign policy. Kenya will also continue to provide institutional support and capacity building in the region through a regional technical cooperation programme under the Kenya Regional Technical Cooperation Fund.

7.3.3.5 Institutional Framework

To achieve Kenya's foreign policy objectives and priorities, the following institutions are fundamental: The Executive, comprised of the Presidency, the Cabinet, Ministry of Foreign Affairs and International Trade and relevant Ministries, Departments and Agencies; The Parliament, County Governments, Offices of Retired Heads of State/Government and other Statesmen; and any other relevant institutions, offices and instruments.[345] It remains strong member of EAC, IGAD and UN. It became one of the African Union's three representatives to non-permanent seats of the UNSC from January, 2021.

---

344   Ibid, p.29
345   Ibid, p.30

7.4 Nigeria's Foreign Policy

Foreign policy is implicit in the fact that nations formulate and execute their foreign policies with the ultimate aim of promoting and protecting their national interests, which are always limited by treaty obligations, international law and responsibilities assumed under international organizations while the foreign policy of other states and the circumstances at hand are also considered. The Nigerian nation is known as one, whose foreign policy is essentially tailored to reflect her commitment to the well-being of all African countries, particularly in the areas of peaceful co-existence, prevention of violent conflicts at intra-national and international levels in the restoration of peace where necessary, and maintenance of peace all over the world.

7.4.1 Foreign Policy Objectives

Since independence, Nigeria's foreign policy has been guided by certain objectives such as the protection of the sovereign and territorial integrity of the Nigerian State; the promotion of the economic and social well-being of Nigeria; the enhancement of Nigeria's image and status in the world at large; the promotion of unity as well as the total political, economic, social and cultural liberation of Nigeria and Africa; the promotion of the rights of black people and others under colonial rule; the promotion of international cooperation conducive to the consolidation of world peace and security, mutual respect and friendship among all peoples and states; redressing the imbalance in the international power structures which has tended to frustrate the legitimate aspirations of developing countries; respect for the sovereignty, independence and territorial integrity of all nations; and the promotion of world peace based on the principles of freedom, mutual respect and equality of the world. From 1960 to date, Nigeria has maintained a relatively consistent foreign policy considering the fact that the country experienced varied forms of government within this period. Right from independence, Africa was the centrepiece of Nigeria's foreign policy with emphasis on the emancipation, development and unity of Africans both within and outside the continent. It is delivered to be a frontline state outside the frontline states.

7.4.2 Origin and Development of Nigeria's Foreign Policy

In its ingredients, the foreign policy of all nations, great and small, are the same. In short, the shaping of foreign policy is a dynamic process involving the interaction between a country's internal and external environments. Below is the historical development of Nigeria's foreign policy over time.

7.4.2.1 Pro-British Epoch: 1960-1966

Fresh from colonial rule and basking in the euphoria of a newly independent nation, Nigeria made certain pronouncements that had stuck with her until the present, and perhaps, have been responsible for her foreign policy thrust to present. Nigeria's foreign policy immediately after independence till the first military coup was predominantly pro-British and guided by British interests. While claiming non-alignment as one of her policy objectives, Nigeria was clearly pro-British and pro-West generally. The government was responsible for its action, but would not allow the infiltration of communism into Nigeria. The British government was consistently teleguiding Nigeria's new leadership and actions towards rejecting the Soviet Union's communist ideology and even seeking or accepting any type of aid from them.

During this period, Nigeria's foreign policy was conservative, reactionary, Pro-Western under an uncertain and timid administration that was totally aligned to the West in every trade and diplomatic relation. According to Egbo (2003), "all sectors of the economy were not only controlled by the West, but were entirely dependent on their capitalist orientation for the country's consumptive patterns and developmental efforts." However, there were many inconsistencies and contradictions in foreign policy, as could be seen from the following actions he took within the period:

- Severing relations with France over their testing of an atomic bomb in the Sahara Desert in 1961 just three months after independence;
- Refusal to attend the maiden conference of the Non-aligned Movement in Belgrade;
- Prevarication over the establishment of formal diplomatic ties with the Sino-Soviet bloc until December 1961;
- Acceptance of the Anglo-Nigeria Defence Pact until he was forced to abrogate it by students and the opposition;
- Refusing to train armed militia for Angolan national fighters waging a war against Portuguese colonialists despite Nigeria's avowed resolve to rid the continent of colonialism.
- The above show that while the Africa policy was still intact, there were still a lot of other inconsistent components of that government which believed its definite foreign policy thrust.

7.4.2.2 The Tribulation Epoch: 1966-1975

During this period, Nigeria's civil war and the oil boom "provided Nigeria a new impetus to practice her non-aligned stance and position of neutrality in international events."[346] The government of the day was involved with the civil war and the attitudes of former and new entrants into the alignment scope of the Nigerian State. For instance, faced with the British initial hesitation at supplying arms to the government to launch the war against Biafra, the government had to turn to the Soviet who supplied all the weapons needed for the onslaught. This seeming advantage of the USSR in ideological warfare led Britain to get involved in the war, so as to stave off the Soviets' increasingly communist influence in Nigeria. Thus, the period was devoted to winning the civil war and maintaining the integrity of the Nigerian nation. The period was a very vibrant decade of interesting foreign policy learning as propaganda became a major aspect of Nigeria's foreign policy. Coming out from a sapping civil war, Nigeria learnt many lessons:

- There was need to come closer in cooperation to other African states on matters that could promote both political and economic freedom to the continent;
- Nigeria need not unnecessarily reject overtures of friendship from the Soviet Union; and
- Nigeria could disagree with Britain on issues it felt strongly about and still retain her status.

The period was one of self-confidence, a period when Nigerian foreign policy that was previously personalized especially by Gowon now turned to a low-profile policy deliberately made so for maximum effect and attention by world leaders. It was also very vibrant in the sense that far-reaching decisions were made at this time, which have stood the test of time.

7.4.2.3 Refining the Policy Epoch: 1976-1979

This period saw a true manifestation of the Africa policy of Nigeria as the regime gave a well-defined, articulate, coherent and explicit policy for Africa that was not tainted with fear or deference to any bloc or country. The boldness exhibited by the Nigerian leadership has been given as perhaps one of the many reasons for his untimely elimination from the political scene. There was an issue of conspiracy by the West that could not stomach a revolutionary leader, a

---

346   Egbo, (2003), p. 65

staunch believer in Africa and a soldier who was ready to do all it took to wrest Africa from the wrenches of the capitalist West that had continued to control the continent's destiny many years after the declaration of independence. Mohammed did not help matters with his forceful sparring with the United States on the Angolan crisis between UNITA and MPLA, where Nigeria recognized and supported the MPLA government as against the American support for UNITA.[347]

The short-lived leadership of Murtala Mohammed did not in any way derail Nigeria's foreign policy, as his successor, General Olusegun Obasanjo, vowed to and followed the same trend. He was dedicated to the African spirit and was bold to take actions independent of Western influence. Obasanjo, to his credit, did a lot in terms of pushing Nigeria to the front-burner in international affairs by telling Britain and America some home truths despite the closeness, though without antagonizing them, and he went beyond that to the Soviet/Communist bloc to cultivate friendships that have endured to date.[348] Although the domestic policies did not materialize a lot of visible developmental progress, Nigeria's foreign policy under Mohammed/Obasanjo regimes is the best so far as it received wide acceptability and respect in the global community.

7.4.2.4 Afro-Centric Epoch: 1979-1983

The rationale was the maintenance of the Afrocentric foreign policy by trying to keep up with the already established policy but could not be possible because of series of problems that faced the country. This policy resulted into spearheading Africa's commitment to peaceful settlement of inter-state disputes like the Somalia/Ethiopia; Morocco/Polisario Movement over Western Sahara; and the Hissene Habre/Guokonni Weddeye crises in Chad.[349] Rather, the government was known to have caused bad blood and hostility towards Nigeria by some neighbouring states in the African continent with the expulsion of illegal aliens especially from Ghana. Moreover, it was during this time that the corruption in government led to the downward spiral in the Nigerian economy. As succinctly noted by Egbo who reiterated that, to any casual observer, the steam had gone out of Nigeria's foreign policy. The momentum and zeal which had characterized Nigeria's foreign policy in the previous five years, was eventually replaced with a lack of forthrightness and excessive caution in approaching issues. The regime lacked definite focus and fundamental framework, lapsed into unenthusiastic

---

347   Ezirim, Gerald Ekenedirichukwu, (2016), p.5-6
348   Ibid, p.6
349   Egbo, (2003), p. 77

conceptualization and incoherent policy vacuum. The innovativeness and assertiveness of the last two regimes was lost. Shagari's foreign policy became a flash-back to the conservatism and legalism of the Balewa era, such that while lots of noise was made for good measure, the reality was one of incompetence and impotence borne out of indifference, confusion and political foot-dragging.[350] This attitude created the opportunity for the military to come back into the political scene with the coup d'etat of December 1984.

7.4.2.5 Good Neighbourhood Epoch: 1983-1993

During this period, the foreign policy priority was to have more peace in Africa starting with her neighbours as seen in what it conceptualized as the 'concentric circle'. As clearly adumbrated by Gambari (1989), the pattern of concentric circle may be discernible in our attitude and response to foreign policy issues within the African continent and in the world at large. At the epicentre of these circles are the national economic and security interests of the Federal Republic of Nigeria, which are inextricably tied up with the security, stability and the economic and social well-being of our immediate neighbours. One of our principal priorities is to put on a more constructive footing relation with our neighbours with whom we share identical goals of regional stability and peace.[351]

It was during this period that the Quadripartite Agreements involving Nigeria and her three neighbours to the West (Benin, Ghana and Togo) were signed. But then, the regime showed inconsistency by indefinitely closing down Nigeria's borders as a measure against smuggling and money laundering in her much-vaunted fight against corruption. This action caused a serious infraction in the diplomatic relations between Nigeria and Britain. Moreover, the highhandedness and unbending and unyielding resolve of the regime in some of its actions brought about his overthrow; Buhari was accused of running a two-man show of himself and Idiagbon.[352] Babangida also went beyond the continental level by taking bold steps such as restoring relations with Israel that had been severed since October 1973 over the Arab-Israel conflict. Thus, in all, Babangida's regime was credited with some achievements such as:

- The revival of Nigeria's active commitment to ECOWAS by lifting boundary closures and restoring free movement within ECOWAS countries;
- Nigeria's active intervention in inter-African affairs and conflicts, especially

---

350   Ibid, p.78
351   Gambari (1989), p.3
352   Ezirim, Gerald Ekenedirichukwu, (2016), p.6

in West Africa, in the border wars between Mali and Burkina Faso and in the strained relations between Sierra Leone and Liberia;

- The establishment and funding of Nigeria's Technical Aids Corps (TAC) which provides highly trained Nigerian personnel at little or no costs to needy African states;
- The formation of the Lagos Forum of Medium Powers; and
- The use of Nigeria's foreign policy to support and promote Nigeria's domestic economic policy.

Moreover, it was during this era that Nigeria received the most representation in the international scene through the United Nations. It was during this period that Obasanjo was selected as one of the three pioneer members of the International Eminent Personalities mandated to arbitrate in the South African political debacle by the Commonwealth; in 1989, Nigeria's permanent representative to the United Nations Joe Garba was made President of the General Assembly in its 44th meeting of 1990 where Emeka Anyaoku was elected as the Secretary-General of the Commonwealth of Nations. Despite all the above minimal successes, Babangida's regime is not taken to be the best time for Nigeria's foreign policy because "rhetoric, emptiness, inaction, policy somersault and indecision were to mark the second half of his tenure.

7.4.2.6 Reaction and Isolation Epoch: 1993-1999

Thus, foreign policy during this period was "reactive and isolationist For him, there was a need to fashion out a new foreign policy thrust for the country as the traditional position had become more or less in his estimation, thus, the constitution of a 50-member committee of every other interest group apart from career diplomats, intellectuals and experts in the field of international relations and foreign policy. This deliberate action showed his hand early enough that he did not want anything except to direct what should happen without recourse to what had been the tradition. Moreover, the regime was so brazen in disregard of diplomatic norms and showed marked disdain for finesse in relations with the diplomatic corps of other countries that left them stunned. Such traditional allies as Britain, United States, France, Germany, Canada and South Africa and many others temporarily withdrew diplomatic representations and support for Nigeria; and in response to the isolation from the West and its associates turned to Asia. This further alienated Nigeria from dominant powers of the world as Asia did not really do much for the foreign policy objectives of Nigeria.

7.4.2.7 Democratization and
Shuttle Diplomacy Epoch: 1999-2019

Nigeria's foreign policy after the successful transition to democratic governance was more of shuttle diplomacy beyond Africa embarked upon by President Obasanjo in order to win over a world that had overlooked Nigeria and would rather not have anything to do with her. Thus, the foreign policy, according to Agbu (2001), extends far beyond the concern for the well-being of the African continent. The debt burden, for instance, is not an exclusive African predicament, and many countries in Asia, the Caribbean and South America face similar problems, hence the need for the harmonization of efforts.

This was corroborated by the former Foreign Affairs Minister Sule Lamido's comments that while it may appear improper to dismiss Africa as the centrepiece of Nigeria's foreign policy, the core issue in contemporary international relations, which is economic, makes that prevailing doctrine inappropriate. Thus, Nigeria's foreign policy in this era, rooted in support of democratic values, the principle of self-determination, human rights, rule of law, was bound to strengthen and institutionalize the culture of good governance and democratic culture at the domestic level. At the regional level, Nigeria did not move away from her traditional Afrocentric stance. According to Obasanjo (2005), Africa should remain the centrepiece of our foreign policy. The renewed determination of African leaders, our strengthening of regional economic communities, the restructuring of the OAU into the AU, and a better global disposition towards Africa, the AU and the AU's programme, NEPAD, are indicators that we are indeed a new Africa, the Africa that should be united, integrated, devoid of conflicts and violence, especially in the contemporary global system where there is no chronic conflicting ideological divide.

Thus, Nigeria created structures that would help in further bringing the country into greater reckoning in Africa, thereby making for peace and development in the continent. This was done through the creation of such important offices as the constitutional provision for the promotion of African integration and support for African unity – shown through the Ministry of Cooperation and Integration in Africa, maintenance of peace and security in the West African sub-region as shown by Nigeria's leadership role in the formation of ECOMOG, and her membership of the Gulf of Guinea Commission. Also, Nigeria played a key role in the "conceptualization of the New Partnership for African Development (NEPAD) and shift its focus from conflicts to economic development.

7.4.3 Pillars of Nigeria's Foreign Policy

Some of the vital factors that gave rise to this kind of foreign policy are namely the symbiotic relationships, religious affiliations, economic affairs and historical background. The implication is that Nigeria cannot afford to be hostile to these other countries if only because a large number of her citizens benefit from symbiotic relationships, just as nationals of these other nations reside and make a living in Nigeria.

7.4.3.1 Religious Affiliations

Nigeria is a secular state where freedom of religion is guaranteed. But then, the country has a predominance of Christians and Muslims, the two major religions. This is not to suggest that there are no other religious groups, but they are not as prominent as the Muslims and Christians. The preponderance of the two religious groups has serious implications for the nation's foreign policy, since any noticeable policy perceived to be unfavourable to any of the two religious blocs can create problems domestically.

For example, the nation's peace was relatively threatened when the federal government of Nigeria, during General Ibrahim Badamosi Babangida (IBB)'s administration, announced that Nigeria was going to become a member of the Organisation of Islamic Countries (OIC). The southern Christian population saw the move as a betrayal in a country whose constitution clearly declares a secular state. They also saw the military President, a Muslim, as using his position to drag the nation along to Islam, being the dominant religion of his people in the northern part of the country. There was uproar and widespread condemnation of the Babangida administration for this.

Therefore, even in deciding what relationships to maintain with other countries, the Nigerian government has a duty to weigh the implications of such decisions on the domestic front as policies tilting too closely to the side of countries professing either of the two religions could lead to disruption of peace within the country.

7.4.3.2 Economic Affairs

Even now after more than 50 years of her political independence, Nigeria is still far away from economic independence, as the nation remains a raw materials producer for the manufacturing economies mainly of the Western world. The discovery of petroleum in large quantities, for instance, on the Nigerian soil in

1958 is a natural blessing, which ought to have changed the nation's economic situation for the better, but for lack of foresight by successive leaderships.

At the moment, over 90 per cent of the national budget is tied to revenue generated through sales of crude oil. What this means is that Nigeria cannot make policy decisions that may injure or offend countries that buy her crude oil. If for reasons beyond her control she has to take injurious decisions affecting such countries, the aftermath will be a devastating economic crunch which could cause serious threat to national peace and stability at home.

7.4.4 Principles of Nigeria's Foreign Policy

Nigeria's foreign policy principles consist of careful statements and pronouncements in respect of our national interests. According to Nwibor Lucky Barika, the following are the key principles of Nigeria's foreign policy.[353]

7.4.4.1 Non-Alignment

This is a foreign policy principle which rejects a formal military alliance with and routine political support for either the West or East as to bloc politics especially in the light of the post-World War II ideological cold war between the West and the former Soviet Union.

7.4.4.2 Legal Equality of States

This principle makes Nigeria believe that a well ordered and peaceful community at the global and continental levels needs mutual and reciprocal respect for the views and interests of all peoples and as such she should continue to re-assure the world that she has no intention of dominating or embarking on aggressive military policies against smaller and weaker nations despite her relative advantage in size, population and resources. Nigeria believes in playing a leadership role within the context of Africa but not an imperial type.

7.4.4.3 Non-Interference in the
Domestic Affairs of Other States

Without prejudice to this principle, experts argue that as dominant power in West Africa, her security boundaries are not expected to be synonymous with

353   Nwibor Lucky Barika, (2014), p.54

her territorial boundaries but should extend to the territorial boundaries of her contagious neighbours with other states especially the Francophone states in Africa who use this threat of domination and interference to further consolidate their economic and diplomatic pressure on France.

7.4.4.4 Multilateralism

This principle calls for Nigeria's membership of major international organizations at the sub-regional, regional and global levels and the need to initiate new ones. This is predicated on the fact that membership of such organizations affords her the opportunities for multilateral negotiations and collaborations so as to moderate international political games as they are able to use such fora to articulate and aggregate their views and collectively give legitimacy to their foreign policy goals.

7.4.4.5 Africa as the Centre Piece

This implies that in all issues of foreign relations, those involving Africa would always take precedence. This Afro-centric position makes Nigeria initiate policy choices and antagonises Nigeria to subordinate any extra African powers for the attainment of her national interest. This position demonstrates her absolute support for OAU, AU, OPEC which she has frequently used as a diplomatic strategy to drive African interest in the United Nations (UN). One can now recall why the organization of African Unity (OAU) stood steadfast with Nigeria during the civil war and facilitated her victory. Nigeria has relatively and consistently antagonized African enemies and support African through the initiation of policy choices and options to drive home African demands as was the case of the struggle and dismantling of apartheid in South Africa before 1994.

7.4.5 Determinants of Nigeria's Foreign Policy

From the foregoing, an understanding of Nigeria's national interest has been examined, which of course put Nigeria in good stead towards understanding the policy direction which underpins its foreign and defence priorities. Foreign policies are not made by any state in isolation of the prevailing situations in the international system. Therefore, determinants are the factors both internal and external that have conditioning effects on the foreign policy of a country. To this end, in formulating her foreign policy a nation does not consider the goals she wants to achieve alone but takes cognizance to certain basic facts within the international scene that affects its existence. These special considerations and cognizance are:

7.4.5.1 Affiliations

Like any other nation in the world, Nigeria's foreign policy has a base in her historical affiliations and experiences. First, it is clear that many of the countries in the West African sub-region had similar experiences. For instance, all the British West African countries of Nigeria, Ghana, Sierra Leone and the Gambia emerged as independent nations after years of foreign rule. Incidentally, all of them had been colonized by the same colonial master, Great Britain; therefore, they had gone through similar treatments and experiences in the hands of one and the same colonial authority. As a result, the affinity created by similar colonial experiences had a pull on the subsisting subsequent relationships between the African countries when they eventually became independent in quick succession in the late 1950s and early 1960s.

7.4.5.2 Nationalism

Before the advent of independence from the colonial masters, certain things had happened to serve as gravitational pulls for many of the West African countries. Most of those who subsequently became national leaders in the West African sub-region had met in foreign countries where they studied. The long-time dream of the Africans was a self-governing federation of all British West African territories, a dream which faded when they realised the consequences of the fact that Nigeria was much more populous than the rest of British West Africa put together.[354] Therefore, Nigeria was not supposed to join a federation in which her voice was not proportionate to her size; the other territories would not join a federation in which Nigeria would have a permanent majority. This clearly was the beginning of nationalism of individual countries of the West African sub-region and, indeed, all African countries.

However, before the formation of sub-continental bodies, there were two power blocs; the Casablanca bloc and the Monrovia bloc. The two blocs were perceived to be representing different ideologies. The Casablanca Group, which had Ghana as its arrowhead was noted for radical approach to issues; while the Monrovia Group led by Nigeria, was known to be conservative in its approach to issues.

---

354   Ibid, p.28

The two blocs operated along their "leftist" and "rightist" approaches until the formation of the Organisation of African Unity (OAU) in 1963. Countries in the Casablanca group included Mali, Guinea and so on while the Monrovia group had Nigeria, Sierra Leone, and the Gambia to name but a few. It is to be noted, that even when the groups had disbanded, attitudes remained generally the same as voting on issues in the OAU now African Union (AU); reflected former bloc convictions and actions happenings following the termination of the 2nd World War in 1945, thereafter, fanned the embers of nationalism, particularly among the nations of British West Africa. Thousands of able-bodied, young men from Nigeria, Gold Coast (currently Ghana), Sierra Leone, The Gambia and Liberia were recruited to fight on the side of the Allied Forces, of which their colonial master, Britain, was one.

The young Africans, as soldiers, were mobilised to fight in East Africa, North Africa and South-East Asia. During training and subsequent war actions, the soldiers were taught that they were fighting for freedom and that good and comfortable resettlement that awaited them whenever they returned to their respective countries at the end of the war. Moreover, fighting men in Asia were exposed to information through pamphlets circulated among them. The pamphlets, however, contained what demobilized British troops would get; and since the West African soldiers believed they qualified for the same entitlements, "they had high expectations only to be demobilized and abandoned on return to base in their respective countries."[355]

Of course, the United Nations Organization, which replaced the League of Nations shortly after the 2nd World War, had made reference to the Freedom of colonial people. In its Treaty. That alone also created "a mental climate favourable to ideas of self-determination among West Africans of the era. The similarity of treatment under the colonialists engendered the series of constitutional developments which eventually led to the attainment of independence by many West African countries between 1957 and 1965. In a nutshell, this shows that the commonality and similarity of experience in political, social and economic development of West African countries served as a binding force, which subsequently informed their foreign policy outlooks even after independence.[356]

7.4.5.3 Public Opinion

Equally important in the determination and processing of foreign policy is the factor of the public as nations listen to opinions of her citizens on crucial issues.

355   Ibid, p.128
356   Nwibor Lucky Barika, (2014), p.55

This was the case when Nigeria intended to go to war with Cameroon: the students' association of the Cross River State cried out opting for diplomatic measure as against the war as they would be adversely affected. Truly, the students' and other opinions were heard.

7.4.5.4 Information as Source of Intelligence

The translation of information into alternative courses of action followed by decision-making resulting in the adoption of policy guidelines even though there is no strict uniformity among nations on the institutions for the processes of formulating and executing foreign policy. The ministry is collectively responsible to the parliament for whatever decision it takes. The president therefore depends on heads of major ministries as External Affairs, Defence, Petroleum resources, and Trade for advice on foreign policy related issues. The Ministry of External Affairs is a highly hierarchical administrative structure which assists the Executive in the foreign policy planning and execution in Nigeria. The minister of External Affairs is the primary person who relays/conveys to the president or senate committee on foreign affairs. Apart from administering his ministry, he supervises the diplomatic and consular services of the country.[357] The National Assembly is the body with constructional powers to support, modify or defeat proposals of the executive including foreign policy proposals. In a democratic society like Nigeria, the legislature assumes the role of shaping policy through its committee on foreign affairs as the Assembly gathers information, listens to the views of specialized interest groups and carefully weighs alternative courses of action. Also, through the power of approval of appropriation, the legislature could increase or decrease or eliminate executive proposals to enable it implement foreign policy programme.

7.4.5.5 Pressure Group

These groups are otherwise known as interest groups. The main thrust of their activities is to reach and influence decision-making agencies of the government towards pre-determined goals. One can see various categories of interest groups clusters around areas of public policy. They are usually organized around economic groups, religious, socio-cultural, academic and other professional groups.[358] They include Nigerian Manufacturing Association, churches and mosques, Nigerian Bar Association, Academic Staff Unions of Universities and

---

357		Ibid, p.55
358		Ibid, p.55

Polytechnics etc. The attribute of public opinion is that it is not static as they respond to occurrence of events at hand.

7.5 South Sudan's Foreign Policy

Historically, South Sudan foreign policy commenced immediately after the declaration of independence on 9th July, 2011. Sudan was the first country to recognize South Sudan's independence, which cemented her foreign relations. The basis of two country's relations was mediated by the 1 January, 1956 alignment, with final alignment pending negotiations and demarcation to avoid aggression from each state in accordance with disputed or porous borders. The boundary that separates Kenya and South Sudan's sovereignty is unclear in the "Ilemi Triangle," which needs a serious decision and shuttle diplomacy between Juba and Nairobi. Sudan seems to have been supporting some rebel militia groups in South Sudan, which led to conflict and human rights abuses. The good news was that the conflicting parties in South Sudan have signed the Revitalized Peace agreement through Sudan's facilitation and South Sudan has reciprocated it by spearing Sudan peace talks in Juba. South Sudan became a member of the United Nations on July 14, 2011 barely 5 days after independence. The Security Council established the UN Mission in the Republic of South Sudan (UNMISS) in July 2011 to consolidate peace and security and to help establish conditions for development.

The youngest world state was midwifed by the United State of America making her the highest foreign policy priorities for the U.S. Government in Africa. The United States recognized South Sudan as a sovereign, independent state on July 9, 2011. The U.S. government is the leading international donor to South Sudan by contributing more than $10 billion in humanitarian, development, peacekeeping and reconstruction assistance.

In the immediate aftermath of South Sudan's independence, her foreign policy prerogative was seen as a challenge in the quest to balance relations between the West, East, African and the Arab states. South Sudan sought to shed its reliance on Sudan by basing her foreign relations on the Sudan foreign policy doctrine and strategy which was pro-Arab while forging new relations with East African countries. Both before and after South Sudan's admission to the UN, many states issued official explicit statements about its diplomatic recognition and some established diplomatic relations with it. In less than half a year, five countries recognized the Republic of South Sudan and 50 among them had established diplomatic relations.

The government of the Republic of South Sudan reciprocated by opening eight missions in Europe, one each in Washington, DC. and New York, two in

Asia, three in the Middle East, and nine in Africa. Although the country has a number of diplomatic missions abroad, South Sudanese diplomacy remains shackled by the inexperience of its diplomats, lack of a clear understanding of the role of the ministry of foreign affairs, endemic corruption, and the conspicuous absence of a well-articulated foreign policy. Hence, the country's diplomacy has consisted of a series of disjointed reactions. However, the advent of peace provides an opportunity for policymakers to craft a foreign policy which takes into account major policy determinants.[359]

7.5.1 Foreign Policy Objectives

Every country has a goal to achieve by executing her foreign policy and South Sudan should not be an exception. The major rationale of South Sudan's foreign policy is to advance the national interest in a manner compatible with the prevailing climate of international milieu. At the centre stage of the national interest lies a key objective of defending the state's sovereignty by safeguarding its territorial integrity, prestige, achieving economic and security well-being of the citizenry.

7.5.1.1 General Objectives

The transitional constitution of the Republic of South Sudan proposes an outline of the new Republic's foreign policy, its objectives, and the manner in which the policy should be conducted.[360] It states that the foreign policy of the Republic of South Sudan shall serve the national interest and be conducted independently and transparently with the view to achieving the following:

i. Promotion of international cooperation, especially within the United Nations family, African Union and other international and regional organizations, for the purposes of consolidating universal peace and security, respect for international law, treaty obligations and fostering a just world economic order;

ii. Achievement of African economic integration within the ongoing regional plans and fora as well as promoting African unity and cooperation as foreseen in those plans;

iii. Enhancement of respect for human rights and fundamental freedoms in regional and international fora;

iv. Promotion of dialogue among civilizations and establishment of

---

359   Akol, Moses, (2015), p.4
360   Ibid, p.5

international order based on justice and common human destiny;

v.   Respect for international law and treaty obligations, as well as the seeking of peaceful settlement of international disputes by negotiation, mediation, conciliation, arbitration and adjudication;

vi. enhancement of economic cooperation among countries of the region;

vii. non-interference in the affairs of other States, promotion of good-neighbourliness and mutual cooperation with all neighbours and maintaining amicable and balanced relations with other countries; and

viii. combating international and trans-national organized crime, piracy and terrorism.

The above-mentioned goals form a wide basis for a foreign policy framework, with each goal requiring robust and constantly evolving strategies. The above objective could not be effective without a development of a national foreign policy strategy which should state how each objective should be accomplished within the international arena. It is now the duty of the Ministry of Foreign Affairs and International cooperation in collaboration with the presidency and national legislative assembly as well as the council of ministers as well as other stakeholders to develop and streamline a workable foreign policy strategy for the attainment of these noble goals.

7.5.1.2 Short-Range Objectives

These objectives are also known as core objectives, and are attained at all costs. A combination of military power and diplomacy is necessary to secure these objectives, which include the protection of political independence (sovereignty) *and* the defence of territorial integrity. The primary commitment of many modern governments must be to pursue those courses of action that have the highest impact on domestic, economic and welfare needs and expectations. It may be difficult to gain much public support for other types of objectives such as glory, territorial expansion or power for its own sake. The middle range goal has no particular time element, but most of today's leaders in developing countries hope that they can begin to catch up with more economically advanced countries within their own lifetimes.[361] The middle range objectives include international cooperation, prestige and protection of national interest. Therefore, South Sudan's Foreign policy framework should be based on how to manage her porous borders by concentrating the defence

---

361   K.J. Holsti, (1978), p.149.

synergies along Uganda, Sudan, Congo and Kenya. This policy should help the government to align its interest to the current context of the unipolar world system. The protection of citizens abroad especially in the west and East African communities should be paramount.

7.5.1.3 Middle-Range Objectives

These are objectives that have to be achieved within a specific timeframe otherwise they lose their real value, causing dire consequences either at home or abroad or both. The targets of these middle range objectives are usually more than one entity, and they could be carried out simultaneously as is the case of trading with a number of states and trade blocs, exporting raw material to multiple destinations, or diversifying a country's export base by exporting a variety of goods and products to multiple or specific destinations. In the case of the new Republic, this category may include economic uplift, raising the standard of living, respect for human rights, international law and treaty obligations, non-interference in the affairs of other states and combating international and transnational organized crimes, terrorism and piracy.

It is worth noting that some middle and long-range objectives are elastic enough to change categories at a given time, depending on the gravity of the state's national interest.

7.5.1.4 Long-Range Objectives

These are objectives that embody the ideals and values of the state for the realization of which the state invests in a long-term strategy unbounded by the constraints of time. Dissemination of capitalist economy, democracy, and American values are some of the long-range goals of the foreign policy of the United States of America. The spread of communism was the long-term policy of the former Soviet Union. Other countries pursue long range objectives aimed at gaining territorial and ideological expansions at the expense of other nations. Such expansions are sought in order to gain natural resources or military advantage against another state. Although the implementation of such expansionist policies may not bear any outward resemblance to the crudity of the nineteenth century's European scramble for Africa, the end result of such rapacious policies remains as inhumane. Based on the interim constitution, the long-range objectives of the foreign policy of the Republic of South Sudan would include the promotion of international cooperation, especially within the United Nations family, African Union and other international and regional organizations, for the purposes of consolidating universal peace and security, respect for international law, treaty obligations and fostering a just world economic order; achievement of African economic integration, within the ongoing regional plans and fora as well as promoting African unity and cooperation as foreseen in those plans; promotion of dialogue among civilizations and establishment of international order based on justice and common human destiny; enhancement of economic cooperation among countries of the region; and promotion of good neighbourliness and mutual cooperation with all neighbour's and maintaining amicable and balanced relations with other countries.

All foreign policy objectives call for well-thought out strategies that in turn demand enormous perseverance and fortitude, bearing in mind that some of the objectives may prove partially elusive at best or totally unachievable at worst. But since total failure is never a viable option in foreign policy, and since the ever-present threat of failure lurks at every turn in the diplomatic arena, it is perhaps prudent for policymakers to take a long view even when challenges threaten to derail important short-range policy objectives. This is better achieved not through sheer stubborn optimism, but rather by exercising rational flexibility while at the same time presenting alternative strategies that, although barely indistinguishable from the original ones, are more realistic and a great deal more efficacious. How has the world's youngest state fared so far in its efforts to achieve its foreign policy objectives? The country has fared poorly on almost every count.

7.5.2 Foreign Policy Determinants

Having identified and placed the objectives of the foreign policy of South Sudan in their respective categories, the next task is to examine the factors or determinants that are both most likely to shape these objectives and also influence the successful implementation of the resultant foreign policy. While some of them are static and others are in a state of flux, the general determinants of foreign policy are either factors emanating from outside the borders of the state (external) or those attributable to the domestic environment (internal) as explore herein:

7.5.2.1 External Determinants

South Sudan has some international determinants to her foreign policy that, if given attention, could revitalize the national image abroad as follows:

A. World Order

The prevailing world order into which the Republic of South Sudan is born is as deceptively orderly as it is Orwellian in its perception of the equality of all mankind. Ushered in by the collapse of the Soviet Union in the early 1990s, the current world order inspired hope for a better world so much so that Francis Fukuyama declared perhaps prematurely "the end of History". Nonetheless, in the emerging international order, in the words of Henry Kissinger, "nations have pursued self-interest more frequently than high-minded principles, and have competed more than they have cooperated an age-old phenomenon not about to change."[362]

Operating in a unipolar world order, South Sudanese diplomacy has to be constantly cognizant of the influence of the prevailing international environment on the young state's pursuit of its national interests. It is a truism that the health of both the world order and that of individual states, such as South Sudan, depends on collaborative efforts undertaken by countries to address a set of global issues, including the environment, nuclear proliferation, population explosion, money laundering, terrorism, illegal migration, human trafficking, and drug smuggling. This world order gave rise to unipolar system by elevating the United States of America as the superpower which South Sudan should reckon with. South Sudan being midwifed by America gave her a comparative advantage which, if utilized well in the region, could be an epitome of power.

B. Regional and Multilateral Organizations

Actions of a host of organizations may have a negative or positive influence on the viability of foreign policy objectives. Although the government of South Sudan seem to enjoy good relations with major international and regional organizations such as the United Nations, African Union, and IGAD, among others, South Sudan can ill-afford to grow complacent about the state of these relations in the immediate future. Hence, no effort should be spared to promote good relations with these organizations. In the meantime, the new Republic may deem it in its national interest to conduct in-depth, objective evaluations and assessments prior to ascending to full membership in multilateral organizations, especially those that are not organically affiliated with the United Nations system. A good number of, if not all, multilateral organizations are deeply grounded in some philosophical thought, and are bent on achieving their goals at all costs, including at the expense of unscrupulous entities that join the ranks of such organizations in haste.

---

362   Kissinger, Henry (1994); p.19

The youngest state in the world experienced baptism by fire barely six months into its independence. It shut off its 350,000-barrel-a-day oil operations in January 2012, accusing the Sudan of illegally commandeering $815 million worth of the country's oil. To add fuel to the fire, the South Sudanese army launched a surprise attack on the oilfields in Panthau (Heglig) on 26 March 2012. Asserting that Heglig was a South Sudanese territory, world leaders, including the Secretary-General of the United Nations, US President Barak Obama, and other world leaders, called on Juba to withdraw its troops from Panthau unconditionally, causing the first open friction between the new state and the international community.

Subsequent skirmishes along the expansive border, sober rattling, and a vocal war of words between the two Sudan's threatened to bring the two countries to the precipice of war. The African Union came to the rescue with the famous, but now stalled, Nine-point Cooperation Agreement for the resolution of the outstanding issues between the two countries. As a result of this agreement, signed on 29 September 2012, South Sudanese oil began to flow overseas through Sudan's Red Sea port of Bashayer, and by the end of August 2013, cash-strapped Khartoum and Juba reaped the dividends of the sale of South Sudan's crude oil for the months of June and July 2013, with Juba receiving $630 million and Khartoum pocketing $170 million in transit fees.

Internally, the country was smarting from rampant corruption, general insecurity, lack of service delivery, and a boisterous armed rebellion in Jonglei State that the government said was aided and abetted by Khartoum. Furthermore, malfeasance and malevolence in the upper echelons of the government, the army, and the ruling party reached climax, prompting President Salva Kiir Maryardit's surprise but widely popular move to dismiss his entire government on July 23, 2013. The Chairman of the ruling party also suspended the party's Secretary General.

Government's relationships with the United Nations Mission in South Sudan (UNMISS) deteriorated precipitously following the outbreak of armed rebellion in December 2013, in which Juba claimed UNMISS was complicit. Some UN officials were expelled from the country, including the head of UNMISS who departed unceremoniously on the eve of the country's third birthday celebrations.

i. The East African Community (EAC)

South Sudan was admitted to be the sixth member in this regional body. The EAC should be South Sudan's most important foreign policy vehicle for promoting trade and investment policies. South Sudan vision of shared prosperity and peaceful neighbourhood as outlined in the interim constitution will enable her to continue in strengthening ties with the EAC countries. South Sudan will therefore continue to play its rightful role in fast tracking the EAC integration through the full implementation of the provisions of all common instruments.

ii. *The Intergovernmental Authority on Development (IGAD)*

This regional organization has been very instrumental in bringing internal stability to South Sudan. It was through the Intergovernmental Authority on Development (IGAD) effort that led to Comprehensive Peace Agreement between the government of Southern Sudan and Khartoum based government. South Sudan, as a member of the IGAD, should continue to provide leadership and support to the IGAD as an effective regional tool for confronting challenges to sustainable development in the region. Strategic interventions include mobilization of international support to enable the IGAD to consolidate regional peace and stability and strengthen its capacity to effectively address regional environmental issues. This will enable the IGAD countries to take South Sudan issues seriously and give them due attention such as the current internal political crisis which is under mediation of the IGAD.

iii. *The Great Lakes Region*

South Sudan is currently an active member of the International Conference on the Great Lakes Region (ICGLR) and a signatory to the Peace and Security Pact that seeks to achieve sustainable peace and stability in the Great Lakes Region. South Sudan's current political instability could be treated as a violation of this peace pact in one way or another. Sustainable peace in South Sudan is critical to the development of the region. South Sudan should aspire to get sustainable peace and security as a critical prerequisite for participation as the development agent in the Eastern and Central African countries by seeking to promote her regional peace agenda.

C. Counter-Diplomacy

Owing to the fact that foreign policy is concerned with the manner in which the central government of sovereign states relate to each other and to the global system in their attempt to further their respective national interests, it goes without saying that the reaction of a state to policy objectives of another state affects the viability of these objectives. Excellent diplomatic relations notwithstanding, the reaction of other states to policy objectives of South Sudan will always be informed by the self-interest of these states. Therefore, and regardless of how sure we are about the way we think and behave or even know what we want, it is imperative to gain accurate knowledge of the interests of both friendly and other states. Understanding the behaviour of other states is intrinsic to the efforts of ensuring the successful implementation of foreign policy objectives.

D. World Public Opinion

In the course of pursuing its foreign policy objectives, especially *core* and *middle-range* objectives, the new republic will most definitely encounter circumstances where the success of its policy options may hinge on the preponderance of world public opinion. This reaction is not confined only to the reaction of individual governments to our policy objectives, but it extends also to public opinion by non-government actors and polity. Managing world opinion requires a great deal of patience and diplomatic acumen, especially when that public opinion is misguided or adversely ill-informed. Government reaction to a serious border dispute with one of the new Republic's neighbours or a response to an unfortunate episode of human rights violation, for instance, may attract world public opinion. In this case, the ability of the state to sway world public opinion in its favour would certainly ensure the success of its foreign policy options or, at least, defuse any unwarranted tension and condemnation.

E. Building Alliances

Forming alliances with other similar-groups is another determinant of foreign policy that deserves attention. Although alliances entered into by states are crucial for the advancement of foreign policy objectives, they are two-sided swords. On one hand, they enable states to achieve objectives (especially core and long-range objectives) which they could not otherwise attain on their own efforts. On the other hand, members of alliances are required to act in concert with their allies on matters of mutual concern to the overall objectives of the alliance. Hence, some foreign policy objectives of a member state may, for better or worse, be influenced by the virtue of its membership in an alliance. Therefore, the decision to enter into alliances should be scrutinized and weighed methodically before appending signatures to documents. All things considered, the advantages of membership in a carefully selected alliance outweigh the occasional inconveniences that result from the exercise of benevolent dictatorship by the majority.

7.5.2.2 Internal Determinants

Since the theories of foreign policy sits at the junction between the theory of international relations and that of public policy, it is only reasonable that in addition to the aforementioned external determinants a number of domestic factors be also universally recognized for their considerable influence on the foreign policy objectives of states. These internal determinants include a state's historical influences, size and geography, natural resources, economic development, industrial development, military power, quality and size of population, the media, think-tanks, political organization, good governance, and quality of diplomacy.

While the influencing power of some of these determinants is usually self-evident and can easily be traced to readily discernable sources, other domestic determinants are rather subtle and draw their influences from more complex sources such as history, geography, population, the media, politics, and diplomacy. The latter category of domestic determinants merits serious attention, objective comparative analysis, and a more nuanced synthesis in order to assess and appreciate their potential influence on foreign policy objectives of the Republic of South Sudan. In fact, it will be very useful to conduct a detailed case study of the determinants of South Sudan foreign policy five years after independence. In the meantime, it is useful to shed some light on the conceptual basis for some of the subtlest internal determinants that might exert considerable influence on the success of the objectives of South Sudan foreign policy. These determinants include, but not limited to, South Sudan's size and geography, quality and size of population, historical influence, good governance, and quality of diplomacy.

A. Size and Geography of the State

Occupying an area of 700,000 square kilometres, the Republic of South Sudan is a noticeably large sized country. Its large size implies that the new Republic has enough economic, political, and diplomatic potential to enable it to grow into an important regional and international player. Consequently, the nation's ability to successfully implement its foreign policy objectives is greatly enhanced.

The location of a country imposes a particular psychological mind-set as well as physical realities and limitations that greatly influence the implementation of government policies, including defence and foreign policies. Henry Kissinger argues that American and European approaches to foreign policy were an outcome of their geographical realities. Occupying a sparsely populated vast territory insulated from aggressive imperial powers by Atlantic Ocean in the east and the Pacific Ocean in the west and neighboured by weak countries, America did not feel the need for collective security or 'balance of power' with which feuding European states busied themselves in the aftermath of the collapse of the 'medieval universal empire.' America did not preoccupy itself with 'balance of power' since it was not faced with a foreign power that needed to be balanced. Ironically, when America entered world politics 150 years later, it was to rescue Europe the fangs of two wars that broke out in 1915 and 1943 as a result of the collapse of the 'balance of power' in Europe.[363] Therefore, the fact that South Sudan is totally surrounded by its neighbours was bound to pose serious economic and security challenges in the years immediately following the country's declaration of independence. These challenges have been made all the more daunting by the fact that most of South Sudan's neighbours are plagued by political and economic instability. Although by no means insurmountable, these challenges have forced the hands of foreign policymakers, leaving them with very limited options for manoeuvring with South Sudan's neighbours. The best option for safeguarding the national interests of the new nation in this regard would be to work tirelessly toward the development of a pragmatic long-term plan that would enable the new Republic to pursue mutually beneficial diplomatic relations with all of its neighbours. South Sudan's relations with its neighbours are both the curse and gift of geography and size of the new country.

B. Quality and Size of Population

South Sudan is blessed with a decent-sized and culturally vibrant population. If the level of education were the only criterion to measure the quality of population, the population of the new Republic (89% illiterate), would rest comfortably at the bottom of the ladder, handing elitist foreign policymakers the pretext they crave to develop and implement a foreign policy that is far removed from the heartbeat and aspirations of the society. The population of the new nation possesses a treasure of indigenous souls which could be put to good use in matters of negation and conflict resolution, which are essentially at the core of the statecraft of diplomacy. The challenge is to harness this indigenous knowledge and the myriad ethnic cultural values in order to weave them into a strong national fabric of shared common values and identity. A population imbued with a strong sense of national pride and identity is most likely to exert a positive influence on the implementation of foreign policy objectives through a variety of activities, including providing a support base for foreign policy at home in South Sudan.

C. Historical Influence

South Sudan belongs to a generation of countries that have seceded in the last two decades, and whose foreign policies are also manifestations of the

---

363   Kissinger, Henry, (1994); pp. 18-22.

burden of history. Since the amicable secession of Eritrea from Ethiopia in 1994, Ethio-Eritrean relations have remained anything but cordial. On the other end of the spectrum, East Timor, which also separated amicably from Indonesia in 2002, has pursued a realistic, albeit constrained, foreign policy with moderating influences not only on East Timorese-Indonesian-Australian diplomatic ties but also on Indonesian-Australian relations as well as on the calm inside the regional Association of South East Asian Nations (ASEAN).

If the foreign policy of a state is essentially a legacy of the history of the state, then the foreign policy of the Republic of South Sudan stands to inherit the genes of a very complex past where many currents had caused cataclysmic upheavals at various epochs. On one hand, the history of the people of South Sudan is a narrative about a fiercely independent, free-spirited, and proud people who lived in splendid harmony with both the visible and invisible forces of nature. It is a history of a people who are too spiritual to be caught in the rapture of feign religiosity. On the other hand, theirs is also a tortured history haunted by the scrooge of the slave trade of the nineteenth century, rendered all the more scandalous by the rapacity of triple colonialism and exacerbated by the callousness of state-sponsored violence in the twentieth century. Therefore, when all is said and done, the history of the people and land of South Sudan is essentially a history of an innocent people locked in a two-century long fierce struggle for survival in the face of some of the ugliest tools of repression and death that man has ever known.

Since both the distant and recent histories of South Sudan represent two faces of the same coin of repression and resistance, it is most certain that many subtle elements of our history will, for better or for worse, continue to manifest themselves in one way or another whenever we consider decisions pertaining to our future. The challenge is how to accurately identify and safeguard against the aspects of our decisions and decision-making that are dictated by negative historical influences on one hand, and to remain committed to the pursuit of certain national ideals, on the other hand.

History has proven to possess an amazing capacity to hold foreign policies of many nations hostage for a long time. South Sudan policy leaders should know that, "the absence of intellectual roots was a principal cause of the aimlessness of the German foreign policy, the legacy of having been Europe's battlefield for so long caused a deep-seated sense of insecurity, it relied more on military power."[364] By the same token, nations have also proven that history can be overcome in a spectacular fashion while at the same time maintaining national ideals. In the same note, "the American foreign policy efforts were inspired by

---

364   Ibid; p.170.

utopian visions of some terminal point after which the underlying harmony of the world would simply reassert itself. American foreign policy torn between America being a beacon of democracy for the rest of the mankind, and being a crusader for American values abroad- isolationism and commitment."[365]

Ultimately, the impact of historical influences on foreign policy of a nation is identifiable and can be ignored only at one's own peril. Furthermore, "Foreign scepticism about American idealism of Woodrow Wilson, Franklin Roosevelt, and Ronald Reagan spurred America's faith that history can be overcome."[366]

History has naturally crept into our foreign policy in the past four years. While that is neither unusual nor altogether unwarranted, it is a truism that too much dose of anything, including that of a good thing, produces unintended consequences. Hence, if the foreign policy of a state is essentially a legacy of the history of that state, then the foreign policy of South Sudan stands to inherit the genes of a most complex history punctuated by state-sponsored violence whose wounds are too fresh to overlook. It is, therefore, necessary to identify and highlight the size and the potency of the dose of history that has found its way into the formulation and the conduct of the country's foreign policy in the past four years.

D. Quality of Diplomacy

For all their positive and negative influences on the implementation of foreign policy objectives, external and internal policy determinants owe their success (or failure) to the quality of diplomacy of the state. Well-equipped diplomacies have the capacity to both identify determinants of foreign and also to deal effectively with the negative influences of such determinants. Hence, if good diplomacy is the first line of defence against negative influences of policy determinants, well-trained diplomats are the foot-soldiers that man that battle front both at the home front and behind enemy lines.

7.5.3 Pillars of South Sudan Foreign Policy

In the context of South Sudan, most diplomats do not have special training in subjects related to international relations and this makes them unreactive to sensitive issues affecting the nation regionally and globally. The effectiveness of South Sudan's Foreign policy should be based on rejuvenating the pillars of her foreign policy as explored herein.

---

365   Ibid; p. 836
366   Ibid; p. 18.

7.5.3.1 Gender Mainstreaming

In aligning gender issues into government policies, the question here should be "how does the government of South Sudan care about gender balance in appointment of ambassadors but at the same time determine the ratio of gender mainstreaming at the ministry of foreign affairs and embassies abroad?" The government should be much aware that women are excluded from the institutions, which affects the conduct and implementation of South Sudan's foreign policy. So many people believe that women are not so capable for certain types of professions.

These peoples are aggrieved that the values, norms and morals of our society are restricted. Maybe the government was of the view that foreign policy is preserved for men. This has made it very difficult for women to break into the institution, which determines the nation's relations with other countries. The government of South Sudan should know that the foreign policy decision-making could not be achieved without the participation of women, who are the majority within the country according to the national census conducted in 2008.

7.5.3.2 Military and Security

South Sudan, like any other country, has an abiding stake in peace and stability in its neighbourhood for its long-term security and projection on the regional and eventually the world scene. One of the objectives of South Sudan's foreign policy should be the intensification and consolidation of ties with its neighbours and strengthening of peace and security in the region as a whole through mutually beneficial cooperation. However, the nation of South Sudan can engage in joint military training, arms transfer and joint intelligence sharing with neighbouring and advanced states.

One of the key pillars that should underlie South Sudan foreign policy is peace and security diplomacy because its recognition of peace and stability as necessary conditions for development and prosperity will earn South Sudan respect as well as recognition from the neighbouring countries and region at large. South Sudan should have a conviction that its own stability and economic wellbeing are dependent on the stability of herself which should be extended to the neighbours in the Great Lakes region and the Horn of Africa.

Underpinning South Sudan's peace and security diplomacy are the following mutually reinforcing objectives. First is the resolution of internal conflicts by peaceful means. Second, creating capacity to effectively support peace processes by coordinating the training of diplomats from the region through the Foreign Service Institute, appointing and deploying special envoys, and working with independent mediators to resolve regional conflicts. This can happen through working with other African countries to strengthen the conflict prevention capacity of regional institutions, including the EAC, IGAD, COMESA and the African Union. Thirdly, support peace efforts by the African Union and the United Nations through contributing troops and providing leadership in peacekeeping missions within the continent and globally. Mobilize support and resources for peace consolidation and development in African countries emerging from conflict through bilateral networks as well as regional and international peace building mechanisms.

7.5.3.3 Utilization of Diaspora Population

To begin with, South Sudan foreign policy should focus on South Sudanese in the diaspora by tapping into their potential to facilitate the country's political, economic and cultural regeneration and development. South Sudan could utilize the availability of lost boys and girls who understand major problems facing South Sudan from inside the story to renew South Sudan's image in the West. The total number of these lost boys and girls who went to Ethiopia was 26,000 but 5, 000 are expected to have gone abroad.

If South Sudan recognizes that lost boys and girls as well as other South Sudanese in the diaspora have a potential to mobilize resources for the realization of the country's national development goals, then the country will creatively explore the various ways and frameworks of effectively promoting, utilizing and enhancing the contribution of this important resource. The government of South Sudan should tap new skills and resources by enabling the Ministry of Foreign Affairs and International Cooperation to work with other ministries to invite nationals in the Diaspora to invest their skills and resources in the various sectors of national development and create incentives and policies to encourage them to invest in the country.

7.5.3.4 Economic Diplomacy

It is a fact that friendly diplomatic activities between South Sudan and other advanced countries can overcome institutional weaknesses in South Sudan. In other words, strong economic diplomacy would result in increased FDI flows to South Sudan. Integrating with the regional economic blocs and also having multilateral economic agreements with other states outside the region can achieve this. Therefore, the main missions of South Sudan diplomacy should be to safeguard national sovereignty, to create a favourable external environment for building a well-off society and accelerating modernization and to actively promote world peace and development.

South Sudan's pillar of economic diplomacy should be a tool for advancing the goal of becoming a middle income and industrialized economy. South Sudan's quest for a stable environment should be linked to social economic development and prosperity. A robust economic engagement is necessary to secure South Sudan regional and wider economic objectives. South Sudan has an advantage of having natural resources such as gold and oil, which if utilized well could promote diplomatic ties abroad.

The availability of oil resources could increase capital flows to South Sudan and the East African region by exploring alternative non-traditional sources of development assistance and foreign direct investment. The presence of non-oil resources could promote the country to be a favourite destination for foreign direct investment, tourism, and conferencing. These resources tend to expand access to traditional markets and explore new destinations for products in emerging markets in Africa, Europe, Latin America, Asia and the Middle East. Therefore, South Sudan has great potential to strengthen strategic ties with emerging economies in Western and Eastern Europe, Asia, Middle East and Latin America, and consolidate its traditional markets in America, China and Europe by entering into new genuine frameworks for cooperation and strengthening existing ones.

7.5.3.5 Cultural Diplomacy

South Sudan should continuously emphasize cultural recognition and understanding as the basis for dialogue to resolve both internal and external conflict. It is a great resource when effectively using languages such as Arabic and English, known to many South Sudanese, and other cultural attributes such as value systems, food, wine, art, music and dance to build friendships and foster mutual understanding at the local, regional and global levels.

South Sudan's promotion of cultural diplomacy as one of its pillars of their foreign policy will ensure that culture contributes to science, technology and socio-economic development, as well as position South Sudan as a cultural hub internationally. Cultural diplomacy should be a linchpin of public diplomacy among her citizens and foreign nationals because cultural activities are a nation's idea of itself. If applied appropriately, cultural diplomacy could uniquely reach out to people of all occupations from young people, to non-elites, to broad audiences. Cultural diplomacy could also reach influential members of foreign societies who may be out of reach through traditional embassy functions. It can provide a positive agenda for cooperation in spite of policy differences and create a neutral platform for people-to-people contact. Cultural diplomacy serves as a flexible, universally acceptable vehicle for engagement with countries where diplomatic relations are strained or are absent. It provides awareness of the cultural richness of our nation and generate interest in South Sudan's cultural heritage.

South Sudan cultural diplomacy should promote the exchange and sharing of ideas, information, art, lifestyles, value systems, traditions, beliefs, languages and other aspects of cultures. This is essential because culture plays a vital role in international relations and the struggle for space and cultural influence takes the centre stage in the global context. South Sudan has a strong and valuable cultural practice that could be promoted internationally such as traditional wrestling, food such as walwala, akop, and dodo among other foods, liquor such as white bull, and Club special, and serious dancing styles such as Lotuko, Acholi, Dinka Ngok, Dinka Bor and Malual Dinka. The display of traditional attire such as Shilluk, Dinka, Nuer, Lotuko and Toposa outfits has a great influence on understanding South Sudanese way of life and interaction with neigbouring communities.

7.5.3.6 Building Ties with Social Group

These ties may be based on a single issue, ethnic identification, religious affiliation, or economics and political pressure groups. For example, nongovernmental organizations focused on human rights are becoming increasingly visible in countries in political crisis such as South Sudan. The split of SPLM into SPLM in Government, SPLM former Detainees, SPLM Democratic Change and SPLM in opposition has a lot to say about the current South Sudan foreign policy. Sometimes, the government blames SPLM opposition and former political detainees for external pressure exerted on the government on issues to do with AIDS, humanitarian assistance, donation for development, and accessibility to loan for development projects from international financial institutions such as IMF, WB, AfDB among others.

Economic interest groups within South Sudan could be an important societal source of foreign policy because they help in generation of wealth, and economic welfare has become one of the primary functions of the modern state. Economic groups often have an interest in foreign relations as they seek to promote their foreign business adventures abroad or to protect markets from competitors at home. For instance, business groups in Japan have often been considered partners with the bureaucracy on foreign, economic, policymaking, and a wide range of business, labour, financial, and trade groups. These partners have been meant to actively attempt to influence Japan's foreign policy and other countries like South Sudan in learning from Japan by adopting the same strategy.

7.5.3.7 The American Factor

From 1983 to 2005 and during the time of independence in 2011, the United States, headed by Dr. John Garang Mabior, was a friend of South Sudan during the liberation struggle. During this period, the US was antagonistic to the Khartoum regime in Sudan because of discriminatory Sharia Law adopted by the Sudan government.

The important question which requires consideration in this connection relates to the reason why the US was a friend of South Sudan during the liberation movement but later became hostile to independent South Sudan when both were promoting the same ideology of freeing the people of South Sudan from discrimination through race and religion.

The reality shows that the reason for the hostility of the US to Kiir's government seems to rest on violation of the US ideological interest of promotion of democracy internationally. It seems that President Kiir and his allies took anti-United States moves in some instances, such as the 2014 invitation of the Russian president, to deter the US from being close to South Sudan as well as the coming of China.

7.5.4 Conclusion

South Sudanese diplomacy has fared fairly during the last four years. It has been shackled by, among other things, the inexperience of its diplomats and the absence of a well-articulated foreign policy. The short-range, middle-range and long-range foreign policy objectives outlined in the draft transitional constitution of the Republic are yet to be translated into a coherent foreign policy guided by international and domestic determinants. Consequently, the diplomacy of the young state has been conducted on an ad hoc basis, and at an exorbitant financial and diplomatic cost.

Although the bellicosity of World War II rhetoric and the verbosity of the Cold War era are now distant memories, the prevailing unipolar world order, ushered in by the collapse of the Soviet Union in the early 1990s, is no less slippery than its predecessor. As a result, less powerful, resource-rich states such as the young Republic of South Sudan can ill-afford to be complacent and casual in the conduct of its foreign policy. The advent of peace in the months ahead should provide policymakers with the opportunity to formulate a sound foreign policy capable of achieving regional and international rapprochement. To that end, the Ministry of Foreign Affairs and International Cooperation should assert its role as the government entity that implements the country's foreign policy.

7.6 South Africa's Foreign policy

Any country's foreign policy should be the result of the interplay of a large number of factors which determine its nature or outcome. It is, nevertheless, a general rule that each factor individually and collectively affects major problems of foreign policy. This was affirmed by Paddleford and Lincoln who reiterated that, fundamentally, foreign policy has its roots in the unique historical backgrounds, political institutions, traditions, economic needs, power factors, aspirations, peculiar geographical circumstances and basic set of values held by a nation.[367] In the same note, James Rosenau writes that geography, size, economic development, culture and history, great power structure, alliances, technology, social structure, public opinion and governmental structure as inputs of foreign policy.[368]

Although leaders are quick to take credit for foreign policy successes and the public is often quick to blame them for failures, leaders rarely make foreign policy alone. Advisory systems and government bureaucracies may be organised differently in different countries, but they always play some role in foreign policy decision making and implementation. Domestic constituencies may vary in influence depending on the attentiveness of a public to foreign affairs or the structure of government in a specific country. Finally, the world beyond the borders affects the possibilities for foreign policy action. It may present opportunities, but it also presents constraints.[369]

The study of foreign policy includes policymakers, interests and objectives, principles of foreign policy, and means of foreign policy. The determinants of foreign policy of a country can be briefly seen as follows: geographical location, history and traditions, political organisation and traditions, military strength, personalities or leadership factors and international environment etc. All these elements are important in varying degrees for a country's national polities and foreign relations.

---

367   Paddleford and Lincoln, (1967), p. 307.
368   James N. Rosenau, (2006), p.157.
369   Marijke Brenning, (2007), p.9.

The external factors like globalisation, the end of the Cold War and emergence of the United States of America (USA) as a world super power, International Organisations like the United Nations (UN), Commonwealth of Nations, Non-Aligned Movements, WTO etc. and African Countries are some of the major determinants of South Africa's foreign policy. The emergence of multi-polar world like European Union (EU), China, Japan and India have also served as important external determinants of post-apartheid South Africa's foreign policy. Below is the brief evolution South Africa's foreign policy and its adaptation in the post-apartheid period.

The process of foreign policymaking in South Africa after the end of apartheid in 1994 has been subject to a complex interplay of competing forces.[370] Policy shifts of the post-apartheid period not only have necessitated new visions for the future but also new structures. The creation of a value-based new identity in foreign policy has called for transformation of institutions relevant for the decision-making process in foreign policy.[371]

The actors in South African foreign policymaking are the presidency, Department of Foreign Affairs (DFA), non-governmental actors such as the African National Congress (ANC), the civil society, business community, labour unions and the public. Since its independence, the post-apartheid South Africa has had three presidents: Nelson Mandela, Thabo Mbeki and Jacob Zuma. Although the Presidency is divided into four branches – the Private Office of the President and Corporate Services, the Office of the Deputy President, the Cabinet Office and the Policy Coordination and Advisory Service (PCAS) – for purposes of understanding the role of the Presidency as an institution in foreign policy formulation, it is the Cabinet Office, and more particularly the PCAS, that is of significance.[372]

This branch is regarded as the engine room of the Presidency's drive for policy integration.[373] It is this unit too that monitors transformation in all government departments, prepares memos to the principals in the Presidency, researches answers to questions tabled in Parliament, and prepares briefing notes and research reports for the Presidency. Significantly too for foreign policy formulation, the PCAS interacts with civil society on matters of policy formulation as well as with 'international experts' to ensure policy relevance and efficacy. Although this is an advisory branch to the president, deputy president and the minister in the Presidency, it also monitors both the debates and the implementation of policy on crosscutting issues. A deputy DG, who is

---

370   Hughes, (2004), p.7
371   Ryan, K Eta al (2013), Pp.246-260
372   Hughes, (2004), p.17
373   Mark and Crichlow, (2002), p.56

in turn served by five chief directors reflective of the cabinet and DG clusters, leads the unit.

The South Africa foreign policy analysis (SAFA) aims to strive for peace, stability, democracy and development in an African continent that is non-sexist, prosperous and united, contributing towards a world that is just and equitable.[374] The mission of the SAFA is the promotion of South Africa's national values, the African Renaissance and the creation of a better world for all. The values of the SAFA are guided by the core values of loyalty, dedication, Ubuntu, equity and professional integrity. However, the SAFA has been criticized on the vagueness and obscurity of South Africa's foreign policy objectives.

Another player in the foreign policy analysis of South Africa is the ANC.[375] This has been the ruling and dominant party from independence. The most important instrument of ANC foreign policy interaction is the national executive committee on international relations. The composition of the committee is significant as it serves to coordinate ANC foreign policy interests and representation from the Presidency, the Ministry of Foreign Affairs, parliament, the Tripartite Alliance and other significant stakeholders.

As a consequence of and consistent with the process of transition in South Africa in the 1990s, foreign policy thinking underwent a profound and refreshing renaissance.[376] This operated at a number of levels and involved a host of initiatives. One of the most encouraging developments was the engagement of the public, the business community and civil society in South Africa's new foreign policy thinking. This manifested in a raft of conferences, workshops, position papers and policy documents that saw existing SAFA officials engaging with ANC international relations experts, as well as with local and international academics, to rethink fundamentally South Africa's role and positioning in the global environment, and also to commence the process of giving a formal structure to post-1994 South African foreign policy.

The major focus areas of South African foreign policy are security, stability, sustainable development and cooperation. In security, the major focus areas are peace and security, conflict management, sovereignty and territorial integrity, arms control and disaster management. Additionally, stability area focuses on crime and terrorist threats and extremism. Further, sustainable development policies stress on trade, investment, integration and cooperation, imaging and branding, and tourism. In cooperation, policies focus on human resource development, health, people-to-people cooperation and security cooperation.[377]

---

374   Hughes, (2004), p.34
375   Mwagiru, (2010), p.239
376   Wendt, (2004), p.293
377   Hughes (2004, p.19).

Looking at the South African foreign policy from independence, the DFA and the Parliamentary Portfolio Committee on Foreign Affairs (PPCA) neither set the agenda nor dominate the discussion; it is mainly the presidency that drives the discourse. Furthermore, the conflict that one encounters between the executive and legislative branches in the realm of foreign policy in consolidated democracies seems to be absent on the South African scene.[378] So far, parliament and South African political parties have remained substantially calm in the discussion on foreign policy. This analysis shows that South Africa foreign policy is dominated by the presidency but seeking the opinion of the parliament, the business community, the civil society organizations as well as the citizen. The origin and Development of South Africa's foreign policy

Under the apartheid regime, South African foreign policy was severely constraint by universal hostility which the country's racial policies generated abroad. It is worth remarking that it was in the 1980s that the burden of external pressure combined with a growing internal opposition became too great to bear.[379] The result was a dawning recognition that the price of external rehabilitation profoundly depressed the economy. The F.W. De Klerk's decision to initiate change was helped by the fortuitous coincidence of a more favourable external climate and in particular the collapse of Soviet Union. Henceforth, the latter could no longer be regarded as a significant threat to the Republic; the traditional prescription of a total strategy to counter a 'total onslaught' from Moscow was patently absurd. The then-National Party NP government recognised that time and demography was against them: in 1990 South Africa's population was 38.1 million; by 2000 the figure would be 47.5 million. A white minority regime with a declining economy could hardly deliver the 3-4 percent growth rate required to sustain numbers on that scale. True, violent revolution in the absence of change might not be overcome, but the spectre of slow, haphazard social disintegration was presumably more than enough to convince De Klerk, a pragmatic realistic. During the three and half years of constitutional negotiation, the major actors concentrated their efforts on devising a new political structure to give expression to black political aspiration. The new state's foreign policy was a matter of debate and argument, but the energies of principal actors, De Klerk and Nelson Mandela, were absorbed in trying to maintain their partnerships through negotiation.

The period 1990-1994 has been well described by Deon Geldenhuys as "a new era of international engagement in South African politics.[380] A variety of external bodies including the United Nations High Commissions for Refugees,

---

378   Mwagiru (2010, p.241).
379   Spence, n.4, p. 222.
380   Deon Geldenhuys, (1993), Pp. 147-155.

the Common Wealth, the Organisation of African Unity (now African Union), and the International Commission of Jurist offered offices to the major

Both leaders, in effect, were using the external arena as a vehicle for their domestic competition; Mandela sought aid packages for the timing mechanism for the lifting of sanctions and to build a supportive international consensus for the ANC's policy of non-racial majoritarian unitary states as the basis for the new South Africa. South Africa's transition to democracy and its nation-building challenges more or less coincided with far reaching and dramatic changes in the global landscape.[381]

It is against this backdrop that South Africa has attempted to build democratic institutions and a new civic culture on the foundation of a bitter history and legacy. Nelson Mandela could assert as early as 1993 that human rights would be the light that guides our foreign affairs.[382] Freed from its apartheid isolationist moorings, South Africa adopted a broad approach of universality. This represented its intention to pursue diplomacy of active internationalism and to open foreign and local doors in the same reconciliatory spirit that had characterised its own domestic transformation. By 1995, South Africa had established ninety-three resident missions abroad. It also established full diplomatic relations with forty-six African countries. Conversely, by the end of 1994, a matter of months after the installation of ANC government, there were 136 countries with representations in South Africa. The country joined or readmitted to 16 multi-lateral organisations. For example, it was readmitted to full membership in the UN, to the Commonwealth, to the Organization of African Unity (OAU) and to the Southern African Development Community (SADC). It concluded 86·bilateral treaties and acceded to 21 multilateral treaties and conventions. This is how the foundations of post-apartheid foreign policy were laid in South Africa. South Africa's Presidential election in April 1994 was one of the most significant events in African democratic transition.

7.6.1 Strategies of South Africa Foreign Policy

Foreign policy adaptation strategies were adopted by the Mandela and Mbeki Administrations in their quest to further strengthen South Africa's ongoing transformations from an isolated international pariah to the leader of African Renaissance. The following are the strategies designed to adapt South Africa's foreign policy to the new realities of post-apartheid era: restoring civilian control over the security apparatus, restructuring the foreign policy establishment,

---

381   Garthle, P. and Anthonivan, N., (2004), p. 119
382   Nelson Mandela, (1993) p. 88.

self-promotion as the leader of African Renaissance, adherence to the foreign policy principle of universality, and assuming a leadership role in international organisation.[383]

7.6.1.1 Restoring Civilian Control
Over the Security Apparatus

One of the most important tasks was the process of demilitarisation to restore civilian control over a security apparatus that had become too powerful in the formulation of South African domestic and foreign policies. An agreement was signed between the military leaders of the apartheid era SADF and the military wing of the ANC prior to the general election of 1994. The process of the demilitarisation also included profound changes in military doctrine. As opposed to the apartheid era's doctrine of being able to launch counter insurgency wars and retaliatory strikes against neighbouring countries, current military doctrines emphasise the overriding importance of national self-defence in South Africa. An important challenge that confronted the new elected Mandela administration was the necessity of integrating previously opposed military forces into the newly created South African National Defence Force (SANDF).

7.6.1.2 Restructuring the Foreign Policy Establishment

The second strategy to adapt South African foreign policy to the post-cold war was complete restructuring of foreign policymaking establishment. The 1996 constitution clearly established the formal role to be played by a wide variety of institutional actors, with the creation and consolidation of democratic practices favouring the foreign policy inputs of different non state actors. One of the most profound examples of institutional change revolves around the restructuring of the former Ministry of Foreign Affairs to ensure that it once again assumed one of the leading roles in the formulation and implementation of foreign policy.[384] An important step in this process was the creation of a new bureaucracy, the Department of Foreign Affairs. This restructuring process was referred to as Rationalisation within South African Policymaking community.

---

383   Peter Schraeder, (2001), p. 229.
384   Chris Landsberg, Garthle, P. and Anthoni, N., (1995), p. 120.

7.6.1.3 Self-Promotion as the Leader of African Renaissance

As the leader of African Renaissance, the strengthening of democratic practices and economic liberalisation throughout Africa since the fall of the Berlin Wall in 1989 constitutes a third important component of foreign policy adaptation in the post-cold war era. Among the most important foreign policy concerns for South Africa are the promotion of regional integration and development as witnessed by South Africa's membership and leadership role in SADC, its support for nuclear non-proliferation, and a willingness to adopt a liberal economic model of free trade and investment. All have gathered strength in the post-cold war era and are invoked by the more technocratic ally-minded Mbeki administration.[385]

7.6.1.4 Adherence to the Foreign Policy
Principle of Universality

The fourth adaptation is designed to bridge the foreign policy gap between the apartheid and democratic eras. The principle of universality underscores the willingness of South Africa to establish diplomatic relations with all countries of the world regardless of the domestic or foreign policy of those countries. In the case of the Middle East, for example, the Mandela and Mbeki Administrations sought to strengthen diplomatic links with Israel while at the same time establishing and strengthening diplomatic ties with Libya and Iran. In some cases, like People's Republic of China (PRC) and Taiwan as to which capital Beijing or Taipei is recognised as the official seat of the Chinese government. The willingness of the Mandela and Mbeki Administrations to choose economic self-interest over regime type in the case of China led to sharp criticism of South African foreign policy. South Africa's diplomatic ties with Cuba and other countries considered by American policymakers to be terrorist states within the international system caused repeated diplomatic tensions between Pretoria and Washington.[386]

7.6.1.5 Assuming a Leadership Role in
International Organizations

The final strategy for adapting South African foreign policy especially to the international realities of the post-cold war era has been a firm commitment

---

385   Graham Evans, (1999) p. 621.
386   Schraeder, n.14, p. 234.

to upholding and strengthening the international norms associated with the UN and its member agencies. The other organisations also include the Non-Alignment Movement (NAM), the British Commonwealth of Nations, and the African Union. One of the most important foreign policy objectives of the immediate post-apartheid era was to ensure that South African Diplomats quickly reasserted South Africa's rightful place as both a member and a leader within the international community of international organisations.

South Africa has particularly focused on its UN membership, joining the Governing Councils of several specialised agencies and organs. Indeed, South Africa's closest rivals for a permanent UN Security Council seat are often dismissed by South African diplomats as either undemocratic (Egypt or Sudan) and beset by internal conflict (Algeria and the Democratic Republic of Congo) or lacking sufficient economic resources. These were some of the strategies designed by the South African leaders to adapt South Africa's foreign policy in the post-apartheid era.

7.6.2 Domestic Determinants

The study of the sources of Africa's foreign policy traditionally has been dominated by three bodies of scholarships. One body of research, often referred to as the big man theory of African foreign policy, emphasizes the overriding importance of the personal whims of authoritarian leaders to explain the formulation and implementation of African foreign policy. The second body of research focuses on the impact of the larger geo-political setting of great power competitions, most notably the Cold War struggle between the United States and Soviet Union. The third body of research emphasizes the constraints imposed on African Foreign Policies by the continuation of dependency relationships between the African States and their former colonial powers. Domestic determinants of South Africa's foreign policy can be examined as follows: geography, demography, historical and political tradition and economic factors.

7.6.2.1 Geography

This includes location, size, state boundaries, population, climate, and soil, and all of these elements are important in varying degrees for South Africa's national politics and foreign relations. The history of international relations shows that location has always been an important determinant of the foreign relation of a state.

South Africa, on the continent's southern tip, is bordered by the Atlantic Ocean on the west and by the Indian Ocean on the south and east. Its neighbours are Namibia in the northwest, Zimbabwe and Botswana in the north, and Mozambique and Swaziland in the northeast. The strategic location of South Africa on the Indian Ocean gives a central position in Africa, Asia and world politics. South Africa and the Indian Ocean are an indispensable link in world trade and commerce. Most of the major air and sea routes of the world pass through South Africa. Any major happening in South Africa would affect the rest of Africa and Asia. South Africa is a major connecting link among the geographical areas of Africa, South Asia particularly India, and East Asia or Far East.

The logic of geography inevitably makes India heavily dependent on the Indian Ocean for her national security as well as her foreign Indian Ocean. Continues to play a vital role in South Africa's foreign policy in the post-apartheid period. The establishment of the Indian Ocean Rim Association for Regional Co-operation (lOR-ARC) in 1997 is a positive response to geopolitical imperative. Therefore, from the above points we can see that the geographical factor is one of the important domestic determinants of Africa's foreign policy.

7.6.2.2 Demography

The demographic features of the population of South Africa, including population density, ethnicity, education level, religious affiliations and other aspects of the population, have their impact on foreign policy. South Africa has an uncommon demographic profile, marked by a heterogeneous population base, social issues brought on by the legacy of apartheid, divisions within ethnic groups, HIV/AIDS, and emigration. Within the Rainbow Nation, demography consequently plays a prominent role in public policy. Blacks compose about 79.7 percent (2007 est.) of the population and represent different ethnic groups, including Zulu, Xhosa, Ndebele, Tswana, Pedi, Sotho and Swazi, as well as recent immigrants from other parts of Africa (particularly Zimbabwe and Nigeria). Whites compose 9.1 percent (2007 est) to 11 percent (CIA 2007), comprising of the descendants of Dutch, French, British, and German settlers who began arriving at the Cape from the late 17th century, immigrants from Europe who arrived in South Africa in the twentieth century, and Portuguese who left the former Portuguese colonies of southern Africa (Angola and Mozambique) after their independence in the mid-1970s. The remaining 2.4 percent are categorized as 'Indian/Asian', including the descendants of Indian-indentured sugar estate workers and traders who came to South Africa in the mid-19th century (particularly around Natal), and a small Chinese population of approximately 100,000 people.

All of these different ethnic groups are important domestic factors in the making of South Africa's foreign policy. For example, the charismatic leadership of the first black President of South Africa, Nelson Mandela, had a deep impact on both the domestic and foreign policy of South Africa.

7.6.2.3 Historical and Political Tradition

The historical and political tradition is another domestic determinant of South Africa's foreign policy. The past, it could be argued, is never entirely wiped clean, whatever the expectations and aspirations a people may have as their society undergoes transformation of the kind affected in South Africa.

This applies to the prospects for the emergence of a democratic tradition of politics in South Africa as much as it does with respect to the formulation and conduct of foreign policy. With respect to the latter, success or failure in policymaking will depend not only on the stability of the polity but also on the extent to which South Africa succeeds in its efforts to establish a democratic tradition of political behaviour. The term 'tradition' implies that the structure and process of a country's politics is the evolving product o f a peculiar history and culture. This explains why a non-political system is identical to another; it also explains why the wholesale transplantation of Western political values and institutions failed to take root in Third World societies such an Angola, Mozambique and Zaire. Jack (1996) expresses that the new South Africa paradoxically has advantages inherited from the past, however traumatic.

The notion of the rule of law is not, after all, a new and exotic foreign import into South African political culture. It has roots in the country's legal history and has also been vigorously attacked and defended. On the other hand, it is because South African statehood is not fragile that negotiators were encouraged to seek the transformation of the state and society within existing boundaries in the hope of avoiding the ethnic fragmentation that has occurred elsewhere.

The new government started, therefore, with the advantage that it does not have to engage in the business of state- and nation-building simultaneously. The hope remains that by a combination of a debate, constitutional revision and learning from experience, a peculiarly South African version of democratic government may well emerge. By the same token, it could be argued that a country's foreign policy is, to a degree, shaped by past preoccupations, not immutable. As Bruce Miller once put the matter in a perceptive analysis: a national interest cannot be separated from the minds of the men who formulate them.......ideas of national interest have a grounding in the facts of geography and economics, but these facts are subject to changes. Thus, it could be argued that while Pretoria's new policymakers have inherited a set of national interest defined by their predecessors and constrained by the facts of geography and economics, those self-same policymakers will nonetheless put their own particular interpretation on those facts and seek to maximise advantage for their country.

7.6.2.4 Economic Factor

Economic development is another important factor of South Africa's post-apartheid foreign policy. Among the major factors which determine the rate of economic development are population, natural resources, capital and technology. Foreign policy is conditioned by these economic factors in national development in different ways. South Africa is an economic giant relative to other African economies. South Africa's gross domestic product (GDP) of US $239 billion is 40 times larger than the average Sub-·Saharan economy. It represents 25 percent of the total African economy and constitutes one third of the economy of Sub- Saharan Africa and almost two thirds of the GDP of Southern African Development Community (SADC).

The policies of President Mandela's government affected the state's capacity to pursue a foreign policy in Africa and abroad. External perceptions, influenced by the performance of the economy and ensuing observation, hoped that it would be helpful in placing foreign policy incentives and constraints in a domestic and economic context. The new government inherited an economy emerging out of long recession and inflation had fallen to single figures while exports of commodities increased by 25 percent in the first three months of 1994; agricultural products improved. With respect to relations with European Union, the precise form of the relationship between Pretoria and Brussels had yet to be worked out.

According to Martin Holand (1994), the options were as follows; the standard 'Most Favoured Nations' (MFN) status within GATT framework, Generalised System of Preference (GSP), the full Lome Status, Associate Lome Status, a Non-reciprocal association agreement and (6) a Reciprocal Association Agreement. In a detailed analysis Holand contended that the most likely outcome was a bi-lateral agreement that offered reciprocal terms. This would mean the negotiation of a free trade agreement geared specifically to South Africa but in time this would require South Africa to abandon certain protectionists' measures in exchange for access to the EU market, assuming such a forthcoming EU policy would stress promoting economic co-operation, trade and investment promotion.[387]

---

387   Holland, M., (1994), p. l33.

7.6.3 External Determinants

External factors have also served as important sources of South Africa's foreign policy. Among the important external factors of South Africa's foreign policy are: market economy and globalisation, emergence of the USA as only world power, strategic position in the African continent, multinational corporation involvement in South Africa, impact of African Union (AU), rise of Middle Power (IBSA) International Organisations, and emergence of multi-polar world. Having emerged from the international isolation of the apartheid era, South Africa has become a leading international actor. Its principal foreign policy objective is to develop good relations with all countries, especially its neighbours' in the Southern African Development Community and the other members of the African Union. South Africa has played a key role in seeking an end to various conflicts and political crises on the African continent, including in Burundi, the Democratic Republic of Congo, the Comoros, and Zimbabwe. Swaziland has asked South Africa to open negotiations on reincorporating some nearby South African territories that are populated by ethnic Swazis or that were long ago part of the Swazi kingdom.

South Africa's transition is taking place at a time where there are enormous changes in the international system. There is no longer any alternative socialist bloc of countries to allow developing countries and countries attempting the transition to democracy to structure their trade, aid and investment relations. At the same time, powerful forces of globalisation and liberalisation are changing the capitalist world economy. Understanding these changes is essential in defining policy options across the board including our economic policy and social policy and policy on the role of the state.[388]

The United Nations Development Programmes (UNDP) 1997 Human Development Report points out that the term *globalisation* both describes and prescribes the system of economic relations in the world today. The description refers to the fact that international flows of trade, finance and information are being integrated into a single global market. Globalisation, therefore, is a process which is aimed at integrating the world market where national commodity capital, financial and currency markets are joined together into a single market which operates according to a set of rules whose applications are universal. Transnational corporations, multi-lateral institutions and governments of advanced industrialised countries are driving globalisation. This is happening in a context where there are major advances in technology, particularly in the

---

388   Rob Davies, (1998), p. 170.

information and communication industries. These technologies have made capital, financial and commodity flows much quicker.

But globalisation cannot be reduced to technicist changes alone. Globalisation is much more fundamentally a process of restructuring the entire way in which global capitalism works. Globalisation has transformed the way in which dominant forces in the global economy have defined their interests in the world outside of their own home base. The agenda of transnational capital is to look for a very broad and far-reaching breakdown of barriers to the free movement of commodities and capital across national borders as well as removing obstacles to setting up production processes in any part of the world.[389]

7.6.3.1 Emergence of the USA as World Power

International factors like the end of the cold war and emergence of the USA as a world's only power, another determinant of South Africa's foreign policy. The disintegration of the Soviet Union into 15 independent States in 1991, like elsewhere, had direct impact on the foreign policy of South Africa. The external milieu in which South Africa now has its foreign policy objectives changed profoundly. In the past, South Africa was a beneficiary of the precarious order established by the cold war.

The USA took a pro-active and leading role in supporting South Africa through its transition to broad-based democracy. The administration of President Bill Clinton set great store by the success of the South Africa model of multi-culturalism, a model needed in its own cities across America. The USA anti-apartheid movement, which had played a key role in overturning the Reagan Administration's policy of constructive engagement and imposing sanctions in 1986, had created a political environment in the USA that allowed continued and increased development aid to South Africa.[390]

During Nelson Mandela's administration, President Bill Clinton announced an aid package of $600 million (R 3.9 billion) to be distributed over the following five years. The United States is South Africa's biggest single trading partner. Total trade between the two countries increased steadily, with South Africa holding an increasing trade surplus since 1999. This amounted to just under $1.5 billion in 2001, growing slightly in 2002. The USA has consistently been the largest foreign investor in post-apartheid South Africa, representing some 40 percent of the total FDI since 1994.

---

389   Davies, n. 33, p.172.
390   Britdgment M., (2004), p. 250.

7.6.3.2 Strategic Position in the African Continent

South African leaders especially have been influenced by 'role expectations' within the African continent and the wider international community. Africa in particular has been an important focus of interest, as South Africa has worked to cultivate and consolidate partnerships on the continent. This was intended to distance the new governments' actions from the past behaviour of the apartheid states and to express solidarity with and gratitude to those African leaders who had been sympathetic to South Africa's liberation struggle. As aptly summarised by Aziz Pahad, former Deputy Minister of foreign affairs, there exists a 'tremendous expectation' that South Africa will play a major role in fashioning and directing the new world order at the beginning of the new millennium.[391]

South Africa has been vividly captured in literature which variously refers to the country as a regional, intermediary, middle, or semi-peripheral power. Whereas African countries expect South Africa to take the lead in promoting the most cherished aims of African foreign policy, the northern industrialised democracies expect South Africa to serve as a role model for economic and political reforms throughout the African continent.

South Africa has a dominant position in the African continent because of economic power, political institutions, regional power and active role in international affairs. South Africa's dominant position in the region arises from: the size, experience and operational capability of its security forces, and the economic superiority. A key aspect of South Africa's foreign policy over the last few years has been its role of peacemaker in Africa, promoter of democratisation.[392]

7.6.3.3 Multinational Corporations (MNCs) Involvement in South Africa

Multinational Corporations can have a powerful influence in local economies as well as the world economy and play an important role in international relations and globalisation. The presence of such powerful players in the world economy is reason for much controversy. In the context of South Africa, involvement of MNC has a deep impact on the foreign policy of South Africa. A decade ago, South African companies were chained to their national base through sanctions, political isolation and legislative constraints making anything beyond normal trade relations nearly impossible.

---

391   Chris Landsberg, (1995), p. 124.
392   Adebajo, A, Adedeji, A, and Chris Lansburg, (2007), p. 25.

After the release of Nelson Mandela in 1990, both business and diplomatic relations with the rest of the world began to expand, slowly. Following the democratic elections of 1994, the floodgates opened, and South African corporations moved with alacrity into the rest of Africa and beyond. Today, South Africa-based companies are rapidly expanding their global profile and proving that they can compete with the best multinational companies in the world.

South African firms are more likely than international investors to make investments worth less than $1 million and to form partnerships with local entrepreneurs. It's clear that privatisation has provided an opportunity for South African firms to enter a number of Sub Saharan markets. In terms of operational characteristics, South African firms on the continent have tended to rely very heavily on imports from South Africa, often sourcing less than 10 percent of inputs on average locally. It is useful to contextualise the regional activities of individual firms with regard to their overall international activities

In this respect there seem to be four dominant groups of firms. First, there are those that have so far looked primarily outside of Africa, either as production bases or as markets for services, as in case of Sappi. Secondly, there are those firms, such as SABMiller, with a significant African presence within a much larger international network. Thirdly, there are firms with international operations in Africa and other emerging markets. Finally, there are those firms whose expansion has been essentially limited to Africa to date.[393]

This wide variety would seem to reflect, in part, the unbalanced pattern of South African industrialisation under apartheid, which gave rise to a number of very large firms possessing world-leading technology and providing services tailored to high-income markets. The end of apartheid provided the most important pre-condition for South African firms to invest abroad, as potential host economies were once again willing to receive them. This development was followed by increasing liberalisation of investment and trade restrictions within South Africa. Liberalisation has not only facilitated investment abroad, but has also created new incentives, as growing domestic competition has forced South African firms to look for profitable new markets on the continent. It can be seen that the involvement of the MNCs in South Africa has tremendously expanded its companies to the African continent as well as to the global arena.

---

393   Andrea Goldstein and Wilson Prichard, (2008), p. 129.

7.6.3.4 Impact of African Union (AU)

The establishment of African Union (AU) is an important issue in South Africa's foreign policy. South Africa has been a key player in the formation of· the African Union. It has supported the AU financially and militarily and sent peacekeeping forces to other countries of Africa. South Africa was also the first African state to choose its delegation of representatives to Pan African Parliament (PAP). African countries, in their quest for unity, economic and social development under the banner of the OAU, have taken various initiatives and made substantial progress in many areas which paved the way for the establishment of the AU. The AU is Africa's premier institution and principal organisation for the promotion of accelerated socio-economic integration of the continent, which will lead to greater unity and solidarity between African countries and peoples.

The AU is based on the common vision of a united and strong Africa and on the need to build a partnership between governments and all segments of civil society, in particular women, youth and the private sector, in order to strengthen solidarity and cohesion amongst the peoples of Africa. As a continental organisation it focuses on the promotion of peace, security and stability on. the continent as a prerequisite for the implementation of the development and integration agenda of the Union. In this context, South Africa has focused its policy towards the promotion of peace, security and stability on the continent as one of the foreign policy objectives.

7.6.3.5 International Organisations

Another external determinant of post-apartheid South Africa's foreign policy is international organisations like the UN, the African Union (AU), Commonwealth of Nations, Non-Aligned Movement etc. South Africa is active in the United Nations (UN), the African Union (AU) and the Commonwealth of Nations. On June 1, 1994, South Africa re-joined the Commonwealth of Nations, and on June 23, 1994, it was readmitted to the UN General Assembly. South Africa also joined the Organisation of African Unity (OAU).

For South Africa, reacceptance into the community of sovereign states was contingent upon resuming its place in the UN. In this light, the UN can be said to have occupied a distinctive position in South Africa's early post-apartheid international relations.[394] At the same time, the UN was itself emerging from

394   Lee, Taylor and Williams, P, (2006), p.26.

the bipolar rivalry of the Cold War. By the beginning of the 1990s, the UN, like South Africa, faced the challenge of grafting a new role for itself. In the twelve years since the end of institutionalized apartheid, South Africa had sought to do this by defining itself as a leader of the developing world. The reform of the UN has been one of the issues that developing countries have collectively pursued in recent years. This has also been an issue on which South Africa has attempted to take a leading position.

7.6.3.6 Emergence of Multi-Polar World

The emergence of a multi-polar world with many leaders, like the EU, China, Japan and India, has been another external determinant of South Africa's foreign policy. South Africa has aggressively sought foreign aid, trade, and investment. South Africa's leading economic partners of Member-States of the EU are Germany and United Kingdom. It was way back in 1983 that the EU introduced economic and diplomatic sanctions against South Africa in opposition to its apartheid policies. In 1993, the EU re-established its diplomatic relations with South Africa, when President Nelson Mandela called for lifting of economic and diplomatic sanctions. South Africa's relation with the EU is governed by the EU-SA Trade, Development and Cooperation Agreement (TDCA).

The international community sees the People's Republic of China (PRC) as an important player in the global economy as well as a significant force on the diplomatic stage. Post-apartheid South Africa chose to follow the mainstream international consensus was undoubtedly one of the critical tests in Pretoria's foreign policy. Moreover, both governments demonstrated resounding synergies in their global outlook around South-South cooperation, multiculturalism and the promotion of a fairer international economic order. China is now South Africa's fifth-largest trading partner while South Africa is currently China's biggest trade partner in Africa.

Another external factor of South Africa's foreign policy is the emergence of Japan as one of the global powers. In the 1990s, the Japanese government sought its economic agenda in sub-Saharan Africa through two dual and integrated processes: a vigorous initiative through the TICAD into a system which enhances trade and investment. Japan has also exhibited a distinct developmental interest in South Africa. In 1994, the Japanese government committed an aid package amounting to $1.3 billion. In terms of absolute volume, this presently ranks South Africa as the largest recipient of Japanese aid in sub-Saharan Africa.

Finally, India has been one of the important external determinants in post-apartheid South Africa's foreign policy. This can be examined from the following factors. First is historical. This is when Mahatma Gandhi took part in the struggle in South Africa against racial discrimination and oppression. His philosophy has become the base for the current leaders of South Africa. Second, during the days of apartheid, India was at the forefront of international struggle against apartheid and during that time India formed close links with anti-apartheid bodies including the African National Congress (ANC). Third, in the post-democratic South Africa, India was the first country to establish a relationship with South Africa.

Indian diaspora in South Africa is another factor in post-apartheid South Africa's foreign policy. Since the end of apartheid in the 1990s, the Indian community in South Africa has undergone a significant transformation particularly in socio-cultural fields. In the post-apartheid era, there has been a tremendous scope for Indian settlers to rise up with the structural changes in South African society, polity and economy. Therefore, it can be said that Indian diasporas have always been an important factor in South Africa's foreign policy in the post-apartheid period.

7.6.4 Drivers of South Africa's Foreign Policy

Some of the major drivers of South Africa's foreign policy are as follows:

7.6.4.1 Essence of State Actors

Several state actors have played an important role in the formulation and implementation of South Africa's foreign policy during democratic era 1994 to present. The constitution of 1996 that formulized South Africa's entry into the community of democratic nations clearly stipulates the overriding importance of the President in the formulation of South Africa's foreign policy. Former South African President Nelson Mandela was consistently used as a tool of the Pretoria government's foreign relations.[395] During the Mandela Administration 1994 to 1999, the constitutional prerogative was further strengthened by what is often referred to as the 'Mandela Effect'. Mandela's emergence from nearly 27 years of captivity in apartheid jails was one of the most celebrated, admired and charismatic figures of the 20th century.[396]

The charismatic leadership of Thabo Mbeki has been another factor in South Africa's foreign policy. Mbeki as President in 1999 heralded a greater routinisation and depersonalisation of South Africa's foreign policy more in

---

395   Peter Vale and Ian Taylor, (1999), p. 629.
396   Graham Evans, (1999), p. 621.

line with the 1996 constitution. Having served as the Foreign Minister of ANC during its years in exile, Mbeki was clearly familiar with the multitude of foreign policy issues confronting post-apartheid South Africa. Unlike his predecessors, Mbeki was reportedly more open to compromise and more willing to rely on the expertise of foreign policy experts within the executive branch, most notably the co-ordination and co-operation unit.

The foreign affairs bureaucracies of the executive branch also serve as important sources of South African foreign policy in the democratic era. A fascinating aspect of an emerging bureaucratic blueprint of South African foreign policy is that the existing foreign affairs bureaucracies, most notably the department of Foreign Affairs and Ministry of Defence, were completely transformed. Several trends can be noted in the relative positions of power and influence of individual bureaucracies within the foreign policy hierarchy. This constitutionally independent branch of government plays an important oversight role which, although not as powerful as originally envisioned by ANC stalwarts and members of civil society, clearly goes beyond the foreign policy prerogatives enjoyed by legislatures during the apartheid (1948-94) and pre-apartheid (pre-1948) periods. The leading legislative actor within the foreign policy realm is the Portfolio Committee on Foreign Affairs.

7.6.4.2 Essence of Non-State Actors

Non-state actors also play a significant role in the formulation of South African foreign policy. The ANC is particularly influential due to its status as the ruling party in both the executive branch and Parliament during the democratic era. The ANC's victory in two sets of legislative elections and the alteration of power between the Mandela and Mbeki administrations have even led some scholars to refer to South Africa as a "dominant-party system" in which the ANC will continue to rule for the foreseeable future.[397] Non-state actors such as non-governmental organisations (NGO), conflict management institutions, policy think-tanks and peace and stability organisations have also become important instruments and players in South Africa's foreign policy. The NGO sector is already starting to engage in collaborative interventions with the Department of Foreign Policy (DFA) and other government departments involved in foreign policy.[398]Another South African think-tank that has been of policy value to the DFA is the African Centre for the Constructive Resolution of Disputes (ACCORD) which has in recent years acted as an important focal point in

---

397   Herman, (1998), p. 435
398   Paul Nantulya, (2004), p.15

several fields. The Africa Institute of South Africa (AISA), ·the South African Institute of International Affairs (SAIIA), Institute of Global Dialogue (IGD), and the Centre for Conflict Resolution (CCR), among many others, have been of immense value to the South African government's. foreign policy operations.

One of the features of the South African NGO sector in the first ten years of democracy was been its engagements and visibility in national-policy issues. In the area of conflict management, peace and stability, this growth has been phenomenal. South African NGOs have developed depth and experience in the practice of international conflict management, which has placed them in a strategic position to influence the pattern of South African foreign policy towards Africa. The IGR (Institute for Justice and Reconciliation) is considered a leader in transitional politics and engagement in Africa. It has been involved in working across various transitional settings the DRC, Sierra Leone, Rwanda, Burundi and other countries. SAIIA has monitored the development of South African foreign policy and published world class foreign policy reviews annually.

7.6.4.3 Essence of Multiple Actors

One of the challenges of post-apartheid South Africa's foreign relation was the emergence of many actors who played important roles in shaping, determining and finally implementing policies.[399] It was precisely this multiplicity of players with seemingly conflicting interests, which included President Mandela, Deputy President Mbeki, Cabinet, Parliament, and Parliamentary Committees dealing with foreign affairs, trade and other state departments.

President Harry Truman, the US President (1945- 1952) once declared that "the President makes foreign policy."[400] In case of President Mandela, this was certainly true. His command and seeming domination of every major policy decision and issue was so complete as to almost overshadow the roles of Cabinet and Parliament.

From the above discussion, it can be said that foreign policy of South Africa has been influenced by various domestic and international factors. The foreign policy of South Africa has been transformed into a new dimension in the post-apartheid period since 1994 onwards. Domestic factors include geography, political and historical tradition, economic factors etc. International factors include globalisation, end of the cold war, African continent, international organisations and emergence of multi-polar world. In all these, like elsewhere, the role of leadership has been critical.

---

399   Garthle, P. and Anthonivan, (2004), p. 123.
400   Frankel, (1968) p. 21.

7.7 The Sudan's Foreign Policy

Sudan's interaction with many neighbouring states with different regimes and contradictory interests causes continuous difficulties in the choice of policy action. Probable threats related to economic, political or security interests were many in such a large country with a diverse multi-ethnic population. The inherent weakness of the economic, social and political base required a pragmatic external policy guaranteeing the achievement of national security objectives. However, ideology has always played a central role in Sudanese domestic politics, and is seen as an advantage in countering external complications.

The foreign policies of successive Sudanese governments since the period of self-determination had been characterized by a curious pattern in which policies changed course or were aborted or reversed in a way that indicated the lack of any consistent or long-term foreign policy strategy. The first national government of Isma'il al-Azhari, elected in November 1953 on a platform calling for union with Egypt under the slogan of 'Unity of the Nile Valley', had by December 1955 opted for Sudan's complete independence. The military regime of General Ibrahim Abbud despite, or perhaps because of, its rather consistent record of passive withdrawal and non-involvement in foreign affairs by 1964 had managed to dissipate the goodwill it had initially generated with Egypt, and to alienate Sudan's African neighbours by its harsh and brutal policy in southern Sudan.

The radical foreign policy initiated by the first provisional government in October 1964, had ended by July 1965 in a new retreat to conservatism. The Numayri regime undoubtedly beat all records for policy reversal by making a complete U-turn from a pro-Soviet stance in 1969 to a pro-Western posture by 1976 – a reversal of policy which, not coincidentally, ran parallel to that of Egypt.

The reason behind this phenomenon might be that Sudanese politics had always been buffeted by conflicting interests, both internal and external, which led to a certain ambiguity in Sudan's relations with the outside world. The foreign policies of Sudanese governments since independence had largely been shaped not by the national interest of the country as such, but by the interests of the regime in power. These interests, in turn, were not constant and tended to fluctuate with changing internal circumstances and/or external developments.

7.7.1 Origin and Development of Foreign Policy

This section examines three aspects of Sudanese foreign policy: the isolation epoch, the radicalization epoch, and the Numayri regime epoch as explored herein.

7.7.1.1 The Isolation Epoch, 1958-1964

The main feature of the foreign policy of Abbud's military regime was the lack of any active or long-term involvement in external affairs. The regime maintained the impeccable Third World orthodoxy of previous Sudanese governments – standing for world peace, African unity, Arab unity, nonalignment, all nations struggling to be free, and so on. But in practice the foreign policy of the junta was characterized by a 'lethargic indifference' to world affairs. Sudan remained aloof from the radical North African Arab wing of the Casablanca Charter as well as from the more conservative Monrovia Conference countries.[401]

The main function of the regime's foreign policy was to solicit aid from any quarter that was willing to give it. This made it imperative to adopt a low profile in international affairs. Indeed, the activities of the Foreign Affairs Ministry during that period were more appropriate to those of a Ministry of Foreign Trade. The first foreign policy statement, announced by Foreign Minister Ahmad Khair in November 1958, sounded in parts, like a commercial advertisement. We will endeavour to further political, economic and cultural cooperation with all, the statement said, "we are in need of foreign loans and aid; we shall therefore do our best to create a favourable atmosphere to attract them. In our commercial relations we shall deal with all countries of the world on the basis of mutual interest."[402]

On 29th November, 1958 the military reconfirmed the US aid agreement, which had precipitated a major political crisis in the Sudanese parliament just before the coup, and which might have been a factor in the decision to hand over power to the army. The World Bank, West Germany, Britain and Italy became prominent donors of aid and technical assistance. In keeping with its middle-of-the-road policy, the regime sought to balance its economic connection with the West through soliciting recognition and aid from the Eastern bloc. In one of its first foreign policy acts, the government recognized the People's Republic of China. Trade agreements were negotiated with the Soviet Union, Yugoslavia, Bulgaria and Czechoslovakia and, from 1961 on, the Sudan found itself the recipient of aid from many sources.[403]

Non-alignment was endorsed, not from any ideological conviction but because, as Ahmad Khair later argued, it was just something to be used to win friends. The adoption of non-alignment was essentially a convenient certificate of Sudan's non-commitment in cold-war rivalries. Abbud's visit to the USA in 1961 encouraged good bilateral relations, as did his visit to the USSR in the

---

401   Holt (1961), p.1B4
402   First (1970), p.249
403   Ibid, p.249

same year, and Chou Enlai's visit to the Sudan in January 1964. But in terms of foreign policy orientation these visits meant little, except perhaps to underline Sudan's posture of non-involvement.

This attitude was projected into other areas of foreign relations. Thus, although the Sudan continued to pay lip-service to its allegiances within the Arab world, in practice the emphasis was more on the Sudan as part of Africa, so that it could afford to stand at a distance from the forces competing for leadership in the Arab world.[404]

Relations with Egypt started with a cordial note. Egypt was the first country to extend diplomatic recognition to the new regime. In his first broadcast to the nation on 17th November, Abbud promised to resolve all outstanding problems with Egypt and to remove the artificial cloud' hanging over the relations between the two countries. The conclusion of the new Nile waters agreement with Egypt in November 1959 was one of the few major foreign policy acts undertaken by the military regime.[405] The two sides agreed on an allocation of water, which theoretically increased Sudan's quota, and on the financial compensation for the relocation of Nubians whose land in Wadi Haifa would be flooded on the completion of Egypt's high dam.

The successful conclusion of the agreement could be seen as a positive achievement, considering Cairo's previous refusals to grant any concessions. The agreement removed a bone of contention with Egypt and thus seemed to pave the way for better relations between the two countries. The improvement in relations was symbolized by Abbud's visit to Cairo in July1960, which was reciprocated by President Nasser in November of the same year.[406]

However, the conclusion of the agreement entailed damaging domestic repercussions that outweighed any short-term advantages which the regime might have gained. In the first place, it sent a wave of criticism throughout the country. The resettlement compensation was regarded as unsatisfactory. In fact, the resettlement was eventually to cost double the compensation allotted. Secondly, and more seriously, the conclusion of the agreement precipitated the first open civilian challenge to the authority of the military when, in 1960, violent demonstrations erupted in Wadi Haifa in protest against the government's decision to resettle the 50,000 dispossessed Nubians in Kashm al-Girba.

Although the near insurrection was finally contained, the damage to the regime's authority could not be undone. As one writer noted, in the face of opposition, the military attitude hardened; the resettlement project was one on

---

404   Ibid, p.250
405   Howell and Hamid (1969), p.302-303.
406   Henderson (1966), p.135

which the prestige and authority of the regime would rest. The price of prestige helped to cripple the central treasury. As for the authority of the regime, the myth of its invulnerability had been challenged by the act of Wadi Haifa's defiance and would never be the same again.[407]

In the economic field, the regime was also encountering difficulties. The military had acted effectively when they took power to rectify the deteriorating economic situation. In January 1959, the government abolished the reserve price on Sudanese cotton and offered it for sale at whatever price it could fetch. Since world prices were rising at the time, both the backlog and new crops were sold by August 1959, and the country became economically solvent with a small surplus of revenue. But the improvement in the economic situation and the flow of foreign aid only encouraged the government to embark on economic projects that entailed a heavy expenditure of foreign currency and by 1963 the country was in deep in debt. According to one source, over-estimated revenue and underestimated expenditure had resulted in a deficit of more than £75 million in five years.[408]

Thus, any popularity that the regime might have earned as a result of its initial economic successes was gradually eroded by its failure to handle the political and economic issues confronting it. The junta became increasingly insensitive to popular dissatisfaction with its heavy-handed policies, especially in the south, and with the creeping corruption in its administration. The three main reasons for the popular groundswell against military rule were the failure of the soldiers to create an efficient government, their failure to solve the problem of southern Sudan, and their failure to give the Sudanese people any sense of purpose.[409]

The regime's domestic troubles were reflected in its foreign relations. Sudan's relations with Egypt began to cool considerably after President Nasser intensified, in 1961, the process of socialist transformation in Egypt and assumed a more militant stance against conservative and pro-Western states in the Arab world. Relations were further strained when the Abbud regime demanded the payment of Egypt's outstanding debt to the Sudan, a demand which the Egyptians, not unreasonably, attributed to imperialist influences over the Sudan that aimed to undermine the revolutionary policies of Egypt. By 1964, relations with Egypt more or less reverted to their pre-Abbud state of mutual suspicion. That relations with Sudan's neighbours to the south and east did not deteriorate further was largely due to the realistic and self-serving practice of the military to refrain from supporting secessionist elements from

---

407   First (1970), p.249
408   Ibid, P.251
409   Beshir (1964), p.321

these African neighbours. As one writer observed, in this sense, a thinly-veiled system of deterrence-by-mutual-hostage kept the peace, such as it was, but this was no foundation on which to build good neighbourly relations.[410]

By 1964, the military regime was failing both as a government in the north and as an army in the south, and the latter failure, because of the brutality and harshness that accompanied it, sparked the wave of revulsion and anger in the north that culminated in the October Revolution of 1964. The October tide that submerged the military ended a foreign policy isolation which was perhaps far from being splendid.

7.7.1.2 The Radicalization Epoch, 1964-1965

Compared to previous policy pronouncements, there was hardly anything new in the guiding principles of foreign policy outlined on 30th October, 1964 by Sir al-Khatim al-Khalifa, the Prime Minister of the new Provisional Government. What was definitely new was the revolution itself and the forces which generated and, for a while, directed it. The overthrow of military rule by civilians was, indeed, phenomenal at a time when soldiers had seized and kept power in many countries. As one report noted at the time, "the revolution was an event unique in the history of Africa, if not of the world. It was achieved not by armed force from a rival clique of officers, not by an armed mob, not by politicians with outside support, but by a group of intellectuals, students, lawyers, who quickly mobilized public opinion and persuaded President Abbud that he and his Cabinet must resign."[411]

Indeed, the atmosphere in Khartoum in the wake of the revolution was more akin to that of a newly-independent country than one that had ruled itself for nine years. There seemed to be for the first time, little uncertainty about fundamentals; the profound sense of achievement bred a feeling that there was a mission to be fulfilled, and that the revolution made possible, if not inevitable, the emergence of the Sudan as a dynamic force in the heart of Africa. Tied up with this feeling, or emanating from it, was a determination that there would no longer be that discrepancy between declared ideals and actual practice which had characterized previous foreign policy.

The overthrow of the Abbud regime did in fact signal a decisive break with the attitude of non-commitment and passive withdrawal adopted by Sudanese governments in the past. The involvement of the new regime with the revolutionary movements in neighbouring countries and its commitment

---

410   Bechtold, (1976), p.315
411   East African Standard, Nairobi, 20 January 1965

to radical causes throughout the Afro-Asian world was a natural reaction to the conservatism of the military junta. But it was also explained and justified in terms of self- interest: a revolutionary foreign policy was seen as essential to maintain the momentum of the revolution at home.[412]

The political nature of the provisional government clearly indicated that it would hardly be content with simply marking time. Although it assumed power with wide popular support, the new government was not representative in the normal sense of the word. Most of the ministers were actually nominated by the National Front of Professional Organizations, a political body that had come into existence with the first rumblings of revolution.

It would be wrong, however, to view subsequent foreign policy as part of a communist strategy or conspiracy. "The communists had thrived as usual under proscription. As a result, they had been at the forefront of resistance, and after the revolution they were by far the best organized party. Predictably enough, the Communist Party sought to influence events, in domestic as well as foreign affairs. But with power now in the hands of urban and intellectual groups, the Sudan was bound to move left anyway, and in the new political climate, a fresh approach to foreign policy was inevitable."[413]

The new line in foreign policy was quickly demonstrated when in November 1964, the cabinet decided to deny landing facilities to British aircraft carrying military equipment or personnel to Aden. The government publicly condemned the landing of Belgian para-troops in Stanleyville and the complicity of the USA in it, and called upon the OAU to implement collective action against 'imperialist aggression' in the Congo. Of more consequence was the government's decision to offer immediate and active support to the Congolese rebels (the *Simba*) and the Eritrean liberation movement. By January 1965, Algerian and Egyptian arms were being flown, via Khartoum, to the *Simba* rebels on Sudan's southern borders.[414]

It was unfortunate for the Sudanese government that the arms shipments reached the Congolese rebels at the time they were retreating in disarray and defeat before Tshombe'e white mercenaries crossed the Sudan's borders. Their newly acquired weapons were now of little use to them except perhaps as barter for food and drink. Consequently, the new weapons easily found their way into the hands of the *Anya-Nya* rebels. Thus, the sudden influx of arms tended to strengthen the military position of the *Anya-Nya* who had been badly harassed during the last months of the Abbud regime.

---

412   Howell and Hamid (1969), p.300
413   Ibid, p.312
414   Ibid, p.332

7.7.1.3 Numeiri's Regime Epoch 1969 - 1986

The coming to power of the Numeiri regime in May 1969 constituted a new point of radical departure in Sudanese politics. Domestically, the ideological orientation and the political procedures and institutions of the regime were closely cast after, if not out-rightly copied from, the Egyptian model. From the beginning, the foreign policy of the Numeiri regime was marked by a close identification with Egypt which was to remain the touchstone of Sudan's external relations. Indeed, Sudanese-Egyptian relations assumed a pattern which, in our new of this writer, strikingly resembled the relationship of Finland with the Soviet Union. Such a trend constituted a drastic break with previous foreign policy traditions, which had maintained a fairly independent foreign policy orientation, whether passive or not, and an invariably strict neutrality in the important field of inter-Arab affairs. In the pre-1969 period, Sudan had kept on reasonable terms with all Arab states, a stance which had made it acceptable to all sides as mediator in inter-Arab conflicts.

Since 1969, the close association with Egypt had taken various forms, ranging from the Tripoli charter and the abortive Federation of Arab Republics to the Sudan's rather solitary support of Egypt's peace process with Israel. This does not necessarily mean that there were no differences or strains in Sudanese-Egyptian relations during this period. In 1972-1973 bilateral relations cooled after Numayri decided to opt out of his commitment to join the Federation of Arab Republics in order not to jeopardize the delicate quest for a peaceful settlement of the southern problem. Again in 1972, the Egyptians were dismayed by the Sudan's decision to resume diplomatic relations with the USA. Relations with Egypt also became sour in 1979 over Egypt's unilateral peace process with Israel.

But all these differences were of a rather transient nature and did not seriously affect the established pattern of the new relationship. Indeed, it was a measure of Numeiri's Sudan foreign policy that such strains in bilateral relations, particularly the latter ones, were quickly resolved, more often than not with Sudan conforming to the Egyptian position.

The setting in of Numeiri should not be taken to imply that Sudan has abdicated its sovereignty or that Cairo now dictated Sudan's foreign policy. Such a situation is the function of a satellite rather than a Finlandized relationship, nor does it mean that the new pattern of relations had been motivated by Sudanese fears of Egyptian invasion or intervention if Sudan took a different view in foreign affairs. Finlandized was derived from Finlandization which refers to the process or result of being obliged for economic reasons to favor, or at least not oppose the interests of the former Soviet Union despite not being politically allied to it. According to Ekholm, Kai (2001), it is the process by which one powerful country makes a smaller neighboring country abide by its foreign policy rules, while allowing it to keep its nominal independence and its own political system. The term literally means "to become like Finland" referring to the influence of the Soviet Union on Finland's policies during the Cold War.[415]

On the contrary, Egyptian intervention had been invited by the Soviet Union government in 1970, 1971, 1976 and 1981 to have discussion on the bilateral relations between the two countries. Indeed, the new approach to Sudan's foreign policy becomes easily explicable in terms of the security considerations that had made such interventions necessary.[416]

In May 1969, the ideologizing of Sudan's foreign policy along the lines of Nasse's radical Arab nationalism was, in many ways, reminiscent of the early radicalism of the October revolution. But the death of Nasser in 1970 set the scene for drastic changes in Egypt which were to have profound repercussions in Sudan. While Sadat's move in May 1971 against the so-called centres of power initiated a process of de-Nasserization that was reflected in Egyptian foreign policy, Numeiri's success in defeating the communist coup in July 1971 marked a sharp shift in Sudanese politics from an ideological posture to a pragmatic one, that was also mirrored in Sudanese foreign policy.

Both moves entailed drastic domestic and foreign policy reappraisals, which pointed in the same direction and which, thus, provided a common ground of mutual interest. When in July 1971 Sadat moved to help Numeiri crush the communist putsch, he was doing so as much for the interests and security of the Sudanese regime as for his own. Just as Moscow would never tolerate an anti-Soviet regime in Helsinki, Cairo would do all in its power to thwart the installation of an anti-Egyptian regime in Khartoum. The other side of the coin was that since the interests and the security of the Numeiri regime had become so intertwined with those of Egypt, Sudan would not, indeed could not, take a foreign policy stand unacceptable or actually hostile to the Egyptian regime.

After the abortive communist coup, there followed a brief period of relative disengagement from external affairs during which the regime concentrated on the internal consolidation of its authority, and on the successful conclusion of the Addis Ababa agreement of February 1972 that settled the long-standing southern conflict on the basis of regional autonomy for the south.

Sudan reactivated its close ties with Egypt in early June 1973, and the bilateral relations were further consolidated by the conclusion of the economic and political integration agreement in February 1974. Sudan continued backing

---

415   Ekholm, Kai (2001).Pp. 51-57
416   Ibid, P.303

Sadat's pro-Western policies and by its support of the Sinai disengagement agreement of September 1975, put the Numeiri regime in the so-called 'moderate' Arab camp of Egypt and Saudi Arabia, and on the side of American-sponsored Middle East policies.

Sudan's increasing identification with Egypt and Western allies was underlined by Numayri's fierce anti-Sovietism, which could be attributed to a number of factors. Firstly, it could be interpreted as a reflection of Egyptian and Sudanese perceptions of real or imagined Soviet threats to the two regimes. Secondly, Numeiri might have thought that an anti-Soviet posture could be a useful device to please the Saudis and win the support of the Americans. Thirdly, Numayri's anti-Sovietism could be seen as a projection into foreign policy of his intense personal dislike of communism and the Soviet Union, dating back to the 1971 abortive communist coup against his regime. Whatever the causes of Numayri's anti-Sovietism, it had a negative impact not only on Soviet-Sudanese relations but also on Sudan's relations with some of its neighbours. It tended to invite pressures and reprisals from Soviet allies on the Sudan's borders thus creating the very security problem that drove Numeiri still closer to Egypt and that provoked him to take an even more strident anti-Soviet posture.

7.7.1.4 Islamic Ideology Epoch 1989 – Onward

Control of state institutions in parallel with Islamization and Arabization policies reflected the convictions of the NCP's elite in constructing a model that could inspire other Islamic states. Decision-makers advocate that revival of Islamic glory in the international arena should begin with the implementation of domestic policies that would induce Muslim communities to mobilize around the Islamic agenda. The rigid and fundamentalist government policies and the government's tolerant nature that required inclusive policies encompassing all existing cultures and traditions contravened the diversity of Sudanese society. It also demonstrated how the NIF elite looked towards the Islamic Umma as a united front in the effort to challenge the international system's status quo.[417]

This outlook created a new direction in the form and shape of Sudanese engagement in both the region and the international sphere. The urge to back Islamist groups stemmed from the government's objective to advance these groups politically in their respective countries. The NCP's elite viewed the weakness of the Muslims around the world as having a direct link with the 'Christian' West's attempts to control and undermine Muslims. There are three crucial themes that need to be explored when debating the regime's overarching

---

417   Sharfi, M, H (2015), p.524

external agenda at the time, including the regime's revolutionary claims, the leadership of political Islam and the alternatives for political survival. These themes generated a new style of politics that the Sudanese state currently continues to endure.[418]

The impact of the regime's foreign policy during its initial years continues to have an ongoing resonance within the Sudanese political context. The current domestic and external landscape has been shaped to a larger extent by the consequences of the NCP's early agendas. Survival continues to be key for the policymakers and necessitates renouncing the earlier revolutionary agenda. The abandonment of radical agendas was directly linked to the shift in the frame of mind of the regime's inner clique, especially the military. However, certain quarters within the regime felt the government went too far in its attempts to improve relations with the US Administration, which contradicts the stance on the issues of Islamic Umma.

This early fragmentation within the ruling political movement still and will continue to reverberate forcefully within Sudanese political dynamics. One of the outcomes of the political rift is the disintegration of the NIF and the creation of a new force in Sudanese politics – the Popular Congress Party (PCP) – opposing the regime led by former ideologue Dr Al-Turabi. This split was one of the factors that triggered the ongoing Darfur crisis with the political, financial and ideological support of the PCP for the Justice and Equality Movement in its early insurgence in 2003.[419]

The cumulative government policies of the 1990s in the external sphere will continue to be a thorny issue with respect to the regime's image on the international stage. Similar issues of that period continue to shape NCP relations and make it an outcast in the international sphere. These include internal political reform, with Sudan still being on the list of states sponsoring terrorism since October 1993; the human rights situation worsened with the International Criminal Court indictment of President Omar Al-Bashir for alleged war crimes and crimes against humanity.

7.7.2 Determinants of Sudan Foreign Policy

Sudan continues to face an array of sanctions and prohibitions to international economic and development aid despite the April 2011 Revolution.

---

418   Ibid, p.524
419   Ibid, Pp. 529-532

7.7.2.1 Domestic Politics and International Relations

Diplomacy is the implementation of foreign policy, as distinct from the process of policy formulation. Diplomacy has two facets. First, a state asserts itself and represents its concerns to the world through this vehicle. Second, it is also a principal means for conciliating competing national interests. In other words, diplomacy aims at achieving the goals of state whilst preserving 'international order'.[420] Modern international negotiation does represent a meshing of great systems. It is commonplace today to observe that the world is becoming interdependent.

One system of this interdependence is the fact that complex political and economic problems are increasingly handled at the level of international negotiation rather than exclusively at the domestic level. Negotiators nowadays perform those functions, which are construed as the extension of national policymaking processes rather than mere formal diplomatic representation between the two sovereign states. International negotiation is currently becoming a more politicized affair. The distinctions between foreign and domestic affairs are consequently being blurred.[421]

Domestic politics and international relations are thus entangled in some or the other way.[422] Explaining as to how the domestic politics of several countries became entangled via an international negotiation, the main purpose of all strategies of foreign economic policy is to make domestic policies compatible with the international political economy.[423] He stressed that the central decision-makers, i.e. state, must be simultaneously concerned with domestic and international pressures. A more adequate account of domestic determinants of foreign policy and international relations meanwhile takes into account political parties, social classes, economic and noneconomic interest groups, legislators, and even public opinion and elections, not simply executive officials and institutional arrangements.

At the national level, domestic groups pursue their interests by putting pressure on the government to adopt favourable policies, and politicians seek power by constructing coalitions among those groups. At the international level, national governments seek to maximise their own ability to satisfy domestic pressures, while minimising the adverse consequences of foreign developments. Some scholars stated that prediction of international outcomes is significantly improved by understanding internal bargaining, especially with respect to minimally acceptable compromises.[424]

---

420   Martin Giffiths and Terry Callaghan (2004), pp. 79-80.
421   Gilbert R. Winham (1977), p.88.
422   Robert D. Putnam (1988), p.27.
423   Peter 1. Katzenstein (1978), p. 4;
424   Glenn H. Snyder and Paul Diesing (1977), , pp. 510-25.

Central decision-makers strive to reconcile domestic and international imperatives simultaneously. This is more pertinent in negotiation on trade and investment partnership. The relationship between foreign investor and the host country, as postulated by Bargaining Theory is based on the 'problem of joint-maximization.'[425] The foreign investor has capital, organisational resources, expertise, international access to express markets, and marketing ability while the host government has control of natural resources such as ore and crude oil as well as the labour force, and control over taxation, the trade and foreign exchange regime, and other laws and regulations.[426]

The Sudan government uses oil as a major instrument of external negotiation to pursue its foreign policy objectives that are manifested in the military, economic and politico-diplomatic interests of its regime. First, the military components of Sudan's foreign policy calculus indicate the external procurement of arms to strengthen the security apparatus in the midst of prolonged civil war. Second, the economic aspect refers to receiving financial credit and assistance on favourable terms at a time when the country's economy is severely affected due to massive war expenditure and American sanction. Third, politico-diplomatic interests of the regime imply evoking support for Sudan in the international platforms on the controversial issues of territorial conflict and human rights violation. These regime interests have become subjects of negotiation during the bargains for oil production partnership. That the oil industry is itself embedded in the territorial conflict makes the task of negotiation much more complex for the regime.

7.7.2.2 Sudan's Relations with West

Oil production activity was initiated by Sudan by means of facilitating the participation of western players equipped with effective exploration and production technology. The multinational oil firms from North America and Western Europe undertook exploration and development of oil fields, carried out oil production, extended their involvement in the building of oil infrastructure, and moreover performed retailing function of the oil business in Sudan. The rise in oil production gradually enabled Sudan to begin oil exports in the year 1999. Thus, Sudan became integrated with the expanded world oil regime as an upcoming oil producer by forging partnerships with Western oil firms.

The oil industry became very crucial for the economy by contributing the maximum share of export revenues to the country's exchequer. The expansion

---

425   Robert Curry and Donald Rothschild (1974), pp. 173- 89
426   Ronald T. Libby and James H. Cobbe (1981), p. 725.

of Sudan's oil sector, however, coincided with the resurgence of civil war in the 1980s. The revival of intra-state territorial fighting has placed Sudan in an adverse position vis-a-vis the Western powers. They have accused the regime in Khartoum of using oil revenues for strengthening its security apparatus against rebels in the south. The American comprehensive trade sanction was meanwhile a turning point for the Sudanese oil industry.[427] The US' hostility towards Sudan is indeed an extension of the latter's adverse relation with the West that led to the withdrawal of major Western oil firms from its oil industry. Asian oil importers have simultaneously replaced their Western partnerships with several oil fields in Sudan.

7.7.2.3 Sudan's Relations with Asia

There is a time coincidence in the expansion of Sudanese oil industry with rising Asian interest in African oil. The Asian quest for African equity oil provides concrete ground for the current regime in Sudan to diversify the pattern of its transnational production linkage through consolidation of multiple Asian participants in its oil sector. The shift that Sudan's foreign oil policy behaviour has undergone is due to the withdrawal of major Western oil firms which have initiated the exploration and production activity in its oil field. The underlying rationale for such approach, therefore, lies in the intents to ensure that Sudan's oil production remains less dependent on the partnership with West, and at the same time to foreclose an eventuality where any single Asian player does monopolise its oil sector. Asian orientation has consequently become the dominant trajectory of the transnational production partnership that Sudan is currently forging for its oil industry.[428]

Asian countries including not only China, India and Malaysia but also Japan, South Korea, Singapore, Indonesia and Taiwan, have come to be the most important investors in Sudan, an increasingly significant source of Sudan's imports and a dominant feature of Sudan's export profile, largely through oil. Over the past decade, in Sudan the declining economic role of the West has been counter-posed against an increase in Asian importance.[429] The impact of sanctions on Western companies has been reinforced by the high-profile American-led divestment campaigns initiated during the war in Southern Sudan and reinvigorated over Darfur.

Very different and consequential politics have, however, developed since

---

427   Ismail S.H. Ziada, (2006), p.12
428   Daniel Large (2008), p.4
429   Ibid, p.5

the early 1990s and has accelerated through oil cooperation. The historical backdrop before the take-off of relations in the 1990s is thus important in certain respects. It plays a role in framing relations and informing the language of official interaction. However prominent the role of history, the period of substantive Chinese involvement in Sudan is comparatively short and would deepen progressively over the 1990s until the present moment largely because of oil. China's role in Sudan today is different from that during previous phases of relations as it is more far-reaching and involved than at any period in the past. This underlying trend is one reason why China's position in Sudan has become more challenging for the Chinese government.[430] China's politico-diplomatic support to Sudan is meanwhile a major factor that has sustained the oil partnership between the two countries. China has generally vetoed or otherwise opposed UN Security Council measures to hold Sudan accountable.

Thus, Sudan has been able to deepen its engagement with the Asian partners in the wider domains of military linkage, economic exchange and politico-diplomatic relations because the Asian orientation fits African oil production. The multiple Asian participants in its oil industry is the result of a conscious foreign policy decision on the part of the current regime in Sudan. The underlying rationale for such approach lies in the intents to ensure that Sudan's oil production remains less dependent on the partnership with West, and at the same time to avoid a situation where any single Asian player monopolises its oil sector.

All in all, following the April 2019, revolution that overthrew the almost 30 years military rule of Bashir, it is likely that the new government in Khartoum will reassess its foreign policy. There may be major shift and re-orientation of its foreign policy to make room for the new political dispensation within the region and beyond.

---

430   Ibid, p.1-2

CHAPTER EIGHT

AFRICAN DIPLOMACY

The origin of African diplomatic relations can be traced to early times of its existence until the period of the Trans-Atlantic trade in slaves, ivory, beads and other goods. Treaties were ratified solemnly, protocol widely accepted, negotiations regulated, sanctions provided for the observance of treaties, and embassies sent to Europe with emissaries performing official diplomatic duties. These diplomatic activities went on in the pre-colonial period covering a period of four or five hundred years up to the last decade of the nineteenth century before the partition and the establishment of colonies. Pre-colonial Africa too could trace the origin of its diplomatic relations to the same period.

Diplomacy and foreign policy are often conflated, mainly because both terms describe the interaction between actors in the international system. Diplomacy is generally used with the aim of achieving specific objectives through peaceful means and it is often explained in relation to foreign policy. The term foreign policy depicts the policy as targeting actors beyond the borders of the territorial state. While foreign policy exclusively describes interactions beyond the state, diplomacy may apply in both international and domestic environments. In the African context, therefore, diplomacy may include interaction between the state and actors both within and outside its borders. A state aiming to end insurgency within its territorial borders requires diplomacy to conduct negotiations.

Therefore, the application of negotiation to resolve intra-state conflict in Africa by IGAD and AU is a good example in utilization of African diplomacy as a foreign policy tool. Similarly, the resolution of conflict between two warring constituencies within a state requires the use of diplomacy. As a general rule, foreign policy, like diplomacy, is aimed at achieving specific objectives although there are differences in their application. For example, in foreign policy a state could use the concept of threat perception in the form of military or economic to get what it wants, while diplomacy uses negotiation and mediation to achieve what it wants through peaceful means.

The idea that African diplomacy presents a distinct form or style of diplomacy is rather recent because the majority of African states gained political independence only during the past five (5) decades. Indeed, the youngest member of the United Nations (UN) is an African state, South Sudan, which achieved its sovereign status as recently as July 2011.

When the UN was founded in 1945, Africa had the least representation in the organization: a mere four (Egypt, Ethiopia, Liberia, and South Africa) out of 51 founding member states. This profile has changed dramatically and, in the second decade of the 21stcentury, Africa has more sovereign states than any other region in the world, amounting to more than 25% of UN membership.

An historical perspective is essential to explain the guiding themes in African diplomacy: the pursuit for equality and justice in international relations; the overriding imperative of development, peace and security for the continent; and inclination towards diplomacy that binds up African solidarity, unity, and integration. Indeed, much of the rhetoric of African diplomacy is informed by its history of marginalization and exploitation: a relationship that infers continental vulnerability vis-a-vis the rest of the world. But contemporary African diplomacy is not just born of negative experiences. It is also infused with traditional values that Africans and the diaspora share: a seamless approach to the passage of time, respect for culture tradition and authority, predilection for collective, unhurried decisions, and the prioritization of community rather than individuals. The latter approach finds expression in concepts that promote societal selflessness, such as *Harambee* (Swahili word for "pulling together") and Ubuntu (Ngun word for "*being human*"). Thus, for example, the South African government's most recent foreign policy document gave emphasis to Building a Better World or the Diplomacy of *Ubuntu*. In addition, the concept of cultural variation in diplomatic negotiations has enriched African diplomacy in that it takes into consideration other people's way of thinking based on their own culture and understanding of the issue being discussed.

It is this idea of empathetic common human interaction and interest that correlates with enduring value of diplomacy at regional and international levels. The practice exists because of the continuous and constant need for intermediation and negotiation among human groups. Africans tend to approach concepts holistically, and "diplomacy" is therefore a normal part of life; even a part of death. In many parts of Africa, communication with ancestors is a respected tradition, regardless of the state's religious or political dispensation. In Swaziland, for example, the *Incwala* is an elaborate ritual that involves 'negotiation' with ancestors in order to increase the welfare of the nation. All over the continent, diplomacy is a seamless venture, non-linear; involving all levels of diverse societies including those that have departed the temporal world.

8.1 Origin and Development

The continent of Africa is known as a "cradle of humanity," home of the earliest human settlements and the place where language, as a means of communication, first developed. The human instinct to communicate, negotiate, cooperate, and trade across boundaries is fair indication, therefore, that Africa was also the birthplace of democracy. Oral histories and anthropological evidence confirm this assumption, despite the lack of documented sources during the Stone and Iron ages.

The earliest records of diplomacy on the continent are inscribed in clay tablets that date back to antiquity. The cuneiform writing on these tablets provides details of Egypt's relations with the neighbours, manifesting in trade agreements, political alliances, and peaceful resolution of conflict. The first ever codified peace agreement in human history, 1100 BCE was a treaty between Pharaoh Ramesses II of Egypt and the King Hittites.[431] As happened all over the world for centuries thereafter, diplomacy was often accompanied by symbolic gestures and high-profile visits. The Bible, Talmud, and Quran all mention such examples, including legendary diplomatic relations between Israel's King Solomon and the Queen of Sheba who is widely believed to have been a ruler of ancient Aksum (Ethiopia), located in the Horn of Africa.[432]

State-like entities (some of which, like Egypt and Aksum, where among the earliest in the world) shared the diplomatic norms and conventions that started in antiquity, and which continue to characterize civilized inter-group relations across the world. The use of intermediaries, observance of ceremonial protocol, presentation of credentials, and respect of customary legal norms such as the sanctity of treaties and inviolability of envoys are rooted in African diplomacy.

The Aksumite Empire, which reached the pinnacle of its influence during the 1st century BCE, engaged in diplomacy with the Kingdoms of the Arabian Peninsula and further afield. The state minted its own currency and became a major geo-political link in the trade route between the Roman Empire and

---

431   Shaw (2008), p. 14
432   Marsh (2013), p. 59

India. In Central and Southern Africa, early pro-states included chieftaincies with limited or no centralized bureaucracy. Nevertheless, as in the rest of Africa, some of these pro-states evolved into sophisticated empires that grew through conquest, migration, trade, alliances and integration of other nations. Just like the West African Ashanti (Asante) Empire (eighteenth to twentieth century), spectacular natural recourses, notably gold, made the Southern African Kingdoms of Mapungubwe (11th-15th century) and Zimbabwe (12th and 15th century) not just wealthy, but irresistible to traders from other parts of Africa and beyond the continent.

Intercontinental diplomacy was as vibrant as Africa's burgeoning relations with explorers, missionaries, and traders from Europe and Asia. From coast to coast, Africa was teeming with trade, and politics often benefited economically from their geographical position on particular trade route. Thus, states such as Mali, Ghana, and Songhai (in the Western Sahel, 15 – 16th century) were terminals of Saharan trade routes. But rivalry and conflict also shaped the structure of intercontinental relations. In West Africa, the huge Oyo Empire (15 – 19th century) at various times enforced tributary relations on other kingdoms, including Dahomey (17 – 19th Century, in the area of present Benin). The famed city of Timbuktu was unilaterally incorporated by the Songhai empire in 1468 as just one of many external occupations of that Islamic centre of scholarship. A later example would be the Zulu monarchy which transformed the political landscape of Southern Africa during the 19th century through ruthless but masterful empire-building.

It is thus clear that pre-colonial Africa, far from being a chaotic, backward "dark continent" as depicted by early colonial historians, was home to sophisticated political organization, ranging from Empires and Kingdoms to city-states and chieftaincies. Democracy among these centrally organized political entities produced a rich tapestry of relations and was facilitated by abundant trade and the existence of customary law.

8.2 Segregation of African and Western Diplomacy

This section tries to highlight the difference and similarities between the African and Western concept of diplomacy. It should be known that diplomacy has been popularized in the West but African has their means of utilizing diplomatic practices based on the African context. Therefore, this section draws a parallel between the definition of Western Diplomacy and African Diplomacy as follows:

In the West, diplomacy is seen as the conduct of business between states by peaceful means, which is not different from what Africans have been doing in their cultural context in whereby neighbouring villages use peaceful means of resolving conflict. Therefore, in Africa before the colonial period, diplomacy was carried out as the same as elsewhere in the world by negotiating treaties, delimiting frontiers of trade and authority, settling past disputes and peacefully monitoring and managing potential crises.

In the West, diplomacy uses coercive means, methods and strategies to get state business done in the international community of conflicting and competing interests, making African diplomacy a veteran. The Africa before colonial periods sent representatives as both ad-hoc and semi-permanent, gave presents as symbols of common interest and respect, and regularly used courier services between monarchs, royalties and kingdoms.

In the West, appointed officials referred to as Ambassadors carry out the business, while Africa made use of emissaries, envoys and representatives to facilitate the easy conduct of diplomatic relations.

In the West, diplomacy has been guided by International law and Conventions which are binding on actors, while African diplomacy uses experience of the customary laws acceptable to all actors formulated to guide diplomatic relations.

8.3 Tools for Conduct of African Diplomacy

What then were the methods, procedures and means by which pre-colonial African diplomacy was carried out? This question would be answered in the subsequent discussion. However, one major obstacle that would have hindered the flourishing of African diplomacy was communication; this issue was tackled therefore through employing negotiators who were skilled in foreign tongues.[433]

8.3.1 Espionage

The first diplomatic tool which pre-colonial African states used in their international intercourse was espionage. King Agaja's secret agents known as Agbajigbeto were good examples. King Agaja, was a 'politick Prince', who through his spies was able to discover how much the great men and people of Whydah 'were divided, and that the king was only a Cipher in the Government' formation which decided his invasion of that country in 1727.[434] The Agbajigbeto, apart from gathering intelligence, were also sent abroad usually in the guise of merchants, and were also required to create the impression

---

433   Ibid. p.8
434   Akinjogbin, A., (1967). p.124

that Dahomean intentions were peaceful and then, on their return home, to manufacture suitable pretexts for aggression after collecting information on the weaknesses and vulnerability of the other side.

In certain African societies, espionage seems to play dual roles. It was custom of the court of Ardra (Allada) to make strangers wait a long time for an answer.[435] Some of these delays are attributed to their religious observances which according to Dupuis restrict activities to specific days. There were, for instance, only 150 to 160 days in the Ashanti year which were considered propitious for diplomatic business. In short, the Ashantees are slow, and I believe, cautious in cabinet; they are slower, however, in war-like movement.

8.3.2 Bargaining

Bargaining is defined as a discussion of prices, conditions etc. with the aim of reaching an agreement that is acceptable to all concerned. African states bargain for prices of commodities, boundary concession, land delimitation, trade frontiers, political jurisdiction and other issues in order to reach collective acceptable agreement among all parties concerned. The bargaining power depended on the amount of control one state had when trying to reach an agreement in a business or political situation. Some states had what was referred to as a "bargaining chip" which means a fact or a thing that a person or a group can use to get an advantage for them when they are trying to reach an agreement with other groups. This advantage was widely used to get concession from other groups.

The militarily strong states of Mali, Shongai, Kanem-Bornu and Ghana for instance could use their military strength to their advantage when bargaining. The economically viable states of the Niger Delta, the East African states, and other prosperous states could use their buoyant economies to their advantage. In pre-colonial Africa, there were things which a particular state had but which were lacking in another and if these things were to go around in the inevitable situation of interdependence, each state would have to use its bargaining chip. Even some Hausa states like Katsina and Daura were centres of learning and culture and this they also used to their advantage in bargaining.

8.3.3 Dialogue

A dialogue is a formal discussion among groups of people or countries when they are trying to reach an agreement over problematic issues. Dialogue was

---

435   ASTLEY, J., (1746). Voyages and Travels, London.

effectively used during the pre-colonial African era to facilitate diplomacy and enhance negotiation. The choice of words and language used were formal, clear and understandable. It was through dialogue that pacts were reached, agreements formalized and treaties ratified. Sanctions were provided for the observance of the mutual agreement reached and each pre-colonial African state concerned took the mutual agreement as binding.

8.3.4 Compromise

Simply put, compromise is an agreement made between two people or groups in which each side gives up some of the things they want so that both sides benefit at the end. In compromise, there is a connotation that two things cannot exist together as they are not compatible until they are changed or reduced so they can exist together.

Compromise is an age-long system in diplomacy. Even the Biblical Abraham, Isaac and Jacob had to compromise before they could dwell peacefully and happily in the land of Canaan. In pre-colonial Africa, it was not always that agreement could be reached in situations as they originally were. There was always the concession to let go of some privileges or modify a state's interest to meet the needs of the other. For instance, the Niger Delta states had to cut down their production and sales of palm oil to the British to allow for other competing states among their cartel to sell. Mai Idris Aloma of Kanem-Borno had to concede some disputed territories to his vassal states in order for hitch-free diplomacy to thrive. The East African states had to delimit their trade with Portugal and Oman among one another and this enabled diplomacy and cooperation to flourish.

The unalloyed spirit of interdependence among pre-colonial African states made compromise inevitable. For a state to have some of the things of the other, the state should be willing to let go of some things of its own too. There should be a compromise for barter to be achieved. This informed the principle of trade by barter.

8.3.5 Threat

Threat is a situation whereby a message of punishment or unpleasant consequences is portrayed to another if one's wish is not carried out or if the other side does not change its behaviour. Military or economic threat is used in international relations to get things done based on power politics. Threat can only be credible and effective when the state issuing the threat has the military or economic capacity to carry out the threat. In this regard, African diplomacy was no exception. The strong military make-up of well organized, centrally based pre-colonial African states was used to threaten weaker states into submission during negotiation.[436] These weaker states found themselves helpless in such situations and since most of them wanted protection from such strong states, they had to dance to their tune. Also, economic power foreign aid and grants, which are the mainstay of any political make-up especially of greater powers, became a handy tool in threatening poorer states into agreement over boundary and trade issues.

8.3.6 Establishment of Embassies

Another important method that sustained African diplomacy was the establishment of embassies in other states. "Inter-African Embassies enjoyed a degree of prestige and immunity compared to that which protected European diplomacy."[437] He further stresses that embassies were also set up in Europe and adjacent European possessions and settlements, North Africa and the Near East and they were received on a proper footing.

Although it was later on in the nineteenth century that the development of the resident embassy came to Africa, there were in existence the sending of ad hoc and semi-permanent embassies abroad. Notable rulers like Idris Aloma of Bornu built residences in Cairo to cater for pilgrims from Kanem-Bornu, and this later served as an embassy. The pilgrimages of Mansa Musa of Mali, Askia the Great of Shongai and other eminent African rulers served as an attraction to other states which maintained trade and diplomatic contact with these Empires. Embassies were thus sent to the Empires to cater to the foreigners attracted to Mali and Shongai respectively. This in no small measure enhanced African diplomacy.

8.3.7 Exchange of Presents and Gifts

The exchange of gifts was peculiar to pre-colonial African people and this enhanced pre-colonial African diplomacy and cooperation. This was used to seek favour and recognition. This can be likened to giving of aids, grants and financial assistance to win favour to one's side in a matter of international policy. Pre-colonial African states and their rulers exchanged gifts on regular

---

436   Aron, R. (1967), p. 111.
437   Smith, R. (1973), pp. 599-621.

basis to seek political relevance, recognition, sustained growth and development without fear of attack or invasion. It was a method used to solicit continuous peace, cooperation, friendship and to make treaties of peace and amity. Allies were made and, the quality and largeness of the gifts and presents willingly given dissuaded armed conflict. After all, most wars were fought for spoil and booties but once these were willingly parted with, there might be no need to risk a war. This method was also extended to the Europeans and the Muslim Arabs who were attracted to Africa to trade. They exchanged gifts and presents with one another and this brought profound alliance among them.

8.3.8 Usage of Regular Courier Services

A very effective method in pre-colonial African diplomacy was the sending of messages between and among African states. Goodwill messages were sent from one ruler to the other and this facilitated peace for the smooth conduct of pre-colonial African diplomacy. Regular courier services were used for this purpose. Clear messages were sent and sometimes symbolic ones. Special items were used as messages between Dahomey and Oyo, among the Yoruba and Fante states, among the non-centralized peoples of Igboland, among the Niger Delta states, between groups of states in East and South Africa, among the Hausa states, and between Ashante and other states related to it. These respective states had common ancestry and had once belonged to the same Empire, and thus they understood the symbolic messages sent. They knew what the items meant and represented and they responded appropriately to the messages.

The messengers in such situations had certain attributes that made them suitable for the regular courier services and most of them were members of the ad hoc or semi-permanent embassies sent to other states. These messengers were accorded respect, privileges and immunities as the case might be in the state where they delivered messages. What should be noted here is that the use of regular courier services kept mutual agreement intact and dissemination of information easy. It enabled pre-colonial African states enjoy unity, oneness and deep alliances. It kept them abreast of local and international news and potential crisis which might have been caused by lack of information or if contact was forestalled.

Blood friendship performance was the most applied tool of diplomacy among the Azande and their neighbours. This can be illustrated by the alliance between Riwa and Bantu tribal groups when the successor of his brother Barugba decided to deprive him from administration of the territory. Riwa was one of the powerful sons of Nunga who established his authority over the Abakpa, Abadugu and the Aubari Bantu stock in the mountain ranges in Tambura following mistreatment under Sanango after his brother's death. Records indicate that Riwa rebelled against Sanango at Barugbo's death. He moved away from Ri- Manzangba, an affluent of Namutina to the territory of Apambia to become their prince in a blood-friendship pact.

Gbudue reverted to tradition in expressing his disapproval of the proposal of his ruling cousin. Traditionally, a Zande king sent his emissary with a symbol of declaration of war in the form of spear to the other king to accept or reject the offer. In the case of acceptance, the king in question will retain the spear and send back the emissary with a message of alliance/friendship.[438] If the king disagrees, the spear is broken and sent back through the same emissary and war will be declared. In the situation of the message of King Tambura concerning the British plan, King Gbudue took an exceptional measure to mutilate the emissary as a message of disapproval. The revelation of Santandrea demonstrates the anger of Gbudwe towards Tambura's message: "Tambura, knowing that the two armed expeditions had already met with fierce opposition, sent Yambio [Gbudwe] a message advising him to take the same unavoidable step he had taken: to surrender. Yambio sent the man back with his ears and hands cut off."[439]

8.4 Qualities of Emissaries

It was well known that the appointment of emissaries during the pre-colonial era was by the ruler of a state in consultation with the council of state. In performing their assigned duties, emissaries should possess and exhibit certain qualities needed for the smooth operation of pre-colonial African diplomacy. These qualities include:

8.4.1 Education, Training and Experience

Before the evolvement of Islamized states, emissaries might not be scholarly but in place of education, they must be vast in wisdom and intelligence. They must virtually know the customs, cultures and behavioural patterns of other people they were dealing with. They must be well experienced and widely travelled. It was well known that most of these emissaries were once itinerant traders and this experience in their travels was applied to their tasks as emissaries. With the evolvement of Islamized states and impact of Christianity however, educated elites became envoys and representatives of their states in other states. Education

---

438   M-H Lelon (1946). Mes Frères du Congo, Vol.II, Algiers, p. 79
439   Stefano Santandrea (1964). p.43.

became necessary to make envoys more knowledgeable, more experienced and more relevant to written form of treaties and pacts. Most Islamic states like Shongai, Mali, Kanem-Bornu and the Hausa states used Islamic scholars as their advisers and mediators in inter-state crisis. They also served as negotiators in time of conflict and peace.

8.4.2 Tact

Another important quality that an emissary should possess was tact. Tact is defined as the ability to deal with difficult or embarrassing situations carefully and without doing or saying anything that will annoy or upset other people. Emissaries were representatives and messengers of states during the pre-colonial African era and in delivering messages to other states carefully without provoking others through inflammatory statements. Diplomacy entailed peaceful co-existence and these emissaries always seek to maintain that peace through cooperative engagement.

8.4.3 Eloquence

Emissaries should be fluent and be able to carry along their audiences. One who stammers is not fit to be an emissary. An emissary weighs his choice of words (diction) in any circumstance of discussion. He should speak with clarity and use signs that would be understood clearly by the receiving state. He should not be ambiguous. That was the situation during the pre-colonial Africa.

8.4.4 Multilingual Quality

A good emissary understands and speaks many languages fluently. The advent of English, French and Arabic languages into Africa helped a lot in this regard. People with the knowledge of those international languages were commonly used as emissaries during the pre-colonial Africa period. This made communication easy and the gathering of information handy. There were also official interpreters between rulers and visitors to the states during the pre-colonial era but it was common knowledge that an emissary who does not need an interpreter would be more preferred than the one who needs one.

8.4.5 Sociability and Decency

An emissary during the pre-colonial African era was sociable and decent. He attracted people through his character and bearing. He dressed and spoke decently. He composed himself in a dignified manner. This ought to be so because he is a representative of his king in another state and all glamour of his state had to be portrayed through him. Recall that African rulers like Mansa Musa, Askia the Great and Idris Aloma exhibited great pomp and pageantry in their pilgrimage to Mecca. Such was the attitude of African rulers to portray great opulence to the outside world and their representatives had to portray same. This attracted investors, traders and great wealth and respect for pre-colonial African states. Furthermore, emissaries made decent friends in the state they were sent to. This will enable them gather information for their home states and they would be able to get support for their negotiation bids. In all things they did what would be beneficial to their home states and put them in a comparative advantage over others.

8.5 Immunity for Emissaries

African diplomacy had deep respect and immunity towards the emissaries. Just like diplomats in modern day have diplomatic immunities, so were respect and honour accorded to the emissaries during the time of peace in pre-colonial Africa. Even emissaries carrying messages of wars were not harmed except in a few extreme cases like that of Kurunmi of Ijaye killing the emissaries of Alaafin of Oyo. Kurunmi was severely punished for this for he had violated a very solemn custom of the peoples. Forces teamed up against him until he was destroyed. Such was the sacrosanct opinion which pre-colonial African culture held about diplomacy. Emissaries could not be hurt or harmed. They were not treated with contempt or in an undignified manner. Any treatment meted out to an emissary was indirectly meted out to his state. A disdain on an emissary was a disdain on his boss and state. Emissaries were accorded profound respect and they were always received officially with much pomp and grandeur by the ruler of the receiving state himself, with his sub-chiefs and full court in attendance.

8.6 Functions and Responsibilities

An emissary is a person who delivers an official message from his state to another. He is what can be called a messenger of the state. They are envoys or ambassadors of their countries. They have certain functions which include:

8.6.1 Courier Services

They were used for regular courier services during the pre-colonial African period to sustain diplomatic relations. They were messengers of state. They made communication and information channels between states that had diplomatic relations with one another. They filled the vacuum and uncertainty that would have occurred because of lack of proper information. The messages they carried were very official and classified. It might be written or unwritten or even symbolic. Before the advent of Islam and Christianity in pre-colonial Africa, the messages were unwritten or symbolic but they were understandable by all parties concerned.

8.6.2 Representation

Emissaries were representatives of their countries or states in other states. During the pre-colonial period, they were the mouth, ears and eyes of their states. They were vested with authority by their home states to represent them in all or some areas of inter-state affairs. It should be noted however, that during the pre-colonial period, emissaries had no permanent representation. The representation might be ad-hoc or semi-permanent as the situation might call for – just as inter-state embassies were ad-hoc or semi-permanent.

8.6.3 Communication Agents

Communication and information agents of their states during the pre-colonial African era delivered information and brought feedback. A diplomatic communicator is someone who can get their message across and convince people to change without damaging the relationship. Diplomatic communicators use reason, politeness, and compassion. They show respect for the other person. Diplomatic communication is about being honest, but not compromising the interest of one's state.

8.6.4 Negotiators

Negotiators were officials vested with the authority to negotiate or bargain on behalf of their states in other states. They bargained with tact, discerning the situation that called for compromise or the one that called for threat. Threat and not inflammatory statements could cause war or crisis but only to make the other side change his way of doing things or behaviour. The issuance of threat either economic or military was intended to remind the uncompromising rival state of the facts on the ground that there would be consequences if he did not change his behaviour. For instance, an emissary of Mai Idris Aloma of Bornu would only remind an economically and militarily weaker state that his boss would not like to use force in getting a disputed land because of his magnanimity, and hence he was resorting to negotiation. The weaker state would get the message and respond accordingly. It helped to maintain its dignity as a stronger state. The weaker state would "peacefully" hand over the disputed land. In negotiating, emissaries should be careful about their choice of words. In all situations, the issuance of compromise or threat should be for the mutual interest of the home state of the emissary. Emissaries always tried to win advantage to their sides through official dialogue during the pre-colonial African period. They also argued away potential crisis by issuing threats.

8.6.5 Courier of Gifts and Presents

A diplomatic gift is a gift given by a diplomat, politician or leader when visiting a foreign country on behalf of his state. Usually the gift is reciprocated by the host. The use of diplomatic gifts dates back to the ancient world and givers have competed to outdo each other in the lavishness of their gifts. Emissaries always led the team or delegation that carried gifts and presents to other states from their home states. This was an expression of love and goodwill, as well as a desire for continued peaceful co-existence between pre-colonial African states; a gesture for the undesirability of crisis.

8.6.6 Signing of Treaties and Pacts

Treaty-making practices between European colonial powers and African rulers have the legal dimensions of colonialism and explore grounds and possibilities on which the law during the colonization of Africa can be based. The contracting parties of the protectorate treaties were on the one hand representatives of European States, and on the other hand, African rulers. Objects of transfer of these treaties were either all-comprehensive or partial sovereign rights over the territory. It has to be noted that many other agreements alongside treaties were concluded during the Age of New Imperialism between Europeans, whether or not as delegates of the State, and African people(s).

The character of these agreements was diverse. Some bore a highly public character and could be considered genuine treaties under international law, whereas others had more of the characteristics of private law contracts, with many shades of grey lines in between. The same diversity and duplicity exist in relation to the status of the signatories of the agreements, both on the side of the colonizers and the colonized. To make and keep this study manageable, the focus will be on treaties concluded between representatives of European States and African rulers which involved transfer of the partial or full sovereignty over territory.

After due consultation with the home state, emissaries might be mandated to sign treaties of amity and pacts of alliance with other states. They might also be instructed to rectify agreements. Amongst the aforementioned pre-colonial African diplomatic tools used were respect and adherence to treaties or agreements. Treaties were designed to end hostilities between states. A treaty for instance, brought to an end a long series of wars between the Hausa states of Kano and Katsina, C. 1650, while the boundary agreement in the late sixteenth century intended to end Idreis Alooma's Kanem Wars, an agreement which has been described as the first written border agreement in the history of Central Sudan.

One important feature of treaties in mostly West Africa was their sacrosanct nature. African customary law shares similar customary international law principle of *pacta servanda sunt* as a basis for assurance of a valid world order. To make the treaties binding, oaths, which were often formidable undertakings, were sworn to. The nature of oaths taken varied from society to society. Solemnization of treaties among the TIV, for example, entailed the killing of an elephant and a slave, followed by the preparation of sacred emblems and potions and the mingling and consumption of the blood of the parties.

8.7 Credentials and Diplomatic Symbols

The status of diplomats in African states varied. In some states they were among those close to the rulers of the country, often members of the royal household. In Oyo state (Nigeria), people called 'Ilari' ran diplomatic errands for the Oba, had servile origin, and were mainly slaves from neighbouring countries.[440] In some states, they were great men of the land, and sometimes, princes from the royal family sent them on missions abroad. In the sixteenth century, Congolese emissary was sent to Rome and in the seventeenth century, Ashante an representative was sent to the Coast. Toward the end of the seventeenth century, the kings of Denkyira and Ashanti were said to have sent some of their wives as ambassadors to each other. Among the Ibo, priests were appointed

---

440   Adegbulu, F. (2011), p.34

as ambassadors in negotiations to end small-scale inter-communal wars.[441] It is worth mentioning that some of the diplomats were of humble but free birth, who had achieved distinction by their talents. Similarly, the linguists at Kumasi were required to "take fetish oaths to be true to each other and to report faithfully. African diplomats often carried credentials or badges of office. These credentials could be in form of a fan, a cane, a baton, a whistle or a sword. The Ashante and Dahomean ambassadors were noted for their unique credentials. They were often covered in gold silver leaf and decorated with symbolic emblems. The staff of the chief linguist of the Ashante here was called Asempatia, "a true account is always brief."[442] It is believed that such objects, by extending the power of the ruler beyond his normal reach, were intended to ensure the safe passage of his envoys through alien territory. Some wore specially made diplomatic uniforms, such as black caps which according to Bosman, ensured an effectual free pass everywhere. The Dan people in modern Liberia wore special peace-making masks "with animal-like features and a moveable jaw.

Another important aspect of African diplomacy was the immunity which the diplomats enjoyed in the course of their duties. In fact, immunity seems to have been part and parcel of West African diplomacy and was well recognized. This was so particularly when diplomats carried credentials which identified them as state officials representing their sovereigns. Diplomatic immunity in Yorubaland (western Nigeria) is permissible in native law and assures the ambassador's safety, but he must not act as a spy or in a hostile way. Apart from hospitality to strangers, the Yoruba of pre-colonial times had a way of accommodating those who otherwise would have been persona-non-grata in the society. For instance, criminals and others who incurred the wrath of the authorities sought refuge in recognized sanctuaries, including the king's palace.[443]

8.8 Norms and Patterns of African Diplomacy

As noted earlier, state sovereignty in Africa was a contested issue due to historical experiences with colonialism and neo-colonialism during the Cold War. African states thus developed diplomatic norms and principles connected to their low standing in world politics and international relations.

The first African diplomatic norm is anti-imperialism, the movement by African states to rid the continent of external and foreign forces that seek

---

441   MEEK, C. K., (1937). p.224.
442   Ibid. p.23
443   Adegbulu, F. (2011)., p.7

to exploit the African population and resources. It is important to note that even though anti-European liberation movements ended with the political independence of Zimbabwe in 1980, the rhetoric of African leaders continued to advocate for economic autonomy in the decades after self-rule began. Anti-imperial rhetoric continues today, and while often used to cover domestic failings of autocratic or corrupt leaders, this usage and resonance with African constituencies in fact proves the longevity and pervasiveness of the norm. This poses a challenge to integrationists because small states may perceive the transfer of sovereignty to Addis Ababa as a neo-imperialist threat if they perceive the more powerful African states are forcing integration.[444]

8.8.1 Regional Integration

The second norm that integration at the AU confront and oppose is the vehement adherence to the political borders left by the colonial powers. The OAU enshrined this norm of *uti possidetis* in its charter and in subsequent meetings, and this has made a substantial impact on the continent for the nearly 50 years. This has meant the lines drawn on the continent by European powers in Berlin in 1884 and 1885 remain in place despite the irrationality of the borders. The consequences have been the inability of secession movements to gain support among other African states. The OAU supported the national sovereignty of state by working towards compromises retaining the integrity of the colonial borders. African integrationists will confront African publics that see the lasting reputation of the regional body as stifling self-determination and political rights. The norm had the chance to evolve with the successful independence of South Sudan in 2011, but the AU-backed military invasion into northern Mali reinforces this norm.

8.8.2 The Solidarity of African States

The third norm of African diplomacy is the solidarity of African states on the world stage. The power of the region's voting bloc at multi-national organizations, numerically the largest in the world, remains a key feature of the Pan-Africanist movement. Nkrumah's belief in the need to speak with one voice was in an effort to make up for the diplomatic, economic, and political weakness of individual African states was present at independence and remains today. Though a common refrain at regional meetings, this norm is best seen

---

444   Laverty, A. (2013), p.4

in action at the United Nations, where the bloc of African countries makes up 28% of the UN membership. Solidarity in voting at the UN began soon after independence, and extended to issues beyond those on the African agenda.[445]

The last norm promises well for a potential AU foreign service. If all African countries are committed to coordinating their foreign policies, then the current Addis-based integration would be permitted to shape more of the diplomatic agenda on the supra-national level, allowing them to put more comprehensive integration on the agenda.[446]

8.8.3 Pan-Africanism and Multilateralism

The vulnerability of African states has been a powerful incentive for the continent's international relations to be expressed "collectively". In diplomatic terms, this has amounted to a preference for multilateralism, a modern mode of diplomacy that is known for multi-stakeholder, shared common interests, involvement, and a transparent process. Indeed, the global diplomatic impact of post-colonial Africa can be attributed almost exclusively to its group efforts through multilateralism rather than bilateralism, the diplomacy of individual states. It has offered not only a practical advantage but has also been a matter of historical redress with beneficial effects.

It is only a century ago, after the carnage of the First World War, that multilateral diplomacy gained traction in the global arena. Disillusionment with the secretive and exclusive nature of traditional diplomacy the manipulation of international relations by a club of European powers that led to the catastrophic war among themselves prompted calls for "new" diplomacy. US President Woodrow Wilson, in his famous "Fourteen Points" address to the US congress on January 8, 1918, expressed the sentiments of the entire colonized world when he called for norms and equity in international relations. Wilson also pro-founded the idea of a "League of Nations," and chaired its meetings to formulate the rules of a permanent international organization with universal membership.

Wilson's speech was based on a set of proposals for such an organization that had been drawn up by a statesman from Africa, General Jan Smuts from the Union of South Africa (Smuts 1918:vi). The League of Nations was subsequently implemented after the 1919 Paris Peace Conference which deliberated on the post-war dispensation. It died in 1946 after its members could not agree on the implementation of its Charters provisions.

---

445   Chamberlin, W., Hovet, T., & Hovet, E. (1970). P.55
446   Laverty, A. (2013), p.4

At that stage, Africa was still under mass colonization, and remained so for the duration of the League's twenty-year life-span. Until the advent of decolonization in the second half of the twentieth century, the continent played a minimal role in formal global diplomacy. However, outside the state-centric diplomatic system, African intellectuals were mobilizing and laying the groundwork for institutionalized African multilateral diplomacy. Born of the yearning for liberation from foreign oppression, the African diaspora became deeply involved. It was a British-trained lawyer from Trinidad, Henry Sylvester Williams, who coined the expression "Pan-African" – a term that would become, and remains, a leitmotiv in African diplomacy.

The fifth Pan-African Congress took place in 1945 in Manchester, and set out in more detail Africa's plans for the post-war world order. From an African diplomatic perspective, this gathering was as seminal as the deliberations in San Francisco during that same year on the founding of the United Nations. Ironically, the intellectual architect of the League of Nations, Jan Smuts, was once again involved in the planning and contributed to write the Preamble. Yet in South Africa at the time, the vast majority of black people were excluded from governance and diplomacy. Equally so, most of the African countries were excluded from this process.

On March 6, 1957, Ghana became the first sub-Saharan African state to declare independence, under the leadership of Dr. Kwame Nkrumah. Nkrumah was a passionate Pan-Africanist, augmenting the ideas of anti-colonial philosophers in the African Diaspora such as Frantz Fanon who had been instrumental in the Algerian revolution.

Nkrumah led a group of African leaders, among others Egypt's Gamal Abdel-Nasser and Guinea's Ahmed Sêkou Touré that became known as the "Casablanca Group". They insisted that decolonization be followed by radical integration of the continent, to the point of advocating for a "Union of African states" or "United States of Africa." The argument was that Africa should speak with one voice when engaging with the rest of the world in order to counter marginalization, an approach known as multilateralism in international diplomacy.

A more moderate association of African leaders, the Monrovia Group, advocated for close cooperation rather than integration among the newly independent African states. Inclusive of prominent states such as Nigeria and Liberia, they were supported by yet another coalition of leaders, the Brazza-Ville Group, which essentially comprised the African Franco-phone. Notwithstanding the differences among the groups, and after intensive consultation led by Emperor Haille Selassie of Ethiopia, the Organization of African Unity (OAU) was founded in Addis Ababa on May 25, 1963.

The host city, Addis Ababa, would become the head office of the OAU and eventually as from 2000 of the fact that OAU was transferred into African Union (AU) in Durban, South Africa.Over the decades Addis Ababa has attracted observer missions from states and organizations across the world. Even though African diplomacy at least at the rhetorical level was initially driven by Pan-Africanism, the continent's quest for integration has manifested in a multitude of smaller integration projects. It is perhaps a metaphor for Africa's quest to transcend the divisive history institutionalized by its arbitrary borders that the continent has both the oldest existing customs union in the world – the Southern African Customs Union (SACU), dating back to 1910 – and the largest number of regional economic communities (RECs): no fewer than fourteen such schemes. However, despite the proliferation of RECs, only eight (8) of them are recognized by the African Union as its building bloc.

In 1980, the OAU's *Lagos Plan for Action for the Development of Africa* (UNECA 2016) declared the RECS essential to facilitate regional economic integration. They have since then acted as catalyst for intra-African diplomacy, but also have a drawback that is unique to the continent: the zeal of integration has resulted in most African states belonging to two or more of these groups. Overlapping membership taxes the already strained capacity and resources of member-states and creates legal-bureaucratic complexity in coordination of policy. Moreover, the small RECs struggle to maintain a united front in separate negotiations with much stronger economic blocs, such as the European Union. However, the agreement to create the African Continental Free Trade Agreement (AfCFTA) in March 2018 in Kigali-Rwanda, which entered into force on 30 May 2019 bringing together 55 African countries with a population of more than 1.2 billion people, will go a long way to overcome the problem of negotiating separately with stronger economic blocs.

Institutionalized Pan-Africanism was revived after the end of the Cold War to seek more pragmatic and more focused continental integration, free from the interference of feuding superpowers. When Tanzanian top diplomat and statesman Dr. Salim Ahmed Salim became the Secretary-General of the OAU in 1989, he immediately commissioned a report on the changes in the global structure of power and proposed ways in which Africa could take control of its own destiny. This vision was expressed when the OAU adopted the Abuja Treaty in 1991, establishing the African Economic Community (AEC). It became clear, however, that the OAU was neither capacitated nor mandated, in terms of its 1963 Charter, to implement the economic integration agenda set by the Treaty. After the transition to majority rule in South Africa in 1994, the OAU had all but exhausted its political liberation agenda and had to face up to its relatively poor record in fostering good governance and peace and security on the continent.

There were many catastrophic failures of mediation during the Cold War: the civil war in Nigeria, DRC, Somalia are cases in point. The 1994 genocide in Rwanda was a turning point. With Africa dominating the Post-Cold War agenda of the UN Security Council (almost 60% of the issues are on Africa), a new, better capacitated, wider mandated, and much more dynamic supranational organization was required. A new generation of African leaders, individuals such as Nigeria's Olusegun Obasanjo and South Africa's Thabo Mbeki, Ethiopia's Meles Zenawi, Senegal's A.Wade and Tanzania's Benjamin Mkapa, started to conceptualize a successor organization, and found common ground with Muamar Gadafi, the idiosyncratic of Libya, who bank-rolled much of the initiative. In July 2000, the Constitutive Act of the African Union was adopted in Lome, Togo by the continent's heads of state and government, and the new organization set out to nurture an integrated, united, peaceful, and prosperous Africa. Ironically, the very membership profile of the AU reflected a less-than-unified continent. It maintained exactly the same membership as its predecessor, the OAU, from which Morocco pulled out when the organization admitted the contested state of Western Sahara as a full member in 1982. As of today, AN has 55 member states following of the admission of Morocco in 2018.

8.8.4 African Security

Africa's post-colonial political landscape has been dreadfully insecure with security scourge raging from intra-state wars and foreign intervention to predatory governance. The new global security paradigm known as "human security" emphasizes peace and security. It is a development nexus in recognition of the extent to which economic deprivation fuels political conflict, and a number of individual Africans have pioneered efforts to place human security at the centre of the global diplomatic agenda.

Boutros Boutros-Ghali, during his tenure as UN Secretary-General, published the "Agenda for Peace" (UNGA 1992) and made the case for United Nations conflict-resolution to be a holistic, long-term project promoting the idea of peace-building rather than once-off peace-making. In the mid-nineties, then Sudanese diplomat Francis Deng was a pioneer of the normative regime that would later become known as the Responsibility to Protect (R2P).

R2P holds that governments cannot hide behind the principle of state sovereignty when it comes to humanitarian protection, and the AU embraced this new norm within its Constitutive Act of 2000, five years before world leaders endorsed the norm at the UN's sixty-fifth anniversary (in the World Summit Outcome Document of 2005).

Yet another diplomat from North Africa, the Algerian Lakhdar Brahimi, chaired a UN Commission that was tasked to investigate ways in which to strengthen the UN's peace operations. The "Brahimi Report" of 2000 (UNGA 2000a) made wide-ranging recommendations on institutional reform, many of which were incorporated into the world summit's Millennium Declaration (UNGA 2000b) that was adopted later the same year.

The UN Secretary-General at the time, Kofi Annan, acutely aware of the fact that his home continent suffered from recurring intra-state violence, made the case for a UN Peace-Building Commission in 2005. The same year, he tabled several proposals for reform of the UN Security Council, *inter alia* to ensure that Africa, the continent that continues to dominate the agenda of the UNSC would, for the first time ever, be represented in a permanent capacity.

In this regard, Africa had achieved yet another distinctive multilateral feat: the AU's Ezulwini Consensus of 2005 made Africa the only continent with a collective policy on Security Council reform, a position it retains. The AU Committee of ten on UN reform reports to the summit every year. To date, the AU is also unique in the sense that it is the only regional organization that has confronted the International Criminal Court (ICC) on its mandate. African states, which in large numbers supported the establishment of the court through the Rome Statute of 1998, have become disillusioned with the manner in which the continent has turned into an ICC focus area.

They point out that the five permanent members of the UN Security Council have the institutional power to veto their own (or their allies') referral to the ICC, just as their superior military and economic power shields them from interference by other states. The AU has thus become a diplomatic mouthpiece, not over Africa but the broader developing world, to challenge the structure of global power relations by pursuing the concept of multilateralism in world politics for the realization of common goals which humanity so dearly wants.

Apparently, the diplomacy of unity in Africa has tended to be elitist. Comradeship among incumbent African leaders continues to shield illegitimate regimes and tarnishes the pioneering success of Africa's collective diplomacy. Moreover, sub-regional hegemons such as South Africa, Nigeria, Egypt, Algeria and Libya under Gaddafi often stand accused of bullying smaller African states. Despite its success, particularly the liberation struggle for Africa, Africa's collective diplomacy is thus not immune to the *realpolitik* of the continent. Within Africa, the AU struggles to transcend the sum of its parts, and the organization's continental authority is arguably validated more by the wider international community than its own membership.

The UN Security Council's first ever hybrid peacekeeping mission, UNAMID, approved in 2007 and deployed in Darfur with the cooperation of the AU, was hailed as a landmark security joint venture with a regional organization. Yet the AU's independent peacekeeping missions on the continent are fraught with contention and often stillborn at the level of rhetoric. As many critics contend, the AU's biggest problem is neglect – both material and moral – by its own members.[447]

The goal of the African Unity continues to be diluted by divided loyalties, with ruling elites prioritizing relations with former colonial rulers or new external partners rather than their own neighbours. At the same time, foreign intervention in (or subtler diplomatic courting of) Africa in the twenty-first century has not subsided. To the contrary, a rising number of emerging powers have joined the traditional powers in engaging the continent, prompted by interests that range from security concerns (terrorism, illegal migration, transnational crime) to economic profit especially in extractive industry. China is one such external actor that has made inroads in Africa the past few years, in a diplomatic sense most symbolically through 2012 "gifting" of a new headquarters for the African Union. The "new scramble for Africa" will be testing Africa's diplomatic acumen, not just beyond the continent but also, crucially, at the intra-African level. It is here that Africa faces its greatest diplomatic challenges, and where it needs to find its greatest strength. Unity in diversity.

8.9 Setbacks to African Diplomacy

Although military force as an instrument of diplomacy has been used effectively in ending conflicts in Liberia, Sierra Leone, the Ivory Coast and Burundi, it has failed to restore peace and security in several other conflict areas. The AU failed to resolve the Libyan conflict in 2011, Somalia has not known peace for over two decades, and conflict continues to rage in Eastern DRC and in Northern Nigeria, where Boko Haram, the militant Islamist group, has proved a hard nut for the Nigerian government. Similar situations are evident in Cameroon and Central African Republic (CAR) which remain unstable. In some cases, post-conflict peace arising out of military intervention remain fragile at best. In Lesotho and Zimbabwe, SADC efforts at instigating reforms on governance and human rights have yielded limited outcomes, while Gambia and Togo, two small states, thwarted ECOWAS' efforts at passing a resolution to limit presidential terms to two. Diplomacy, whether pure or mixed, has not appeared to have been effective in achieving desired results in most cases in Africa as indicate by a number of related factors explored herein.

---

447   Abatan and Spies (2016), Pp. 30-31

8.9.1 Absence of Diplomatic Instruments

A leading cause of diplomatic failures is the absence of effective instruments. While the use of military intervention remains a popular diplomatic instrument, peace-making and peacekeeping forces are often ill-equipped, under financed and poorly trained. In some cases, too, the forces lack the numbers required for success. In 2004, for example, the AMIS force in Darfur initially numbered a paltry 7,000 troops but grew to 9,000 by October 2007. Yet, this number of soldiers was still too small to be effective in a land area as large as Texas or Spain.[448] This challenge has been exacerbated by the unwillingness of African states to provide troops after initially committing themselves.

The inevitable consequence has been for regional organisations and the AU to rely on extra-Africa actors for funding and other forms of support. ECOWAS frequently relied on France in conflict intervention. This development often exposes the myth of the much-trumpeted slogan "African solutions to African problems". The AU peacekeeping operations (PKOs) for a long time have relied on external support. Intervention as an instrument of diplomacy is awed, failing to address the structural causes of conflicts and typically imposing peace rather than allowing contending factions to resolve long-standing issues. In the words of Adebayo Adedeji, interventions fail to "master and comprehend" the causes of conflict.[449]

Similarly, former South African president Thabo Mbeki, who served as the AU mediator in various conflicts, can only boast of mixed results as a peace envoy. Influenced by the successful but ephemeral inclusive Government of National Unity (GNU), formed in the immediate post-apartheid years, Mbeki seems to believe that the solution to every post-election conflict in Africa lies in the formation of a GNU. As the chief SADC mediator in the Zimbabwean crisis, Mbeki advocated and indeed succeeded in engineering a GNU between President Robert Mugabe and the ZANU-PF, who lost the polls, and the opposition Movement for Democratic Change (MDC) under Morgan Tsvangirai in early 2009. It was clear though that the Zimbabwean GNU was never united. Inspired by the apparent success in Zimbabwe, Mbeki proposed the formation of a GNU in the Ivory Coast when he was dispatched to Abidjan as the AU envoy in the country's post-election conflict in 2010.[450] However, Mbeki's idea of a unity government was rejected, not only by Alassane Ouattara, who was widely known to have won the election, but also by ECOWAS, which feared it would encourage sitting presidents who lose elections to continue in

---

448   Akokpari (2012), p.59
449   Adedeji (1999), p.3
450   Martins (2011), p.81

office through unity governments. In opting for such short-cuts, which in most cases were temporal solutions, Mbeki was shying away from confronting the truth and condemning the loser.

A disturbing feature of Mbeki's diplomacy has been his preference for short-cut approaches to conflict resolution, underscored by a willingness to empathise with, even protect, errant leaders in the name of African solidarity, anti-imperialism and old-style sovereignty.[451] Seeking a shortcut approach, the AU instigated a GNU in Kenya following violence in the aftermath of the presidential polls in 2007.[452] Since the Kenyan case was successful, this concept of GNU should be embraced as best practices in Africa if the South Sudan case becomes successful too. Endemic mutual suspicion, fragility and ephemerality underscore the bankruptcy of unity governments as diplomatic options in post-conflict African countries.

8.9.2 Political Instability

Political instability further compromises the credibility of Africa's diplomacy. Africa remains a leading theatre of conflicts, recording the highest number globally over years. Africa's conflicts have, since the 1960s, been estimated to have claimed 10 million lives and cost the continent over US $250 billion.[453] The prevalence of political instability present challenges to diplomacy. The determination to resolve multiple, some intractable, political instability at the same time stretches the diplomatic resources of regional organisations and the AU. The need to assemble peacekeepers for deployment into conflict zones and to garner resources and logistics place massive constraints on the already overstretched resources of the AU. Historically, the AU has struggled to timeously assemble a force for dispatch to areas of conflict. It is even more difficult to find peacekeepers for two or three conflicts raging simultaneously. In turn, such constraints may lead to either the fashioning of half-baked solutions to protracted political instability, or the prioritisation of one conflict over the other.

8.9.3 Power Dynamics in the International System on Diplomacy

Africa remains a vulnerable continent, lacking political and economic influence in the international system. Accordingly, it has limited diplomatic options when

---

451   Geldenhuys (2010), p.166
452   Mapuva (2013). P.105
453   Murithi (2005), p.82

dealing with actors within, and especially external to the continent. Within the continent, sanctions or threats of sanctions do not serve as sufficient impulses to cause changes in the policies of errant states. Delinquent countries hardly take regional and AU threats seriously. Threats to suspend Zimbabwe from the SADC and the AU failed to induce political reforms.

The tendency of African leaders to empathise rather than criticise culpable peers has not helped the outcome of diplomatic efforts. The AU has so far not mastered the courage to chastise African leaders who clearly threaten the security of their citizens or pursue policies that can potentially generate conflict. On the contrary, the AU has appeared to accommodate and, in fact, side with such leaders. For instance, in 2007, African leaders threatened to boycott the Euro-African Summit in Lisbon, Portugal, following the EU decision to exclude Robert Mugabe, who was under EU travel ban. The ban was imposed on the Zimbabwean leader and his top government officials in 2002 for presiding over allegedly grotesque human rights abuses in his country. The collective threat by African leaders to boycott compelled the EU to allow Mugabe into the summit. Worth noting, the former Sudan President Al Bashir was indicted by the International Criminal Court. The AU stood by him arguing that a seating President should be tried.

Africa's lack of influence is even more apparent in its interactions with external actors. Africa is generally weak, pliable and tends to dance to the tune of external actors. Consequently, it has weak bargaining power vis-à-vis external actors. The price of primary commodities, the chief export of most African countries, is determined not by Africa, but by actors external to the continent. The 2014 signing of the Economic Partnership Agreement (EPAs) with the EU by nearly all sub-Saharan Africa countries typifies Africa's lack of bargaining power. In their current design, EPAs not only balkanise Africa further, but they also compel the continent to liberalise its market to make it easily accessible to Europe. With such clear knowledge of the potential harm of EPAs, the AU sanctioned the signing of the agreement. Even more remarkable and disturbing, the EU imposed arbitrary deadlines for the conclusion of the negotiations without due regard to the objective conditions on the ground. In the process of negotiation, Africa hardly presented a coordinated position on the EPAs.[454]

Lacking sufficient leverage, it is unclear if Africa's non-permanent members in the UN Security Council vote objectively on the merit of issues. African members have tended to vote in ways that are consistent with the foreign policy objectives of the permanent members. In March 2011, the AU took a collective

---

454   Mutume (2008), p.16

decision not to support the imposition of a "no fly zone" over Libya. A few days later, on 17 March, 2011, South Africa, along with Nigeria and Gabon, Africa's non-permanent members of the Security Council, all voted in favour of the resolution, which also called for the use of "all necessary measures" to protect civilians. Pretoria justified its support for the resolution on grounds of protecting civilians. It was less surprising that Nigeria and Gabon, who are comparatively less autonomous in their foreign policies, voted along with Western countries in support of the resolution. However, it was shocking that South Africa, which has a greater capacity to follow an independent foreign policy and defend Africa's interest, contradicted the collective position of the continent. Prior to the "no y zone" vote, Africa proposed a "Road Map to Peace" for Libya, which called for talks between Gaddaffi and rebels that would lead to democratic reforms. This position was trampled. The diplomacy of the AU thus failed to resolve the Libyan conflict.

8.9.4 Dependence on External Actors

Africa's vulnerability and lack of influence has been exacerbated by its notorious dependence on external actors for markets, aid and investments. The continent presently relies heavily on external markets to sell agricultural commodities. According to WTO data, intra-Africa trade in 2014 stood at a paltry 12%. This figure pales when compared to 60% and 30% in the EU and the Association of South East Asian Nations (ASEAN) respectively.[455] The bulk of Africa's trade is with the EU. This has arisen from at least two interrelated factors; the first is what Thomas Callaghy (1994) referred to some two decades ago as the "fallacy of agricultural composition", which describes Africa's production of similar agricultural commodities.[456] This phenomenon offers little opportunities for marketing agricultural products, mostly raw materials, on the continent. Secondly, the obvious, yet disconcerting, truism is that there are few or no industries to process the primary agricultural raw materials produced in Africa. With the exception of the few oil-producing countries, the structure of production in Africa has not seen significant diversification since independence. Most African economies still display the trappings of the colonial economy, which place an emphasis on extractive resources. The inevitable consequence is for Africa to find markets beyond the continent. In addition, Africa depends on external actors for information and technological knowledge. While science remains the driving force of growth and development

---

455   Bridges Africa (2014b).
456   Thomas Callaghy (1994), p.241

in industrialized countries, it has been missing in Africa. Africa thus suffers from a "deficit" of technological information. The ultimate effect of suffering multiple deficits markets, aid, investments and technological knowledge is to depend on external actors, which inevitably diminishes Africa's diplomatic leverage in bargaining and negotiations on the international scene.

CHAPTER NINE

TRADE DIPLOMACY: REFLECTIONS ON AFRICAN CONTINENTAL FREE TRADE AREA

In the 21st century, trade and commerce plays a critical role in shaping the foreign policy of a country. Indeed, it has been prioritized over all other aspects of a foreign policy agenda. With the liberalization of the economy and market, it has been given great importance. More trade has taken place between countries that have subsequently enhanced their foreign relations. Multinational companies (MNC) attempt to influence government institutions in making favourable policies, including foreign economic policies. Negotiating trade agreements is a key aspect of diplomacy, and this is where trade diplomacy plays a vital role in business transactions within international milieu. Moreover, the government often consults the business houses and trade unions before signing any foreign agreement. As a result, gradually trade and commerce become the most influential variables in Foreign Economic Policy Decision making.

The concept of trade *diplomacy* focuses on the development of business between two or more countries. The essence deals with generating commercial gains in the form of trade through inward and outward investment by means of business entrepreneurship promotion and facilitation activities in the host country. Therefore, trade diplomacy is designed to influence foreign government policy and regulatory framework that affect global trade, investment and commerce. It is concerned with government regulations and actions that affect international trade such as the standards in health, safety, the environment, and consumer protection; banking, telecommunications, accounting; agricultural support programs and industrial subsidies.

Trade diplomacy has well been illustrated through the African Continental Free Trade Area as detailed in this chapter. However, the future of the global multilateral system faces significant uncertainty with the escalation of trade tensions between leading economies and the rise of nationalistic inward-looking policies.

The shift towards unilateralism and preference for bilateral over multilateral engagements is in stark contrast to a global policy and trade environment which has governed international relations since World War II and deepened the process of globalisation to integrate goods and capital markets across the borders, thereby fostering global value chains. Going against that emerging development at the global level, Africa has responded by deepening the process of continental integration through the African Continental Free Trade Agreement (AfCFTA), one of the flagship projects of the African Union Agenda 2063. The AfCFTA, will create an integrated market of over 1.2 billion people with a combined gross domestic product (GDP) exceeding US $2.5 trillion. Furthermore, trade diplomacy has been demonstrated well by strengthening Africa's bargaining power in international trade negotiations; the African single market would provide the region with economies of scale denied for decades by colonial balkanization and market fragmentation.

This chapter attempts to shed some light on recent developments in international trade arrangements and provides the rationale for the establishment of AfCFTA. It reviews the drivers of multilateralism in an increasingly challenging global environment while looking at Africa's own integration experience from an historical perspective.

9.1 Historical Background

Following the harsh lessons of the Great Depression in the late1920's, high tariffs, retaliatory currency devaluations, discriminatory trading blocs and a devastating global conflict led leaders to conclude that economic cooperation was the only way to achieve both peace and prosperity. Agreement was finally reached by 44 nations that met in Bretton Woods, New Hampshire at the July 1944 United Nations Monetary and Financial Conference.

The two major accomplishments of the Bretton Woods conference were the creation of the International Monetary Fund (IMF) with the responsibility to foster global monetary cooperation, secure financial stability, facilitate international trade, promote high employment and sustainable economic growth, and reduce poverty around the world. The International Bank for Reconstruction and Development (IBRD), alias, the World Bank, was responsible for reducing poverty in the developing world.

Notwithstanding this success, reaching an agreement on international trade proved more difficult to achieve given the system of preferential tariffs established among the members of the British Commonwealth and the high Smoot Hawley tariffs implemented by the United States. After more than four years of negotiations on this and other issues such as the rules that would govern tariff and the structure of a proposed new organization to oversee international trade, an agreement was finally reached in 1947.

Leaders of 23 nations met in Geneva and concluded the first post-war round of tariff negotiations leading to reductions as well as a draft charter for a new institution: the International Trade Organization (ITO). Participants signed the General Agreement on Tariffs and Trade (GATT), designed to implement the agreed tariff cuts and serve as some interim commercial relations until the ITO was created.

However, strong opposition from the United States' Congress meant that the ITO never saw the light of the day. Instead, it was the GATT that governed post-war international trade relations until it was replaced by (WTO) in 1995 membership which has since grown to 164 states.

Despite these developments, which were driven by economic, political and security considerations, multilateralism and especially the promotion of regional integration became a global phenomenon. For instance, Free Trade Agreements (FTAs) and Preferential Trade Agreements (PTAs) and other forms of integration like customs and monetary unions became a strategic imperative for various countries and regions culminating in the establishment of among others: the European Economic Community (EEC) in 1957, the Latin American Free Trade Association in 1960, the Central American Common Market in 1961, the Association of South East Asian Nations (ASEAN) in 1967, and the Caribbean Free Trade Association (CARIFTA) in 1968.

However, after achieving sustained progress in the six decades after the Second World War, the multilateral global order is currently confronted with challenges: the rise of populism and nationalist sentiment, most notably Brexit and the imposition of tariffs outside the WTO framework by leading economies, the withdrawal from multilateral trade agreements, and the increasing preference for bilateral ones.

The election of Donald Trump in the United States threw the future of multilateralism into question. These developments reflect increasing dissatisfaction with multilateralism and are aggravated by the accumulation of structural trade deficits and declining manufacturing output in a number of leading economies which championed global trade integration and globalisation for decades.

Another major factor driving the retreat from multilateralism has been shifts in the global geo-economic and geopolitical arena, which has seen economic balance shift from developed economies toward emerging and developing market economies. The rise of the developing South has led to the emergence of a multi-polar world with Brazil, China, India, Russia and South Africa (BRICS) and others emerging as global economic and political power houses.

The dramatic shift of the economic balance from developed countries toward developing and emerging market economies is evident from their relative shares in global GDP and trade. For instance, in 1992 developed economies accounted for 84 percent of global GDP, with developing and emerging market economies nations accounting for only 16 percent. By 2018, this changed significantly with developing and emerging market economies nations now accounting for 40 percent of global GDP while the contribution by the developed economies declined to 60 percent. Global trade also witnessed seismic shifts during this period, with developing countries increasing their share in global trade from around 20 percent in 1992, to 39 percent in 2018.

China nears the forefront of this shift in global economic power with its share of global GDP growing from around two percent in 1992 to around 16 percent in 2018, while its share in global trade increased from 2.2 percent to around 12 percent during this period. But the contribution of other developing and emerging countries to global trade and growth over the decades of accelerated globalisation has increased as well, resulting in increased global income convergence. The rise of trade tensions and weakening global trade arrangements triggered by a shift towards beg-thy-neighbour policies threatened progress.

9.2 Multilateralism and Regional Integration in Africa

Newly independent Africa came into existence during the post-second World War golden age of multilateralism and regional integration, and virtually all newly independent African countries embraced the concept of multilateralism and regionalism. The commitment to continental integration and the vision of an integrated Africa led to the creation of the Organization of African Unity (OAU) in 1963.

Apart from efforts to address the impacts of colonialism and apartheid, the main objectives of the OAU included promoting unity and solidarity among African States, organizing and strengthening cooperation for development on the continent, protecting the sovereignty and territorial integrity of member states, and encouraging international cooperation as outlined by the United Nations (OAU Charter). In addition, the Lagos Plan of Action (LPA) was adopted as the continent's blueprint through which Africa could, based on the principle of collective self-reliance, achieve rapid economic and social development.

Subsequently, regional integration arrangements were also formed across the continent. In 1975 fifteen West African states met in Lagos, Nigeria to sign the ECOWAS Treaty which created the Economic Community of West African States. Six years later, in 1981, the Preferential Trade Area for Eastern and Southern Africa was established; it later became a Common Market and was renamed as the Common Market for Eastern and Southern Africa (COMESA) in 1993. The Southern Africa states (excluding apartheid South Africa which joined in 1994) formed the Southern African Development Coordination Conference (SADCC) in 1980 which was transformed into the Southern African Development Community (SADC) in 1992. In 1986, six Eastern African states (Djibouti, Ethiopia, Kenya, Somalia, Sudan and Uganda) formed an intergovernmental body for development and drought control in the sub-region called Intergovernmental Authority on Drought and Development (IGADD). In Central Africa, the Economic Community of Central African States (ECCAS) was created in 1983 by the leaders of the pre-existing Customs and Economic Union of Central Africa.

These arrangements were expected to function under the framework of the Lagos Plan of Action. The commitments in the Lagos Plan of Action and the Final Act of Lagos were translated into a specific agreement in Abuja, Nigeria in June 1991, when OAU Heads of State and Government signed the Treaty Establishing the African Economic Community (alias The Abuja Treaty), which formalized the notion of Regional Economic Communities (RECs) as building blocks of the African Economic Community (AEC).

While the Abuja Treaty did not specify the membership of the RECs, it indicated that the regional communities would cover Northern, Western, Central, Eastern and Southern Africa. This led to the designation of the Arab Maghreb Union (AMU), the Economic Community of West African States (ECOWAS), the Economic Community of Central African States (ECCAS), the Common Market for East and Southern Africa (COMESA), and the Southern African Development Community (SADC) as the pillars upon which the African Economic Community was to be built.

The Pan-African ideal of continental integration was further reaffirmed by the transformation of the OAU into the African Union (AU) in 2002, with the Constitutive Act of the AU fully incorporating the provisions of the Abuja

Treaty. As a sequel to the establishment of the AU, three additional RECs were given formal recognition: the community of Sahel-Saharan (CEN-SAD), the East African Community (EAC), and the Intergovernmental Authority on Development (IGAD). Since then, the total number of AU-recognized RECs are eight.

The Lagos Plan of Action and the Abuja Treaty therefore embraced a bottom–up approach to continental integration with RECs as building blocks for the African Economic Community. Article 6 of the Abuja Treaty provided for the establishment of the African Economic Community in six stages over a period not exceeding 34 years, as follows:

- Stage One: Strengthening existing RECs and establishing of new RECs in regions where they do not exist;
- Stage Two: each REC stabilizing tariff barriers, and non-tariff barriers, customs duties and internal taxes;
- Stage Three: the gradual removal of tariff barriers and non-tariff barriers to intra-REC trade and the establishment of a REC free trade area and subsequently a REC customs union with a common external tariff;
- Stage Four: Coordination and harmonization of tariff and non-tariff systems among the various RECs with a view to establishing a Continental Customs Union with a common external tariff;
- Stage Five: establishment of an African Common Market through the adoption of common policies in several areas; harmonization of monetary, financial and fiscal policies and the application of the principle of free movement of persons; and
- Stage Six: consolidating and strengthening the structure of the African Common Market and setting up of a Pan-African Economic and Monetary Union, a single African Central Bank and a single African Currency.

However, the pace and level of integration among the RECs differed whilst overlapping memberships posed a challenge for further integration both at the REC and continental levels to date.

The significance of the AfCFTA to Africa's integration of economic history is full of examples of the substantial benefits that countries have registered from enhancing their integration into the world economy. The emphasis on trade liberalization, particularly export orientation, in the past three decades has led to a phenomenal growth in the world merchandise trade and improvement in living standards. Most recently, several East Asian economies that pursued the export–led growth model saw a dramatic reduction in poverty levels, especially China where over half a billion people raised their income above the poverty line.

The convergence of income levels between Asia and advanced economies has been accelerated by the impressive growth of Asia's contribution to global trade. Between 1980 and 2018, Asia's share of global trade increased from 4.4 percent to around 20 percent. In contrast, Africa followed a completely different path with its contribution to global trade falling over the same period. Africa's share in world exports fell from about 4 percent in 1980 to 2.3 percent in 2018, and its share of world imports fell from about 4.4 percent in 1980 to 2.5 percent in 2018. Its combined share of global trade declined from 4.2 percent to 2.4 percent over the same period (2017).

The marginalization of Africa in global trade are the consequences of a number of factors, most notably the continued reliance on the exports of primary commodities and natural resources in a world where global trade is increasingly dominated by manufactured goods with technological content. Whilst this bias towards the extractive sectors and consequently extra-African Trade has helped Africa achieve among the highest growth rates in recent years, it also increased the region's exposure to global volatility and adverse terms of trade shocks.

The excessive reliance on primary commodities and stubbornly low levels of intra-African trade despite the integration efforts undertaken since independence and the establishment of RECs means that Africa's economic fortunes remain contingent on commodity price movements and external shocks.

During the most recent episodes of globalisation, the structure and patterns of African trade were further exacerbated by premature deindustrialization, which led to a sharp decline in the contribution of manufacturing value-added to GDP across the region. Even though Africa's exports have in recent years witnessed a reorientation away from stagnating OECD markets toward emerging and fast-growing markets in the South, especially China and India, the composition of Africa's export basket has not changed significantly. Primary commodities and natural resources continue to account for a significant share of total African exports.

Most countries in the region have a commodity export dependence of more than 80 percent, whereas industrial products and manufactured goods account for the lion's share of African imports. The challenges facing Africa on the path to greater integration are therefore not only due to the skewed nature of the composition of its terms of trade, but also a result of the extroverted nature of its trade.

*Table 2: export trade of the regional economic
communities by partner, 2010-17 average (%)*

REC	Intra-REC	Africa	China	EU	US	Rest of the World
AMU	3	2	5	63	8	19
COMESA	9	8	12	37	4	30
CEN-SAD	7	5	5	40	9	34
EAC	20	18	5	19	4	34
ECCAS	2	4	34	20	15	25
ECOWAS	9	7	3	29	12	40
IGAD	14	12	21	16	3	34
SADC	19	3	20	20	8	30
AFRICA AVERAGE	10	7	12	31	8	30

Source: AUC/UNECA – 2018

*Table 3: Import trade of the regional economic
communities by partner, 2000-17 average (%)*

REC	Intra-REC	Africa	China	EU	US	Rest of the World
AMU	3	2	5	64	8	18
COMESA	9	5	13	38	5	29
CEN-SAD	6	4	5	41	11	33
EAC	17	14	14	19	5	31
ECCAS	3	5	34	31	13	26
ECOWAS	8	6	4	16	13	38
IGAD	14	12	21	16	3	34
SADC	16	3	27	21	8	25
AFRICA AVERAGE	9	6	17	31	8	28

Source: AU/UNECA - 2018

Addressing the dichotomy in African trade has been central to all national and continental development strategies. However, and despite the progress made under the RECs to dismantle trade restrictions in order to boost trade, barriers to intra-African trade persist and have impacted the level of intra-African trade, which has remained stubbornly low (Tables 2 and 3). Whereas intra-regional trade in Europe and Asia, which are the leading drivers of globalisation, have averaged 69 and 59 percent of total trade over the last decade respectively, the performance in Africa has been dismal, averaging around 16 percent despite efforts at regional integration.

Whilst some progress had been achieved by the RECs in boosting intra-REC trade, most notably in SADC and the EAC (Table 3 and 4), the performance of the RECs has been disappointing. This is particularly the case for the AMU and CEN-SAD countries which continue to trade more with the EU than with each other. At the same time, a further complication to integration arose as RECs were beginning to overlap, creating what has come to be termed a "spaghetti bowl" of overlapping regional arrangements as some countries were members of more than one REC and had committed to join more than one customs Union (Table 4). To overcome this conundrum and rationalize the regional integration process, Ministers of Trade and Industry of SADC, EAC and COMESA initiated the process of building an FTA between the three RECs. In June 2011 Heads of State of SADC, EAC and COMESA launched the Tri-Partite Free Trade Agreement (TFTA) negotiations at a Summit in Johannesburg. The agreement between SADC, COMESA and the EAC set the platform for African leaders to launch their most ambitious trade integration project, recognizing that boosting intra-African trade will mitigate against global volatility and help promote specialization amongst African countries and develop regional value chains to enhance diversification and competitiveness.

During its 18th Ordinary Session in Addis Ababa, Ethiopia in January 2012, the Assembly of the Heads of State and Government of the African Union adopted the decision to establish a Pan-Africa Continental Free Trade Area by an indicative date of 2017 and also endorsed an Action Plan for Boosting Intra-Africa Trade (BIAT). While the AfCFTA was conceived as a time-bound project, the BIAT was planned as a continuous one with the concrete target of doubling intra-African trade flows from January 2012 to January 2022.

According to AUC, the BIAT contains seven major clusters aimed at addressing the key constraints and challenges of intra-African trade and at significantly enhancing the size and benefits of the trade for the attainment of sustainable economic growth and development.

Table 4: AU recognized RECs as pillars for
the African Economic Community (AEC)

REC	Other sub-Regional	Membership	Free Trade Area status	Customs Union Status
AMU		Algeria, Libya, Mauritania, Morocco, and Tunisia	Stalled	Stalled
CEN-SAD		Benin, Burkina Faso, Cape Verde, the Central African Republic, Chad, Djibouti, Egypt, Eritrea, the Gambia, Libya, Mali, Mauritania, Morocco, Niger, Nigeria, Senegal, Somalia, Sudan, Togo, and Tunisia	Stalled	Stalled
COMESA		Burundi, Comoros, DRC, Djibouti, Egypt, Eritrea, Ethiopia, Kenya, Libya, Madagascar, Malawi, Mauritius, Rwanda, Seychelles, Somalia, Sudan, Swaziland, Tunisia, Uganda, Zambia and Zimbabwe.	In force	Partially in force
EAC		Burundi, Kenya, Rwanda, South Sudan, Tanzania, and Uganda.	In force	In force
ECCAS	CEMAC	Cameroon, the Central African Republic, Chad, Equatorial Guinea, Gabon, and Republic of Congo	In force	In force
	ECCAS wide	CEMAC+ Burundi, DRC, Angola, and Sao Tome and Principe	In force	Delayed
ECOWAS	WAEMU	Benin, Burkina Faso, Cote d'Ivoire, Guinea Bissau, Mali, Niger, Senegal, and Togo	In force	In force
ECOWAS	ECOWAS Wide	WAEMU + Cape Verde, the Gambia, Ghana, Guinea, Liberia, Nigeria and Sierra Leone	In force	CET Adopted
IGAD		Djibouti, Ethiopia, Eritrea, Kenya, Somalia, Sudan, South Sudan and Uganda	Stalled	Stalled
SADC	SACU	Botswana, Lesotho, Namibia, South Africa and Swaziland	In force	In force
	SADC Wide	SACU - Angola, DRC, Madagascar, Malawi, Mauritius, Mozambique, Seychelles, Tanzania, Zambia and Zimbabwe.		Stalled

Source: AU/ UNECA 2018

The main objectives of the AfCFTA are to create a single continental market for goods and services, with free movement of business persons and investments, and thus pave the way for accelerating the establishment of the Custom Union. The AfCFTA is also an important step towards rationalizing Africa's regional trade arrangements to deepen economic integration and draw on economies of scale and development of regional value chains to accelerate the process of structural transformation of African economies.

Preliminary estimates and simulations suggest that the AfCFTA could significantly expand industrial production and Intra-African trade. Estimates from the Economic Commission for Africa (UNECA) suggest that the AfCFTA has the potential to boost intra-African trade by 52.3 percent and to double it in addition to eliminating import duties if measures are taken to remove non-tariff barriers. An integrated African market is also likely to see enhanced flow of foreign direct investment (FDI) to the benefit of participating economies and could shift FDI from natural resources to industry and manufacturing as investors seek to take advantage of increased market size.

Implementation of the AfCFTA and the broader Agenda 2063 will also enhance the integration of African economies into the global economy and strengthen the process of engagement between Africa and its main trading partners multilaterally within the WTO framework and bilaterally with other trading partners such as Brazil, China, the EU, India and the US.

9.3 Status in Africa

Negotiations for the establishment of the AfCFTA were officially launched in June 2015 in Johannesburg, South Africa. Also adopted during the Summit were the objectives and principles of negotiating the AfCFTA, the indicative roadmap for the negotiation and establishment of the AfCFTA, the Terms of Reference for the AfCFTA Negotiating Forum, and the institutional arrangements for the AfCFTA negotiations (Figure 4).

Figure 4: AfCFTA Negotiating Structure:

AU Assembly of Head of states and Government

↑

AU Ministers of Trade

↑

Committee of Senior Officials

↑

CFTA Negotiating Forum

↑

**Stakeholders   Continental Task force
Technical Working Groups**

The following principles guided and continue to guide negotiations of the AfCFTA: (i) negotiations shall be AU Member States/RECs/Customs Territories driven with support of the African Union Commission and its structures; (ii) the Free Trade Area arrangements of RECs would serve as building blocks for the AfCFTA; (iii) preservation of "acqus", meaning that what has already been achieved as part of the implementation of REC obligations will have to be respected; (iv) variable geometry, allowing negotiations of one or more particular issues to lead to an agreement that is not binding on all of the parties; (v) flexibility and special and differential treatment; (vi) transparency and disclosure of information; (Vii) most-favoured-nation (MFN) treatment; (viii) national treatment; (ix) reciprocity; (x) substantial liberalization; (xi) adoption of best practices in the RECs, in the State Parties and International Conventions binding the African Union.

Negotiations towards the AFCFTA have been divided into two phases: Phase one covers Trade in Goods and Services and Dispute Settlement, while phase two negotiations address Intellectual Property, Investment and Competition Policy. The Negotiating Forum was tasked with the responsibility of conducting trade negotiations at the technical level and reporting to the Committee of Senior Trade Officials on its negotiation activities. The Negotiating Forum also has the responsibility of preparing quarterly reports on progress made in the negotiations highlighting areas, requiring higher level intervention by the Committee of Senior Officials, Ministers of Trade Committee and the Assembly of Heads of State and government of the AU.

In January 2017, H.E. Mahamadou Issoufou, President of the Republic of Niger, was mandated by the 28th Ordinary Session of the AU Assembly of Heads of State and Government to champion the process of the AfCFTA. The Negotiating Forum held eight meetings towards finalizing the draft modalities for negotiations on both tariff liberalization and trade in services.

The 8th Negotiating Forum in 2017 arrived at three outcomes: a Framework Agreement on the AfCFTA, a Protocol on Goods, and a Protocol on Trade in Services and a built-in agenda. The three documents were formally approved and adopted by African Trade Ministers in Niamey, Niger in December 2017. African Union Ministers of Trade (AMOT) subsequently adopted the legal instruments constituting the African Continental Free Trade Area (AfCFTA), in Kigali, Rwanda from 8 to 9 March 2018, namely (i) the Agreement Establishing the AfCFTA, (ii) the Protocol on Trade in Goods, (iii) the Protocol on Rules and Procedures for the Settlement of disputes.

History was made on March 21, 2018 in Kigali, Rwanda at an Extraordinary Summit of the AU on the AfCFTA where the Agreement establishing the AfCFTA was presented for signatures along with the Kigali Declaration and the Protocol to the Treaty Establishing the African Economic Community relating to the Free Movement of Persons, Right to Residence and Right to Establishment. In total, 44 out of the 55 AU member states signed the consolidated text of the AfCFTA Agreement, 47 signed the Kigali Declaration and 30 signed the Protocol on Free Movement. The general objectives of the AfCFTA as captured in the Agreement include:

a. Creating a single market for goods, services, facilitated by movement of persons in order to deepen the economic integration of the African continent and in accordance with the Pan-Africa Vision of "An integrated, prosperous and peaceful Africa" enshrined in Agenda 2063;

b. Creating a liberalized market for goods and services through successive rounds of negotiations;

c. Contributing to the movement of capital and natural persons and facilitating investments building on the initiatives and developments in the State Parties and RECs;

d. Laying the foundation for the establishment of a continental Customs Union at a later stage;

e. Promoting and attaining sustainable and inclusive socio-economic development, gender equality and structural transformation of the State Parties;

f. Enhancing the competitiveness of the economies of State Parties within the continent and the global market;

g. Promoting industrial development through diversification and regional value chain development, agricultural development and food security; and

h.   Resolving the challenges of multiple and overlapping memberships and expediting the regional and continental integration processes.

The Specific objectives of the AfCFTA are stated as follows:

a.   Progressively eliminate tariffs and non-tariff barriers to trade in goods;
b.   Progressively liberalize trade services;
c.   Cooperate on investment, intellectual property rights and competition policy;
d.   Cooperate on all trade-related areas;
e.   Cooperate on customs matters and the implementation of trade facilitation measures;
f.   Establish a mechanism for the settlement of disputes concerning their rights and obligations; and
g.   Establish and maintain an institutional framework for the implementation and administration of the AfCFTA.

Following signing, AU members, individually or as part of a customs union, started developing and submitting schedules of concessions for trade in goods, detailing the 90 percent of products that are to be liberalized, the sensitive products to be liberalized over a longer period of time (7 percent), and the excluded products that are to be exempted from liberalization (3 percent)`. A related complement to the schedules of concessions for trade in goods is the list of product–specific rules of origin which is still being negotiated, as is the protocol on dispute resolution.

In December 2018, a roadmap was adopted to finalize outstanding work on the AFCFTA negotiations. On rules of origin, negotiators were expected to submit an agreement by June 2019. Negotiations are continuing and are expected to be concluded in 2020. AU member states also agreed on a January 2020 deadline to submit their negotiated market access offers for goods.

For trade services, scheduling will call for a review of the regulatory framework of the identified sectors in view of preparing the initial market access offers, which will then be subject to negotiations. AU member states agreed to submit their schedules of concessions for five priority services sectors by January 2020: transport, communications, financial services, tourism, and business services. Phase two negotiations on the Protocols on Investment, Competition Policy and Intellectual Property Rights is expected to be concluded by 2021.

Institutional arrangements to support implementation of the AfCFTA were also agreed. These include a dedicated Secretariat to be hosted in Ghana; the African Business Council, which will aggregate and articulate the views of the private sector; as well as a Trade Observatory, which will ensure effective monitoring and evaluation. Regional economic communities (RECs) will also remain important partners coordinating the implementation and measures for resolving non-tariff barriers, harmonizing standards and monitoring implementation. In accordance with the Agreement, the AfCFTA was entered into force in 2019 after 22 Member States submitted their instruments of ratification. The 22-country threshold was reached on April 29, 2019 when Sierra Leone and the Saharawi Republic deposited their instruments of ratification, allowing the Agreement to enter into force on 30 May, 2019.

The 12th Extraordinary Session of the Assembly of the African Union on the AfCFTA in Niamey, Niger on 7 July, 2019 marked the launch of the operational phase of the AfCFTA Agreement. To date, 28 countries have ratified the agreement and of the 55 AU member states, only Eritrea is yet to sign the Agreement

Table 5: Status of AfCFTA

1.Burkina Faso	8.Ethiopia	15.Niger	22.Sao Tome and Principe
2.Chad	9.Eswatin	16.Mali 23.Senegal	23. Senegal
3.Congo	10.Kenya	17.Mauritania	24.Sierra Leone
4.Cote D'lvoire	11.Gabon	18.Mauritius	25.South Africa
5.Djibouti	12.Ghana	19.Uganda	26.The Gambia
6.Egypt	13.Guinea	20.Rwanda	27.Togo
7.Equetorio Guinea	14.Namibia	21.Saharawi Republic	28.Zimbabwe

Source: Report by H.E Issoufou Mohamadou, President of Niger and leader of AfCFTA process to 33rd ordinary session of AU assembly 2020, Addis Ababa.

While negotiations are continuing, AfCFTA already started to produce results even before it entered its operational phase. The first was the successful hosting of the Intra-African Trade Fair (IATF) held in Cairo, Egypt from 11 to 17 December, 2018. The Fair, organized by the African Export-import Bank in collaboration with the African Union and the Government of the Arab Republic of Egypt, attracted 1,086 exhibitors from 29 African and non-African countries. By facilitating the dissemination of information and investment opportunities, it created a platform for exhibitors to showcase their goods and services, engage in business (B2B) exchanges, and strike deals. Business to business transactions during the Fair were above US $30 billion. Building on the success of IATF (2018), the second edition of the Intra African Trade Fair is planned for 2020 in Kigali, Rwanda.

In order to facilitate trade and address liquidity constraints and exchange risk, the African Export-Import Bank worked with the African Union to establish a Pan African Payment and Settlement System (PAPSS). PAPSS, which is conceived as a digital platform, was launched during the 12th Extraordinary Session of the Assembly of the African Union on the AfCFTA in Niamey, Niger on 7 July 2019.

A Continental Platform on e-commerce has also been established by the African Union Commission in partnership with a member of the African Diaspora. This Platform will create 600,000 small and medium enterprises in four years (2019-2023) and complement other efforts like the AfCFTA Business Forum, integration of African Financial markets and commodity exchanges.

In addition, African manufacturers are working towards the establishment of a continental association that will drive the development of regional value and supply chains and through them, joint ventures to enable them to produce to the scale of the AfCFTA market.

9.4 Challenges and Prospects

Historically, an important challenge to the economic integration process in Africa has been political stability. The quest for political stability is still a challenge for several countries and has undermined integration at the sub-regional and continental level and is a reflection of the nexus between security and development. While there is no development in the context of a security vacuum, sustainable development driven by robust and inclusive growth can act as a catalyst for long-term stability and peace. The 33rd African Summit adopted a theme the year to be silencing the gun by 2020. This is a step in the right direction.

Another key challenge is overcoming the myth of national sovereignty that is often used to undermine the regional integration. In effect, in the medium and long term, national and regional interests are always more aligned than "national" interests, which tends to weaken the bargaining power of countries. Implementation of the AfCFTA and the broader Agenda 2063 will enhance the integration of African economies into the global economy and strengthen the process of engagement between Africa and its main trading partners multilaterally within the World Trade Organization (WTO) framework and bilaterally with other trading partners such as Brazil, China, the EU, India and the US on a win-win basis.

The approach to integration in Africa has also traditionally been top-down with governments emerging as the main actors. Governments initiate the establishment of RECs and are by and large responsible for the implementation of integrative measures and development programmes. Under that top-down model, the participation of non-state actors including the private sector and civil society in trade negotiations between African countries and with external parties have been very limited, making it difficult to mainstream the process of integration across the region. The AfCFTA seeks to reverse this with a bottom-up approach.

In the absence of private sector operators, who to a large extent have the ultimate responsibility of operationalizing integration either through intra-African trade or cross-border investment, implementation has remained a major challenge. The Pan-African Private Sector Trade and Investment Policy Committee (PAFTRAC) and the institution of the AfCFTA Civil Society and Business Forum will be especially important to ensure that non-state actors play a more important role in trade negotiations undertaken by African governments.

In addition, the realization of the potential offered by the AfCFTA and deeper integration will hinge on a supportive and conducive trade environment. In particular, effective implementation of the AfCFTA will require investments in trade facilitating infrastructure to ensure that market access benefits are fully realized, implementation of the AU's Action Plan for the Accelerated Industrial Development of Africa (AIDA), and effective implementation of the programme for infrastructure Development in Africa (PIDA). Implementation of the BIAT Action Plan will provide the framework for the supportive policies and environment that are key to the AfCFTA's success.

Strengthening regional and continental institutions leading and managing the process of regional integration also needs to be addressed as does national capacity for the implementation of protocols and agreements. Regional institutions do not have enough manpower capacity to lead the implementation of measures on integration and development. They also lack sufficient financial resources for the implementation of regional integration and development programs. Committing regional resources and mobilizing domestic resources to overcome these challenges will therefore be critical to ensure the success of the AfCFTA. Creating conducive environments and right policies will be imperative.

9.5 Underlying Issues

Over and above those challenges, Amb. Albert M. Muchanga the commissioner for Trade and Industry correctly underscores a couple of underlying issues that cannot be ignored. The first issue here is that in opening for signature the AFCFTA Agreement and launching its operational phase in Niamey, Niger where it was decided; among others that the start of trading would be 1ˢᵗ July 2020, Africa laid out for the whole world to see, her ambitious transformational agenda of creating one African market to usher in inclusive prosperity.[457] This bold move has also raised high expectations for decent livelihoods among ordinary Africans. The underlying tasks here are to transform this ambition into tangible results and in the process, meet the expectations of the African people. Failure would create a crisis of expectation.

The second underlying issue is that in making this bold move, African within the continent and in the other parts of the world where they live, as we as the African diaspora, have placed their honour and integrity to public scrutiny. Failure to implement the AfCFTA Agreement will undermine them. On the other hand, success will enhance them. In this respect, the momentum that has been built in the negotiation, signature, ratification and launch of the operational phase of the AfCFTA Agreement must not just be sustained during its implementation but also be enhanced.

The third underlying factor is that we are on the eve of starting implementation of the AfCFTA Agreement with the backdrop of Africa being well known for crafting well intended agreements, resolutions, and declarations but falling short in their implementation. AfCFTA must not suffer the same fate.

The fourth underlying factor is the need to be fully aware that there are some cynics within Africa and outside who believe that we lack the capacities to deliver on the commitments that have been made in the AfCFTA Agreement. In addition to this, there are also several detractors whose aim is to slow the momentum in the implementation of the AfCFTA Agreement and preserve the status quo of the weak and fragmented African economies. Furthermore, among us, we also have skeptics and people with self-doubt about our individual and collective capacities to fully and effectively implement this Agreement. With self-doubt comes a fixed mindset that with or without the AfCFTA, it is business as usual. In connection with this is the underlying conviction in those quarters that national markets should co-exist with the AfCFTA market when the agenda for transformation dictates that the AfCFTA market is the new and larger domestic market for each and every African country.

457   AU ECHO, 2019. pp. 20-21

The fifth underlying issue is the need for Africa to meet the expectations of investors for stability, scale, predictability, fair treatment, combating corruption and among others an enabling environment in the AfCFTA market in order to attract them to deploy large-scale and long term investments. These are critically important to create job opportunities for Africans, thereby offering alternative solutions to young Africans who risk their lives in search of decent livelihoods outside the continent. This is a mixed bag of perspectives.

African Countries began officially trading under a new Continent-wide Free Trade area on Friday, 1st January 2021 after months of delays caused by the global coronavirus pandemic. But experts view the New Year's Day launch as largely symbolic with full implementation of the deal expected to take years. The African Continental Free Trade Area (AfCFTA) aims to bring together 1.3 billion people in a $ 3.4 trillion economic bloc. This will be the largest free trade area since the establishment of the World Trade Organization (WTO).

Backers say it will boost trade among African neighbours while allowing the continent to develop its own value chains. The World Bank estimates it could lift tens of millions out of poverty by 2035. "There is a new Africa emerging with a sense of urgency and purpose and an aspiration to become self-reliant," Ghana's President Nana Akufo-Addo said during an online launch ceremony.[458] Ghana is the hosting headquarters of the AfCFTA.

However, obstacles-ranging from ubiquitous red tape and poor infrastructure to the entrenched protectionism of some of its member states must be overcome if the bloc is to reach its full potential. Both tariff and non-tariff challenges are abound.

Trade under the AfCFTA was meant to be launched in July 2020, but was pushed back after COVID-19 pandemic made in-person negotiations impossible. The pandemic also gave the process added impetus. It demonstrated that Africa is overly reliant on export of primary commodities, overly reliant on global supply chains. This means that when global supply chains are disrupted, Africa suffers.

As stated above, every African country except Eritrea has signed on to the AfCFTA framework agreement, and 34 have ratified it. Critics say the real work begins now. They argue that they would be surprised if they could have everything set up within 24 Months. In their view for long-term success and based on European experience, it is a must start somewhere. Historic challenges including African's poor road and rail links, political unrest, excessive border bureaucracy and petty corruption will not disappear overnight. An annex to the deal outlining the rules of origin-an essential step for determining which

---

458   No.1 Citizen, 4th Jan, 2021

products can be subject to tariffs and duties is yet to be completed. It is work in progress. As the adage goes, Rome was not built in one day.

Meanwhile, 41 of the zone's 54 member states have submitted tariff reduction schedules. Members must phase out 90 percent of tariff lines- over five years for more advanced economies or 10 years for less developed nations. Another 7 percent considered sensitive will get more time, while 3 percent will be allowed to be placed on an exclusion list. Finalizing those scheduled and communicating them to businesses must be done quickly.

But efforts to implement the deal will also likely face resistance from countries' domestic interest groups. Fears of losing out more competitive neighbours initially made some countries including West African giant Nigeria, skeptical of the pan-African project. Still, proponents of the zone are confident that initial steps towards its implementation will already allow member states to quickly boost intra-African trade which is currently very low. Economic integration is not an event. It is a process. AfCFTA must start from somewhere despite the challenges.

9.6 Conclusion

The launching of Agenda 2063, the adoption of the BIAT Action Plan, the establishment of a single Air Transport Market, and the adoption of an African Union Passport all demonstrate the continent's progress and commitment to working together to achieve an integrated and prosperous continent. In particular, AfCFTA holds tremendous potential for boosting intra-African trade, accelerating the process of structural transformation of African economies and reducing their vulnerability to external shocks.

The historic signature of the AfCFTA Agreement was an important milestone in the process of economic integration and development. The speed of ratification – the Agreement entered into force slightly more than a year later on May 30, 2019 – is a testament to Africa's collective will to overcome the historic fragmentation of its economies and open a new chapter in Africa's development.

Pundits have argued that Customs Union should be prioritized in executing the AfCFTA. However, this assertion raises more questions than answers. For example, how can this be achieved when the present regional economic communities are yet to become full-fledged Custom Unions, when SADC is challenged by the existence of SACU, when COMESA still struggles to achieve a free trade regime with Egypt, and when South Africa and Kenya fight it out for superiority? In 2007-2008 COMESA, EAC and SADC thought they had successfully crafted Tripartite, and then at Summit in Kampala Tanzania's President Kikwete called for the creation of Customs Union for the three economic regions and even a merger of the three RECs. This turned out to be a far-fetched dream: How realistic is AfCFTA considering present challenges, growing nationalism, and inequality to 'America first' a la Trumpism? But we cannot be oblivious of realities that undermine political ambitions and dreams.

Indeed, the launch in May of the African Continental Free Trade Agreement (AfCFTA) created a single market of 1.3 billion people that will grow to an estimated 2.5 billion by 2050. This is a market where 60% of the population is under 25 and where there's an appetite for high levels of consumption of fast-moving consumer goods. The challenge is how do we make it work?

The AfCFTA has been signed by 54 of the 55 countries in Africa (only Eritrea has not signed it) and ratified by more than half of the signatories. It creates a real opportunity for Africa to liberalize more than 90% of intra-Africa tariffs and deliver growth on the continent. Successful implementation of the agreement has the potential to establish Africa as a global manufacturing centre and could, ultimately, result in an estimated 80 million jobs in Asia being transferred to Africa. CEOs of African businesses have their fingers crossed that this is, finally, tangible progress towards a homogeneous market. But they remain sceptical that such an ambitious agreement can be successfully implemented given the limited success of previous African regional free-trade zones and initiatives.

The first step to successful AfCFTA was a high level of participation which, against all odds, has been achieved. The second step, due to be taken in July 2020, is the implementation and practical adoption of the trade practices, processes and infrastructure required to establish a working free zone across 54 countries. A precedent model for such a Herculean task exists: the Asian free trade zone has been a notable success, creating a platform for manufacturing, regional trade and stimulus for jobs and prosperity in Asia. By 2040 Africa will have a larger working population than China and India combined.

Much of the momentum to date has been driven by the African Union and the continent's development of finance institutions, which have ushered in the process forward, often having to use all the leverage and persuasion they have available. Encouragingly, they are now fully committed to implementation, resourcing and supporting a launch and delivering achievable steps by July 2020. The agreement will take until 2030 to be fully operational. Africa has the lowest inter-regional trade in the world. Only 15% of African trade is cross-border between neighbouring countries, whereas cross-border trade represents about 65% of the trade in developed markets. The free movement of goods has the potential to trigger a manufacturing boom and establish Africa as a world centre for manufacturing.

Asia's transformation into a global economic engine began with the production of cheap goods in countries where wages were low and workers abundant. What followed was the development of sophisticated regional value chains, knowledge transfer and up-skilling, and the transition from export-led economies to more balanced ones with rising domestic consumption. Africa has yet to experience anything like that. The lack of cross-border trade today stifles manufacturing across the continent, constraining production to local markets that are difficult to scale. The elimination of tariffs will stimulate trade, enabling companies to expand and develop as they address larger regional markets. The manufacturing sector will also begin to draw foreign direct investment. This, in turn, will lead to larger production volumes and bring about new efficiencies, enabling African manufacturing to finally have the ability to compete not only in domestic and regional markets but also be more competitive with global manufacturing.

By 2040, Africa will have a larger working population than China and India combined. Low wages on the continent are attracting manufacturers from high employment industries such as the apparel sector. This can be manufactured at a lower cost in Africa than in traditional Asian production centres. The current slowdown in developed markets means that increasing numbers of multinational companies are becoming interested in the African opportunity as a market and as a global manufacturing base. For Africa, successful implementation of the AFCfTA is a game changer with the potential to move millions from rural subsistence agriculture-based society to an early-stage industrial society. Manufacturing wages are five times more productive for GDP growth than agriculture.

Many of the criteria needed for Africa to prosper finally appear to be aligning. This includes a competitive young workforce that is willing and able to adopt new technology and embrace the fourth industrial revolution combined with increasing political stability across the continent and vast, untapped energy resource discoveries that are attracting billions of dollars of foreign investment.

China is first out of the blocs. It is interacting with the private and public sectors in Africa to realise the benefits anticipated from the AfCFTA. Already at the forefront of infrastructure projects in Africa, Chinese manufacturing initiatives are spreading across the continent. Chinese companies are relocating their manufacturing hubs from China to Africa in the expectation of tariff-free regional trade and competitive export markets. The alignment of Africa with the Chinese Belt and Road Initiative is at the forefront of Sino-African intergovernmental discussions. If Africa can implement the agreements in practice and other countries and trading blocs follow China's lead, the AfCFTA has a good chance of living up to its promise, propelling Africa to the forefront of global manufacturing. The AfCFTA, might only need to operationalize a continent-wide customs union area, at least for the moment. Whether it is done on RECs basis or a one-step move remains a major challenge to be addressed. However, regardless of how it is achieved, the necessity of a continental Customs Union to protect nascent industries which Africa is striving to build cannot be over emphasized. The continental foreign policies will have to reflect these fundamental principles and objectives. As aptly captured in Agenda 2063, that will be the only way to realize the Africa we want.

CHAPTER TEN

REVAMPING AFRICAN FOREIGN POLICIES

Interdependence among states has been an incontrovertible fact of international relations. This compels African states to get essentially involved in the process of establishing and conducting relations with other states across the globe. Each African state has been establishing inter alia the diplomatic, economic, trade, educational, cultural and political relations with other nations. For giving meaning and direction to African relations with other states, each country has been formulating and adopting a foreign policy strategy. It is through its foreign policy that it tries to secure the goals of national interest in international relations because the behaviour of each state in an international milieu is always conditioned by its foreign policy.

Making a difference in African approach to foreign policy should be done by revamping the available strategies. Therefore, revamping foreign policy in this context means changing or re-arranging existing policy strategies to reflect the African case as in the interest of the people by improving where Africa has been disadvantaged. Thus, revamping African foreign policy refers to an improvement of an old idea or a newer into a better version from something that was disfavoured to get new life through repair and restoration.

Suffice to note and underscore the fact that the new millennium has come up with new challenges. Yet Africa has no alternative except to rise to the occasion. It is in this context that the African Union as well as Agenda 2063 were conceived. The AU agenda 2063 is the current blue print which guides both aspirations and flagship projects of the continent. Fortunately, all 55 AU member states have signed, ratified, acceded and domesticated the blueprint into their National Development programmes. Apparently, some of them coincide with the UN- SDGs. In this regard, and as we shall see, their foreign policies must be realigned to accommodate the Agenda 2063, for example, programmes like African Peace and Security Architecture (APSA), Programme on Infrastructure Development in Africa (PIDA), Common African Agriculture Development Pragramme (CAADP), African Continental Free Trade Area (AfCFTA) etc.

Foreign policy is a fundamental concept in the theory of interactions in the international system. It consists of a range of actions taken individually by a state or collectively by intergovernmental organizations corresponding to actions of other states or international actors. Theorists argue that each nation determines and defines its foreign policy, but practically, collective policy directives do prevail. In the case of Africa, a history of humiliation and subjugation determined the direction and trends of foreign policy. Africa suffered the humiliation of slavery and the subjugation of European colonialism and neo-colonialism after independence. Africa and its diaspora embarked on the search for unity under the ideologies of Pan-Africanism formulated from the London Conference of 1900 to Manchester Congress of 1945.

Decolonized countries sought ideas about continental unity in different platforms like the Monrovia Group, the Brazzaville Group and the Casablanca Group as an expression of Pan-Africanism. The latter is such a complex set of ideas that some scholars referred to it as having no single definition. There are as many ideas about Pan-Africanism as there are thinkers who had their perceptions of the ideology. Rather than being a unified school of thought, Pan-Africanism is more of a movement which has as its common underlying theme the struggle for social and political equality and freedom from economic exploitations and racial discrimination.[459] African countries expressed social and economic emancipation through philosophies like Umbutu in South Africa, which underscores solidarity. The Tanzanian philosophy of Ujamaa emphasizes collective work or cooperative movement.

After the wind of independence blew across Africa, the new states adopted and sharpened those ideas of Pan-Africanism to forge them into ingredients of foreign policy suitable for African countries. As mentioned earlier, differences occurred about the form of unity. During the May 1963 conference in Addis Ababa, the idea of immediate continental unity was substituted with that of gradual continental unity. African states established the Organization of African Unity (OAU) on the basis of gradual unity. The foundation of African foreign

---

459   Murithi, Tim, (2015)., pp. 217-233.

policy lay in the struggle for social and political equality and freedom from economic exploitations and racial discrimination. The cornerstones of African foreign policy was the liberation of African territories still under colonial rule to full independence, the struggle against apartheid and settler colonialism in South Africa, and continuous struggle against neo-colonialism.[460] African countries got their independence during the period of Cold War. Politics of the Cold War divided nations between supporters of Western imperialism and Soviet communism. The newly independent African in the 1960s became active members of the Non-Aligned Movement (NAM) born at the 1955 Bandung Conference in Indonesia, which developed into a Third World Movement.

Although African foreign policy varied from one country to another, scholars found a consistent set of directives formulated by states, which was directed to target foreign policy issues lying beyond African territorial legitimacy. The OAU encouraged its members to support liberation movements in Southern Africa in countries like South Africa, Zimbabwe, Namibia, Angola, Mozambique and Western Sahara. African countries coordinated their foreign policy actions in international organizations like the United Nations to secure independence of colonial territories, and to impose sanctions against apartheid South Africa and its isolation from the international system.

The African Union (AU), which succeeded the OAU in July 2002 in Durban, continued to institutionalize Pan-Africanism in its structures. The organization has instituted principles of peace in the Protocol on Peace and security, principles of post-conflict reconstruction and principles of development by establishing the New Partnership for Africa's Development (NEPAD). The AU has introduced principles in the area of governance, which have implications for African foreign policy. They are the African peer-review mechanisms and unprincipled and unconstitutional changes of government. African countries are careful about their policy directives outside their territorial boundaries. Overall, this analysis serves as the overarching foreign policy, explaining how African states interact in the continent and beyond.

Throughout history of state relations, the debate of foreign policy conduct has evolved in different environments and circumstances in which the country has undergone in realization of its interests. When cooking, the application of each ingredient used serves a particular function, reacting with others to produce new combinations and create the structure, flavour and texture of the finished product for human consumption.

In the context of foreign policy, experts and technocrats are expected to apply some tools and instruments for flavouring as well as giving texture to

---

460   Young, Crawford, (2017). pp. 11-22.

the nature of national interest accomplished abroad. Tools in this regard refer to an instrument or implement that empowers the foreign policy expert and professional to align their national interests in accordance with the norms of the international system. In the context of the African experiences, tools are meant to empower policymakers with appropriate toolkits for formulation and execution of national foreign policies. The ingredients refer to foreign policy constituents, components, elements, sections, strands, portions, units, items, features, aspects and attributes employed by foreign policy experts to determine success, failures and effectiveness of a national policy abroad. In the context of African experiences, ingredients exhibit the potential for creating an African foreign policy taste that suits norms, culture, and values for overcoming the challenges of the international system.

The title of this book is the revamping of foreign policy ingredients, tools, dynamics, and the African experiences. We explore various techniques and conceptualizations of foreign policy in an African perspective for revamping foreign policy in Africa as illustrated in the following domains:

First, for African countries to rejuvenate their foreign policies, experts in the Ministry of Foreign Affairs and diplomatic and consular missions abroad should, generally, familiarize themselves with nature, meaning and conceptualization of foreign policy. This could be accomplished by understanding the historical development of foreign policy, the essence of the policy in the international politics as well as the theoretical underpinning of foreign policy as a practice.

Secondly, the essence of decision making by the national expert has a great influence in the formulation and conduct of foreign policy in Africa. The technocrat's comprehension of international relations in decision making and models of decision making in foreign policy could promote good relations with other states as well as membership in regional and global institutions.

Thirdly, African foreign policy technocrats understand that level of analysis would play a vital role in making and executing each African state foreign policy. For these technocrats to revamp domestic policies, they should comprehend three level of analysis: idiosyncratic, state, and system levels. Understanding of key ingredients at each level determines the success and failures of domestic strategy in influencing international regimes and states within the international milieu. Foreign policy should be seen as one of several venues or opportunities for leaders to engage in the politics of state survival. The leader and the leader's circle extract resources to maintain rule from both domestic and international sources which determine the nature of African states' foreign policies.

Fourthly, there are many avenues of formulating and conducting foreign policy within African states. Some states have a well-defined foreign policy strategy while others respond to foreign policy issues as they arise without a well-coordinated mechanism for executing national interest. In most African States the decision for foreign policy formation and execution is vested in the authority of the President and sometimes in the Minister of Foreign Affairs and International Cooperation. This book would enable the president and ministers of foreign affairs of the African states to understand various instruments of foreign policy for revamping national abroad.

Fifth, the concept of formulating and executing foreign policy is a universal phenomenon for all sovereign states in the world. However, there is variation in each state's approach to the achievement of national interest abroad. In revamping African state foreign policies, the states should be mindful of domestic and international factors influencing their interest in the international arena. Therefore, each African state should be mindful of domestic factors such as the geography, the form of government, public opinion, social groups and public diplomacy. In the same note, the state should be considerate of international factors such as regional integration, international organization and the nature of international system.

Sixth, this section deals with how foreign policy ingredients should be properly utilized in accordance with national interest. The formulation and conduct of foreign policy would strengthen African countries' relations with other continents by identifying key national interests to be executed abroad. This would help the African states revamp their foreign policies through the formulation and execution of a well-designed and nurtured national foreign policy that could promote African heritage and norms in the international milieu.

Seventh, studies on African foreign policies, especially their formulation, have received less attention in comparison to other areas over decades. We agree with East (1973) who described small state foreign policies as exhibiting low levels of overall participation in world affairs, high levels of activity in intergovernmental organizations, high levels of support for international legal norms, avoidance to the use of force as a technique of statecraft, avoidance of behaviour and policies which tend to alienate the more powerful states in the system, a narrow functional and geographic range of concern in foreign policy activities and frequent utilization of moral and normative positions on international issues.[461] Therefore, the essence of African experiences in formulation of a national foreign policy is a litmus test for revamping other states' foreign policies which are not explored in this book.

Eighth, generally speaking, diplomacy has its ancient roots firmly in Africa, the cradle of humanity, but the idea of "African diplomacy" surprisingly has

---

461   East, (1973), p.557

been seen as new concept because African states are very young compared to those in the rest of the world. However, the legacy of colonialism put together with the damage caused by intra- and interstate wars in Africa have infused the continent's diplomacy with a collective memory of subjugation and marginalization. In revamping African foreign policies, all states should have a common understanding that the continent of Africa is known as the "cradle of humanity" or "home to the earliest human settlements" where language as a means of communication first developed. Therefore, all the aspects of the current diplomacy such as the human instinct to communicate, negotiate, cooperate, and trade across boundaries is a fair indication that Africa was the birthplace of diplomacy.

The vast majority of African states were *decreed* sovereign on a particular date, in contrast to states in the rest of the world that *evolved* over centuries into sovereign statehood. Furthermore, the colonial state's institutional grooming and training of indigenous African officials for post-colonial self-governance were done in haste. African countries should comprehend that the autonomous conduct of diplomacy in the international domain is a highly competitive practice which requires foundation in a functioning civil service at the domestic level and nascent statehood. African technocrats have very little foreign policy infrastructure, bureaucratic know-how, and skilled human resources; the new African states ventured into the global diplomatic arena at a disadvantage.

The developing states of Africa have also battled to reach levels of diplomatic representation that would enable them to participate equitably in global forums. Diplomacy is a costly enterprise and the maintenance of numerous resident missions is simply not an option for the majority of African states. The tendency is therefore to prioritize multilateral diplomatic missions which is accredited to intergovernmental organizations in order to maximize diplomatic opportunities in a single location. African diplomacy has not only changed the "demographics" of international relations, but also impacted the substance of the global diplomatic agenda. From the moment they gained independence, African states campaigned to be treated as equals in a world where they had experienced the brunt of subjugation. Obtaining sovereignty provided equality in terms of international law but much more than abstract status was required: it was essential that the new states also develop socio-economically, so as to break the cycle of asymmetrical relations with the rest of the world. This chapter gives solution to the poor African foreign policy approach. Therefore, the effectiveness in formulation and conduct of African countries' foreign policy should be based on the African Union Agenda 2063 as explored herein:

10.1 The Foci of African Foreign Policy: The Agenda 2063

A quick look at the Agenda 2063 in nutshell reveals that it has seven aspirations namely: (i) A prosperous Africa based on inclusive growth and sustainable development, (ii) An integrated continent politically united, based on the ideals of Pan-Africanism and the vision of Africa's renaissance, (iii) An Africa of good governance, democracy for human rights, justice and rule of law, (iv) A peaceful and secure Africa, (v) Africa with a strong cultural identity, common heritage, values, and ethics., (vi) An Africa whose development is people driven, relying on the potential of African people, especially its women and youth, and caring for children, (vii) Africa as a strong, united, resilient and influential global player and partner.

Equally, the Agenda AU 2063 has 15 fast-track or flagship projects which have been identified as key to accelerate Africa's economic growth and development as well as promoting a common identity by celebrating Africa's history and vibrant culture. The flagship projects are: Integrated High Speed Train Network (aims to connect all African capitals and commercial centres), Pan African Virtual and e-University (PAVeU), African Commodities Strategy, African economic Forum, African Continental Free Trade Area, (AfCFTA), African passport, and Free Movement of People, Silencing the Guns by 2020,Grand Inga Dam Project, Pan African e-network, (PAeN), Africa Outer Space Programme, Single African Air Transport Market, (SAATM), African Financial Institutions, Great Museum of Africa, Cyber Security, and Encyclopedia Africana Project (EAP).

It is in light of agenda 2063 that one needs to situate and interrogate the revamping of African foreign policies in the 21st century. A close scrutiny of the agenda 2063 reveals that there are lot of commonalities in the agenda that with the requisite commitment, visionary, and dedicated leadership, coupled with self-reliance and sacrifice spirit, so it is possible to haul the socio-economic development from low to high level. This can be attested by examining a few sectors that can impact and turn around the current problems of unemployment, industrialization and infrastructure.

10.1.1 Aspirations of Agenda 2063

In view of the foregoing, besides the Constitutive Act of the African Union, Agenda 2063 is built on the AU Vision, the 50th Anniversary Solemn Declaration, the seven aspirations, and national plans as well as regional and continental frameworks from which specific goals, priority areas and strategies have been developed to facilitate their achievement. Africa aspires that by 2063, Africa shall have: an entrenched and flourishing culture of human rights, democracy, gender equality, inclusion and peace; prosperity, security and safety for all citizens; and mechanisms to promote and defend the continent's collective security and interests. From Agenda 2063, seven aspirations were distilled, demonstrating what the African citizenry wanted to be pursued and achieved by Agenda 2063. In revamping African foreign policies, we urged all the states in Africa to adhere to the aspirations of the Agenda 2063 as follows[462]:

i.   Aspiration 1: A prosperous Africa based on inclusive growth and sustainable development: Africa will by 2063 be a continent of shared prosperity, which finances and manages its own growth and transformation.

ii.   Aspiration 2: An integrated continent, politically united based on the ideals of Pan Africanism and the vision of Africa's Renaissance: By 2063 Africa will have emerged as a united, strong, sovereign, independent and self-reliant continent that realizes full economic and political integration.

iii. Aspiration 3: An Africa of good governance, democracy, respect for human rights, justice and the rule of law: By 2063, Africa will have undergone a deepening of the culture of good governance, democratic values, gender equality, respect for human rights, justice and the rule of law.

iv.   Aspiration 4: A peaceful and secure Africa: By 2063, Africa will emerge as a peaceful and secure continent, a conflict-free continent with harmony and understanding among communities at the grassroots level.

v.   Aspiration 5: An Africa with a strong cultural identity, common heritage, values and ethics: Africa, as the cradle of human civilization, is custodian of a cultural patrimony that has contributed enormously to human progress. African cultural identity, values and ethics as a critical factor in Africa's re-emergence on the global stage in the decade of the 2010s will be promoted and strengthened by 2063.

vi.   Aspiration 6: An Africa whose development is people-driven, relying on the potential of African people, especially its women and youth, and caring for children: By 2063, Africa will be a continent where all citizens will be actively involved in decision-making in all aspects of development, including social, economic, political and environmental. Africa will be a continent where no child, woman or man will be left behind.

vii. Aspiration 7: Africa as a strong, united, resilient and influential global player and partner: Africa will emerge as a strong, united, resilient and influential global player and partner with a bigger role in world affairs.

---

462   Au Agenda 2063, Pp. 6-7

10.1.2 Industrialization/Infrastructure/Employment

To begin with, Africa must industrialize to end poverty and to generate employment for the 12 million young people who join its labour force every year. One of the key factors retarding industrialization has been the insufficient stock of productive infrastructure in power, water, and transport services that would allow firms to thrive in industries with strong comparative advantages.

The continent's working–age population was projected to increase from 705 million in 2018 to almost 1.0 billion by 2030. As millions of young people join the labour market, the pressure to provide decent jobs will intensify. At the current rate of labour force growth, Africa needs to create about 12 million new jobs every year to prevent unemployment from rising. Unemployment is a time bomb. Strong and sustained economic growth is necessary for generating employment, but that alone is not enough. The source and nature of growth also matter.

Africa has achieved one of the fastest and most sustained spurts in the past two decades, yet growth has not been pro-employment. A 1 percent increase in GDP growth from 2000 – 2014 was associated with only 0.41 percent growth in employment, meaning that employment was expanding at a rate of less than 1.8 percent a year, or far below the nearly 3 percent annual growth in the labour force. If this trend continues, 100 million people will join the ranks of the unemployed in Africa by 2030. This is a time bomb. Without meaningful structural change, most of the jobs generated are likely to be in the informal sector, where productivity and wages are low and work is insecure and unpredictable, making the eradication of extreme poverty by 2030 a far-fetched dream.

One of the most salient features of labour markets in Africa is the high prevalence of informal employment, the default option for a large majority of the growing labour force. On average, developing countries have higher shares of informal employment than developed countries. While data on informal employment are sketchy, it is clear that Africa has the highest rate of estimated informality in the world, at 72 percent of non-agriculture employment and as high as 90 percent in some countries. Furthermore, there is no evidence that informality is declining in Africa.

On rough estimates, the continent loses an average of 176,000 private-sector jobs every year because of each of the business obstacles examined, for a total of 1.2 - 3.3 million jobs lost every year. The number of estimated jobs lost ranges from 74,000 due to customs and trade regulations to 264,000 due to licensing and permitting. These rough estimates are indicative only, and actual and potential job losses could be much higher. They do, however, indicate how detrimental the obstacles are to both creating new jobs and maintaining existing high-quality jobs in the formal sector. Licensing and permitting, courts, political instability, and corruption are associated with the highest number of private sector jobs lost in Africa. Related to governance, these obstacles are thus amenable to reform. Africa's common and collective foreign policies need to address these issues when engaging Investors to come and invest into Africa.

Despite the potential long-term benefits, the share of resources allocated to infrastructure was cut sharply by African governments and their development partners in the 1980s and 1990s, prescribed by the Structural Adjustment Programs (SAP) most African countries adopted under the so-called Washington Consensus. That partly explains Africa's current lag in infrastructure relative to other regions. It was imposed on Africa, which swallowed it wholly without considering its impact on the dire economic situation in the continent. While capital accumulation started to pick up again in the early 2000s, the pace has been too slow to close Africa's infrastructure gap. New estimates by the African Development Bank (AfDB) suggest that the continent's infrastructure needs amount to $130 - $ 170 billion a year, with a financing gap in the range $67.6 - $107.5 billion. But African countries do not need to fill these gaps before proceeding with their economic transformations.[463] The economic costs of Africa's insufficient stock and poor quality of infrastructure are as big for the continent as the size of the potential impacts of resolving the problem. Funding infrastructure in Africa and around the world should not be an issue of financial resources from the public sector in advanced economies; rather, institutional investors such as insurance companies, pension funds, and sovereign wealth funds which have around $100 trillion in assets under management globally could step in.

A small fraction of the excess global savings and low–yield resources would be enough to plug the financing gap and finance productive and profitable infrastructure in the developing world. That would boost aggregate demand, create employment in poor and rich countries alike, and move the world toward peace and prosperity. In ideal political circumstances, a global pact between rich and poor nations would codify a "grand-bargain" based on infrastructure financing. But the world does not have ideal political circumstances. Economic decisions are rarely rational in the realm of dreams, and without the interference of political subjectivities and irrationalities. It is worth noting that when one dreams must wake up and act on the dreams.

---

463   African Economic Outlook, (2018); p. 64

African countries facing mammoth infrastructure need to have to change their focus and strategy. In fact, even if the continent had the resources, it should not devote them to financing infrastructure. No country or region in world history has ever had to fill its entire infrastructure deficit before igniting and sustaining high rates of growth. Indeed, in the 19th century's industrial revolution and the 20th century's miracle economies, countries from several global regions grew at high rates for long periods while having wide infrastructure deficits.

With an estimated infrastructure gap up to $107.5 billion a year and urgent needs in health, education, administrative capacity, and security, Africa has to attract private capital to accelerate the building of critical infrastructure needed to unleash its potential. This calls for a common position as a continent. The revamped foreign policies of the continent must reflect this position and the messaging out there need to be the same crystal clear to potential investors.

African countries need to accelerate their investments in infrastructure, but in a smarter way. And they need to find new mechanisms and instruments to fund their most urgent needs – infrastructure and otherwise. African countries can jump directly into the global economy by building well-targeted infrastructure. For example, Grand Inga Dam project, with a capacity of 43,200 megawatts (MW), can support current regional power pools, and their combined service can transform Africa from traditional to modern sources of energy and ensure clean and affordable electricity. Similar strategic and targeted project may support competitive industries and sectors in industrial parks and export – processing zones linked to global markets.[464] Using their limited resources for infrastructure more wisely for new investments and maintenance, all African countries can leverage these zones to attract light manufacturing from more advanced economies, as East Asia economies did in the 1960s and China in the 1980s.

By attracting foreign investment and firms, even the poorest African countries can improve their trade logistics, increase the knowledge and skills of local entrepreneurs, gain the confidence of international buyers, and gradually make local firms competitive. This strategy is already being used with great success in Bangladesh, Cambodia, Ethiopia, Mauritius, Rwanda, and Vietnam. The strategy need not be limited to traditional manufacturing but can also cover agriculture, services, and other activities. Africa is well placed to help the global economy. It is up to the world leaders to put forth the policy framework to make it happen.

---

464   Ibid, p.64

The positive impact of infrastructure on economic growth and inclusive social development has been well documented by researchers in several social science disciplines. Infrastructure affects productivity and output directly as part of GDP formation and as an input to the production function of other sectors.[465] It does so indirectly by reducing transaction and other costs, thus allowing a more efficient use of conventional productive inputs. Poor energy quality, for example, can impose additional costs on firms such as idle workers, lost production, or damaged equipment. But modern transport systems could increase manufacturing competitiveness cheaply and quickly, moving raw materials to producers and manufactured goods to consumers.[466]

High-quality infrastructure is essential for Africa to achieve the Sustainable Development Goals (SDGs) of the United Nations (UN), Agenda 2063 of the African Union (AU). It is needed for raising economic productivity and sustaining economic growth. Good infrastructure has an impact on growth directly and indirectly. It increases total factor productivity (TFP) directly because infrastructure services enter production as an input and have an immediate impact on the productivity of enterprises. It thus fosters aggregate economic output given its contribution, on its own, to GDP.[467]

Good infrastructure can also raise TFP indirectly by reducing transaction and other costs, allowing a more efficient use of conventional productive inputs. It does this by being a factor of production for virtually all goods and services generated by other sectors.[468] In addition, it can affect the adjustment costs of investment, the durability of private capital, and the demand for – and supply of – health and education services. If transport, electricity, or telecom services are absent or unreliable, firms face additional costs (buying power generators, for instance) and struggle to adopt new technologies. Better transport increases the effective size of labour markets.

By lowering transaction costs, infrastructure fosters more efficient use of productive inputs such as land, labour, and physical capital assets, which translates into higher TFP and expands the production frontier and profitable investment opportunities. For example, reducing the cost of broadband internet could foster the development of e-commerce and a digital economy. Other transmission channels include facilitating trade flows, stimulating aggregate demand, and improving a country's attractiveness as an investment destination.

As a short-term effect, infrastructure projects create jobs during construction, and by extension contribute to growth as illustrated by Tanzania's recent

---

465   Baro and Sala, (2004)
466   African Economic Outlook, ibid.
467   African Economic p 66.
468   Aschauer,(1993).

experience under the 5th Administration of President Dr. John Pombe Joseph Magufuli, whereby Nyerere Hydro Electric Power Plant and the Standard Gauge Railway (SGR) are under construction. Other such constructions include: Grand Ethiopian Renaissance Dam (GERD), and the crude oil pipeline project from Hoima (Uganda) to Tanga (Tanzania). All these projects have impacted positively on the economies of the respective countries.

Africa has a compelling case for accelerating infrastructure development. First, it is a continent of small, open economies that will rely on trade as the main engine of growth for the foreseeable future. For much of the period since World War II, there has been an intellectual consensus that barriers to market access – tariffs, quotas, and nontariff measures disadvantaging foreign firms; safety and sanitary requirements; local content and the like – were the main barriers to trade and to foreign direct investment in Africa. That view still has some validity, but the global landscape for production and trade has changed considerably in recent decades.

International trade is no longer about manufacturing a product in one country and selling it in another. It is about cooperating across boundaries and time zones to minimize production costs and maximize market coverage. Value chains (the networks of activities for producing and getting a product to consumers, spanning the manufacturing process and transport and distribute services) are the dominant framework for trade.

Reducing supply chain barriers could increase global GDP up to six times more than removing all import tariffs. Poor quality infrastructure services can increase the input material costs of consumer goods by up to 200 percent in certain African countries. In Madagascar for instance, supply chain barriers can account for about 4 percent of total revenues of a textile producer (through higher freight costs and increased inventories), eroding the benefits of duty-free access to export markets. Small and medium enterprises (SMEs) tend to face proportionally higher supply chain barriers and costs. Even a less ambitious set of reforms that moves countries halfway to regional best practice could increase global GDP by 2.6 percent and world trade by 9.4 percent. The main implication of this huge paradigm shift in global trade is that Africa policymakers should devote more time and resources to building some well-targeted infrastructure that can connect their economies to global value chains.

Africa's infrastructure stock is low, particularly in power; more than 640 million Africans have no access to energy, giving an electricity access rate for African countries at just over 40 percent – the world's lowest. Per capita consumption of energy in sub-Saharan Africa (excluding South Africa) is 180 kWh, against 13,000 kWh per capita in the United States and 6,500 kWh in Europe.

Access to energy is crucial not only for attaining health and education outcomes, but also for reducing the cost of doing business and unlocking economic potential, creating jobs. Insufficient access to modern energy causes hundreds of thousands of deaths each year due to the use of wood burning stoves for cooking, handicapping the operations of hospitals and emergency services, compromising educational attainment, and driving up the cost of doing business. Thus, energy access for all is one of the key drivers of inclusive growth because it creates opportunities for women, youth, and children in urban and rural areas.

As stated earlier, referring to the Grand Inga dam project, Africa's energy potential, especially renewable energy, is enormous, yet only a fraction is employed. Hydropower provides around a fifth of current capacity, but not even a tenth of its potential is utilized. Similarly, the technical potential of solar, biomass, wind, and geometrical energy is huge. Based on preliminary results, it is expected that Africa's investment needs for infrastructure overall will be in the range of $130 -$170 billion a year.[469]

The Africa Infrastructure Development Index (AIDI), produced by the African Development Bank, serves three main objectives: to monitor and evaluate the status and progress of infrastructure development across the continent, to assist in resource allocation within the framework of African Development Bank replenishments, and to contribute to policy dialogue within and outside of the Bank. The AIDI also serves as a key tool in evaluating and monitoring the continent's progress toward attainment of the "High 5s," the number one priority being to "light up and power Africa." The indicators produced by the AIDI also generate other indices relating to High 5s, namely the "Feed Africa Index," "Industrialize Africa Index," and "Integrate Africa Index."

The AIDI has four main components: transport, electricity, ICT, and water and sanitation. These components are disaggregated into nine indicators that have a direct or indirect impact on productivity and economic growth (AfDB,2013). A data reduction method generates a single index, normalized to lie between and 100. Thus, the higher the value of the index, the better a country's readiness in meeting its infrastructure needs for development.

In the updated version, there is a wide variation among African countries in their infrastructure gap, with a range of more than 90 percent between the country at the top having good infrastructure (Seychelles) and the country at the bottom (Somalia). The countries at the top are mostly from North Africa, with a few in Southern Africa. The rest of the continent is in very bad shape.

---

469   Ibid, p. 66

There is a high correlation between inequality in assets and the infrastructure index, suggesting that improving infrastructure leads to inclusive growth as well.

Although Africa, Asia, and Latin America started at similar levels in 1960, fixed capital formation (a proxy for infrastructure) declined in the 1980s and 1990s in Africa, partly due to Washington Consensus policies. While capital accumulation started to rise again from 2002, the pace is still much slower than in other developing regions.

This is partly due to this lack of investment in infrastructure building, Africa's infrastructure lags behind of other regions on quantity, affordability, and quality. For example, at the same level of GDP per capita, China and India both had higher access to electricity and water than most African countries.

In 2014, the share of population in Africa with access to electricity was estimated 47 percent, around half the 97 percent in Latin America and 89 percent in Asia. There are also stark regional differences, with access in North Africa around 98 percent (the highest) and 26 percent in East Africa (the lowest). Electricity access also varies greatly within countries: Urban consumers are typically better served than rural consumers, and across Africa in 2014, average electricity access was about 72 percent in urban areas, more than double rural Africa's 33 percent. The largest difference was in East Africa, where urban access was about 73 percent, nearly seven times the 11 percent in rural areas.

Access to improved sanitation also tends to be higher – though less starkly than for electricity in urban Africa (47 percent) than in rural Africa (34 percent). For Africa as a whole, access to improved sanitation was 36 percent in 2015, far lower than in Latin America (83 percent) and Asia (62 percent). This rate was lowest in West Africa (25 percent). The share of population using improved water sources (70 percent) or using basic drinking water services (63 percent) was the lowest in Africa, against more than 90 percent on Asia and Latin America. Despite rapid expansion in the use of mobile phones and mobile technology applications in Africa, internet penetration – a lifeline for modern trade, communications and technology applications in almost all sectors – has been progressing extremely slowly in the past decade.

Affordability is also a challenge. Infrastructure service costs in Africa are several multiples higher than in other developing regions, whether for power, water, transport, or ICT.[470] Energy is particularly expensive, notable for countries running small or isolated electricity grids and for net fuel importers. The average effective cost of electricity to manufacturing enterprises in Africa is close to $0.20 per kWh, around four times higher than industrial rates elsewhere in the world. This reflects both high–cost utility power (of around

---

470   Foster and Briceno, (2010)

$0.10 per kh), and heavy reliance on emergency back-up generation during frequent power outages (around $0.40 per kWh). Road freight tariffs in Africa are two-to-four times higher per kilometre than those in the United States, and travel times along key export corridors two-to-three times higher than those in Asia.

Africa's telecommunications costs have been falling sharply in recent years, but are still higher than those in other developing regions. Mobile and internet telephone charges in Africa are about four times higher than those in South Asia, and international call prices are more than twice as high. Connectivity of African countries to international broadband networks is nearly complete, but cost is a key factor affecting adoption. In Africa 1GB of data costs an average citizen nearly 18 percent of average income in 2016, against only 3 percent in Asia. Uncompetitive pricing policies of mobile telephone operators, such as charging more for calls to competitive networks, also making ICT relatively expensive.

Besides access, adequacy, and cost, the quality of infrastructure services is crucial for productivity and economic growth. Compared with other developing regions, electricity in Africa is not only scarce and expensive but also unreliable. Between 2006 and 2016, 79 percent of firms in sub-Saharan Africa experienced power outages – on average 8.6 power outages a month, with an average duration of 5.7 hours. Although roads are the predominant mode of transport, much of Africa's road network is unpaved, isolating people from basic education, health services, transport corridors, trade hubs, and economic opportunities, particularly in regions with high rainfall. Road safety is worrisome, with the region recording the highest rate of fatalities from road traffic injuries worldwide, at 26.6 per 100,000 population for 2013. Furthermore, the constant problem of highway-ambushes is petrifying.

Similar quality constraints are seen in port infrastructure where, in addition to limited capacity in terminal storage, operation, and maintenance, many ports lack the capacity even to handle large vessels. Several of them are hamstrung by inadequate infrastructure networks in the hinterland, such as railway lines and roads linked to ports, often leading to long delays at the ports. In 45 African countries, neither the current stock nor the access nor the quality of infrastructure drives economic growth in a context of low basic infrastructure endowment.

Poor infrastructure shaves up to 2 percent off Africa's average per capita growth rates. Only firms that have very high returns and engage in well-controlled markets can make a profit by operating in Africa: notably extractive industries in mining, oil production, and allied activities. Firms with high value addition, broad job opportunities, and wide sectoral linkages face serious setbacks.

Firms in Africa face adversities due to difficulties in powering their production operations. On average, power outages occur a quarter of the year, significantly increasing down time or exposing firms to costly energy substitute such as private generators. Progress thus far in this area has been very slow. Close to 60 percent of firms operating in Africa consider infrastructure (power shortages and costs and transport bottlenecks) as the most binding constraint they face in their daily operation. Even if most African countries have enhanced their electricity generation capacity, their progress in power distribution has been painfully slow, making the generated electricity unusable for productive purposes.[471]

The consequences of poor infrastructure are not just the opportunity costs of lost growth. They also include retard human development. Higher child mortality is driven by low access to basic services such as electricity and clean water.

The productivity loss and the cost to human development brought about by poor infrastructure will not go away without commitments by policymakers and leaders to embark on ambitious investments in the sector. First, African countries on average had lower access to electricity irrespective of the level of development, suggesting that what really matters is the political will and committed determination of countries to invest in power generation rather than their ability to afford it. Second and strengthening this point, some African countries provided access to electricity for large segments of their population, almost close to the East Asia average, while being relatively poorer.

10.1.3 Factors Explaining the Low Infrastructure Provision in Africa

10.1.3.1 Weak Legal, Regulatory, and Institutional Frameworks

Africa's legal, regulatory, and institutional frameworks are major constraints to attracting private capital to infrastructure. Ineffective or non-existent institutions also pose a challenge. Even when laws are enacted, they may not be implemented or may lack the implementation decrees. In the energy sector for instance, strong and credible financial institutions are required for the sector to work. Private sector players tend to participate in power generation as independent power producers (IPPs) and in the distribution to final consumers

---

471   Ibid, p. 73

(DISCOs). Between the two, a public company often owns the transmission lines and purchases the power produced by IPPs (off-taker) to sell it to DISCOs. The off-taker typically guarantees the payment of the IPPS production at a pre-agreed rate. The lack of a financially credible off-taker is often a major constraint for IPPS to negotiate and sign power purchase agreements, which can be mitigated through government guarantees backed by guarantee schemes from development finance institutions. This increases project costs and off-take tariffs.[472]

The often-inappropriate regulatory framework also limits private sector participation in infrastructure funding. For example, a large number of pension funds in Africa are not allowed to invest in infrastructure projects, even less so outside their countries. Given the small size of most economies and the cross-border nature of many infrastructure projects, this obstacle is crucial. When allowed, institutional investors may find it difficult to invest as they are often subject to stringent guidelines, such as those for the credit ratings of facilities they invest in, except in Botswana, Mauritius, Seychelles, and South Africa. Most pension funds lack the technical skills to assess complicated infrastructure. Fixing these failures would allow African pension funds to allocate up to $ 4.6 billion a year to infrastructure.

Another area that requires strong institutional intervention is the PPP framework. PPP agreements are often poorly structured and drafted due to lack of skills or experience in government departments. Lacking actual PPP laws, each project is then subject to individual workaround existing public investment laws and procurement regulations case by case. In the worst-case scenario, all project elements have to be developed at all levels of government, adding to uncertainty and extending project development times and complications in procurement. Overall, however, interest is growing for PPPs to support infrastructure in Africa, as reflected in the development of regulatory and institutional frameworks, with many African countries passing laws, national policies, regulations, and PPP units for implementation over the years.

10.1.3.2 Weaknesses in Infrastructure Planning and Project Preparation

The absence of well-defined infrastructure programs and bankable project pipelines is also a major issue in many African countries. At the core of the challenge: the private sector is not prepared to access, develop, and prepare infrastructure projects, given the costs, risks, and long-time horizons. That means governments, donors, and international financial institutions (IFIs) need

---

472   Ibid. p.77

to take action through long-term infrastructure planning based on population growth and development objectives and taking into account the economic importance of different regions of a country.

A lack of planning may also prevent a government from taking a programmatic approach to building infrastructure and implementing complementary projects to maximize benefits. For instance, a national highway passing through an agricultural region can be built or upgraded along with rural roads to ensure that farmers benefit from the highway: the multiplier effect at its best.

Even with infrastructure plans, individual projects need preparation to demonstrate their bankability and reach financial viability. Project preparation includes project identification, prefeasibility and feasibility studies (proof of concept), detailed studies (feasibility environmental and social impact, design), project structuring, and procurement concession agreements (including contract negotiation). Strong administrative capacity may also be required for setting up the laws, regulations, and institutions necessary for a specific project. This step can be challenging for African countries due to their lack of capacity and financing. Sometimes, an African country may lack the human capital in the public sector to undertake infrastructure project preparation, which can require highly skilled professionals, so many must seek external expertise.

The more complex the PPP structure, the more extensive the advisory service required. Even if a sufficiently skilled workforce exists in the public bureaucracy, it may be dispersed among multiple ministries and agencies and unable to work well together. Poor coordination between ministries can make this process complex and time consuming, therefore discouraging investors.

Another constraining issue in infrastructure development is the lack of funding for project preparation. In general, the preparation phase can be very risky for private entrepreneurs if they are not compensated when projects do not reach financial completion; this may happen with relatively high probability due to various obstacles. According to the NEPAD infrastructure Project Preparation Facility (IPPF), project development costs in Africa average 10 -12 percent of total project costs. At that rate, the cost of preparing the PIDA projects alone could be as high as $ 2.5 billion a year, far more than the $91.8 million currently available in the IPPF or $126 million for InfraCo Africa.[473] Given the estimated infrastructure funding need of $95 billion, project preparation costs can range from $9.5 billion to $11.4 billion, so the funding facilities are well below the needs.

During the operational phase, pricing of user charges by a regulator is often compromised by political motives without taking into consideration

473   Nepad Infrastructure, November, (2017)

the real cost of infrastructure service and the market pricing of the associated risks. Indeed, African countries have followed a distinct trend when pricing infrastructure services. Services are considered basic rights, and those with strong public-good characteristics have been provided below cost, including water, roads, commuter rail services, and to a varying degree, electricity. Road infrastructure services, for instance, have traditionally been provided toll-free. In the power and water sectors, illegal connections and under-collection of bills add to losses that undermine the financial stability of utilities.[474]

10.1.3.3 Governance and Corruption

Poor governance and political economy issues can be major bottlenecks for infrastructure development in Africa, frequently because these projects are complex. They require heavy and long-term investment, have strong public-good characteristics, a long-life, and high sunk costs. They are also very sensitive to local political conditions. These issues naturally affect private investors' risk perceptions of infrastructure funding in Africa.

Political rather than economic and social considerations may dictate where infrastructure projects are executed. In many African countries, airports, paved roads, and power plants are built to yield political benefits in the regions of powerful politicians, and end up as "white elephants". This was particularly common in the 1980s.[475] Political bias in project selection also leads to a large number of unfinished projects as new governments fail to complete old projects given their lack of economic returns or their perceived benefits favouring constituencies that may not support them.

Elections and political considerations can shift the composition of public spending toward "more visible" current expenditure instead of capital expenditures. A major infrastructure project can easily take more than five years from inception to commissioning. In this case, governments might prefer not to undertake such projects in one or two years since they will not be able to show outcomes ahead of the next election. In addition, political considerations may favour constructing new infrastructure as opposed to optimizing the use of what is already there.

The negative consequences of political considerations are often worsened by rent-seeking and corruption, lowering the quantity of productive public investment. Corruption also reduces the efficiency of public investment as corrupt officials give priority to projects that generate higher private material

---

474   Ibid. p.78.
475   Arezki et al. (2017)

and political gain over projects with higher social returns. In such circumstances, projects take a long time to develop and involve multiple stakeholders. Civil servants at different levels of responsibility play critical roles at various stages in the project development cycle, which increases their opportunities to seek bribes. Projects involve large sums of money and cumbersome regulatory systems with ambiguous rules, leaving room for subjective interpretations, weak accountability, and ineffective transparency mechanisms.[476]

Widespread corruption in infrastructure increases projects costs, lengthens delivery times, reduces output quality, and thus lowers benefits. It also undermines infrastructure maintenance and sustainability of benefits. In many countries, not only is there an infrastructure deficit, but the existing infrastructure, such as power plants and paved roads, is not regularly maintained. Bureaucrats may let the infrastructure deteriorate so that renovation and redevelopment will require more funds to siphon off. Vested interests may also stall critical infrastructure projects that displace rent-seeking activities. Strong political will and leadership at the highest level of government is necessary to overcome the powerful forces trying to keep the status quo.[477]

Political considerations and weak management capabilities can also lead to soft but pervasive forms of populism where households and firms do not pay bills, starving public utilities of revenue. Power and water infrastructure tend to record significant wastage. Transmission and distribution losses can be as high as 50 percent of the power output in many sub-Saharan African countries. In addition to those losses, illegal connections and under-collection of bills hamper the financial stability of utilities in Africa. Utilities typically collect only 70 to 90 percent of billings, and distribution losses can easily be twice as high as technical best practice. It is not unusual for revenues lost as a result of these inefficiencies to exceed the current turnover of the utilities. In the power sector, these losses have been estimated on average at 1.9 percent of GDP. For water utilities, the absolute value of the inefficiencies is smaller, with the average at 0.6 percent of GDP.

These quasi-fiscal costs represent a real financial burden on the public budget, since utilities that incur such deficits must ultimately resort to the state for investment finance and periodic bailouts. They may also represent real economic burden for the country, as underfunded utilities tend to run down their assets and provide low quality services. The revenues lost as a result of under-collection, distribution losses, and other inefficiencies amount to $6 billion a year.[478]

---

476   Stansbury, (2005).
477   African Economic, (op.cit.).
478   Foster and Briceno, (2010).

10.1.3.4 Regional Integration

A borderless Africa is the foundation of a competitive continental market that could serve as a global business centre. This would allow agricultural and industrial production across national boundaries and therefore offer economies of scale to investors while creating much bigger markets and providing new opportunities for small firms and large firms. Multiplier effects are best. Sustainable peace is paramount. The linkage of PIDA, CAADP, APSA is best. It would help eliminate monopoly positions while enhancing cross-border spill-overs between coastal and landlocked countries like South Sudan. At a deeper level, regional integration can improve regional security, since the expansion of international trade often correlates with a reduced incidence of conflict. Continental common foreign policies must therefore be geared towards promoting regional integration. As argued elsewhere, regional integration in this regard remains imperative.[479]

10.1.3.5 Increasing Labour Mobility

Migration is happening in Africa even if not all free movement of persons are ratified and implemented. Fully implementing all of them might increase flows among African countries. That makes it important to focus on what prevents countries from implementing the protocols. The Africa Union Passport, launched in July 2016 at the African Union Summit in Kigali, encourages the free movement of people in general and labour mobility in particular. Also, the first objective of the African Continental Free Trade Area is to "create a single continental market for goods and services, with free movement of business persons and investments, and thus pave the way for accelerating the establishment of the Continental Customs Union and the African customs Union. These are the two flagship projects of the agenda 2063 currently being implemented.

For these initiatives to be successful and effective, it is useful to proceed by first improving the effectiveness of the policies within each regional economic community (REC) before scaling up efforts to the continent. And because integration should happen not only in the goods market but also in factors of production, discussions should attend more to the free movement of persons.

---

479   Biswaro, (2012).

10.1.3.6 Integrating Financial Markets

Despite progress, financial markets in Africa are still weakly integrated. Bold reforms, especially at the institutional level, are needed to synchronize financial governance frameworks across the region and to remove any remaining legal restrictions to cross-border financial flows and transactions. It is important to pursue stronger technological advances in the harmonization of payment systems across the continent, as this would facilitate actual movement of funds across borders.

While the treaty creating the African Union envisions a single currency for Africa, and many RECs have plans to create regional currencies, these plans are in most cases more aspirational than concrete guides to national policy. Countries need to implement the institutional building needed to make a monetary union successful, such as close coordination of banking supervision, a willingness to come to the assistance of countries in economic crisis, and political federation to coordinate fiscal policies and control deficits.

10.1.3.7 Enhancing Cooperation for Regional Public Goods

Regional integration has always been about more than market access. Regional cooperation has always been important, if only because of the need for rail, roads, and other means of communication, and is now attracting more attention on several fronts. Beyond the eight RECs and seven other regional organizations aiming at deepening intra-regional trade, the majority of regional organizations deal with regional public goods: 5 deal with energy, 15 with the management of rivers and lakes, 3 with peace and security, and 1 with the environment.

Collective action by governments in the region should create positive spill-overs across the region that are greater than the spill-overs that individual governments acting alone could generate. This requires regional governance (approach) by a regional body with real authority over member states to deliver regional public goods. States must be willing to cede a significant amount of sovereignty to the body, something that has so far occurred only in the European Union. That is why most regional cooperation is intergovernmental. Each state retains veto power, and the regional organization is a secretariat to coordinate and harmonize policies set standards and provide services but without authority.

10.1.3.8 Focusing on the World Trade Organization's Facilitation Agreement

Reducing supply chain barriers to trade could increase global GDP up to six times more than removing tariffs. If all countries could bring border administration, together with transport and communications infrastructure, up to just half the level of global best practice, global GDP would grow by $ 2.6 trillion (4.7 percent), and total exports would increase by $ 1.6 trillion (14.5 percent).

Clearly, global value chains are now the dominant framework for trade. African countries such as Rwanda (Ethiopia and Morocco) are already taking advantage of this paradigm shift. Rather than wasting time in unproductive policy discussions over tariffs, they are redirecting their strategies to focus on trade facilitation.

The reduction in fixed trade costs related to time in customs and the associated monetary costs should encourage greater diversification of trade to other markets and in other products to the same market. It should also lead to greater participation in supply chain trade at both the regional and global levels, where goods have to cross borders multiple times.

Because duties and import restrictions may depend on the origin of imports, criteria are needed to determine the country of origin of a product. These are referred to as rules of origin, and they are an integral part of all trade agreements. Preferential rules of origin are used to enforce preferential schemes by establishing which products can benefit from preferential access.

Rules of origin will also have to deal with the regime-wide rules covering certification, verification, and cumulation. Because there are few differences in certification and verification methods across the African RECs, agreeing on them should be relatively easy – especially if, as recent evidence suggests, administrative costs are not as high as previously estimated. Thus, it might be easier to agree first on harmonizing rules governing certification and verification. In contrast, provisions on cumulation (treating of intermediates from other countries in the bloc or countries with special cumulation status) differ across RECs.

10.2 Features for Revamping African Foreign Policy Goals

10.2.1 The Situation Analysis

In foreign policy formulation, the definition of the situation includes all domestic and external, historical and contemporary conditions which are relevant and vital to policymakers in the face of foreign policy formulation challenges. Challenges can emanate from events abroad, domestic political needs, degree of threat or opportunity perceived in a situation, social values and ideological imperatives, availability of capabilities, expected outcomes or costs - benefits of proposed courses of action and so forth.

10.2.1.1 Images

Statesmen act and react according to their perception (or misperception) of their political environment; and as far as foreign policymakers are concerned, it is not the state of the environment that really counts, but what policymakers believe the state to be. According to Holsti (1967); "image means an individual perception of an object, fact or condition, his evaluation of that object, tact or condition in terms of badness or goodness, friendliness or hostility, or value, and the meaning ascribed to, or deduced from, that object, fact or condition". The discrepancy that exists between image and reality is due in part to physical impediment to the flow of information, arising from time, faulty communication, censorship, lack of competent advisors and intelligence source. It can also be as a result of distortion of reality caused by attitudes, beliefs and so forth. There have been instances where policymakers twisted and disregarded information that contradicted their preferences and values, thereby allowing their psychological environment to color the definition of the situation and physical environment

10.2.1.2 Attitudes

Hitler, in his totalitarian system, backed by this foreign number, relied on his images and attitudes to push all the decisions that eventually led to the Second World War. Attitudes are viewed as general evaluative propositions about a particular object or situation, factor or condition, more or less friendly, desirable, dangerous or hostile. In international relations or politics, policymakers operate or function with the framework of evaluation assumptions, or hostility or friendship, trust or distrust, fear or confidence toward other governments and people. Thus, attitudes are related to how policymakers react to external stimuli (i.e., others states' behavior, actions demanded). This reaction is grounded in their perception of other states' intention and capability, and then defines or formulate their own objectives vis-à-vis others.

10.2.1.3 Values

The nature and manner of our family values, political socialization, indoctrination, and our personal experience shape our values because they form the standards against which conducts of others are weighed. In the process of formulation of foreign policy, therefore, values serve justification for actions and goals for policymakers. Beliefs could be viewed as propositions that policymakers hold to be true, even if they cannot be verified. In a foreign-policymaking context, such beliefs are valuable because they become the unexamined assumptions upon which numerous policy choices are made.

10.2.2 Structure and Conditions in the International Political System

Policymakers of different nations perceive major structural changes in the international political system in almost the same way, and through a series of gathered information tend to attune their states' foreign policies to fit that structure. For instance, in a "polar" structure, policymakers of some newly independent countries have calculated that their security can best be achieved by alliance with one military bloc leader or other, without an option of neutrality. Thus, they are compelled by conditions in the international political system to either on the United States or Russia to safeguard their national security interest in order to survive as nations.

Therefore, the structure and conditions in the international political system have manifested significant influence on the newly independent states that they adjust their foreign policies in conformity with the rules and obligations of the alliance. This in effect establishes the limits of what general foreign policy orientations of the new states are. A major shift in international politics can bring in new power configuration that creates new opportunities for many states to recover their freedom from old limitations imposed by unfavourable balance of power in favour of constructing countervailing balance to deter new threats. Here we once again confirm that in international politics, there are no permanent friends (or enemy) but permanent interest. In contemporary time, development in the external environment can also influence a state's foreign policy because the international system possesses some doctrine which transcends national doctrine. The predominant international doctrine and value have come in the form of economic development. The prestige of a nation-state is closely related to the level of its military capability, technology and industrialization. Based on successes of the Western world, nation-states place high value on their influence in the international system.

10.2.3 Capabilities

The ability of a nation-state to significantly achieve its foreign policy objective greatly influences foreign policy decision-making. Most significant capabilities available include: diplomatic personnel and quality of diplomacy, military capability, technology communication, level of industrialization and so forth. These strongly determine the policy to be formulated within a time frame. Indeed, it is for this reason that developing countries are encouraged to define their interest and objective in terms of nation-building and economic development, and be content with neutrality (non-aligned). It is reasoned that the development of political and economic infrastructure would form a better base for the takeoff of other elements of power and capability. These are believed to underpin the process of formulation of foreign policy, which in turn projects a nation's interest abroad. The above suggest that a country's size, population, distribution of natural resources; climate and topography (geopolitics) influence socio-political and economic development, including access to other areas of the world. Also, these have military and defense policy implications.

10.2.4 Prevailing Domestic Needs

Foreign policy formulation focuses on general social needs and specific interest of domestic groups, political parties and economic organizations because demands and expectations are placed upon the government (state) in its interaction with others. Examples are when a government negotiates a tariff agreement (bilateral or multilateral) to protect its domestic industries, or intervene diplomatically or militarily in another country to protect the lives and property of its own citizens. Another is when country A establishes trade links with country B to create an avenue for a steady supply of a natural resource (from country B) population can influence (from process of formulation of foreign policy).

10.2.5 Public Opinion and Organizational Structures

In a political system where fundamental human rights and freedom of expression form part of the national life, the role of public opinion in the process of formulating foreign policy is formidable. There have been instances where public opinion has influenced foreign policymaking. Highly structured and developed bureaucracies play a role in the process of foreign policy formulation. Traditionally, information comes from and must have already been debated by officials of the relevant agencies that reflect all shades of views. In other words, factors that define a situation are usually complex and diverse because this involves a myriad of rival and competing institutions and interests. Examples of such government agencies include the Ministry of Foreign Affairs, the Institute of International Affairs (IIA) in most countries in Africa, and the National Advisory Committee on Foreign Affairs or Policy (NACFP).

10.3 Emerging Ingredients, Tools, and Issues for Revamping African Foreign Policies

An instrument of African foreign policy is a set of conventional principles, guidelines, strategies, rules and norms of African governments that define their external relations with other countries. These tools serve as instruments to achieve the national interests of the African nation. In implementing their foreign policy, African governments should continue to manage their 21st century relations worldwide through foreign ministries, embassies and consulates. In general terms, the tools/instruments of African foreign policy would be promoting national interests such as economic, political, and security interests. In achieving their foreign policy, governments use several approaches that range from peaceful negotiation and diplomacy to the use of military power.

Africa has 55 independent countries with different foreign policies. Taking this fact into consideration, one can argue that it is difficult to establish one foreign policy for all African countries' interests. Each country has its own characteristics. They are not all homogeneous, but rather heterogeneous. In spite of this heterogeneity, nonetheless, there are matters of fundamental and mutual common interests that they ought to pursue collectively in their foreign policy. Some of the common interests of African countries are the security and stability of the continent, sustainable economic development, good governance, democracy and human rights, technology transfer, development of culture, environment and the like UNSC reforms, Climate Change, Corruption etc. These matters of common interest can be translated into a single foreign policy document of the continent. Such foreign policy would help Africa be more proactive than reactive to the policies and interests of other countries.

A quick look at the current trends and interaction of the African Union member states with other big countries in the world, one can infer that the latter develop their own foreign policies towards the former and either a forum or a partnership will be established. This means that Africa is fulfilling the agenda of the great countries. But this does not mean that Africa is not getting some benefit from such interactions. Through such forums Africa could get political, economic and social benefits as well as experience-sharing in various fields. Just to mention one example, and despite the criticism, China built the new conference building of the African Union based on the partnership which has been established between them.

The vision of the African Union is to have "an integrated, prosperous and peaceful Africa, driven by its own citizens and representing a dynamic force in the global arena."[480] From this vision it is clear that the African Union should not be driven by the agenda from outside. The presence of a common foreign policy will help Africa have a clearly defined strategic partnership and approach to external relations. In designing a common foreign policy there is a need to have a consensus among member states of the African Union. However, the policy of the continent should not go down to specific policy details. Africa should develop its own foreign policy which is a mechanism for adopting common principles and guidelines in interacting with other countries. Currently, the African Union is promoting the active participation and contribution of African peoples in the development and integration of the continent. The following are some of essential ingredients, tools and issues that can constitute common African position and by extension, African foreign Policies which are vital for revamping any state's external relations. Further, it is worth noting that, they are dynamic and applicable in specific material conditions.

10.3.1 Silencing the Guns in Africa

Peace and stability are key ingredients for any nation to achieve its social and developmental goals. When there is peaceful coexistence between the citizens of a nation and between its neighbours, the opportunities for social, culture and economic interaction and integration increase. Promoting peace, security, and stability on the continent is one of the key activities of African Union (AU), as the linkages between peaceful environment and sustainable development are naturally evident.

---

480   AU Agenda 63

The AU agenda 2063 places importance on the aspiration for a peaceful and secure Africa and one of the flagship initiatives is that of Silencing the Guns by 2020 which aims to drive the African agenda to end wars and civil conflicts, and prevent genocide.

Significant progress has been made towards Silencing the Guns in Africa in spite of the common narrative of Africa being a continent always at war with itself with severe humanitarian consequences. In 2002 when AU was formed as a successor to the Organization of African Unity (OAU), there were around 28 conflicts/crises. By 2009 these had reduced to around seven, due to initiative of the AU Peace and Security Council (PSC).

The achievements in the reduction of conflict is the result of the efforts deployed by Members of the AU promoting peace, security, stability development to all African citizens by forming dialogue-centred conflict prevention and reconciliation as well as peacebuilding efforts in member states emerging from violent conflicts. Specific strengthening of national infrastructures for addition, the AU deploys troops for the protection of citizens in conflict zones to maintain peace and stability in the continent. However, the era of terrorism and violent extremism affecting Northern Africa, the Sahel, western and Central Africa has changed the nature of armed conflict, requiring strategies to identify and address the causes leading to armed conflict.

The African Peace and Security Architecture is the African Union's blueprint for peace, security, and stability in Africa. The Centre of the APSA is the PSC, which is the AU's decision-making organ for the prevention, management, and resolution of conflicts as well as on post-conflict Reconstruction and Development. The PSC is supported, in the discharge of its mandate, by various structures, namely: the AU Commission, the Panel of the Wise, the Continental Early Warning System (CEWS), the African Standby Force (ASF), and AU Peace Fund. The PSC has developed the AU Master Roadmap (AUMR) on practical Steps to Silence the Guns in Africa. The Master Roadmap is premised on the principle that Africa should assertively assume total responsibility for its destiny, which contributes to building prosperity and the wellbeing of African citizens. The Roadmap is geared towards effective interventions on conflict prevention, management, resolution and post-conflict reconstruction and development, which would contribute to the goal of Silencing the Guns in Africa. Within the framework of APSA, the AU continues to work with strategic partners such as the European Union (EU), United Nations (UN) and other bilateral partners in its efforts towards attaining peace on the continent.

The Peace and Security Council meeting held in June 2017 made several recommendations on working towards Silencing the Guns including:

i.   African Member States to sign, ratify and implement all relevant AU and international instruments related to silencing the guns in Africa, in particular the Arms Trade Treaty, which will play a great role in this initiative;

ii. Encouraged political actors, especially political partners and parliaments, to foster conducive conditions that contribute to the preservation of peace, security, and cohesion and encouraged them to use Agenda 2063, as a guide for elaboration of their manifestos and programs.

iii. Highlighted the need to capacitate law enforcement agencies to enable them effectively contribute to stopping inflow of illicit weapons into Africa, and at the same time curb the circulation of illicit weapons within the continent, and also enhance capacity, seize and destroy illicit weapons;

iv. Recommended the declaration of the African day,25 May, as an Amnesty Day for surrender and collection of illegally owned weapons/arms to designated national law enforcement agencies;

v. Multi-stakeholder collaborative effort –AUC, Regional Economic Communities (RECs), policymakers, civil society organizations, private sector-to take all necessary measures to fully implement the AU Master Roadmap to find sustainable solutions to conflict/crises situations in the continent.

Some of the ongoing actions being taken by the AU to deliver on Silencing the Guns include:

a. Establishment of the AU Peace Fund to secure financing for Africa's peace support operations and to promote Africa's ownership of its peace and security agenda by establishing a foundation for creating a more responsive international peace and security architecture.

b. Establishment of the Nouakchott and Djibouti Processes for the enhancement of security cooperation and intelligence sharing in the Sahel and Eastern Africa regions, respectively, to respond to existing and emerging security challenges such as extremism, terrorism, and transnational threats.

c. Appointment of H.E. Ramtane Lamamra of Algeria as the AU High Representative for Silencing the Guns in Africa,

d. Declaration of September of each year, until 2020, as "Africa Amnesty Month" for the surrender and collection of illegally owned weapons and arms. During Africa Amnesty Month:

- Persons who surrender their illegally owned weapons/arms shall not be subjected to disclosure, humiliation, arrest or prosecution;
- Persons who fail to surrender their illegally owned weapons/arms beyond the Africa Amnesty month shall automatically be considered to be in violation of national laws of Member States.

- All members States, RECs/RMs as well as civil society organizations shall give wide publicity to the Africa Amnesty Month through media networks within their territories and regions;
- Member States will adhere to and promote Africa Amnesty Moth, September each year, and mobilize their citizens to actively participate in the efforts to silence the guns.

In respect of the AU flagship project on "Silencing the Guns in Africa by 2020" and implementation of the African Union Master Roadmap (AUMR) of Practical Steps to Silence the Guns in Africa, the timeframe for its full implementation should be extended to give additional time for Member States and Regional Economic Communities and Regional Mechanism (RECs/RMs), with the support of relevant stakeholders such as civil society organisations and the private sector as well as the United Nations (UN) system to continue implementing the various aspects in the AU Master Roadmap. This extension should be informed by a review of what has been done on this issue thus far. In addition, within the framework of the ongoing laudable efforts on silencing the guns in the Continent, there is a need to create conducive conditions for sustainable development, promotion of inclusive political dialogue for the settlement of disputes using AU mechanisms on mediation, good neighbourliness, dialogue, reconciliation and pacific settlement of disputes provided for within the framework of the African Peace and Security Architecture (APSA) and African Governance Architecture (AGA). In this regard, efforts towards silencing the guns should ensure the rejection of all forms of external military intervention and interference in the continent's affairs.

The African Union's campaign on Silencing the Guns in Africa by 2020 aims at achieving a conflict-free Africa, preventing genocide, making peace a reality for all and ridding the continent of wars, violent conflicts, human rights violations, and humanitarian disasters. The campaign aims to promote prevention, management and resolution of conflicts in Africa. Silencing the Guns is a slogan of a project that targets silencing all illegal weapons in Africa. September 2020 was declared amnesty month where those with illegally-acquired guns could hand them in to the authorities without penalty. The campaign targeted member states because the primary responsibility of providing peace and security and the overall protection of citizens lies with governments. It is also putting an emphasis on the youth.

10.3.2 Combating Climate Change

Concern over the negative impact of climate change has strengthened fears that environmental degradation and demographic pressures will displace millions of people in Africa and create serious social upheaval. Most scientists studying the potential impact of climate change have predicted that Africa is likely to experience higher temperatures, rising sea levels, changing rainfall patterns, and increased climate variability, all of which could affect much of its population. Higher temperatures, the drying up of soils, increased pest and disease pressure, shifts in suitable area for growing crops and livestock, increased desertification in the Sahara region, floods, deforestation, and erosion are all signs that climate change is already happening and represents one of the greatest environmental, social and economic threats facing the continent:

The impact of climate change will follow disproportionate on the world's poorest countries, many of them in Africa. Poor people already leave on the frontlines of pollution, disaster and degradation of resources and land. For them, adaptation is a matter of sheer survival. Africa is the least emitter of carbon dioxide gas (or source of pollution) compared with the industrialized countries. Yet it seems to be the most affected.

As observed above, the African continent as a whole is facing unprecedented pressure owing to various extreme weather events and slow-onset events accentuated by climate change, including flash floods, heavy rainfall, water scarcity and drought, displacing thousands of people and causing deaths in North Africa; landslides, which have caused thousands of deaths in Central Africa; severe drought, affecting livestock, water, crops, wildlife and the energy sector in East Africa; extreme events in the Western Africa region, which have caused flash floods, resulting in the loss of lives, displacing thousands and destroying infrastructure; and cyclones and drought, which have caused the deaths of thousands and destroyed homes and properties in southern Africa.[481]

Advancing Africa's Climate Change Agenda, including supporting Africa's negotiations on climate change at global level, through facilitation of effective coordination around African Common Position on Climate Change, and formulation of an African Climate Change Strategy is crucial. This includes: enhancing capacities of member states and RECs to access near-real time environmental, natural resources, and climate information for policy and decision-making, and development planning by improving Africa's exploitation of earth observation technologies through the implementation of the Monitoring for Environment and Security in Africa (MESA) programme

---

481   AU 33 Summit Rpt.

formerly called the African Monitoring of the Environment for Sustainable Development (AMESD) Program; and operationalizing, in partnership with UNECA and AfDB, the program on Climate for Development in Africa.[482]

Building Member States' capacities for improved performance in terms of discharging their responsibilities and deriving benefits from Multilateral Environmental Agreements (MEAs) is crucial. Implementation of the Great Green Wall for the Sahara and Sahel Initiative (GGWSSI), as part of the efforts to combating land degradation and desertification, is inevitable. The Initiative serves as an important platform and instrument towards bringing together key actors and partners at various levels for a concerted action. Advancing the African Water and Sanitation agenda, in terms of implementation of the Sharm El-Sheikh Commitments on Water and Sanitation, and supporting the Water Basin initiatives is important.

The responsibility of spearheading climate change was given to H.E. Cyril Ramaphosa, the President of the Republic of South Africa. He was to supervise the outcomes of the 25th Conference of the Parties to the United Nations Framework Convention on Climate Change (COP 25); 15th Meeting of the Parties serving as the Conference of the Parties to its Kyoto Protocol (CMP 15) and the Second Session Conference of the Parties should serve as the Meeting of the Parties to the Paris Agreement. The AU has unwavering common position on this matter.

10.3.3 Enhancing United Nations Reforms

In promoting the reformation of the United Nations, the African Union adopted the Ezulwini Consensus. The consensus is a position on international relations and reform of the United Nations, agreed by the African Union, that calls for a more representative and democratic Security Council in which Africa like all other world regions is represented.

The consensus is named after Ezulwini where the agreement was made in 2005, a valley in central Swaziland now known as the Kingdom of Eswatini with several tourist hotels. Some of us participated in this meeting, and naming the consensus was our brain child. The consensus was then adopted at an Extraordinary Session of the Executive Council of the African Union in March 2005 in Addis Ababa. African countries' demand in reforming the United Nations includes getting at least two permanent seats (including veto power), and five non-permanent seats on the Security Council. The African Union would choose which African governments get the seats and calls for ECOSOC to be strengthened.

---

482   ClimDEV Africa.

The Ezulwini Consensus was followed by the Sirte Declaration of July 2005, which required at least two permanent seats and two non-permanent Security Council seats for African states. It is important that a balance be maintained between the consideration of security and development issues at all levels. To this effect, an African Union Standing Committee of Ten led by Sierra Leone is responsible to follow up inter alia, this matter within the broader context of UN reforms. The special needs of Africa, as recognized in the Millennium Declaration, also ought to be taken into account in this context. In addressing poverty, it is important to welcome the innovative idea of a timetable for fulfilling the commitment of 0.7% of GDP as Overseas Development Assistance (ODA) and to take into consideration the recommendations on ODA within the larger framework of the Millennium Declaration's focus on Africa's Special Needs. In addressing this issue, the Secretary-General, in the preparation of his report, should take into account the recommendations of the Report by the World Commission on the Social Dimension of Globalisation, entitled: "A Fair Globalisation: Creating Opportunities for All", as it provides a crucial base for addressing poverty and other systemic issues that impede Africa's development.

The power of the Security Council to impose sanctions should be exercised in accordance with the United Nations Charter and international law. Sanctions should be considered only after all means of peaceful settlement of disputes under Chapter VI of the United Nations Charter have been exhausted and a thorough consideration undertaken of the short-term and long-term effects of such sanctions. Sanctions should also be smart and targeted to mitigate their humanitarian effects.[483] In this regard, there is need for the UN to define the objectives and guidelines for the imposition of sanctions.

As part of the support of the international community to peacebuilding in post-conflict countries in Africa, there is need for the Bretton Woods institutions, in particular, to show sensitivity in demanding macro-economic reforms that have a potential for social upheaval. This underlines the necessity for the Bretton Woods institutions, which are part of the United Nations system, to become more accountable, democratic and transparent in their structure so that their operation will enjoy the full confidence of the entire world. It is important to lay down clear rules for the deployment of UN peacekeeping operations to avoid arbitrary use of the right of veto that may delay or obstruct such deployment when the need for deploying peacekeeping forces arises. This task was given to the Republic of Sierra Leon to lead the AU Committee on UN reform. It dutifully reports to every AU summit on the progress and has been doing well.

---

483   Biswaro, (2013).

10.3.4 African Asset Recovery

The African Union advocates for strengthened tax cooperation to stem Illicit Financial Flows (IFFs) through the High-Level Panel on Illicit Flows from Africa. The Panel, which was established to improve the knowledge of the nature, scale and impact of illicit financial flows and to track and stop the outflows, estimates that the continent loses over 50 billion dollars annually to illicit outflows.

The estimates that commercial activities are by far the largest contributor to IFFs, accounting for 65% due to abusive transfer pricing, trade mispricing, over invoicing of the services and intangibles, equal contracts and tax evasion. Criminal activities account for 30% percent due to money laundering, trafficking and smuggling of people, drugs and arms. Corruption and abuse of office account for 5 percent of the illicit outflows.[484] These figures highlight the urgency to identify modalities and steps that must be taken to radically reduce these outflows and to ensure that these development resources remain within the continent as well as the need to improve and enforce good governance and sustainable improvements in the business environment.

Reflecting on the effectiveness of the approach to fight corruption on the continent, the AU report on the progress on implementation of the 2018 theme of the year gives a preliminary assessment of the implementation of the activities towards the fight against corruption and similarly concludes with some key findings and recommendations. The report by H.E. Muhammadu Buhari, President of the Federal Republic of Nigeria and Champion of the AU theme of the year 2018 "Winning the Fight against Corruption: A sustainable Path to Africa's Transformation," identifies key priorities, notably, the development of a Common African Position on Asset Recovery: the development of an African Anti-Corruption Methodology as well as continued advocacy on the issue of Illicit Financial Flows through the Consortium on Illicit Financial Flows.[485]

Following on the commitment to stem graft on the continent in 2019, the AU Assembly adopted the Nouakchott Declaration on the African-Anti-Corruption Year, in which AU member states committed to progressively abolish bank secrecy jurisdictions and tax havens on the continent, establish public beneficial ownership registers and ensure that public officials declare their assets. The Assembly also called allies to agree on transparent and efficient timetable for the recovery and return of stolen assets to Africa while respecting the sovereignty of States and their national interests.

---

484   AU ECHO, (2020), p. 12
485   ibid

In seeking a common framework to enable the fight against illicit financial flows, the swift recovery and return of African Assets and transparency in the utilization of returned assets, the AU, through its organ, the African Union Advisory Board on Corruption (AUABC), has embarked on a progressive approach for the development of the Common African Position (CAP) on assets recovery, an institutional framework to support coherent and stream-lined administrative strategies on the recovery of stolen assets. The development of a common African Position on Assets Recovery is timely and critical in ensuring that Africa presents a united front in dealing with internal and external challenges being faced in the recovery of African assets.

In 2019, the AUABC embarked on a consultative process to establish the legal, policy, procedural and institutional framework regulating asset recovery in all 55 AU member states. The process included the collation of information from member states as relates to initiative undertaken to asset recovery, the challenges encountered and the measures of redress as well as recommendations. As of October 2019, fifteen member states had submitted their data. Those countries were: Benin, Ghana, Cote d'Ivoire, Kenya, Lesotho, Malawi, Mali, Mauritius, Mozambique, Namibia, Senegal, South Africa, Togo, Zambia and Tanzania.

The data will be key in unpacking the numerous internal and external obstacles faced by African countries in recovering the stolen assets. The absence of comprehensive policies, lack of technical capacity and ineffective inter-agency cooperation have often been cited as main challenges hampering recovery efforts of stolen assets. Other constraints include: moderate investigative knowledge, the inherent secrecy of the activities, inadequate resource allocation to financial aspects of the crime, inadequate use of reports by investigators, and customs agencies on suspicious transactions. Other constraints as per the Mbeki Report (AU/ECA,2015) are: over-reliance on unpredictable foreign assistance, duplication, and overlapping of functions. The development of the CAP will also be key in defining effective collation between African states and external agencies such as Interpol, money transfer agencies and central bank in their respective countries to ensure assets recovery.

The 3rd edition of the African Anti-Corruption Dialogue, convened in 2019, focused on the development of the Common African Position on Asset Recovery. The dialogue brought together the AU Permanent Representative Committee; national Anti-Corruption agencies, civil societies, media, academia, and international organizations to deliberate on the development of a Common African Position on Asset Recovery. Held under the theme "Towards a Common African Position on Asset Recovery," the meeting made the following eight critical observations towards developing the CAP:

- The quest for the recovery of African Assets must be situated and contextualized in the broader historical, political, economic and social narrative of Africa including demands for the return of stolen African artefacts and reparations for slavery and colonization of Africa.
- The technical and legal processes involved in recovery of African assets are complex and unduly lengthy and CAP must ensure that legal and other processes are streamlined and simplified.
- While noting that the development of the CAP is in part a technical process, it must further be recognized that it is also fundamentally a political one. Therefore, the CAP shall require a strong political will and ownership by African Leaders and its development shall be conducted in accordance with the African Union's policymaking processes.
- The CAP should address measures to prevent further loss of African assets. It should propose mechanisms and strategies to ensure that financial institutions identify and refuse to accept Illicit Financial Flows.
- The CAP should prioritize the creation and establishment of an asset recovery database including information required to facilitate asset recovery such as the legal framework and applicable processes in the destination countries, the requirement's for mutual legal assistance and list of experts. In addition, there is need for further research and data into the field.
- The CAP should incorporate five pillars namely asset identification, asset repatriation, asset management, applicable legal frameworks and institutional mechanisms.
- Inter-agency collaboration and mutual legal assistance, experience sharing and learning remain key in asset recovery processes. The inclusion and participation of all stakeholders such as the Legislature, Civil Society Organizations, regional Economic Communities, the media, the Academia will enhance its development and implementation.
- The CAP should be accompanied by a robust communication and implementation strategy and action plan which is well resourced and has support at the highest level in order to promote better understanding of the Common African Position and its role in the transformation of African lives under agenda 2063.

The report with these far-reaching recommendations was submitted for consideration by the AU policy organ in 2020. Worth noting is the fact that Africa has experienced strong economic growth with an average of around 5% since 2000. However, the growth has not substantially reduced poverty and inequality nor led to job creation on the continent.

In recognition of limited budgetary resources, scarcity, volatility of development assistance, the scale of socio-economic destruction evidence by sluggish or ceased development plans and programmes due to undue diversion of resources through corruption, the AU has, over the years, deepened the resolve, focus and expertise for addressing the many facets of corruption on the continent as a prerequisite for the realization of the goals articulated in "Aspiration 3" of Africa's development framework, Agenda 2063, which seeks an Africa of good governance, respect for human rights, justice and the rule of law. Strong institutions have often been cited as a necessary condition in the fight against corruption.

It is quite evident that corruption has a devastating impact on marginalized communities, especially the youth, women and children. Corruption breeds unequal societies, renders vulnerable groups prone to human trafficking, and recruitment into armed groups and militia. In effect, corruption deprives our young citizens of opportunities to develop meaningful livelihoods. We must therefore, work together to defeat this evil.

The designation of year 2018 as the African Anti-Corruption year and annual commemoration of the 11th of July as the African Anti-Corruption Day, therefore, have been among the deliberate actions by the AU to scale up advocacy efforts and broaden partnership towards the realization of tangibles efforts in the fight against graft. These actions have also been crucial in supporting the implementation of policy framework, such as the African Union Convention on Preventing and Combating Corruption (AUCPCC) adopted in 2003.

Efforts have yielded commendable policy action by member states on the implementation and monitoring of anti-corruption strategies. As of October 2019, 43 member states had ratified the African Union Convention on Preventing and Combating Corruption while another 25 member states had also undertaken to implement domestic reforms to strengthen anti-corruption measures. Lessons from the African Anti-Corruption year 2018 showed that there is a need to strengthen and further capacitate national anti-corruption agencies and related institutions to ensure their functional autonomy as well as capacitate the African Union Advisory Board on Corruption (AUABC) to understand the challenges of member states in ratifying and domesticating the convention.

The AU has been keen to rally citizens' participation on AU-led anti-corruption initiatives across the continent and a correlated increase in knowledge on the dangers of corruption on socio, economic and political transformation of Africa. This has also provided a platform for strengthened partnership with key stakeholders including national anti-corruption agencies, supreme audit institutions, civil society organizations and the media. It is through the deepened collaboration that the Africa Group at the United Nations successfully led an initiative to have a resolution on IFFs adopted by the UN general Assembly.

Various youth-led activities such as the African Youth Congress Against Corruption (AYCAC) have since adopted the Youth Declaration against Corruption and endorsed the establishment of the African Youth Community of Practice on Anti-Corruption (AYCPAC) as a framework for coordination of youth-led efforts in the fight against corruption in Africa. The consultative process has been critical in consolidating the gains and in driving momentum for the legal and political frameworks to enhance the fight against corruption and accountability and transparency in the continent. Furthermore, the Common African Position on Asset Recovery is viewed as a continental policy and advocacy tool to strengthen the combat of illicit financial flows.

African countries are now implementing Agenda 2063 and the Sustainable Development Goals (SDGs), both of which highlight the importance of domestic resource mobilization (DRM) as a core priority for sustainable development. For instance, the 2015 Addis Ababa Action Agenda (AAAA) on Financing for Development emphasized that "for all countries, public policies and the mobilization and effective use of domestic resources, underscored by the principle of national ownership, are central to our common pursuit of sustainable development, including achieving the sustainable development goals."[486] Moreover, DRM is also a priority for the Africa Union (AU)'s Agenda 2063 as African countries resolved "to look inwards to mobilize domestic resources to finance and accelerate its transformation, integration, peace, security, infrastructure, industrialization and democratic governance and strengthen continental institutions."[487] It is planned that DRM should account for 75% to 90% of the Agenda 2063 financing for every country, with other sources (official development assistance and international financial markets) contributing the remaining capital requirements.[488] At the continental level, High Level Panel on illicit Financial Flows from Africa established in 2011 has received a lot of attention while raising awareness on the strategic importance of IFFs and related issues. Under the auspices of the AU/African Commission (AUC), various conventions such as the Convention on Preventing and Combating Corruption (CPCC) and the Younde Declaration on Combating Illicit Financial Flows (YDCIFF) from Africa have been adopted but not ratified by all African countries. Other Africa specific initiatives include the African Tax Administration Forum (ATAF) and the Collaborative African Budget Reform Initiatives (CABRI) aimed at ensuring financial reforms.

---

486   UN, (2015).
487   AUC, (2015a).
488   AUC,2015b; Nnadozie et al.,(2017).

10.3.5 Preservation of African Arts, Culture and Heritage

The tool promotes the unprecedented initiative by the champion to establish a panel of peers on arts, culture and heritage in charge of formulating strategic orientations, ensuring that the orientations are taken into consideration in the activities of the African Union, and at the regional level, playing the role of leadership, advocacy and facilitation. The importance of culture, arts and heritage in the achievement of the objectives and the flagship projects of African Union Agenda 2063 is understood. The emphasis was that the rich and diverse African heritage is an essential asset to profile the continent in the global arena and to build sustainable development, integration and peace in Africa. Mali remains the leader in this regard. This tool was put under the flagship of President of the Republic of Mali to act as an African Union Champion for the Promotion of Arts, Culture and Heritage on the Continent.

10.3.6 A Friendly Migration Framework

Throughout its history, Africa has experienced migratory movements, both voluntary and forced, which have contributed to its contemporary demographic landscape. In many parts of the continent, communities are spread across two or three nation-states, and movement is often not limited by political boundaries. Cross-border migration in Africa is an important livelihood and coping strategy during times of ecological and economic downturn and lack of employment and decent work, and is key to understanding, as well as forecasting, the onset and evolution of humanitarian disasters.

The globalisation process has also facilitated the movement of people across the various regions of Africa and to other regions outside the continent, as the number of migrants continues to increase. Due to these trends, migration is a major issue in the 21st Century, and poses social, economic and political challenges for policymakers engaged in the management of migration for the betterment of the continent.

In light of the challenges posed by migration and its ramifications (socio-economic, political etc), the OAU Council of Ministers adopted Decision CM/Dec 614 (LXXIV) during the 74th Ordinary Session in Lusaka, Zambia in July 2001, which called for the development of a Migration Policy Framework, and mandated the following:

- To develop a strategic framework for migration policy in Africa that could contribute to addressing the challenges posed by migration and to ensure the integration of migration and related issues into the national and regional agenda for security, stability, development and cooperation;

- To work towards the free movement of people and to strengthen intra-regional and inter-regional cooperation in matters concerning migration, on the basis of the established processes of migration at the regional and sub-regional levels; and
- To create an environment conducive to facilitating the participation of migrants, in particular those in the Diaspora, in the development of their own countries. This culminated in the AU Migration Policy Framework (MPFA) which was adopted in Banjul, Gambia in 2006.

The 2006 MPFA provided comprehensive and integrated policy guidelines to AU Member States and RECs, which were encouraged to take into consideration in their endeavours to promote migration and development and address migration challenges on the continent. It provided policy guidelines in nine thematic areas, namely: Labour Migration; Border Management; Irregular Migration; Forced Displacement; Human Rights of Migrants; Internal Migration; Migration Data Management; Migration and Development; and Inter-State co-operation and partnerships. Global inequality, the lack of employment and decent work, poverty, conflict, gender inequalities and discrimination, terrorism and climatic pressure continue to drive people to search for a better life abroad. Mixed flows, consisting of different types of migrants and asylum seekers that use the same migration routes and means, have been on the rise, as legal migrants are falling prey to smugglers and human traffickers.

Consequently, the lack of legal pathways for migration has contributed to record numbers of deaths in the Mediterranean Sea, with more than 5,000 people losing their lives in 2016 alone. Reliable data on migrant deaths on other routes remain scanty, which means that even more people may be dying crossing the Red Sea and the Sahara Desert. These dynamics have strained and called into question the world's refugee system, which is struggling to provide adequate protection to more than 21 million refugees. In addition, the notion of a growing migration "crisis" and international terrorism have led to policies that seek to deter migration and jeopardize the protection of the rights of migrant women and men.

The AU launched Africa's development strategy for the next half century, Agenda 2063, which aspires to an integrated and politically united Africa and calls for the free movement of people, capital, goods and services.

Continental economic integration builds on the work of the RECs, and the implementation of their free movement of persons protocols will serve as legal instruments for managing migration and mobility on the continent. Cross border trade and development is hampered by Africa's stringent visa regimes, which are expected to be liberalized incrementally through the implementation of the AU Free Movement of Persons Protocol. Migration and mobility within the context of Africa's integration will play a key role in unleashing the continent's growth potential.

Agenda 2063 advocates for the free movement of people as part of the continental integration agenda to contribute to significant increases in trade and investment among African countries, which would in turn strengthen Africa's position in global trade. Globally, and in Africa, states need to cooperate to harness the development benefits which migration brings, and to control who enters and stays on their territory. The free movement of persons in Africa, effective migration governance and strengthened interstate cooperation on migration should aid Africa's development and security.

10.4 Conclusion

The thrust of our discussion in this work, has significantly centred on revamping foreign policy ingredients, tools and dynamics in Africa from theoretical and practical perspectives. Its formulation, decision, conduct and goals have been interrogated, the fundamental question of national interests and the debate surrounding its objectivity as well as subjectivity featured. The crucial tools among which diplomacy plays critical role as a first line of defense is highlighted. As argued, these tools are not new to Africa. Pre-colonial Africa had its diplomacy, though not much documented. With the coming of foreigners, this practice was relegated to the barricade of history. However, the nationalism that followed colonialism and consequently postcolonial Africa saw the formation of the then OAU with principal agenda of liberation of the continent from the yoke of colonialism and apartheid system. This struggle that assumed different forms reached its logical conclusion towards the end of the 20th century. The foreign policies of independent Africa, to a large extend, reflected these historic struggles for emancipation. The new millennium witnessed fundamental changes in the globe.

The African continent had to respond to these new realities. Therefore, it transformed the OAU into the African Union (AU) in 2002 which has an expanded mandate. The new organization came with Agenda 2063, which is the blueprint of the continent referred to as "*the Africa we want*". As aptly captured in this book, the agenda has comprehensive aspirations and flagships. Its implementation depends largely on Africans themselves. The spirit and policy of self-reliance is high on the agenda. Between 75% and 90% of its implementation costs have to be domestically mobilized. Given human and material capital, this is possible. Africa is not poor though Africans are poor because billions of dollars continued to be siphoned from Africa, day in, and day out, mainly to enrich former colonial powers and keeping the continent underdeveloped. The continent is endowed with a lot of resources. The reports on the IFF speaks volumes. Plugging these holes could be a great game changer. All that is needed is a proper harnessing, nurturing and utilization of those resources, because the capacity is there.

This new way would include taking on board the private sector in the context of public- private partnership (PPP). African countries should embrace the private sector which accounts for over 80% of the total gross national product, two-thirds (2/3) of total investment, and three-fourths (3/4) of lending within the economy. It also provides jobs for about 90% of the employed working-age population. Small Medium Enterprises (SME) should be the backbone of the African private sector accounting for over 90% of the businesses in Africa and translating to 63% of the employment in low-income countries while contributing to over 50% of the growth domestic product of the African states. Although trends in the intra- African trade point toward progress, trade within Africa remains very low in proportion to total global trade highlighting the need for enhancing intra-African trade. The tides, however, look promising with the operationalization of the AfCFTA. The AfCFTA is expected to increase intra-African trade by over 50% and will boost the continent's GDP by more than $40 billion and exports by more than $55 billion. The common market is expected to upscale the prospect in the agriculture sector, a bedrock of employment for the majority of Africans, by improving regional market access thereby stimulating growth. Visionary and committed leadership is critical. Above all, political will is crucial. This prospect underscores the need to leave no one behind in moving forward with the agenda of the "Africa we want".

To achieve this, regular training and refresher courses in negotiation and communication skills of the staff in the foreign services and relevant institutions are required. This should involve everybody across the board whether a career diplomat or what other scholars have referred to step children of the foreign service. This training should cover all fields and disciplines related to international politics. Preparation will be critical. Above all, proper staffing of our institutions, embassies and missions based on meritocracy will be necessary. Wining and whisking must be accompanied by productivity.

While regional and international partnership is crucial to the development of Africa, and therefore a principal objective of African foreign policy, the core principle of foreign policy as an extension of domestic policy must remain pivotal to a well-grounded, confident, sovereign, internationally respected and effective foreign policy. Africa must know itself, its unifying identity, and the core cultural values of that identity as bases for engaging with international partners. Africa must prioritise developing its vast natural resources to achieve at least food sufficiency, and promote prosperity for its people. Africa must end its current image as the richest continent of the poorest populations. From a foundation of rich natural endowment and well-grounded self-confidence, Africa can then reach out to partners in trade and economic cooperation on the basis of mutual respect, shared interests and responsible sovereignty.

There can be no pride in a sovereignty that depends on foreign handouts to meet basic needs and even to keep domestic peace and security. Africa now depends on international peacekeeping operations that are often tenuous, not entirely dependable, and get terminated in a panic when the going gets tough. Under those exigencies, foreigners that are supposed to provide protection barricade themselves or exit the afflicted African country for their own safety, leaving Africans to slaughter themselves, as the world shamelessly witnessed in Rwanda in 1994. Their conduct and lavish lifestyle leave much to be desired. There have been cases whereby they are accused of being involved in act of human rights violations such as raping, killing, harassing and abusing the civilians whom they are expected to protect. Some have been accused of extending their mandate due to this conspicuous consumption. A few cases that could be cited to illustrate these violations are the Democratic Republic of Congo and the Republic of South Sudan. This makes them compromise their professional ethics and therefore become unpopular.

It is not easy to build a sense of pride and dignity in a people whose history has mostly been one of enslavement, domination, humiliation and dehumanisation. But that only makes the challenge of overcoming this dehumanising legacy a formidable task and success in doing so a most rewarding and gratifying achievement. There is no alternative to Africans assuming the front line of the fight against injustice and gross inequality and stopping Africans from continuing to be the primary victims of physical insecurity, gross violations of human rights and suffering the ills of poverty, hunger and disease. Africa must assume primary responsibility for ensuring peace, security, stability, development and prosperity for its people, with external partnership based on equality and mutual respect.

The guiding principle must be to approach 'Sovereignty as Responsibility', and not as a barricade against remedial action by the concerned world when national authorities manifestly fail to protect or assist their own needy populations. The best protection for national sovereignty is to discharge the responsibilities of sovereignty or accept international support in the exceptional case of unmet needs proving to be beyond the means of the state concerned to provide protection and assistance for its needy citizens.

This approach is the surest way for Africa to own its agenda and consequently control and determine its own destiny. This does not mean it no longer needs the international community. Africa is not an autarky. In this regard, its foreign policy must be geared towards achieving that goal. Indeed, engaging our international partners with this state of self-reliance, prudence, tenacity and assurance gives Africa the audacity of doing so based on a win-win situation. They need Africa and Africa needs them. This symbiotic relation is inevitable. However, mutual respect is paramount. It can be done, play your part. Let us walk the talk.

BIBLIOGRAPHY

Adebajo, A, Adedeji, A, and Chris Lansburg, (2007) *South Africa in Africa: the Post-Apartheid Era,* Scottsville: University ofKwaZulu, Natal Press.

Adler-Nissen, R & Pouliot, V (2014). "Power in practice: Negotiating the international intervention in Libya." *European Journal of International Relations,* 20 (1), pp 1–23.

Alden, Chris and Aran, Ammon (2012). *Foreign Policy Analysis: New approaches,* New York: Routledge Taylor and Francis group.

Allen, Louis A., (1964). *The Management Profession.* New York : McGraw-Hill, ,

Allison and Zelikow, (1999). *Essence of Decision: Explaining the Cuban Missile Crisis,* 2nd edition. New York: Addison-Wesley Longman.

Allison and Zelikow, (1999). *Essence of Decision: Explaining the Cuban Missile Crisis,* 2nd edition. New York: Addison-Wesley Longman.

Akol Moses M *(2015), Peace and Reinvigoration of South Sudanese Diplomacy: Regional and International Rapprochement, Unpublished, a seminar paper presented at Ebony Centre of Strategic Studies, Monthly, forum.*

Anderson, M.S. (1993). *The Rise of Modern Diplomacy 1450 – 1919,* London: Longman.

Andrea Goldstein and Wilson Prichard, (2008) "South African multinationals: South-South co-operation at its best", in Neuma Grobbelaar and Hany Besada (eds), *Unlocking Africa's Potential, the role of corporate South Africa in strengthening Africa's private sector,* (Johannesburg, SAIIA,

Auger, Vincent A (1996). *The dynamics of foreign policy analysis: The Carter administration and neutron bomb,* Boulder: Rownman &Littlefield publishers.

Axworthy, L. (2003). *Navigating the New World,* Toronto: Alfred Knopf.

Babaci-Wilhite, Z., Geo-JaJa, M. A. & Shizhou, L. (2013). "China's aid to Africa: competitor or alternative to the OECD aid architecture?? *International*

Journal of Social Economics, 40 (8), pp.729 – 743

Badie, D. (2010). "Groupthink, Iraq, and the War on Terror: Explaining US Policy Shift toward Iraq." *Foreign Policy Analysis*, 6, pp. 277–296.

Baumann, A., and Deber, R., (1989). "Limits of Decision Analysis for Rapid Decision-Making in ICU Nursing." *Image: Journal of Nursing Scholarship* 21 (2), pp. 69-71.

Baumann, A., and Deber, R., (1989). "Limits of Decision Analysis for Rapid Decision-Making in ICU Nursing." *Image: Journal of Nursing Scholarship* 21 (2), pp. 69-71.

Beasley, Ryan et al., (2013). *Foreign Policy in Comparative Perspective: Domestic and international influences on state behavior*, Los Angeles: Sage publications.

Beckner, L. R. (2012). *Decision-Making during National Security Crises: The Case of the JFK Administration*, Master's thesis, Virginia Polytechnic Institute and State University.

Below, A. (2008). *Decisions to Ratify the Kyoto Protocol: A Latin American Perspective on Poliheuristic Theory*, Ph.D. dissertation, University of Southern California.

Berding, Andrew. H. (1996). *The Making of Foreign Policy*, Washington, D.C: Potomac Books.

Berridge, G. R. (2005). *Diplomacy: Theory and practice, 3rd edn.* Houndmills, UK: Palgrave Macmillan.

Bidabad, (2012). "Foreign policy principles: An Islamic Sufi approach – Part II." *International Journal of Law and Management*, 54 (3), pp.173 – 196.

Biswaro, J.M. (2012). The quest for Regional Integration in the Twenty First Century: Rhetoric Versus Reality; Mkuki na Nyota Publishers Ltd, Dar es salaam, Tanzania.

Biswaro, J.M. (2013), The Role of Regional Integration in Conflict Prevention, Management, and Resolution in Africa; FUNAG, Brasilia, Brazil.

Boote, D. N., & Beile, P. (2005). Scholars before researchers: On the centrality of the dissertation literature review in research preparation, *Educational Researcher*.

Bowie, R. R. (1960). "Formulation of American Foreign Policy." *American Academy of Political and Social Science*, 330, pp. 1-10.

Breuning, Marijke (2007*). Foreign policy Analysis: A comparative introduction*, Hampshire: Palgrave Macmillan.

Brummer, Klaus, & Thies, Cameron G. (2014). "The contested origins of national role conceptions: Lessons from Germany." *Foreign Policy Analysis*, doi: 10.1111/fpa.12045.

Buckley, P.J. et al., (2007). "The determinants of Chinese outward foreign direct investment" *Journal of International Business, Studies*, 38 (4), pp. 499-

518.

Bueno de Mesquita, B. (1989). *The Contribution of Expected-Utility Theory to the Study of International Conflict,* In *Handbook of War Studies,* ed. Manus I. Midlarsky, Ann Arbor: University of Michigan Press.

Bueno de Mesquita, B. & Lalman, D. (1990). "Domestic Opposition and Foreign War." *American Political Science Review,* 84, pp. 747–765.

Buthe, T. and Milner, H.V. (2008). "The politics of foreign direct investment into developing countries: increasing FDI through international trade agreements?" *American Journal of Political Science,* 52 (4), pp. 741-762.

Byman, D. L., and Pollack, K. M. (2001). "Let Us Now Praise Great Men: Bringing the Statesman Back." *International Security,* 25, pp. 107–146.

Cardozo, H.M. (1962), Diplomats in International Cooperation: Stepchildren of the Foreign Service, Cornell University Press, Ithaca, New York, USA.

Cashman, Greg, (2000). *What Causes War? An Introduction to the International Conflict.* Lanham, Maryland: Laxington Boobs.

Chapple-Sokol, S. (2013). "Culinary diplomacy: Breaking bread to win hearts and minds." *The Hague Journal of Diplomacy,* 8 (2), pp. 161–183.

Chen, K. Z. Hsu, C. & Fan, S. (2014). "Steadying the ladder: China's agricultural and rural development engagement in Africa." *China Agricultural Economic Review,* 6 (1), pp.2 – 20.

Clinton, H. R. (2014). *Hard Choices,* New York: Simon and Schuster.

Conciliation, Resources, (2013). *Innovation in mediation support: The International Contact Group in Mindanao,* London: Conciliation Resources.

Cooper, A. F. (1997). *Niche-Diplomacy Middle Powers after the Cold War,* Basingstoke: Macmillan.

Courmont, B. (2013). "What Implications for Chinese Soft Power: Charm Offensive or New Hegemony?" *Pacific Focus,* 28, pp. 343–364.

Cuervo-Cazurra, A., Maloney, M. M. and Manrakhan, S. (2007) "Causes of the difficulties in internationalization." *Journal of International Business Studies,* 38 (5), pp. 709-725

Damodaran A. K. (1987). "Roots of foreign policy." *India International Centre Quarterly,* 14 (3), pp. 53-65.

Davis, C.L. and Meunier, S. (2011). "Business as usual? Economic response to political tensions." *American Journal of Political Science,* 55 (3), pp. 628-646.

Deon Geldenhuys, (1993). "The Changing Nature of Foreign Involvement in South Africa", *South Africa International.*

Desbordes, P. (2010). "Global and diplomatic political risks and foreign direct investment." *Economics & Politics,* 22 (1), pp. 92-125.

Ding, S. (2008). "To Build a Harmonious World: China's Soft Power Wielding in the Global South." *Journal of Chinese Political Science,* 13 (2), pp. 193–218.

Dizard, W. (2001). *Digital Diplomacy,* Westport: Praeger.

Duncan, W. Raymond, Barbara Jancar-Webster and Bob Switky, (2009). *World Politics in the 21ˢᵗ Century.* Boston: Cengage Learning.

Duncan, W. Raymond, Barbara Jancar-Webster and Bob Switky, (2009). *World Politics in the 21ˢᵗ Century.* Boston: Cengage Learning.

Egeland, J. (1988). *Impotent Superpower - Potent Small State,* Oslo: Norwegian University Press.

Faizullaev, A. (2014). "Diplomatic Interactions and Negotiations." *Negotiation Journal,* 30, pp. 275–299.

Fawole, A. (2003). *Nigeria's External Relations and Foreign Policy under Military Rule 1966-1999,* Obafemei: Awolowo University press.

Fearon, J. D. (1998). "Domestic politics, foreign policy, and theories of international relations." *Annual Review of Political Science,* 1, pp. 289 – 313.

Fettweis, C. J. (2013). *The Pathologies of Power: Fear, Honor, Glory, and Hubris in U.S. Foreign Policy,* Cambridge: Cambridge University Press.

Foyle, D. (2003). "Foreign Policy Analysis and Globalisation: Public Opinion, World Opinion, and the Individual." *International Studies Review,* 5, pp. 155–202.

Frankel, (1968). *The Making of Foreign Policy,* London: Oxford Press.

Freedman, L. & Karsh, E. (1991). "How Kuwait Was Won: Strategy in the Gulf War." *International Security,* 6, pp. 5–41.

Friedman, T. L. (1999). *The Lexus and the Olive Tree,* New York: Straus & Giroux.

Friend, J. M. & Thayer, B. A (2012). "Evolution and Foreign Policy: Insights for Decision-making Models." In Albert Somit, Steven A. Peterson (ed.). *Biopolicy: The Life Sciences and Public Policy,* Emerald Group Publishing Limited.

Fukuyama, F (1992). *The End of History and the Last Man,* New York: Free Press.

Gammeltoft, P., Barnad, H. and Madhok, A. (2010). "Emerging multinationals, emerging theory: macro-and micro-level perspectives". *Journal of International Management,* 16 (2), pp. 95-101.

Garcia-Canal, E. and Guillen, M.F (2008). "Risk and the strategy of foreign location choice in regulated industries." *Strategic Management Journal,* 29 (10), pp 1097-1115.

Garrison, J. (2001). "Framing Foreign Policy Alternatives in the Inner Circle: The President, His Advisors, and the Struggle for the Arms Control

Agenda." *Political Psychology*, 22, pp. 775–807.

Gay, L., Mills. G. & Airasian, P. (2006). *Educational research: Competencies for analysis and application (8th ed.),* New York: Prentice Hall.

Geva, N., Redd, S. B. & Mintz, A. (2000). *Evolving vs. Static Decision Dimensions and Decision Processes: An Experimental Assessment of Poliheuristic Propositions,* Monograph: Texas A&M University.

Geva, Nehemia and Alex Mintz ,(1997). *Decision-making on War and Peace: The Cognitive-Rational Debate.* Colorado US: Lynne Renner Publishers.

Glenn, P., and Susskind, L (2010). "How talk works: Studying negotiation interaction." *Negotiation Journal*, 26 (2), pp.117–123.

Gomes-Saraiva, M. (2014). "The Brazilian Soft Power Tradition." *Current History*, 113 (760), pp. 64–69.

Gordon, M. R. (2003). "Iraq Strategy Is Seen as Delay and Urban Battle." *New York Times*, February 16, pp. 1-29.

Gottwald, J. & Duggan, N (2011). "Hesitant adaptation: China's new role in global policies." In Sebastian Harnisch, Cornelia Frank, & Hanns W. Maull (eds.), *Role theory in international relations: Approaches and analyses*, London/ New York: Routledge.

Götz, Norbert (2005): On the Origins of 'Parliamentary Diplomacy' Scandinavian 'Bloc Politics' and Delegation Policy in the League of Nations. Cooperation and Conflict 2005 40: 263.

Greene, Fred (1984). *Dynamics of International Relations: Power, Security and Order*, Chicago: Holt, Rinehart and Winston.

Gries, P. H. (2004). *China's New Nationalism: Pride, Politics, and Diplomacy.* Berkeley and Los Angeles: University of California Press.

Grunig, J.E. (1993*).* "Public relations and international affairs – effects, ethics, and responsibility." *Journal of International Affairs*, 47 (1), pp. 137-162.

Hagan, J. D. (1994). "Domestic Political Systems and War Proneness." *Mershon International Studies Review*, 38, pp. 183–207.

Halliday, Fred (1994). *Rethinking International Relations*, London: Macmillan.

Hamilton, K. & Langhorne, R (1995). *The Practice of Diplomacy - Its Evolution, Theory and Administration*, London: Routledge.

Harnisch, S. (2011). *Role theory: Operationalization of key concepts*, In Sebastian Harnisch, Cornelia Frank, & Hanns W. Maull (eds.), *Role theory in international relations: Approaches and analyses,* London: Routledge.

Hart, P. (1994). *Groupthink in Government: A Study of Small Groups and Policy Failure,* Baltimore: Johns Hopkins University Press.

Hartmann, Frederick H. (1988). *The Relations of Nations*, New York: Macmillan.

Head, K. and Ries, J. (2010). "Do trade missions increase trade?" *Canadian Journal of Economics*, 43, pp.754– 775.

Henrikson, A. K. (2013). "Sovereignty, diplomacy, and democracy: The changing character of "international representation: From state to self?" *The Fletcher Forum of World Affairs*, 37 (3), pp. 111–140.

Herman, (1998))"South Africa's Emerging Dominant Party Regime", *Journal of Democracy*, Vol. 9, No. 3, p. 435

Hermann, M. G. (2001*)*. "How Decision Units Shape Foreign Policy: A Theoretical Framework." *International Studies Review*, 3 (2), pp. 47–81.

Hewitt, P. (2009). *The NIHR research design service for the Middle East*, Nottingham: University of Nottingham.

Hilsman, Roger (1987). *The Politics of Policy-Making in Defense and Foreign Policy: Conceptual Models and Bureaucratic Politics*. Engelwood Cliffs, NJ: Prentice-Hall.

Hocking, B. (2004). "Changing the Terms of Trade Policymaking: From the Club to the Multistakeholder Model." *World Trade Review*, 3 (1), pp. 3-26.

Hollis, Martin and Steve Smith, (1991). *Explaining and Understanding International Relations*. Oxford:Clarendon Press.

Holsti, J. K. (1997). *International Politics: A Framework for Analysis*, New Jersey: Prentice – Hall.

Hudson, Valerie (2014). *Foreign Policy Analysis: classic and contemporary theory*, Boulder: Rownman &Littlefield publishers.

Hudson, Valerie M. and Christopher S. Vore, (1995). "Foreign Policy Analysis, Yesterday, Today and Tomorrow". *Mershon International Studies Review* **39** (2) October, pp. 212-214.

Hudson,Valerie M. and Christopher S. Vore, (1995). "Foreign Policy Analysis, Koontz,

Harold and O'Donnell, Cyril (1972). *Principles of Management: An Analysis of Managerial Functions*. Tokyo: McGraw-Hill Kogakusha.Lovell, John, (1970). *Foreign Policy in Perspective* cited in Morgan, Patrick M., 1977. *Theories and Approaches to International Politics*, 2nd edition. New Brunswick NJ: Transaction Books.

Huntington, S. (1996). *The Clash of Civilizations and the Remaking of World Order*, New York: Simon and Schuster.

James N. Rosenau, (2006). *The Study of World Politics: Theoretical and Methodological Challenges:* Routledge.

James, P. & Oneal, J. R. (1991). "The Influence of Domestic and International Politics on the President's Use of Forc." *Journal of Conflict Resolution*, 35, pp. 307–332.

James, P. & Zhang, E. (2005*)*. "Chinese Choices: A Poliheuristic Analysis of Foreign Policy Crises 1950–1996." *Foreign Policy Analysis*, 1, pp.31–54.

Janis, I. L (1982). *Groupthink: Psychological Studies of Policy Decisions and Fiascoes, (2nd ed)*, Boston: Houghton Mifflin.

Jentleson, B. (Ed.). (2000). *Opportunities missed, opportunities seized: Preventive diplomacy in the post-Cold War world,* Lanham: Rowman and Littlefield.

K.J. Holsti, (1978), International Politics: A Framework for Analysis," Prentice Mall of India Pvt. Ltd., New Delhi.

Kaplan, Martin F, and Charles E. Miller, (1987). "Group Decision-Making and Normative versus International Influence: Effects of Type of Issue and assigned decision Rule". *Journal of Personality and Social Psychology*, Volume 53, pp. 306-313.

Kaplan, Martin F, and Charles E. Miller, (1987). "Group Decision-Making and Normative versus International Influence: Effects of Type of Issue and assigned decision Rule". *Journal of Personality and Social Psychology*, Volume 53, pp. 306-313.

Kaplan, R. (2000). *The Coming Anarchy: Shattering the Dreams of the Post-Cold War*, New York: Random House.

Kendall, J. (2010). "Ashgate Research Companion to US Foreign Policy." *Reference Reviews*, 24 (6), pp.13 – 14.

Kim, W. & Bueno de Mesquita, B. (1995). "How Perceptions Influence the Risk of War." *International Studies Quarterly*, 39, pp.51–65.

Kinne, B. J. (2005). "Decision Making in Autocratic Regimes: A Poliheuristic Perspective." *International Studies Perspectives*, 6, pp. 114–128.

Kissinger, Henry, (1994) Diplomacy, New York: Toughstone

Kolstad, I. and Wiig, A. (2012). "What determines Chinese OFDI?" *Journal of World Business*, 47 (1), pp. 26-34.

Kotur, M. (2010). *Psychological aspect of diplomacy and negotiations: The case of Serbian ego in negotiations over Kosovo's status.* Thesis presented for the Degree of Master of European Studies, College of Europe, Bruges Campus.

Krumbein, F. (2014). "The European's Foreign and Security Policy in a Globalised World." *Journal of European Integration*, 36 (5), pp. 525-53.

Kupchan, C. A. (2002). *The End of the American Era: U.S. Foreign Policy and the Geopolitics of the Twenty-first Century*, New York: Knopf.

Kurtzman, J & Rifkin, G (2001). *Radical E from GE to Enron: Lessons on How to Rule the Web,* New York: Wiley.

Le Prestre, P. G. (1997). *The United States: An elusive role quest after the cold war,* In Philippe G. Le Prestre (ed.), *Role quests in the post-cold war era: Foreign policies in transition,* Montreal & Kingston: McGill-Queen's University Press.

Ledingham, J. A. (2006). "Relationship management a general theory of public relations." In Botan, C. and Hazleton, V. (eds.), *Public Relations Theory*

II, Mahwah Lawrence Erlbaum Associates.

Lee, D. and Hudson, D. (2004). "The old and new significance of political economy." *Review of International Studies,* 30 (3), pp. 343-360.

Leonard, M and Small, A (2003). *Norwegian Public Diplomacy,* London: The Foreign Policy Centre.

Lukes, S. (2007). "Power and the Battle for Hearts and Minds: On the Bluntness of Soft Power." In F. Berenskoetter and M.J. Villians (eds.), *Power in World Politics,* London: Routledge.

MacKenzie, W.J.M, (1975). Power, Violence, Decision. New York: Peregrine Books, pp. 176-179.

Marijke Brenning, (2007). *Foreign Policy Analysis: A Comparative Introduction,* (New York, Palgrave Macmillan,

Mark, S. & Crichlow, S. (2002). "The Process-Outcome Connection in Foreign Policy Decision Making: A Quantitative Study Building on Groupthink." *International Studies Quarterly,* 46, pp. 45–68.

Mattern, B. (2005). "Why Soft Power Isn't So Soft: Representational Force and the Sociolinguistic Construction of Attraction in World Politics." *Millennium,* 33(3), pp. 583–612.

Melissen, J. (2005). *The New Public Diplomacy: Soft Power in International Relations,* New York: Palgrave.

Mintz, A (2002). *Integrating Cognitive and Rational Theories of Foreign Policy Decision Making,* New York: Palgrave.

Mintz, Alex and DeRouen, Karl (2010). *Understanding Foreign Policy Decision Making,* Cambridge: Cambridge University press.

Mitchell, O. S., Piggott, J., & Kumru, C. (2008). Managing Public Investment Funds: Best Practices and Remaining Questions. Available from: http://www.esri.go.jp/jp/workshop/080821/02_02_01.pdf. (Accessed 10 June 2015).

Morgan, Patrick M. (1977). *Theories and Approaches to International politics,* 2nd Edition. New Brunswick, New Jersey.

Morgenthau, H. J. (1993). *Politics among nations: The struggle for power and peace,* New York: McGraw-Hill.

Morrow, James D., (1997). " A Rational Choice Approach to international Conflict. In Geva, Nehemia and Alex Mintz, Decision Making on War and Peace: The Cognitive-Rational Debate. Colorado: Lynne Rienner Publishers.

Morrow, James D., (1997). " A Rational Choice Approach to international Conflict. In Geva, Nehemia and Alex Mintz, Decision Making on War and Peace: The Cognitive-Rational Debate. Colorado: Lynne Rienner Publishers.

Mushi, S.S. and K. Mathews, (1981). *Foreign Policy of Tanzania 1961-1981: A Reader.* Dar es Salaam: Tanzania Publishing House.

Nduwimana, D. (2013). *AMISOM in Somalia: A Ray of Hope?* Nairobi: International Peace Support Training Centre.

Neak, Laura Et al (1995). *Foreign policy Analysis: continuity and change in its second generation*, New Jersey: prentice hall.

Neumann, I B (2013). *Diplomatic sites*, New York: Columbia University Press.

Nye, J. (2008). "Public Diplomacy and Soft Power." *Annals of the American Academy of Political and Social Science*, 616 (1), pp. 94–109.

Nye, J. S. (1990). *Bound to Lead: The Changing Nature of American Power*, New York: Basic Books.

Nye, J. S. (2004). *Soft Power: The Means to Success in World Politics*, New York.

O'Neill, B. (2002). *Honor, symbols, and war*, Ann Arbor: The University of Michigan Press.

Onis, Z. and Yilmaz, S. (2009). "Between Europeanization and Euro-Asianism: Foreign Policy Activism in Turkey during the AKP Era." *Turkish Studies*, 10(1), pp. 7–24.

Paddleford and Lincoln, (1967). *The Dynamics of International Politics*, (New York, Macmillan.

Partowazar, B., Jawan, J. A. & Soltani, F. (2014). "Decision-Making in Foreign Policy." *Pensee Journal*, 76 (4), pp.344 – 353.

Payne, J. W Eta al (1993). *The Adaptive Decisionmaker*, Cambridge: Cambridge University Press.

Payne, J. W. (1976). "Task Complexity and Contingent Processing in Decision Making: An Information Search and Protocol Analysis." *Organizational Behavior and Human Performance*, 16, pp.366–387.

Peck, C. (1996). *The United Nations as a dispute settlement system: Improving the mechanisms for the prevention and resolution of conflict*, The Hague, Netherlands: Kluwer Law International.

Peter Vale and Ian Taylor, (1999)."South Africa's Post-Apartheid Foreign Policy five years on Pariah State to Just Another Country", *The Round Table*, 352.

Petersone, B. (2013). "The role of public relations in foreign policy planning and execution." *Journal of Communication Management*, 17 (4), pp.308 – 323.

Plantey, A. (2007). *International negotiation in the twenty-first century*, Abingdon UK: Routledge.

Pollack, M. A. (2007). "Rational Choice and EU Politics." In Knud Erik Jorgensen, Mark Pollack, and Ben J. Rosamond (eds.). *Handbook of European Union Politics*. New York: Sage.

Qavam, A. A. (2002). *The Principles of Foreign Policy and International Policy*, Tehran: SAMT Publication.

Quer, D, Claver, E. and Rienda, L. (2012). "Political risk, cultural distance and outward foreign direct investment: empirical evidence from large Chinese firms." *Asia Pacific Journal of Management,* 29 (4), pp. 1089-1104.

Ray, James Lee)1979). *Global Politics.* Boston: Houghton Mifflin Company.

Redd, S. B. (2005). "The Influence of Advisers and Decision Strategies on Foreign Policy Choices: President Clinton's Decision to Use Force in Kosovo." *International Studies Perspectives,* 6, pp. 129–150.

Republic of Kenya. (2014). *Kenya foreign policy,* Nairobi: Government Printers.

Reynolds, P. A., (1980). *An Introduction to International Relations,* 2nd Edition. London: Longman Group Limited.

Reynolds, P. A., (1980). *An Introduction to International Relations,* 2nd Edition. London: Longman Group Limited.

Rob Davies, (1998). ANC Member of Parliament, adapted from paper, "Globalisation: The Challenge facing South Africa.

Rosati, J. (2000). "The Power of Human Cognition in the Study of World Politics." *International Studies Review,* 2 (3), pp. 45–75.

Rosenau, James N. (1979). *International Politics and Foreign Policy: A Reader in Research and Theory.* New York: Free Press.

Rosenberg, S. W. (1995). "Against Neoclassical Political Economy; A Political Psychological Critique." *Political Psychology,* 16, pp. 99–136.

Russo, J. E. & Dosher, B. (1983). "Strategies for Multiattribute Binary Choice." *Journal of Experimental Psychology:* Learning, Memory, and Cognition, 9, pp.676–696.

Sabic, Zlatko (2013): International Parliamentary Institutions: A Research Agenda. In: Costa, Oliver, Policy Department, Directorate-General for External Policies 44 Clarissa – Stavridis, Stelios (eds.) (2013): Parliamentary Dimensions of Regionalization and Globalization: The Role of Interparliamentary Institutions. New York, Palgrave Macmillan, 20-41

Sachar, B.S. (2003). "Cooperation in military training as a tool of peacetime military diplomacy." *Strategic Analysis,* 27 (3), pp. 404-421.

Sachar, B.S. (2004). "Military diplomacy through arms transfers: A case study of China." *Strategic Analysis,* 28 (2), pp. 290-310.

Sandal, N. A., Zhang, E., James, C. C & James, P (2011). "Poliheuristic Theory and Crisis Decision Making: A Comparative Analysis of Turkey with China." *Canadian Journal of Political Science,* 44, pp. 27–57.

Schultz, David A., (2004). *Encyclopedia of Public Administration and Public Policy.* New York: Fact on File. Inc.

Schultz, David A., (2004). *Encyclopedia of Public Administration and Public Policy.* New York: Fact on File. Inc.

Shanker, T. & Schmitt, E. (2003). "Firing Leaflets and Electrons: U.S. Wages Information War." *New York Times*, February 24, pp.1-32.

Shell, R. (2006). *Bargaining for advantage: Negotiation strategies for reasonable people*, New York: Penguin Books.

Signitzer, B. and Wamser, C. (2006). "Public diplomacy: a specific governmental public relations function." In Botan, C. and Hazleton, V. (eds.), *Public Relations Theory II,* Mahwah: Lawrence Erlbaum Associates.

Signitzer, B.H. and Coombs, T. (1992). "Public relations and public diplomacy – conceptual convergences." *Public Relations Review*, 18 (2), pp. 137-147.

Simon, H. A. (1957). *Models of Man*, New York: John Wiley.

Simon, H. A. (1990). "Alternative Visions of Rationality, Cambridge, UK: Cambridge University Press.

Simon, H. A. (1992). "Decision Making and Problem Solving." In Mary Zey (ed.). *Decision Making: Alternatives to Rational Choice Model.* Newbury Park CA: Sage Publications.

Simon, Herbert A., (1956). "Rational Choice and Structure of the Environment". *Psychological Review*, **63** (2), pp. 129-138.

Singh, P. K. (2011). "China's 'Military Diplomacy': Investigating PLA's Participation in UN Peacekeeping Operations." *Strategic Analysis*, 35 (5), pp.793-818.

Smith, Steve Et al (2012). *Foreign policy: Theories, actors and cases*, Oxford: Oxford University press.

Snyder, Richard, C., H.W. Bruck, and Burton Sapin (1954). *Decision-Making as an Approach to the Study of International Politics*. Foreign Policy Analysis Project, Series No. 3. Princeton: Princeton University Press.

Snyder, Richard, C., H.W. Bruck, and Burton Sapin (1954). *Decision-Making as an Approach to the Study of International Politics*. Foreign Policy Analysis Project, Series No. 3. Princeton: Princeton University Press.

Stein, J. G & Welch, D. A (1997). Rational and Psychological Approaches to the Study of International Conflict: Comparative Strengths and Weaknesses, In Nehemia Geva, and Alex Mintz (eds.). Decision making on War and Peace: The Cognitive-Rational Debate. Boulder, CO: Lynne Rienner.

Fasil Solomon (2020), Foreign Policy and Diplomacy of Ethiopia Lecture Note, April, 2020

Stein, Janice Gross, (2002). "Psychological Explanations of International Conflict". In Carlsnaes, Walter, Thomas, Risse and Beth A, Simmons, eds. Handbook of International Relations. London: Sage Books, pp. 292-308.

Stein, Janice Gross, (2002). "Psychological Explanations of International Conflict". In Carlsnaes, Walter, Thomas, Risse and Beth A, Simmons, eds.

Handbook of International Relations. London: Sage Books, pp. 292-308.

Stephen, W. (1999). *African foreign policies*, Westview: Westview Press

Stern, E. K. and Sundelius, B. (2002). "Crisis Management Europe: An Integrated Regional Research and Training Program." *International Studies Perspectives*, (3), pp.71–88.

Szalai, A. (2008). *Rational Choice Theory in Early Cold War US Defense Policy - The Role of 'Defense Rationalists*, Monograph: Central European University.

Thies, C. G. (2010). *Role theory and foreign policy*, In Robert A. Denemark (Ed.), *The international studies encyclopedia*, volume X, Chichester: John Wiley & Sons.

Transparency International (2002). *Bribe payers index 2002: explanatory notes and comparative table*, available at: www.transparency.it/upload_doc/bpi2002.en.pdf (Accessed June 6 2015).

Unamete, U Bassey. (1996). *Foreign Policy Decision making in Nigeria*, Cranbury: Rosemont Publishing and Printing Company.

Vogel, J. (2010). *Die indische Chinapolitik seit 1988'*, Master's Thesis, University of Trier. Available from: https://www.uni-trier.de/fileadmin/fb3/POL/Studium/Ausgewaehlte_Abschlussarbeiten/MA_Vogel_-_Indische_Chinapolitik.pdf. (Accessed 8 June 2015).

Vujnovic, M. and Kruckeberg, D. (2005). "Imperative for an Arab model of public relations as a framework for diplomatic, corporate and nongovernmental organization relationships." *Public Relations Review*, 31 (3), pp. 338-343.

Wagner, C. (2005) *Die "verhinderte" Großmacht: Die Außenpolitik der Indischen Union, 1947–1998.* Baden-Baden: Nomos.

Walker, S. G. & Watson, G. L. (1989). Groupthink and Integrative Complexity in British Foreign Policymaking: The Munich Case." *Cooperation and Conflict*, 24, pp. 199–212.

Walt, Stephen M. (1998). "International Relations: One World, Many Theories". In *Foreign Policy No. 110, Special Edition: Frontiers of knowledge*, pp. 30-40.

Walton, Hanes Et al (2007). *The African foreign policy of secretary of the state Henry Kissinger: A documentary Analysis*, New York: Lexington Books.

Wang, J. and Chang, T. K. (2004). "Strategic public diplomacy and local press – how a high profile head-of-state visit was covered in America's heartland." *Public Relations Review*, 30 (1), pp. 11-24.

Weisglas, Frans De Boer, Gonnie (2007): Parliamentary Diplomacy. The Hague Journal of Diplomacy 2, 93-99.

Yun, S. H. (2006). "Toward public relations theory-based study of public diplomacy – testing the applicability of the excellence study." *Journal of Public*

Relations Research, 18 (4), pp. 287-312.

Zairi, M (2012). *Benchmarking for Best Practice*, Keighley: CRC Press.

Zhang, J. (2006). "Public diplomacy as symbolic interactions – a case study of Asian tsunami relief campaigns." *Public Relations Review*, 32 (1), pp. 26-32.

Zhang, J. and Cameron, G.T. (2003). "China's agenda building and image in the US – assessing an international public relations campaign." *Public Relations Review*, 29 (1), pp. 13-28.

Zhang, J., Jiang, J. & Zhou, C. (2014). "Diplomacy and investment – the case of China." *International Journal of Emerging Markets*, 9 (2), pp.216 – 235.

Zoellick, R. B. (2005). Whither China: From membership to responsibility? Remarks to National Committee on US-China Relations', Available from: http://2001-2009.state.gov/s/d/former/zoellick/rem/53682.htm. (Accessed 10 June 2015).

INDEX

www.ingramcontent.com/pod-product-compliance
Lightning Source LLC
Chambersburg PA
CBHW021844020426
42334CB00013B/177